Priests and Prelates

Priests and Prelates

The Daily Telegraph
Clerical Obituaries

Compiled by

Trevor Beeson

continuum
LONDON • NEW YORK

For Hugh Massingberd
writer, pioneer, obituarist, editor
with admiration and gratitiude

Continuum
The Tower Building, 11 York Road, London SE1 7NX
370 Lexington Avenue, New York NY 10017-6503

www.continuumbooks.com

© Trevor Beeson 2002

British Library Cataloguing-in-Publication Data
A catalogue record for this book is available from the British Library.

ISBN 0-8264-633-7-1

Typeset by Kenneth Burnley in Wirral, Cheshire.
Printed and bound in Great Britain by MPG Books Ltd

Contents

Introduction

The clergy are a strange bunch – and I should know, since I have for more than half a century been numbered among them. Our oddity should not, however, be regarded as either surprising or deplorable. After all, we are required by the very nature of our calling to have, more than most, a particular concern for the mysterious, supernatural dimension of life. There is nothing spooky about this, but we are frequently involved in the key moments of human experience – birth, love, suffering, fear, sacrifice, death – and, as we struggle to discover the significance of all this in our own lives, we try to lend others a hand.

There is also the fact that in an increasingly secularised world the cleric, in common with all other Christians, seeks to uphold and promote certain values, personal and social, that are no longer fashionable and are regarded by many as eccentric or even dangerous. In the turbulent societies of Latin America the Church sees itself as "a sign of contradiction" and this is, or ought to be, true of the Church everywhere. The priest and the prelate are called to be challengers – the askers of awkward questions. We are all nonconformists now.

In the Church of England these theological factors have, over the course of many centuries, been reinforced by organisational arrangements which have placed a premium on clerical independence. Designed originally to protect the parish priest against the arbitrary sanctions of lay patrons and, later, Episcopal oppression, the parson's freehold has historically provided the clergyman with a unique freedom. Answerable only to God, via his own conscience, he has been free to exercise his ministry without fear or favour and in accordance with his own understanding of the Church's task.

Thus the parishes have been served by both saints and scoundrels, as the obituaries that follow clearly demonstrate, but for the most part they have benefited by a rich variety of ordinary men (and now of women) who have been admired and loved, and who have contributed something important to the life of the community. This variety owes a good deal, also, to the fact that the independence guaranteed by the freehold has attracted to the ranks of the ordained ministry incorrigible individualists who enjoyed being kings of their own castles and required to collaborate with no one. Before the 1939–45 war the small country parish provided the scholar-parson with both security and time to pursue his studies, and in some instances to make an important contribution to various branches of learning, not all of them religious. William Keble Martin, who died as recently as 1969, compiled his classic *A Concise British Flora* during his years as a priest in Devon.

The arrangements of the Roman Catholic and the Free Churches do not afford their clergy quite the same scope for independence and absurdity as that enjoyed by their Anglican brethren, but fortunately this has not inhibited the emergence of many colourful and fascinating characters in their ranks. Who could ever hope to match Monsignor Gilbey? They comprise a valuable element in this volume, as they did in the Christian witness of their day.

The arrival of a new kind of clerical and lay obituary in the latter part of 1986 was therefore timely. The credit for this is due entirely to Hugh Massingberd, one of the most entertaining of writers, who persuaded the then editor of *The Daily Telegraph*, Max Hastings, to give him the chance to turn the small obituaries section of the paper into a celebration of life, rather than of death. What had previously been a dull backwater soon became a lively river. Hugh, a devotee of P. G. Wodehouse, knew that in human life fantasy is not always far removed from reality and that just below the surface of respectability there is usually something far more interesting. He also had a hunch that by the time readers reached the obituaries columns they might well welcome a relief from the reports of war, crime, politics, sleeze and so forth. If it turned out to be a good read, with a surprising element of humour, so much the better. The truth of this hunch was confirmed when the other broadsheets began to follow the *Telegraph*'s lead and the deceased demanded more space.

My own involvement in the new order came accidentally, as these things tend to do in journalism, and immediately demonstrated the hazards and the joys of the obituarist's art. "Mr Dean", called out a lady of uncertain years as I entered Winchester Cathedral one afternoon in March 1987, "do you realise that you have been insulted in this morning's *Daily Telegraph*? The obituary of your predecessor describes him as 'the last of the gentleman Deans'. What do they suppose you are?" I thought it best not to enlighten her as to the authorship of the offending description.

Anonymity remains an integral element in the *Telegraph*'s formula. How could one ever trust the judgements expressed in a piece signed by a close friend? But now, having written about 500 of the Anglican priests and prelates published during the last 15 years, and consulted so many others in the process, I am aware that my cover has long been blown. I hope nonetheless that it may be possible to continue a little longer without every clergyman I meet becoming unnaturally discreet lest his beliefs, hopes and fears find their way posthumously into print. An obituary is in fact invariably the work of several hands. Although long years in the service of the Church of England has given me a fairly comprehensive knowledge of its senior clergy, I do not – fortunately, some may think – know everything about them. Thus, when a death is announced or sometimes (my voice is now hushed) even before, I turn to their friends and acquaintances for assistance. This is always forthcoming and invariably helpful, though I am often the first to convey the news of a death to them, and telephone conversations have to be brief when deadlines are close. Only once have I had to stop playing in a cricket match in order to deal with an urgent request from Canary Wharf – a former Archbishop of Wales had inconveniently died.

Some of the most interesting and inspiring clerical obituaries concern priests of whom I had no previous knowledge and who laboured long and faithfully without any external recognition apart from the admiration, love and sometimes the exasperation of the communities they served. It is good when the exploits of these hitherto unknown characters are shared with millions. I am sometimes asked if I ever consult the members of the subject's family, to which the answer is – very occasionally. This is because I am reluctant to intrude on the grief of people unknown to me and whose concerns are unlikely to include an obituary in tomorrow's newspaper. Yet, whenever I have telephoned in search of information not available elsewhere, I have nearly always become involved in a long conversation with the widow or one of her children which in the end may, I hope, have been as helpful to them as it was to me.

The issue of candour can be deferred no longer. The old adage *De mortuis nil nisi bonum* must, I believe, be rejected, chiefly because its acceptance can only lead to dishonesty, and also because it is singularly unhelpful to others. Hagiology – the lives of saints which portray them as without stain or blemish – has always been a hindrance to the Christian cause, for it overlooks the fact that unlimited virtue is more likely to repel than to attract, to discourage than to encourage, the sinful pilgrim on his journey through life. Significantly, canonisation as a saint does not require perfection.

Neither does entry to the obits columns of *The Daily Telegraph*, which is just as well, for otherwise these would be either blank or insufferably dull. Those who enter public life, either by choice or interior compulsion, must not complain because their words and deeds are open to public inspection. And if at the time of their death their lives are deemed significant or interesting enough to warrant attention, it is to be expected that the portrait offered to those who buy a newspaper will not be too far removed from the reality. I go further and assert that if a man or woman merits an obituary, the character of such a person will not only be able to withstand references to any of their foibles and failures but actually be enhanced by the lack of distortion. The aim is always a rounded picture, presented with sympathy – and hopefully a little insight. Often enough the reader is left to read between the lines, and if the overall effect of the piece is to raise a smile, this may perhaps help to ease the pain of loss.

All of which has for a long time been acknowledged as applicable to politicians, businessmen, sports personalities, actors and the like, but has yet to win wide acceptance in church circles. There remains the belief that Christian charity requires weakness and eccentricity to be overlooked and that, although priests and prelates generally lack the attribute of infallibility, their lives ought to be beyond honest scrutiny – at least in the public prints. But this is to devalue their office and role. It suggests that they are not significant enough to merit serious attention, yet the increasing amount of space allocated by the *Telegraph* to clerical obituaries during the last 15 years indicates clearly that this has not been the view of its successive editors.

My own anxiety concerns the future. The pages that follow present a rich tapestry of clerical personality and dynamic leadership compiled mainly from the Anglican Church but considerably enhanced by the contribution of other churches. It is becoming less easy, however, to locate such personalities and leaders. Admittedly, ancient scribes such as myself are not always a reliable guide to the present and the future. The temptation to look back to a golden age in which every sphere of public life was led by giants can be irresistible. Our prophecies are rarely fulfilled. Yet facts must be faced by every generation and I cannot help believing that if, as a result of some fearful catastrophe, the entire bench of Church of England

Bishops, together with all the members of the Roman Catholic Bishops' Conference for England and Wales and the chairmen and moderators of the Free Churches, were suddenly wiped out, it would be difficult to compile more than about half a dozen really interesting obituaries.

There are several reasons for this serious decline in the quality and character of church leadership and, although my personal knowledge is confined to the Church of England, I suspect that some at least of these reasons apply also in the other churches. Before explanations, however, it is necessary to note that matters took a serious turn for the worse during the second half of the twentieth century. In 1942 Winston Churchill, when nominating William Temple for the Archbishopric of Canterbury, said, famously, that he had chosen the only half-crown article in a sixpenny bazaar. But the distractions of war evidently caused him to be misinformed. For while William Temple undoubtedly stood head and shoulders over virtually all the bishops of the previous 500 years, he was surrounded by at least 16 colleagues of considerable distinction. Not all of these would have made good Archbishops of Canterbury, but six would, in the absence of Temple, been worth serious consideration and six members of the bench at that time were scholars of the first rank.

The numerical decline of the Church of England which gathered pace after a mini-religious revival in the 1950s was accompanied by a reduction in the size of the ordained ministry and therefore of the pool from which leaders could be chosen. It also led, for manpower and financial reasons, to the amalgamation of the small, rural parishes in which the scholars and colourful parsons had previously flourished. The equalisation of parochial clergy stipends brought about the demise of the able "Prince Rector" who, aided by a few curates, presided over a large central town parish and was a major figure in civic life. Many of these went off to become archdeacons and earned their higher pay by attending endless meetings.

These meetings were a consequence of the centralisation of much decision-making, which gradually eroded the independence of the parish priest. At the same time, the appointment of Priests-in-charge, instead of Rectors and Vicars, reduced substantially the number of clergy with secure freeholds. Unsurprisingly, the closing decades of the twentieth century witnessed a serious decline in the morale of the parish clergy and this, combined with ever-increasing administrative and financial problems, led to a change in the role of the Bishop who became a pastoral-manager, rather than a thinker and strategist. Thus the Episcopal office ceased to be attractive to the scholar and the man of wide vision.

At the same time the reduced size of the Church and the gradual secularisation of society caused the Christian community to become increasingly marginalized. The parish priest lost his central place in the life of the village or market town, while the Bishop ceased to be a county or city leader whose words were listened to with interest and sometimes respect. It would be misleading to suggest that in the past men were attracted to the ordained ministry simply by the social status it conferred, but it would not be surprising if the most able were today disinclined to embrace a vocation in which the possibility of significantly improving the lives of individuals and communities seems somewhat limited. There are many other avenues of service open to the dedicated, and it is noticeable that the public schools and ancient universities are now producing very few ordination candidates.

No assessment of changes in the Church's institutional life during the twentieth century can ignore the effects of the two world wars. Both led to the tragic loss of many potential leaders and to disillusionment with religion. At the same time, however, they inspired in many of the most capable survivors the desire to create a better world based on Christian values. Thus the two post-war periods witnessed the emergence of some outstanding clergy who exercised devoted and imaginative ministries in their parishes and, later, dynamic leadership in their dioceses.

Sadly, this ability and commitment was never satisfactorily harnessed to the institutional life of an essentially conservative body and after the 1939–45 war the failure of reforming movements to make much progress caused some of the most able and visionary clergy to decline leadership positions and others to move to different spheres of Christian service. The lack of such men on the bench of Bishops after the turbulent 1960s resulted in two particular elements of reform being directed in ways that made ordained ministry even less attractive to those whom the Church needed most.

During the inter-war years the attempt to revise the Book of Common Prayer in a way that now seems modest was frustrated by Parliament and, although some strictly illegal changes were permitted by the Bishops, the content of the Church of England's worship was widely believed to be unsatisfactory for the twentieth century. Liturgical change was therefore a high priority when the war ended, as was the case in virtually all the churches of Western Europe. What was not foreseen by the liturgists of the 1950s and 1960s, however, was the degree to which, in an increasingly introverted Church, the devising of new forms of worship would, in the hands of their successors, become something approaching an obsession. Volumes of material consisting of some thousands of pages are now confusing the clergy and confounding the laity, not least those of their number who are occasional churchgoers. And, as in the case of Canon Law revision in the 1950s and 1960s, the enterprise has diverted the Church from the more urgent task of reforming its missionary structure.

After the 1914–18 war there was also seen to be an urgent need to make the Church more democratic by giving the laity a responsible place in its government and ensuring that decision-making at all levels was appropriately shared. There were theological as well as social reasons for this. Some, but not enough, progress in this direction was achieved and during the 1960s there was a strong and largely successful movement for the inauguration of full synodical government. None of us who were involved in that movement foresaw what a monster we were about to release, though it is just possible that had the new arrangements been placed in less bureaucratic hands the consequences might have been more lively. As it is, decision-making is inhibited, often stifled, by endless processes of consultation and innumerable meetings.

None of which provides the soil in which priests and prelates of unusual gifts and high intelligence can flourish. The Crown Appointments Commission, which became responsible, after 1976, for advising on the appointment of Bishops, consists almost entirely of synodical nominees and, predictably enough, is disinclined to take risks. When Prime Ministers made their own choices they made much more imaginative appointments. Again, the reduction in the power of the independent patron and the increased power of parishes to veto the appointment of unusual priests with whom they might not feel altogether comfortable has reduced the scope for the ministry of the prophet and the oddball. More dynamic leadership in the Church at all levels – and a constant supply of interesting obituaries – requires, therefore, a marked change of direction in some key areas of ecclesiastical life.

It would be seriously misleading, however, to suggest that leadership problems are confined to the Church, since they form just one part of a broader picture. As the twentieth century advanced there was a noticeable diminution in the number of men and women of ability who were prepared to embark on careers in the public service. Making money in the City of London and elsewhere held a greater attraction. Hence the current desperate shortage of gifted and inspiring leadership in education, politics, medicine, social service, the police and the prison service. There is not enough talent available to go round.

A healthy society, including a healthy Church, requires wider recognition of the central place of the sacrificial in human experience, and in the obituaries that follow there is ample evidence of its creative power.

The compilation of an obituary is, as I indicated earlier, nearly always the work of several hands and it is to me a delight as well as a duty to acknowledge the part played by others in the contents of this book. The pioneering Obituaries Editor, Hugh Massingberd, and his successors – David (Lewis) Jones, Kate Summerscale, Christopher Howse and the present incumbent, Andrew McKie – must obviously head the bill. A special word of thanks is due also to David Twiston Davies who roped me into this strange but curiously satisfying trade back in 1987 and over the years edited many of my pieces. Some of his own contributions are included in this collection and, after a period of exile as Letters' Editor, he returned to the Obits desk in time to retrieve from the *Telegraph*'s archives a number of items lacking from my own cuttings file. Important contributions have also been made, in a variety of ways, by Mark Bence-Jones, David Bowman, Aurea Carpenter, Will Cohu, Philip Eade, Claudia Fitzherbert, Robert Gray, the late Peter Hebblethwaite, Diana Heffer, George Ireland, Adam McEwen, Desmond O'Grady, Martin Onoh, James Owen, Chris Ralls, Damian Thomson, the late Gordon Wakefield and the late Philip Warner. And, as Hugh Massingberd has been at pains to acknowledge in the previous volumes of this series, we have all depended enormously on the cheerful and dedicated efficiency of Teresa Moore – the secretary of the desk throughout most of the new order.

TREVOR BEESON
Romsey, Hampshire
March 2002

1987

The Very Reverend Hugh Heywood

The Very Reverend Hugh Heywood, who has died aged 90, achieved wide publicity as Provost of Southwell, first by encouraging miners to sing *Roll Out The Barrel* at a service and then by being arrested in Yugoslavia on suspicion of spying for the Russians.

On returning home from Yugoslavia, where secret police suspicions had been raised on finding him inspecting some ruins near the Greek border, Heywood had another brush with higher officialdom when he paid his overdue phone bill, only to be cut off the next day. Recognising that no good could come of tangling with the colourful clergyman, the Post Office apologised profusely.

Heywood strongly believed that a church should be used as widely as possible. He criticised parishioners who hounded a couple out of a service because their baby was gurgling, put up a sign saying "dogs welcome", and organised a pageant in which whistling cyclists, courting couples and even a farmer with a shotgun went down the aisle.

He announced that he preferred to have his letters addressed to Mr rather than the Very Reverend, and was not afraid to reveal the difficulties of living on his stipend of £23-a-week.

That was in 1955. He pointed out that 10 years before, he had employed a man and a boy full-time all week in his three-acre garden, but now only had a single man for half-a-day a week.

There were few subjects on which he could not be relied upon for a sensible, genial opinion, whether it was the advisability of buying a wreath rather than picking wild flowers, or the best kinds of postcards.

He even got Mr Tom Driberg, Labour MP, to raise in Parliament an incident in which he had been refused a glass of beer in Richmond Park because half a round of sandwiches did not legally constitute a whole round and therefore a meal.

But many of his friends felt that the beautiful Nottinghamshire minster over which he presided from 1945 to 1969 was not sufficiently demanding for a man of Heywood's considerable gifts. He had earlier been Dean of Gonville and Caius College, Cambridge, for 17 years.

Born in 1896, Hugh Christopher Lempriere Heywood joined the Manchest Regiment in 1914 and was quickly at the front, where he was wounded and mentioned in despatches.

In 1917, he was transferred to the Indian Army, serving in the 74th Punjabis, and remained in India, where he was a staff captain, until 1923.

He then returned to England to seek ordination and went up to Cambridge as an exhibitioner of Trinity, where he soon became a Scholar. In addition to securing a First, with distinction, in both parts of the Theological Tripos, he carried off the coveted Carus Greek testament prize.

After being ordained at Ely in 1926, Heywood spent his final student year as curate of Greenford. But a year later he returned to Cambridge as Fellow and Dean of Gonville and Caius College.

Here he remained until 1945, serving as a Proctor for several periods and teaching in the faculty of theology as well as in his own college.

During this time, he was in great demand as a university preacher.

His first book, *The Worshipping Community*, was published in 1938, but nothing more was to appear from his pen until 1960 and his later books were somewhat slight.

In 1945 the then Bishop of Southwell, Dr F. R. Barry, who admired men of academic distinction, invited Heywood to become Provost of Southwell, but this quiet rural backwater offered no stimulus to a Cambridge scholar, and the pastoral responsibilities of the Cathedral parish diverted him from sustained reading and writing

To the surprise of many, not least the Bishop and the Chapter, Heywood embarked on his programme of unusual activities designed to enliven the Cathedral community. Most of these were dismissed as gimmicks, and relations between the Provost and his colleagues, especially the Bishop, became strained.

But Heywood continued in office until he was 73, and was much appreciated by lay people as a pastor and preacher. He than spent another seven years very happily as priest in charge of the country parish of Upton, near Howard-on-Trent, Nottinghamshire.

He married Margaret Marion Bizard in 1920 and they had a son and a daughter.

May 11, 1987

The Reverend Christopher Hildyard

The Reverend Christopher Hildyard, who has died aged 86, took part in three coronations and many royal weddings during 45 years as a minor canon of Westminster Abbey, where he was highly influential in developing its dignified ceremonial.

He cared little for the finer points of dogma and ecclesiastical dispute, but was deeply committed to things that were "lovely and of good report."

A descendant of the Elizabethan miniaturist, Nicholas Hilliard, he was also a talented artist whose work included a formal portrait of the legendary Major Purne Rai, the first Gurkha commissioned officer, and several memorable sketches of figures at the 1953 Coronation.

A firm believer that the Church should avoid itself of anything modern, he nonetheless wrote several religious dramas, including "The Mysterious Way," which in 1936 was performed at St Margaret's, Westminster, and "Surrender," put on the following year at Christ Church, Westminster, with himself as the narrator.

In 1946, he became involved in theatrical work of a more frivolous nature when he produced the medical school pantomime at Westminster Hospital, where he was chaplain for 21 years.

Born in 1901 at Windsor Castle, where his father was a Minor Canon of St George's Chapel, Christopher Hildyard has happy memories of his Edwardian Windsor boyhood and was a page-boy at the Coronation of King George V.

After Repton, and Magdalene College, Cambridge, he prepared for ordination at Cuddesdon and served as a curate in the coal mining parish of Glass Houghton, near Wakefield, and then at Guisborough, North Yorkshire.

In 1928, he moved to Westminster where the Sacrist, the redoubtable Dr Jocelyn Perkins, had already made considerable progress in repairing the liturgical neglect of the 18th and 19th centuries. Although the two priests were not always in full agreement, they made a perfect combination, Hildyard demonstrating his fine eye for colour as well as appropriate fabric and furnishings.

Both stayed at the Abbey long enough to win freedom from the authority of changing Deans and Canons, and in matters affecting ceremonial and ornament their word became law.

The Coronation of King George VI in 1937 was carried out with a degree of dignity not previously experienced on such occasions and by the time the television cameras moved in for the Coronation of the Queen, the beauty and drama had raised religious and state ceremonial to the highest level.

For the 900th anniversary of the Dedication of Westminster Abbey in 1966, Hildyard persuaded the Guinness family to present a set of fine chandeliers in Waterford glass and another friend agreed to pay for a set of majestic copes, designed in London but woven on the historic French looms at Lyons.

About the same time Hildyard, while on holiday in the Greek island of Hydra, noticed in a second-hand shop a soldier's uniform which was badly worn but had splendid golden ornamentation. This was purchased "for a song" and brought to London where the ornamentation was re-mounted on blue velvet to provide the Dean of Westminster with his most magnificent cope.

His artistic flair is still to be seen in the design of the Westminster Hospital chapel, where the altar is crowned by a remarkable painting of the Resurrection by Veronese, which a persistent chaplain persuaded the hospital governors to purchase for just a few thousand pounds in the early 1950s.

On his retirement in 1973, Hildyard was appointed Sacrist emeritus of the Abbey and continued to live in his beautiful house in the Cloisters where, with his companion, Professor Norman Ashton, FRS, he loved to share a bottle of wine with old friends and talk of a bygone, more courtly, age. He was appointed Lieutenant of the Royal Victorian Order in 1966.

May 18, 1987

The Reverend Dr Alec Vidler

The Reverend Dr Alec Vidler, the former Dean of King's College Cambridge who has died aged 91, was one of the more picturesque priests in the Church of England

Combining conservative Catholic practice with markedly liberal theological views he once described himself as "a sceptic in faith's clothing". But perhaps his friend Malcolm Muggeridge summed up him up more accurately – as a man who believed with all his heart and doubted with all his mind.

Certainly Vidler's faith had been strong enough to give the young Muggeridge his first nudge towards Christianity.

As Vidler grew older his views, like his famous beard, became more free-ranging. Nevertheless, he remained a faithful priest of the Oratory of the Good Shepherd – the society of celibate clergymen which he joined in 1923.

An American admirer who studied his works remarked that the only item in the Creed which Vidler seemed prepared to endorse was that Christ suffered under Pontius Pilate.

In order to protect himself against possible inhibition by more conservative bishops, Vidler persuaded Cambridge University to revive a right granted by Queen Elizabeth I and to license him to preach without restriction anywhere in England.

To Vidler it appeared axiomatic that Christians, swimming

against the tide of secularism, were the best qualified to estimate its force. Two books of essays which he edited, *Soundings* (1962) and *Objections to Christian Belief* (1963), were important contributions to the theological ferment of the early 1960s.

Such views were not always popular with his ecclesiastical peers. Nor did he win universal approval when, in a 1962 television programme, he displayed a marked lack of horror about fornication and declared himself "bored with parsons".

As a scholar Vidler specialised in modern Church history, having been much impressed by the work of Alfred Loisy and other French Roman Catholic modernists. Among the 20 or so books he published, *The Modernist Movement in the Roman Church* (1934) remains the standard English work on the subject.

Vidler also edited the magazine *Theology* for a quarter of a century. He liked to think of himself as "a theological midwife", and displayed a remarkable flair for discovering and encouraging writers who were looking at old truths from new angles.

But when his books were put away there were few priests who celebrated Communion with greater elegance and panache. He showed himself equally adept ceremonially as Dean of King's and, in retirement, as Mayor of Rye, where his father, grandfather and great-grandfather had held the office before him.

Vidler also started, with modest success, the Cambridge fashion of clergymen wearing a black shirt with a white tie. He declared himself prejudiced against the ordination of women on the grounds that "they go in for the inelegancy of the clerical collar which looks even worse on them than on men".

Alexander Roper Vidler was born at Rye in 1899, and went to Sutton Valence School, where a promising academic career was interrupted by the need to work in the family shipping business during the First World War.

He spent six months in the Army at the end of the war, then went up to Selwyn College, Cambridge, where he met Malcolm Muggeridge. Their friendship proved an enduring one, and 51 years later they made a television programme together about St Paul.

As an undergraduate Vidler was drawn to the Anglo-Catholic movement in the Church of England. After further training at Wells Theological College and the Oratory House, Cambridge, he was ordained to a curacy in a slum parish at Newcastle-upon-Tyne.

Here Vidler became a staunch supporter of the Labour party, often appearing on the platform at its meetings. After two years he moved to another Anglo-Catholic parish – St Aidan's Birmingham, which, soon after his arrival, found itself in conflict with a new bishop, E. W. Barnes, who objected to some of its sacramental practices.

After ill-health forced the vicar to retire, Vidler stayed on for two difficult years since he knew that, when he went, the bishop would appoint a replacement of his own way of thinking. The dispute was eventually resolved through the intervention of the Archbishop of Canterbury.

More than 40 years later, in 1974, Vidler was asked to preach at the service celebrating the centenary of Bishop Barnes's birth – a task he carried out with grace, generosity and truthfulness.

In 1931, after leaving Birmingham, Vidler joined the community at the Oratory House in Cambridge.

Shortly before the outbreak of the Second World War he was invited to take over the editorship of *Theology* and to become Warden of St Deinol's Library – W. E. Gladstone's foundation at Hawarden.

This combination suited him admirably, for he was an admirer of Gladstone, and had ample freedom to write and lecture.

In 1946 he became an honorary canon of Derby Cathedral and two years later he accepted a Royal invitation to become a Canon of St George's Chapel, Windsor. This post again offered great freedom. He took over the leadership of the Christian Frontier Council, and used his large house in the cloisters to accommodate a number of older men ("Vidler's Doves" or sometimes "Vidler's Vipers"), whom he prepared for ordination.

Once again he would have been happy to remain in this work until retirement, but in 1956 he found it impossible to decline a pressing invitation to return to Cambridge as Dean of King's and University Lecturer in Divinity.

His arrival at King's, complete with the 50,000 bees he kept, might have been a cause for some concern. But his style suited the College.

He continued to be in great demand as a lecturer, and, as always, his pen was never idle. His books included *Sex, Marriage and Religion* (1932), *A Plain Man's Guide to Christianity* (1936), *God's Judgement on Europe* (1940), *A Century of Social Catholicism* (1964), *F. D. Maurice and Company* (1966) and *A Variety of Catholic Modernists (1970).*

In 1966 he laid down the Deanship, and next year left Cambridge for good to retire to his old family home, "Friars of the Sack", at Rye.

Here he kept bees, baked his own bread, entertained friends, and wrote a few more books, including his autobiography *Scenes from a Clerical Life* (1977). In 1972 he was delighted by his election to an Honorary Fellowship of King's.

July 27, 1987

Canon Charles Smyth

Canon Charles Smyth, who has died aged 84, was a Fellow of Corpus Christi College, Cambridge, and a distinguished church historian whose somewhat prickly nature stood in the way of his preferment to senior posts both in the academic sphere and in the Church of England.

Fortunately, he lived long enough to be able to come to terms with the disappointment and frustration which dogged most of his days.

Born in China in 1903, where his father was a doctor, Charles Hugh Egerton Smyth was educated at Repton and at Corpus

Christi College, Cambridge, where he was a scholar. At Cambridge he carried all before him, taking a double first in the history tripos, winning the Thirlwall Medal and the Gladstone Prize, and securing, on the same day as R. A. Butler, election to a fellowship of his college.

In the following year, 1926, he went to teach history at Harvard, but soon returned, having decided to enter Wells Theological College to prepare for Holy Orders.

However, ordination in 1929 did not remove him immediately from academic work, for in the same year he was appointed University Lecturer in History at Cambridge. But he left this post in 1932 to undertake parish work as a curate, first in Islington then in Chelsea.

Returning to Cambridge in 1936 as curate of St Giles, he became Dean of Chapel at Corpus Christi College in the following year, and was almost immediately appointed an honorary Canon of Derby Cathedral. Eventually he became a Canon Emeritus both of Derby and of Lincoln.

Smyth's first book, *Cranmer and the Reformation under Edward VI*, had been published when he was only 23, and the early years of the war saw the appearance of two more substantial books: *The Art of Preaching*, a survey of preaching in the Church of England from the 8th Century until 1939, and *Simeon and Church Order*, a study of the 18th Century evangelical revival in the Church of England.

When the Dixie Chair of Ecclesiastical History at Cambridge became vacant in 1944 it seemed obvious to many that Smyth would be appointed to it. But he had made too many enemies in college and university and to his great chagrin was passed over. There is sad irony in the fact that the most widely read of his many books, published in 1945, was entitled *The Friendship of Christ*.

The Crown came to his rescue in 1946 when he was appointed Rector of St Margaret's, Westminster, and a Canon of Westminster. The next 10 years were probably the happiest of his life. Smyth proved to be a parish priest of the highest calibre, and in the immediate post-war era large congregations gathered at St

Margaret's on Sunday mornings to hear his erudite sermons which were expressed with great clarity and fine use of the English language.

During this time he wrote a biography of one of his predecessors, Dean Milman, and a study of church history illustrated by the parish history of St Margaret's.

Once again, however, the old interior enemy began to assert itself. The proximity of his rectory to Westminster School and the penetration of his study by schoolboy noise led to an unedifying battle with the school authorities, and before long he had also crossed swords with most of his colleagues in the Abbey community.

It was now clear that neither a bishopric nor a deanery would come his way, so at the early age of 53 he resigned from St Margaret's, and returned once more to Cambridge to write the biography of Archbishop Cyril Garbett.

When this appeared in 1959 it was immediately recognised as one of the finest episcopal biographies of the present century – scholarly in its detail, beautifully written, and so honest in its portrayal that the tyrannical character of the greater part of Garbett's ministry could no longer be overlooked.

Two more, smaller works were to come from Smyth's pen, but his creative work as a historian had now ended. Unresolved, however, was the paradox of a man whose work as a historian displayed almost perfect balance and objectivity, but whose personal relationships often foundered on the rocks of unreason and prejudice.

Smyth was happily married to Violet, daughter of the late Canon Alexander Copland, of Forfar, who survives him. There were no children.

October 31, 1987

The Right Reverend Thomas Pearson

The Right Reverend Thomas Pearson, who has died aged 80, was the tall, colourful Roman Catholic "Bishop of Lakeland", celebrated for his mountaineering exploits and his penchant for driving fast cars.

Together with Sir Arnold Lunn, he founded, in l945, the Achille Ratti Climbing Club named after the one-time Alpine guide who went on to become Pope Pius XI, which supports climbing huts in the Lake District and Wales. Pearson's appointment in 1967 as Bishop in Cumbria, the leader of the Catholic community in the Lake District, was thus supremely fitting.

Twelve years earlier he had managed to buy his own 1,250ft mountain at Broad Crag, near Ambleside, together with some farm buildings which were developed into a mountain resort.

Because he had no titular see of his own, Pearson was given, in accordance with Catholic tradition, a nominal bishopric, that of Sinda (a place in India). In consequence the Lancaster stretch of the M6 became popularly known as the "Sinda Track" on account of the way the Bishop used to burn it up in his Jaguar. The registration letters on the car were SBF. "People tend to think it stands for 'Sinda, B.F.'", said the Bishop.

His Lakeland diocesan area demanded constant long journeys, and at one time he was clocking up 800 miles a week. The Bishop claimed that in an average year he motored as much as a travelling salesman. Pearson covered the difficult parts of the terrain with practised aplomb, combining hillclimbing with pastoral work. Sometimes, however, the elements got the better of him. On one occasion he was lost with a party of children in a storm; on another he was stuck in huge snowdrifts on his way to say Mass on the shores of Ullswater.

The climbers' chapel he opened in the Langdales in 1967 was the first in England at which the obligation of Sunday Mass could be fulfilled on a Saturday evening.

Thomas Bernard Pearson was born at Preston in 1907 and educated at St Ignatius Selective Central School and St Edward's

College, Liverpool. During his school years he had shown little aptitude for games but when he went to the English College in Rome to pursue his studies for the priesthood, he began climbing the Dolomites.

After his ordination in 1933 Fr Pearson returned to the Lancaster diocese determined to foster mountaineering among young men of an outdoor persuasion. He had the unusual distinction of serving the same parish, St Cuthbert's, Blackpool, first as curate then as priest over a continuous stretch of 33 years.

In 1967 he moved to the parish of Our Lady and St Herbert, Windermere. Having been Auxiliary Bishop of Lancaster since 1949 he was then assigned – in line with the Vatican Council's regionalisation policy – to take pastoral care of a defined area of the diocese.

His intimate knowledge of the Lake District and its people made Pearson a key figure in inter-church relations which he used to lubricate by giving clergy parties in Windermere for ministers and their wives. A devoted educationalist with an active concern for underprivileged children, the Bishop's legacies include Windermere's first Catholic school.

November 27, 1987

1988

The Reverend Dr Bertrand Brasnett

The Reverend Dr Bertrand Brasnett, who has died aged 95, was in his day a considerable theologian.

But his genius was accompanied by a degree of eccentricity, and when his academic career in Edinburgh ended suddenly in 1942 he retired to Oxford, where he spent the rest of his life as a recluse.

His fine trilogy on the nature of God, published between 1928 and 1935, earned him an Oxford doctorate in divinity and has continued to illuminate and exercise the minds of serious scholars, among them the renowned Professor Jürgen Moltmann of Tubingen. His work on the difficult question of whether or not God can suffer was to be of lasting value.

Brasnett was an exacting teacher with more than a touch of the Victorian martinet in his style. As Principal and Pantonian Professor of Theology at Edinburgh Theological College he had a strong sense of duty and was obsessive in his attention to detail in the life of the college and in his own regularity of habit. The college produced high-calibre clergymen, several of whom became important leaders of the Scottish Episcopal Church.

In 1942, however, with a different kind of student in residence and the strain of war requiring some change of priorities, Brasnett was asked to make way for a new principal who would prepare the college for the post-war era. He resigned under pressure, laid down his Edinburgh Cathedral offices, and was deeply wounded psychologically by a sense of rejection.

Thus the bachelor Brasnett returned to his old haunts in Oxford where, sustained by a more than adequate private income, he lived for another 45 years in complete privacy.

At the same time every morning, until infirmity recently intervened, he was to be seen walking to a newsagent for his daily paper. He received no visitors, wrote no more books, sent Christmas cards to a few old friends. For a time he attended the early Sunday morning Holy Communion in the local parish church, but otherwise remained quite isolated, though served by a devoted housekeeper.

Bertrand Rippington Brasnett was born in Norfolk in 1893, but the family soon moved to Oxford. He won a scholarship to Keble College, where he read Greats and, after attending Cuddesdon Theological College, was ordained in 1916 by the famous Bishop Gore.

Brasnett was chaplain and assistant master at Bradfield College for two years before moving into parish life as a curate at Amersham. Four years later he was appointed chaplain of the Theological College at Cheshunt and in 1925 began his association with Edinburgh Theological College.

He succeeded as Vice-Principal his own brother, Canon Leslie Brasnett (now aged 90), and in 1930 became Principal. At the same time he was made a Canon of Edinburgh Cathedral and an examining chaplain to the Bishop. Later he served as Chancellor of the Cathedral.

February 12, 1988

The Reverend Sir Patrick Ferguson Davie, Bt

The Reverend Sir Patrick Ferguson Davie, 5th Bt, who has died in Cyprus aged 78, exercised his considerable liturgical knowledge as honorary chaplain to Robert Mortimer, Bishop of Exeter, throughout whose 24-year reign the two high churchmen laid on ceremonial which would not have displeased a Spanish cardinal.

Sir Patrick, who had recently succeeded his uncle in the baronetcy and family seat of Creedy Park, Devon, was responsible for advising the Bishop on all matters relating to worship.

Soon after his appointment in 1949 instructions were issued to cover virtually every movement of the Bishop during his visit to a parish church, from the moment he arrived at the church gate until he was ready to return to Exeter.

Bishop and chaplain both had an exalted view of the episcopal office, and the proposed ceremonial drew heavily on medieval sources, which on one occasion led to violent opposition. Prayer Books were thrown, chairs overturned and Sir Patrick had his surplice torn when four members of the Protestant Union were ejected from St Peter's Church at Shaldon, Devon, in 1952.

In 1961, Sir Patrick published *The Bishop in the Church*, as a guide for new bishops and others who were concerned with the ceremonial side of their work, and this proved to be useful even for those who did not accept all its recommendations.

Arthur Patrick Ferguson Davie, the son of an Indian Army colonel, was born in 1909 and educated at Wellington, Lincoln College, Oxford, and Ely Theological College.

He was ordained at Exeter in 1934 and spent three years as Curate of Littleham-cum-Exmouth before moving to another curacy in the well-known Anglo-Catholic parish of St Augustine, Kilburn. He also became an enthusiastic Territorial Army Chaplain.

During the 1939–45 War he served with the 4th Devonshire Regiment in Gibraltar, and later in North Africa and Italy. He was a fine chaplain, never anything less than a priest, popular with all ranks and always ready to work hard for the well-being of his regiment.

On leaving the Army in 1945 he returned to Devon to become Vicar of St John, Torquay, but when he inherited his family estate in 1947 he soon found that it was impossible to combine parochial and estate responsibilities, so he sadly left Torquay. Even more sadly, he was driven by death duties to sell his inheritance.

From 1966 to 1968 he was Rural Dean of Cadbury. After the retirement of Bishop Mortimer, Sir Patrick moved to Cyprus where he continued to minister in the English speaking community and also offered valuable advice on all aspects of worship to the Anglican Province of Jerusalem and the Middle East.

He married in 1949, Iris Cable-Buller, who survives him together with their son Antony, aged 35, who succeeds to the baronetcy.

February 22, 1988

Canon Edwyn Young

Canon Edwyn Young, who has died aged 74, was one of the Church of England's most colourful priests and claimed to be the first-ever chaplain to a striptease club, officiating at the Raymond Revuebar in Soho.

His claim was never challenged, and it is certain that he was the only Chaplain to the Queen and Chaplain of the Royal Victorian Order to hold such an office.

Young exercised a remarkably influential ministry among ordinary people in east London and central Liverpool, as well as those in the world of theatre and show business. He belonged to his Church's Anglo-Catholic wing, saw the Mass as the centre-point of parish life, and had an immense love of people which drove him in unusual directions in order to save their souls.

Cecil Edwyn Young was born in Colombo, Ceylon, in 1913 but his parents returned to England before his first birthday and he was brought up in Devon. After Radley, he entered Dorchester Missionary College in 1931 with a view to serving in the Church overseas, but this did not materialise and in 1936 he was ordained to a curacy at St Peter's, Wapping.

When the war came he was very much in the thick of it – ministering, under heavy bombing, to people in air raid shelters; to the dying and others who had lost their homes; and taking occasional breaks to visit parishioners who had been evacuated to the country.

In 1941 he became priest-in-charge of St Francis, near Paddington station, and in addition to tough pastoral ministry was also an air raid warden. On his marriage in 1944 to Beatrice Mary Rees he was appointed rector of Broughton with Ripton Regis, Hunts, but he was in no sense a countryman and within three years was back in London as vicar of St Silas, Pentonville.

In this toughest of all London parishes he soon became the leading figure in the community. He mixed easily with the poor and the criminal, selling his lively parish newspaper in the public houses on Saturday evenings, and befriending stallholders and their customers in the local market.

It was during this time that he was invited to become chaplain to Collins Music Hall and, fascinated by the stage, quickly established a rapport with both performers and managers, the clothed and the unclothed. He also took another music hall, near King's Cross, under his wing and became greatly loved in the show business world.

In 1953 the Bishop of London persuaded him to leave Islington in order to become rector of Stepney, a parish of some 32,000 people and comprising five pre-war parishes. Here he built up a staff of six curates, three women church workers, two club leaders and a secretary, and through a combination of hard work and audacity the Church infiltrated virtually every aspect of Stepney's community life.

At one time Young was a member of 44 committees and for five years was chairman of the Borough Youth Committee. In 1959 he became rural dean of Stepney and also a prebendary of St Paul's Cathedral.

The parish newspaper, reflecting the life of the whole community and once again sold in public houses, was called *Stepahoy*; on one occasion a member of the staff suggested that from time to time it might have a religious supplement.

In fact, it contained many pictures of the rector in the company of actors and actresses, for he was also chaplain of the London Palladium and often invited "stars" to church services and parish events.

Every summer he moved down to Kent for three weeks to minister to East Enders working in the hop fields.

In 1964 he went to Liverpool, spending the next nine years as rector of the parish church and also rural dean, becoming a canon diocesan of the cathedral soon after his arrival.

A city centre parish, with only a small resident population, cramped his style somewhat, but he found plenty of scope for his pastoral energy in the public life of Liverpool and, besides theatre and night-club chaplaincies, inaugurated a new form of ministry in departmental stores. It was sad, but perhaps not surprising, that this vigorous and creative ministry was halted by a severe heart attack in 1973.

On his recovery the following year, Young returned to London as Chaplain of the Queen's Chapel of the Savoy. This was a strange appointment in many ways, but the duties were light and theatreland was on the doorstep. So also were a number of London's leading hotels and soon Young persuaded their managements that no hotel was complete without its visiting chaplain.

He retired in 1983 and last year celebrated the 50th anniversary of his ordination to the priesthood surrounded by a large company of friends and former colleagues.

He is survived by his wife, two sons and a daughter.

March 2, 1988

The Right Reverend Christopher Robinson

The Right Reverend Christopher Robinson, the former Bishop of Bombay who has died in Delhi aged 84, was one of the most universally loved men in India and was believed by many to be a saint.

He first went to India in 1926 as a teacher and identified himself totally with the Indian people and their way of life. Although he belonged to the Catholic wing of the Anglican Church, his sympathies were wide and he played a crucial part in bringing together the six different churches that form the Church of North India in 1970.

New bishops always invited Robinson to preach the sermon when they were installed in their cathedrals. He was also tolerant of other religious faiths and was revered as a man of great holiness and wisdom wherever he went.

Christopher James Gossage Robinson, brother of the economist Sir Austin Robinson, was born in 1903; his earlier years were spent in the Close at Winchester, where his father was a canon. He was educated at Marlborough and Christ's College,

Cambridge, and after taking his degree in 1926 joined the teaching staff of St Stephen's College, Delhi.

Here he came under the influence of the Cambridge Brotherhood of the Ascension in Delhi and he returned to England in 1929 to be ordained into the priesthood. He was a curate of St Mary's, Portsea, for two years, then went back to India to join the Cambridge Brotherhood and to serve first as assistant priest then as Vicar of St James's, Delhi.

There he ministered to the Indian poor and the more affluent British with equal devotion and his reputation soon became known all over India. While still in his early thirties he became Superior of the Cambridge Brotherhood and in 1944, having by this time become Vicar of St Thomas's, New Delhi, he was appointed an honorary canon of Lahore Cathedral.

In 1947 he was consecrated as Bishop of Lucknow and began an episcopal ministry characterised by humility, holiness of life, and love of all who lived in his vast diocese. When his close friend and former colleague of Portsea days, William Lash, retired from the bishopric of Bombay in 1951, Robinson was his obvious successor and so for the next eight years Bombay enjoyed the presence and ministry of a very remarkable Christian leader.

Robinson's life was an example of what he preached and people came from near and far to seek his counsel. Besides helping to bring together the non-Roman Catholic churches of North India, he was deeply involved in the development of the united churches' liturgical life.

When he retired from the bishopric in 1970 he returned to Delhi to live a simple life in the Brotherhood House and continued to exercise a personal ministry that brought many to Christian faith and commitment. He was unmarried.

March 4, 1988

The Reverend Joe Williamson

The Reverend Joe Williamson, who has died aged 92, was a crusading East End clergyman celebrated for his campaigns to save prostitutes.

A deceptively frail figure with a bellowing voice, he regarded himself as "called" – having had "a vision" as he walked along Cable Street in Stepney where he was Vicar of St Paul's. "Suddenly", he recalled, "a woman called out to me: 'You walk past me because I'm a bloody prostitute, don't you?'

"I turned to her and saw she was young and very beautiful. Later I realised she was old and ugly with a razor-scarred face. But my vision was of the lovely girl she had been before prostitution destroyed her. Her name *had* to be Mary.

"It was a message from God", he explained. "I had to help women like her."

Williamson duly proceeded to turn Church House, Stepney, into a hostel for prostitutes; founded the Wellclose Square Fund on whose behalf he constantly toured the country and soon opened two more hostels in Essex and one in Birmingham. Troubled with failing eyesight he eventually had to retire from the parish in 1962 but continued as warden of the hostel.

Joseph Williamson was himself born into poverty in Poplar in 1895, as he described in his graphic autobiography, *Father Joe* (1963). His emancipation owed most to his remarkable mother – "one of Nature's greatest ladies".

At an early age he felt drawn to the priesthood and one day presented himself at the door of the local vicarage to announce this fact. The vicar, who was later to become Bishop of London, thanked him for the information and dismissed him with a curt good afternoon.

But he persevered and after attending St Augustine's College, Canterbury was ordained in 1925 in St Paul's Cathedral as Curate of Fulwell. Following another curacy in Kensington he went to South Africa and served on the staff of Grahamstown Cathedral from 1928 to 1932.

He then returned to England and in the course of his career rebuilt four churches, partly with his own hands. At Fenny Drayton, Leicestershire, he restored the church in the 15 months he was there by spending all his money on the work.

In 1934, when he went to Shimpling Suffolk, he had to stand in water to conduct the services in the parish church. He continued the successful fundraising while he was a chaplain to the forces during the 1939–45 War.

Then Williamson moved to Little Dunham, Norfolk, where he became a spare-time carpenter and bricklayer for months in order to repair the church. He arrived at St Paul's, Dock Street, Stepney in 1952 and undertook a major restoration of the church which had been bombed during the war.

From the platform of his provocative parish magazine, *The Pilot*, Williamson launched a series of outspoken attacks on the appalling conditions that prevailed in Stepney. In 1961 he described his parish to the London Diocesan Conference in a withering tirade: " We have developed into an area of low-level cafe-clubs for drugs, drink, gambling, and women.

"We have a hotbed of vice on gutter level. Humans are like rats, living in filth – two couples, four in a bed.

''We have actually been exhibited to sightseers in this setting. For one day a coach pulled into Ensign Street. They had an American guide; he led them to a Somali cafe-club – 'You'll find everything here!' he shouted – and, indeed, they would!

"At the same spot, one evening before the Street Offences Act, I found a group of my schoolchildren with coloured adults watching a coloured man and a white girl having sexual intercourse.

". . . Girls screaming and fighting for their money, girls taking man after man in the open streets, girls being smashed to the ground by men, thrown down bodily and kicked . . .

"There are people in this hall now who saw three men committing sodomy in the open in Wellclose Square.

"Right now I would move the unemployables, the impotent, and the weakminded not back to Malta or Jamaica or Africa but to hutments around the Houses of Parliament and the Lords, Lambeth Palace Gardens and suchlike. Let Parliament enjoy a bit of 'Sophia Town' under its own nose".

He challenged the then Minister of Housing, Henry Brooke, to join him in a walk around Stepney – "he would be sickened and shocked".

Father Joe was one of the Church of England's great characters. He was rarely to be seen other than in his cassock and biretta and his notable work in the East End also included the chaplaincy of the Sailors Home and the Red Ensign Club.

Among the staunch supporters of Father Joe's campaign to rescue prostitutes was the Queen Mother. He was appointed MBE in 1975.

March 17, 1988

The Right Reverend Lord Ramsey of Canterbury

The Right Reverend Lord Ramsey of Canterbury, 100th Archbishop of Canterbury, who has died aged 83, occupied the Primacy during a period of considerable turmoil in the Church of England and saw more changes in his Church than any other archbishop since the 17th century.

Although a professional theologian by training and inclination, he was nonetheless a churchman of deep spirituality; and the combination of intellectual gifts and interior strength proved to be a great asset to the Church of England at a time when ancient traditions of belief and practice were being seriously, and sometimes recklessly, challenged.

Ramsey also had the considerable advantage of looking like an archbishop. His venerable figure, first noted by the public when, at the age of 48, he occupied the Bishop of Durham's traditional place at the right hand of the Queen at her Coronation, seemed to be that of a mediæval prelate.

His massive frame, dome-like head, fluttering eyebrows and engaging stammer suggested to television viewers a man quite out of the ordinary, who yet fitted perfectly his high ecclesiastical office.

It was with some surprise that most of these viewers discovered that Ramsey, so evidently detached from the world, was also exceedingly shrewd in his judgment of human problems and out-spoken in his denunciation of what appeared to him to be wrong in the behaviour of individuals and nations.

During the 13 years of his Primacy (from 1961 to 1974) Ramsey became the most widely travelled Archbishop of Canterbury in history. He visited all the provinces of the Anglican Communion and was often in Eastern Europe as the guest of the Orthodox Churches, whose spirituality he greatly admired.

His visit to Rome in 1966 was the first to be made officially by an Archbishop of Canterbury since the Reformation; and he and Pope Paul VI not only worshipped together but also signed an agreed statement which led to the setting up of a joint Anglican/Roman Catholic Theological Commission.

His commitment to the cause of church unity in Britain suffered a serious blow with the collapse of the negotiations between the Church of England and the Methodist Church; but he was highly regarded in all the English Free Churches and was a popular, if not particularly energetic, president of the British Council of Churches.

On social and political issues Ramsey was generally of a liberal mind, supporting changes in the laws governing capital punishment, divorce, abortion and homosexuality; his deep concern for racial equality led to his appointment as chairman of the Community Relations Commission in Britain.

There was surprise and controversy when he suggested in 1965 that it would not be inappropriate for the British Government to use military force to deal with the unilateral declaration of independence by the white government of what was then Rhodesia: on the other hand, he was strongly opposed to the grants given by the World Council of Churches to "freedom-fighters" in Africa.

In 1971 he said: "The ordination of women to the priesthood will come. I think it will be seen in time that the objections are not everlastingly valid."

Arthur Michael Ramsey was born in 1904 in Cambridge, where his father was a lecturer in mathematics and later Master of Magdalene College. His paternal grandfather was a Congregationalist minister, and his maternal grandfather was an Anglican clergyman.

Ramsey was educated at Repton – when Geoffrey Fisher, his predecessor as Archbishop of Canterbury, was headmaster – and as a scholar at his father's college, where he obtained a second class in Classics and a first in Theology. He was President of the Cambridge Union in 1926 and the prospective Liberal parliamentary candidate for Cambridge.

At one time he considered reading for the Bar, but he changed his mind and decided to seek holy orders instead. He spent a year at Cuddesdon Theological College and in 1928 was ordained to a curacy at Liverpool Parish Church. Two years later his theological expertise was recognised by his appointment as Sub-Warden of Lincoln Theological College, where he remained until 1936.

During his time at Lincoln Ramsey published his first and most original book, *The Gospel and the Catholic Church*. In it he argued that the structure of the Church is an expression of the Christian Gospel, and although he was to modify this view later it plainly identified him with the high church wing of the Church of England – which, in its liberal expression, is where he remained for the rest of his life.

Ramsey next felt the need for more parish experience, and accordingly spent two years on the staff of Boston Parish Church before moving in 1939 to become vicar of St Benedict's, Cambridge. He stayed at St Benedict's for just over a year, as he was pressed to accept a chair of Divinity at Durham University, with which was linked a residentiary canonry of the cathedral.

Thus began his deep attachment to Durham and its people. The next ten years were probably the happiest of his life. In 1942 he married Joan Hamilton, whose father was a colonel, and who was at that time the secretary of his neighbour, the Bishop of Jarrow;

and while he was at Durham he wrote two more books – *The Resurrection of Christ* and, as a sign of his growing interest in Eastern Orthodoxy, *The Glory of God and the Transfiguration of Christ*.

Ramsey also proved to be a stimulating teacher and became a leading exponent of Biblical theology, to which he had been introduced at Cambridge by Sir Edwyn Hoskyns.

In 1950 he returned to Cambridge as Regius Professor of Divinity and as a fellow of his old college; but after the unexpected translation of Bishop Alwyn Williams to Winchester Ramsey was recalled to Durham in 1952 as its bishop. This was a difficult decision for him to make, and he confessed later that had the diocese been any other than Durham he would have declined.

But he was a churchman as well as a don, and although his tenure of the ancient prince bishopric was to last only four years it proved to be memorable. Durham loved its bishop, and he preached with eloquence in the cathedral, and with moving simplicity in the mining parishes of the diocese.

Wherever he went he spoke of the priority of God in human life and of the need for the Church's spiritual roots to be nourished. When his next book, *Durham Essays and Addresses*, was published in 1956, it attracted attention far beyond its place of origin.

In the same year Ramsey was translated to York in succession to Dr Cyril Garbett, who had occupied the archbishopric until his 81st year. He greatly missed Durham, but he soon became a popular figure in Yorkshire and also began to play an increasing part in the national affairs of the Church of England. He led an official delegation to the Russian Orthodox Church in 1956 and conducted a mission in Oxford in 1960, the addresses at which were published as *Introducing the Christian Faith*.

When Archbishop Fisher retired it seemed obvious to everyone – apart from Dr Fisher himself – that Ramsey should move to the southern Province. Fisher wanted Dr Donald Coggan, who was then Bishop of Bradford, to succeed him, but the Prime Minister, Harold Macmillan, would have none of this.

Macmillan later said to Ramsey: "Fisher may have been your headmaster, but I wasn't going to let him be mine."

So Ramsey went to Canterbury, and Coggan to York – a partnership which proved to be an uneasy one.

In his enthronement sermon in Canterbury Cathedral in June 1961 Ramsey spoke of the urgency of the quest for church unity and also hinted broadly that he was far from happy with the degree of state involvement in the Church of England's affairs. By the time of his retirement the Church had secured a new freedom to order its worship and was soon to be given much greater influence over the choice of its bishops.

There were those who thought that Ramsey did not make sufficient use of the influence he already had. But what he had not foreseen was the theological explosion which followed the publication by Bishop John Robinson of Woolwich of a controversial paperback entitled *Honest to God*.

Ramsey's initial reaction was to censure the bishop: "It is utterly wrong and misleading to denounce the imagery of God held by Christian men, women and children and to say that we cannot have any new thought until it is all swept away." But later he confessed that he had been too critical and conceded that Robinson had raised a number of important questions and may have been helpful to many people.

This particular incident was typical of Ramsey's reaction to most new developments in the Church. His immediate response was generally cautious or even negative, and it was not until he had had time to work through the matter intellectually that he was able to accept any possibility of change.

Similarly, when the proposals for reuniting the Church of England and the Methodist Church were first published Ramsey was not at all enthusiastic about them: but eventually he threw his weight behind the scheme, and was devastated when it was rejected by his Church.

Although this cautious style was often frustrating to those who were anxious for change, it served both to offer reassurance to the many who were afraid of upheaval and to help to maintain unity and stability within the Church of England; in the long run it facilitated rather than hindered reform.

Ramsey was disappointed over unity with the Methodists but he saw significant changes in the pattern of worship in the Church of England, with much greater emphasis on the Eucharist; and steps were taken to secure the more effective deployment of the clergy in both town and country. A strong permanent commission to advise on doctrinal matters was set up, and synodical government of the Church was established.

Throughout the years of his primacy Ramsey felt constrained to comment on political and social affairs both in Britain and elsewhere in the world. He was strongly against the Kenyan Asians Bill in 1968; and condemned the American bombing of North Vietnam. During a visit to South Africa he crossed swords with Prime Minster Vorster and said afterwards: "Violence is inevitable without speedy reforms to end the injustices and inhumanities of apartheid."

Ramsey's powerful speeches in the House of Lords sometimes made him unpopular in government circles; but he always spoke with great conviction, and his interventions sprang from a view of Church and society which owed much to his study of earlier theologians.

With the exception of Anselm in the 11th century and Cranmer in the 16th, no other Archbishop of Canterbury wrote more theological books. Most of these were translated into the main Western European languages, and many are likely to be read for some years to come. One was written jointly with Cardinal Suenens, the Roman Catholic Primate of Belgium. Ramsey's collection of ordination charges, *The Christian Priest Today*, is already a classic.

Among the many honorary degrees conferred on him none gave greater pleasure than the doctorate from the Spanish University of Salamanca. He was created a life peer in 1974.

Ramsey will be best remembered as an Archbishop who, in spite of his high office and its temptations, was never other than himself. The fact that he preferred a Morris Minor to the official

Daimler when travelling to London was unsurprising in a man who once said: "While Christians try to serve every human need they can serve, the greatest is the need to serve the love of God himself."

April 25, 1988

The Reverend John Foote

The Reverend John Foote, who has died aged 83,was awarded the Victoria Cross for his work helping the wounded under heavy fire on the beach during the ill-fated Dieppe Raid.

In eight hours of action on August 19, 1942, he assisted the medical officer in the first-aid post, exposing himself to "an inferno of fire," according to his citation, as he repeatedly went out onto the beach to give first aid, inject morphine and carry men down the shore to be picked up. While the tide went out, he calmly helped to move the post to a beached landing craft, from which he later removed the wounded when its ammunition was set alight by gunfire. Foote saved at least 30 lives. As the boats came in, he lifted the first man onto his back, walked down the beach into the sea and waded out to the nearest boat. Despite the jam around it, he then persuaded others to help him transfer the wounded man on board before returning to the beach to pick up another. For more than an hour the padre sought out boats, calling to all who could hear: "Every man carry a man!" When only one boat remained, two men grabbed his arms and pulled him into it. But as the boat moved away from the shore, Foote leapt into the water and returned to the beach because, as he said, "The men ashore would in all likelihood need me far more in the months of captivity ahead than any of those going home."

The commander of the Royal Hamilton Light Infantry, to which he was attached, had been concerned about the chaplain taking part in the raid, but Foote had reassured him, saying, "I know what's in the wind, I want to go." When Lieutenant-Colonel Robert Labatt jibbed, Foote replied, "Well, I'll make my own arrangements, and if you see me on the beach you can order me off." Somewhere in the columns of dark silhouettes that night the stowaway Foote sat on a hard bench among the men.

John Weir Foote was born at Madoc, Ontario, on May 5, 1904, and educated at the University of Western Ontario, Queen's University and McGill, where he studied to become a Presbyterian minister. He served congregations at Coulonge, Quebec, and Port Hope, Ontario, before enlisting at the beginning of the war in the Chaplain Services.

After Dieppe Captain Foote spent three years in a prisoner-of-war camp and did not gain his VC until 1946. When he first received the news, he thought it was a mistake. He stayed on with the army until 1948 before going to work briefly for the Ontario Liquor Control Board and then entering local politics as a Conservative member of the provincial parliament for Durham. For seven years until his retirement from politics in 1957 he was minister for reform institutions. He then served as sheriff of Northumberland County from 1960 to 1979.

Foote said that he rarely thought of the raid. "I don't like dwelling on unpleasant things. If I did something of value it was in the prison camp. The action at Dieppe was the easy part of it." His fellow prisoners in Stalag Luft 8b at Lambsdorf in Lower Silesia attested to the truth of his statement. The Canadians spent three months tied at the wrist with rope from Red Cross parcels, then 14 months shackled with slightly free-er chains. It was possible to slip the shackles, but the Germans would make offenders stand head and toes to a wall for a minimum of one hour with the threat of rifle butt between the shoulders if they moved.

As the only clergyman in the camp, Foote conducted services attended by all denominations and told everyone to call him just John instead of Padre. He organized baseball, bridge and cribbage tournaments, and encouraged men to take study courses for their return to civilian life. His leadership came to the fore during the fortnight when three prisoners killed themselves by slitting their wrists or throats with razor-blades. The dead men had taken the easy way out, he pointed out in a strongly worded sermon at a special service. They had acted selfishly in failing to show consideration for the loved ones who were waiting for them at home. No further suicides followed.

Foote died just before a meeting of the VC and GC Association in London, whose vice-chairman was Major-General H. R. B. Foote, who was born in India during the same year as John Foote and won his VC in the Western Desert in 1944. They were not related.

May 5, 1988

The Reverend Michael Bland

The Reverend Michael Bland, who has died aged 67, had an unhappy tenure as Rector of Buckland and Stanton with Snowshill, Gloucestershire, which combined the Church politics of a Trollope novel with the social comedy of one by Mrs Gaskell.

A former intelligence officer in the RAF, the bachelor Bland had the physical presence of a heavyweight boxer and what he himself described as "a later Ciceronian haircut".

He was appointed to the living in 1958 and remained there until shortly before his death: but his effective ministry ended in 1969 when he was charged in a Consistory Court at Gloucester for neglect of duties and conduct unbecoming a clergyman.

Wearing full convocation dress of cassock, gown, scarf and hood with white bands, he made Anglican history as the first person to be tried under the Ecclesiastical Jurisdiction Measure of 1963.

He was tried on four charges of neglecting his duties: by leaving church before Divine Service ended; refusing to baptise a baby;

preventing a parishioner from entering the church to declare publicly his dissent to the marriage of his son at the time the banns were published; and repelling another parishioner from Holy Communion without lawful cause.

Furthermore he was alleged to have written rude letters to six people; made offensive and hurtful remarks to parishioners; indulged four times in fits of temper in church, and to have have been generally short-tempered in the course of his dealings.

Under the charge of making offensive remarks, Bland was alleged at a parochial church council meeting to have said in effect that he hated his parishioners.

He was also said to have called one parishioner a liar and to have told him he should be ashamed of himself for taking part in Holy Communion when his purpose in attending church was to hear his daughter's marriage banns read.

Finally, Bland was alleged to have told the council that on the day he found no one in the church when he arrived to conduct a service he would have achieved what he wanted to do: he could then run the church the way he wanted without the local squire's paid servants and tenants.

Bland, defended in court by Geoffrey Howe (now the Foreign Secretary), was sentenced to be deprived of his living. But the verdict was overturned on appeal to the Court of Arches which simply administered a formal rebuke and allowed him to return to his parish. The legal fees incurred by the diocese of Gloucester amounted to some £30,000.

Any hope that once the court case was ended there would be a recovery of pastoral relations between the Rector and his parishioners were quickly dashed, for Bland seemed incapable of carrying out his work in a way that was appropriate and acceptable. Asked about the angry emotions felt by some of his congregation, he said: "Quite right. Get the violence off the streets and into the Church where it belongs."

For many years Sunday services in Buckland were attended only by the Rector's housekeeper. All attempts by bishops, archdeacons and others failed and the sad situation came to an end only recently when Bland was persuaded to accept retirement.

Michael Bland was born in 1921 and read history and theology at St Peter's College, Oxford, before preparing for ordination at Wycliffe Hall.

Curacies at Southampton, Milford-on-Sea and Newbury from 1952 to 1958 were followed by his appointment to Buckland, and Stanton with Snowshill, and quite soon after his arrival things began to go badly wrong.

July 18, 1988

Cardinal Maximilien de Furstenberg

Cardinal Maximilien de Furstenberg, who has died aged 83, was a cardinal whose name and pedigree somewhat overshadowed his achievements, though in 1972 his name appeared among a speculative shortlist of possible papal candidates.

At the time his chief credential was neatly summarised by Norman St John-Stevas in *The Sunday Telegraph* as that of a presence of aristocratic distinction; "If a papal election were a beauty contest – which was once denied by Pope John – Cardinal de Furstenberg would carry away the prize."

Maximilien de Furstenberg was born at the castle of Ter Worm, Roermond, in the Netherlands in 1904. But his family had served in the Belgian diplomatic corps and he felt himself to be thoroughly Belgian.

This feeling was strengthened by his education with the Benedictines at Maredescus near Namur. A spell at the Gregorian University in Rome during the turbulent years straddling the end of the 1920s and the beginning of the 1930s left him a keen observer of the political scene.

He was ordained priest in 1931. Although he would have been admirably suited for the Vatican's school for diplomats – then known as the Academy of Noble Ecclesiastios – he taught theology in the major seminary of Antwerp, moving on to Malines.

After a quiet war he returned to Rome in 1948 as Rector of the Belgian College. Rectors of national colleges often act as unofficial ambassadors of their bishops, a role in which he acquitted himself so well that he was ordained titular archbishop in 1949 and embarked on the career as a Vatican diplomat for which he seemed predestined.

His first posting was to defeated Japan and he became internuncio when it established diplomatic relations with the Holy See in 1952. From 1960 to 1962 he was in Australia, with responsibility also for New Zealand and Oceania. Then Pope John XXIII sent him to Portugal where he remained until 1967.

Paul VI made him a cardinal and Prefect of the Congregation for Oriental Churches of which he had, if the truth were known, little experience. Insiders said the real work was done by the secretary, Archbishop Marcio Brini.

He retired in 1973, but lingered on in Rome as a member of various commissions, one of which was that which supervised the Institute of Religious Works, better known as the Vatican Bank, headed by Archbishop Paul Marcinkus.

De Furstenberg was a man of impenetrable discretion. If he had any secrets or views he has taken them to the grave.

September 24, 1988

The Reverend John Milburn

The Reverend John Milburn, who has died aged 73, was a leader in that exotic fringe of the Church of England which in belief and practice is often more Catholic than the Pope and makes the ethos of latter-day Roman Catholicism seem distinctly Protestant.

He was essentially a parish priest, serving in Liverpool and Brighton, but for 14 years was also the energetic Chaplain General of the Society of Mary – an organisation concerned to foster devotion to the Virgin Mary in the Church of England.

Allied to this was a preference for the Baroque in church vestments and furnishings; following the stripping of many European churches after the reforms of Vatican II, he imported into his own church at Brighton a splendid array of items, many of which were of considerable artistic merit.

On the morning after the bombing of the Grand Hotel in 1984, Father Milburn appeared on the platform of the Conservative party conference to lead prayers for the dead and the injured.

The son of a mining engineer, John Milburn was born in Co. Durham in 1915. He read English at King's College, London, but then decided to seek ordination and in 1940 became a curate at the London parish of St Saviour's, Hoxton, where most of the services were conducted in Latin.

The church was bombed in 1941, and he spent the rest of the war on the staff of St Peter's, Limehouse, also teaching English in East End schools.

After the war he had another curacy in Worcester before becoming chaplain of the Hostel of God, a hospice on Clapham Common. Following four years in this post, where his ministry both to the dying and to the nursing staff was greatly valued, he was appointed in 1953 as Vicar of St Stephen's, Liverpool.

In a city and diocese where the Anglican evangelical tradition was strong, Milburn felt moved to take his own church to a theological and liturgical position close to that of his many Roman Catholic neighbours, and soon it became a well-known Anglo-Catholic centre for the whole of Lancashire.

In 1954 he became Vicar of the famous St Paul's Church, Brighton, and immediately set about the task of renewing its furnishings and fabrics. Not everything he brought back from the sacristies and second-hand shops of Austria and Germany was of equal value, but he had impeccable taste and what was not deemed suitable for Brighton was sold to other, less fortunate churches.

He also raised the standard of music to a high level, so that a visitor to St Paul's could easily believe himself to be in a former age, worshipping in one of the great churches of Saltzburg or Vienna.

Milburn's view of the priesthood also belonged to a former age. He was unmarried and lived a highly disciplined life, with the Mass and the Daily Office at its centre; but he had a multitude of friends and admirers – as well as some enemies who found his rigidity and sharp tongue less than attractive. No one was surprised when he assumed a leading role in opposing the ordination of women.

At one time he was a frequent visitor to Rome where he had several audiences with Pope Paul VI and was more than pleased to receive an honorary Doctorate of Sacred Philosophy from the International Marian Academy in Rome. He retired from his parish in Brighton in 1985.

October 26, 1988

1989

Canon Martin Andrews

Canon Martin Andrews, who has died aged 102, was a priest for almost 80 years and one of Cornwall's best-loved characters.

Andrews was appointed Rector of Stoke Climsland in 1922 after a chance meeting with the then Prince of Wales on the steps of the Duchy of Cornwall office in London, and six years later he prevailed upon his patron to assist him in providing work for some of Cornwall's many unemployed.

The Duchy gave Andrews land near the rectory at a low rent, and he established there, with the help of his former Army batman, a successful flower and vegetable farm where jobs were found for young men who would otherwise have been unemployed. The project lasted 38 years and at its peak employed 45 men and women on 250 acres of land.

Offered grander posts in the church he said "What's to become of my people working on the farms? I can't say, 'Goodbye, chaps, I'm off to be a bishop.'"

The Prince took a particular interest in the scheme – "Why can't this be done everywhere?" he asked – and on his accession as King Edward VIII in 1936 immediately appointed Andrews as one of his chaplains.

Thus began a friendship with the Royal Family which continued through the reign of King George VI and even beyond his retirement from the Royal Chaplaincy.

Andrews also enjoyed the friendship of many of Cornwall's landed families, whose weddings and christenings he conducted, and the rectory saw many fashionable garden parties.

Andrews was an honorary canon of Truro Cathedral for more than 50 years. In his younger days he was an outstanding games-player, representing Cornwall at tennis, competing at Wimbledon and, in 1919, captaining a British Army soccer team against the Belgian Army.

Leonard Martin Andrews was born at Hackney in 1886 and educated at Owens School. His father was in the rag trade, and it was intended that he should follow in his footsteps, but after coming down from Queens' College, Cambridge, in 1909 he was ordained in St Paul's Cathedral to a curacy at Winchmore Hill.

In 1913 he moved to Australia to join the Brotherhood of the Good Shepherd – a community of priests, known as "the Bush Brothers", who served the remote sheep stations and opal fields of the Outback.

At the beginning of the 1914–18 War Andrews joined the Australian Army as a private and went to Gallipoli with the Anzacs as a stretcher-bearer with the 1st Field Ambulance Unit. In 1916, while recovering from a fever, he was persuaded to transfer to the British Army.

On the battlefields of France he was officiating padre as shell-shocked British soldiers were shot for cowardice, and as a chaplain with the Royal Fusiliers in 1917 he was wounded and awarded the Military Cross.

From 1920 to 1922 he was Chaplain of the Cathedral at Khartoum in the Sudan, and it was during the course of a visit to London to play tennis at Wimbledon that he met the Prince of Wales. He spent the rest of his long ministry in Cornwall, where he proved to be a devoted pastor and was in great demand as a preacher, albeit of an emotional style – his sermons were sometimes accompanied by tears.

He founded the Stoke Climsland Football Club for which he played at centre-half until he was 46; and during the 1939–45 War he was a company commander in the local Home Guard. He continued to exercise an influential ministry in Cornwall until shortly before his death.

Andrews was appointed MBE in 1944 and CVO in 1946. In 1974 he published a lively autobiography, *Canon's Folly*, but on his 100th birthday refused all but one of the many requests for interviews from journalists on the grounds that his life story was not worth reporting.

As a young unmarried priest of some style, with a fine military record and even better tennis, he was a more than welcome guest at houses where there were eligible daughters. But he never married and for many years enjoyed the close companionship of a male friend, Vincent Curtis, who died in 1981.

February 16, 1989

Canon Graham Routledge

Canon Graham Routledge, who has died aged 61, was a Canon of St Paul's and before his ordination in 1966 had a distinguished career at the Chancery Bar of Liverpool and the Northern Circuit.

As a churchman he was, in addition to his cathedral appointments, Chancellor of the Dioceses of Ely, Peterborough and Lichfield, and for eight years combined the posts of Director of Studies in Law and Dean of Chapel at Corpus Christi College, Cambridge. He founded the Ecclesiastical Law Society and remained its chairman until his death.

Like others before him, Routledge did not find it easy to marry a finely tuned legal mind to the claims of the Christian religion, and he was generally ill at ease in a church where a legal approach to religious problems won him little sympathy.

This made him a difficult colleague for those who did not share his theological opinions, which were very conservative, and he was a thorn in the flesh to successive Deans of Peterborough and thereafter to Dean Webster of St Paul's, who retired in 1987.

Routledge's appointment by the Crown to a Canonry of St Paul's in 1982 came soon after the controversial Falklands War thanksgiving service in the Cathedral and was widely interpreted as a combined operation by the Prime Minister and the Bishop of London designed to bring St Paul's to heel.

Routledge was a complex personality, with a considerable interest in power, and within a surprisingly short time had welded his fellow Canons into a formidable force opposed to the Dean, leading in the end to a demand for the liberal Dr Webster's resignation.

This was unsuccessful but the incident and other related events soured relations at St Paul's for several years and outclassed anything to be found in the novels of Anthony Trollope and Susan Howatch.

As Treasurer of St Paul's Routledge had a special responsibility for the protection of the cathedral's treasures, a task which he discharged assiduously and independently. His gifts as a teacher were exercised more effectively in study groups than in the pulpit and he led a much valued group on Dostoyevsky, to whose writings he was specially devoted.

He also took great interest in the work of the Friends of the Cathedral and was good company with laypeople in convivial gatherings outside the cathedral precincts. Meetings of the New Right were often held at his home in Amen Court.

Kenneth Graham Routledge was born at Birkenhead on September 21, 1927. He went straight from Birkenhead School into the Army in 1945, serving first in the Royal Engineers, then in the Education Corps.

On demobilisation he read Law at Liverpool University where he took a First, and was called to the Bar in 1952, winning several honours at the Middle Temple. Eleven years of Chancery work in the North West followed and he became much involved in public life.

In the 1959 General Election he was an unsuccessful Conservative candidate at Birkenhead, and he served for three years on Birkenhead borough council. He was also a lecturer in Law at Liverpool University and found time to play rugby football for Birkenhead.

In 1963, to the great surprise of his friends in the legal world, he decided to seek ordination and went to Cambridge to read Theology at Fitzwilliam College and to complete his preparation for Orders at Westcott House.

He was ordained at Chester in 1969 and spent three years as a curate at St George's Stockport with the redoubtable Canon Wilfred Garlick as his vicar. During this time he also taught Law at Manchester University.

When Corpus Christi College, Cambridge, required both a Dean of Chapel and a lecturer in Law they found the perfect combination in Routledge who was soon very much at home in the Corpus tradition of conservative politics and "high and dry" religion.

Routledge's teaching was of exceptional quality and the life of the college chapel was ordered with meticulous care. His home was a place of warm friendship and generous hospitality, and outside Cambridge he made many friends through his highly competent legal work in the Church and his membership of the governing bodies of Haileybury and the Woodard schools.

He became a Canon Residentiary of Peterborough cathedral in 1977 continuing to teach in Cambridge until he moved to London.

Routledge is survived by his wife, the former Muriel Shall-cross, whom he married in 1960. There were no children of their marriage. His sister is the well-known stage and television actress Patricia Routledge.

May 22, 1989

Canon Bill Sargent

Canon Bill Sargent, who has died aged 62, had a fine brain, was a superb preacher and with his broad vision would have made an exciting cathedral dean; but his Left-wing political views, allied to a disdain for the Establishment, made him suspect among those with preferment at their disposal.

It was said that his extreme position disqualified him from any representative office higher than that of Rural Dean of Portsmouth – though health problems in recent years had to be taken into account, and it is doubtful whether he would have been able to work effectively within the constraints of modern episcopal life.

So he gave himself unstintingly to two important parishes, one in London's East End, the other in Portsmouth, and offered powerful leadership in community life as well as in the church.

He was a Labour councillor in Hackney and a pacifist member of CND; he started a Yellow Star movement to support Jews under attack from the National Front; and among much social involvement in Portsmouth pioneered a housing association which now has assets of more than £60 million and a staff of more than 100. But above all he was a caring pastor and a friend to anyone in need.

William Richard Gerald Sargent was born in Suffolk in 1926, and his early promise as a linguist won him a place at the London University School of African and Oriental Studies. But instead he enrolled in the wartime Indian Army, suspending his pacifist convictions for a time.

On demobilisation he joined the police force in Middlesbrough and three years later transferred to the Colonial Police in Malaya.

None of this work won the approval of his increasingly sensitive social conscience, so he returned to England and, after two years at Lincoln Theological College, was ordained to a curacy at Newlands in Hull. Now he had found his true metier and before long he was appointed vicar of Holy Trinity, Dalston, one of London's toughest parishes.

Ten years of outstanding and often highly controversial work there was followed by appointment in 1970 to St Mark's, North End, Portsmouth, where his blunt opposition to the Falklands War in 1982 landed him in much hot water with the naval and dockyard communities.

But he was too good and lovable a priest to hate or despise. He became an honorary Canon of Portsmouth Cathedral in 1983 and was made Rural Dean in 1984.

He is survived by his wife, Jill, and three daughters.

June 10, 1989

The Reverend Paul Kingdon

The Reverend Paul Kingdon, the scholar priest who has died aged 82, was well known in Oxford in the 1930s but never fulfilled his early promise.

Although a Fellow of Exeter College, Oxford, from 1933 to 1945 he had no vocation as a teacher. He was relentless in the pursuit of arcane detail and lectured in terms so obscure that few of his students could understand him.

Sadly, he fared little better as a parish priest. He had a remarkable capacity for creating misunderstanding and often left a trail of havoc behind him. Kingdon did have, though, an unrivalled knowledge of German theology.

His history of the Church in Germany – and the two extracts from Kittel's monumental *Theological Word Book of the New Testament* which he edited and translated into English in 1958 – were models of scholarship and lucidity.

Henry Paul Kingdon was born in 1907 and was educated at Corpus Christi College, Oxford, where he just missed a double first in Greats.

He took the Diploma in Theology with distinction and then studied at Tübingen, where he was introduced to the liberal German theologians of the time.

In 1933 he became Chaplain of Exeter College, Oxford and was elected a Fellow a year later.

He played a full part in the life of the college and served as librarian from 1940 to 1945, during which time he also edited the *Oxford Magazine*.

At the end of the 1939–45 War the college presented Kingdon to the living of Somerford in Wiltshire.

In 1951 he returned to teaching, at King Alfred's College, Winchester. He was not a success there and left in 1956.

Kingdon then became Vicar of Chewton Mendip, near Bath, and was also appointed as a lecturer at Wells Theological College. He was quite unfitted for both these posts, the second of which lasted no more than a fortnight.

Fortunately, he inherited enough money to retire in 1964, to Almondsbury in Bristol, where, relieved of the burden of parochial responsibility, he exercised a much appreciated personal ministry as an honorary curate of the parish church.

His wife, Joan, predeceased him.

June 24, 1989

The Very Reverend Allan Shaw

The Very Reverend Allan Shaw, who has died aged 62, was Dean of Bulawayo from 1967 to 1975, a canon residentiary of Hereford from 1975 to 1982 and Dean of Ely from 1982 to 1984.

Shaw sought to combine in the priesthood the sensitivity of a caring pastor, the flair of a theatrical impresario and the humour of a clown; he was highly successful in all three spheres, but the attempt to hold them together ended in disappointment.

Like many apparently flamboyant figures with theatrical connections Shaw was essentially a lonely and melancholic man; and it was perhaps his longing for acceptance, friendship and love that led to certain indiscretions at Ely which brought his ministry there to an abrupt conclusion.

Charles Allan Shaw was born in humble circumstances at Westhoughton in Bolton in 1927, and was educated at the local grammar school and Christ's College, Cambridge, where he read Modern Languages and Theology. He taught briefly at Tonbridge School before training at Westcott House, Cambridge, and was ordained in 1951 to a curacy at Swinton in Manchester.

Three years later Shaw returned to teaching, as an assistant master at Malvern, and in 1958 he became Vicar of St Ambrose, Pendleton in Salford. The parish was a tough one, and Shaw's ministry lasted only four years; but the care and enthusiasm which he brought to the task are still spoken of. He was also an excellent preacher.

Leonard Wilson, the Bishop of Birmingham, then invited him to become his domestic chaplain and also succentor of Birmingham Cathedral. Thus began an association with cathedrals which was to continue for the next 22 years. In 1967, soon after the Smith regime in Rhodesia declared its independence of Britain, Shaw was appointed Dean of Bulawayo.

The Cathedral congregation was mainly white, and very anxious, and Shaw was able to offer an understanding ministry. He made no attempt to become involved in politics – although his Bishop, Kenneth Skelton, was sympathetic to the claims of the Africans – concentrating rather on raising the money for new cloisters and a chapter house.

In 1975 Shaw returned to England and became a canon residentiary of Hereford. The next year the diocese celebrated its 1,300th anniversary, and Shaw, very much in his element, organised a festival. Such was its success that he went on to establish Shaw's Enterprises, which continued to organise festivities of various kinds on a smaller scale.

Shaw used this opportunity to extend his contacts with the world of the stage and the arts in which he became widely known; and with the aristocracy, many of whom welcomed him to their country homes.

Although by no means an easy colleague on the Hereford Chapter – his love of exotic attire grated on some – Shaw spread cheer wherever he went and was always a good friend to anyone in trouble.

His appointment as Dean of Ely in 1982 was seen as an attempt to introduce fresh air into a distinctly stuffy atmosphere. Those who knew him well, though, dreaded the personal problems that might arise if loneliness and frustration were combined. Sadly, these conditions were evident soon after his arrival in the Close, and his early departure frustrated what might have been a creative ministry in the Fens.

There followed a short and humiliating period of unemployment, until the Marquess of Hertford came to the rescue by appointing him Rector of the attractive Warwickshire parish Alcester with Arrow.

Shaw threw himself into parish life with characteristic zest, and with greater discretion than he had hitherto shown; he concentrated on pastoral work and raising money for the restoration of the church tower, which was successfully accomplished shortly before his death.

He was unmarried.

July 22, 1989

1990

Prebendary Richard Hetherington

Prebendary Richard Hetherington, who has died aged 81, was one of the best-loved priests in the London diocese and numbered among his flock such diverse figures as Princess Marie-Louise, Dame Sybil Thorndike and the Kray Twins.

Violet Kray, the adored mother of Ronnie and Reggie, was a regular church-goer and would sometimes ask Hetherington to "speak to the boys". He duly did so – and to some effect, as he was a physically powerful and verbally forthright man.

The priest remembered the twins with affection: "They were extremely kind boys and would do anything for me except actually come to church. But they were both exceptionally polite, to old folk in particular, and they took trouble over people." He blamed their moral decline on the excessive publicity given to their boxing: "Everything went wrong once the local papers published the twins' photographs and wrote about them as super boxers when they were really two ordinary East End boys."

Reggie called him "the most understanding man I know" and sometimes asked him to pray for him. Their friendship survived Hetherington's refusal to officiate at Reggie's wedding, which he felt should not have taken place at all. His misgivings were perhaps justified when Reggie's bride committed suicide two years later – but he did agree to conduct her funeral, a typically theatrical occasion. And in 1982, keeping a promise made to Violet Kray 30 years earlier, he emerged from retirement to conduct her funeral.

Richard Nevill Hetherington was born in November 1908. He worked for a while in banking, entered Lichfield Theological College in 1930, was ordained deacon in 1932 and priest a year later. His first curacy was at St Luke's, Shepherds Bush (now demolished) and his second at St Barnabas, Ealing – in the days when curates entered the vicarage by the servants' entrance.

After the death of his fiancee Hetherington devoted himself to the Church and celibacy. During the Second World War he served as a chaplain with the RNVR, and after spent his five years at Bethnal Green, as Vicar of St James the Great. In 1951 he returned to Ealing, as Vicar of St Barnabas, where he remained until his retirement in 1976; in 1971 he became a prebendary of St Paul's Cathedral.

It may have been Hetherington's experiences at Bethnal Green, riddled then with protection rackets, that gave him his lifelong disdain for money. He loathed the need for church fund-raising, but when Ealing instituted an annual "Gifts Day" he stood all day at the church gate to accept offerings.

Ealing has seldom seen anything like the stream of taxis that descended on St Barnabas's from the East End, each disgorging a lavish gift – a sack of toys, a valuable antique or simply a wad of banknotes. Ever scrupulous, Hetherington would inquire of each rough-looking philanthropist, "It is a genuine gift? You didn't *lean* on anyone for this, I trust?" to be met with the reply: "Clean as a whistle, Reverend, God's honour."

He was passionately opposed to the tide of laxity which he felt was engulfing the Church. A Prayer Book Catholic, in 1972 he was a founder of the London-based Book of Common Prayer Action Group, which three years later became the national Prayer Book Society, with Hetherington as vice-president.

He was a hospital chaplain in the days when such positions carried no financial reward, and his sympathetic but never less than authoritative insight won many converts. He was always on duty, and once at a dinner party he rebuked a fellow priest for not wearing a dog-collar.

In retirement he lived at Cheltenham, in a home for elderly clergy; and his last days were cheered by the Prince of Wales's speech before Christmas, at a Prayer Book Society event which Hetherington was not strong enough to attend. He died in a nursing home, where the Bishop of London and his wife were among his last visitors; they found him still determined to enjoy God's gifts of tobacco and whisky.

January 14, 1990

The Reverend Joseph McCulloch

The Reverend Joseph McCulloch, who has died aged 81, was a highly gifted Anglican priest, notable for the skill and energy with which he conveyed his sometimes unorthodox views.

He did outstanding work as a parish priest at Chatham and at Warwick, and was responsible for the restoration of the church of St Mary-le-Bow, Cheapside, after its destruction by wartime bombing.

St Mary-le-Bow boasts twin pulpits, which McCulloch used to great effect every Tuesday lunchtime, when he invited well-known figures – writers, broadcasters, politicians and actors – to discuss the issues of the day with him. For the speakers, no less than the audience, he proved an enduring influence.

In earlier days, though, McCulloch had been the *enfant terrible* of the Church of England. In 1932 he found himself obliged to leave his first curacy at Blundellsands on Merseyside after only a few months because his novel *Charming Manners* – although written under a pseudonym – insufficiently disguised the identities of various prominent people in the parish.

Later, he departed from another curacy, in Westminster, when the Rector, who had been absent in Australia, discovered on his return dynamic initiatives which he could not approve.

McCulloch's service as an army chaplain during the Second World War ended abruptly when he sent the Chaplain General a critical report on the conduct of religion in the armed forces. His controversial views also caused him to be banned from broadcasting by the BBC for a year.

These hazards left McCulloch undaunted. He expressed his ideas on Church reform in several widely noticed books, and also published an abridged edition of the Bible, about a quarter of the length of the Authorised Version, presented so as to attract new readers.

Like many prophets and reformers, McCulloch had an independent, impatient temperament. He could be sharply critical of his fellow clerics, and was more relaxed in the company of laymen. Undoubtedly at times he suffered from disappointment that his gifts and ideas were not recognised by more substantial preferment.

Joseph McCulloch was born in a working-class district of Liverpool on August 31, 1908, and, having become closely involved with the local Anglo-Catholic church, went as a scholar to Exeter College, Oxford, to read Theology.

After some hesitation McCulloch decided to enter the Church, under the influence of Dr H. D. A. Major, the Principal of Ripon Hall, Oxford, who was then the leader of the liberal Modern Churchmen's Union.

As a result of the difficulties at Blundellsands with his novel, McCulloch became a figure of some notoriety. He was rescued by Canon F. H. Gillingham, the famous cricketing parson, who took him on as his curate at Lee, in south London.

There McCulloch was happy and repaid the Rector by marrying his daughter. In 1935, after his second ill-fated curacy – this time at St John's, Smith Square – he became Rector of Turweston, a rural parish in Buckinghamshire. He earned the gratitude of parishioners, not only for his spiritual ministrations, but also for his part in bringing water and electricity to the village.

He risked a second novel, *Limping Sway*, which dealt with life in a cathedral close, and then another book, *A Parson in Revolt*, which indicated his position in the Church.

The Rector of Turweston, though, was not really a country-man. When in 1938 he moved to Great Warley in Essex, he eagerly noted that his new residence was only an hour from Broadcasting House, and profited accordingly.

On the outbreak of war, McCulloch took up duty as chaplain to an anti-aircraft brigade, and served with them in the London blitz. By 1941 he was back in his parish, and four more books appeared – *The Divine Drama*, *The Faith That Must Offend*, *We Have Our Orders*, and *The Trumpet Shall Sound*.

These books, together with his broadcasts, made McCulloch a household name, and his projected reforms, which included the disestablishment of the Church, the re-organisation of parishes and the ordination of women, attracted much sympathy.

In 1943 the Bishop of Rochester challenged him to put some of his ideas into practice at St Mary's, Chatham – a huge parish church with a tiny congregation. McCulloch threw himself into the task of revival. Over the course of six years at Chatham he built up a strong core in the church, where he invested the worship with fine ceremonial.

He held a one-man brains trust in the Red Lion Inn on Sunday evenings, established links with other churches in the town, and strove to integrate the life of the church more closely with that of the secular community.

The book he wrote about this experience, *The Medway Adventure*, inspired others to attempt similar approaches in their parishes, though few had the flair and energy which brought McCulloch success. Unfortunately, his wife's ill-health required him to leave bleak Chatham just as the parish was moving into top gear.

In 1949 McCulloch became the Rector of St Mary's, Warwick, where for the next 10 years he worked at reordering and refurbishing the interior of the ancient church, a task which involved him in a Consistory Court battle.

He established the Eucharist as the main act of worship, and cherished a deep attachment to the Book of Common Prayer and to the Authorised Version, the language of which he held to be more inspiring than any of the modern translations.

When McCulloch moved to London in 1959 as Rector of St Mary-le-Bow, very little of the church remained from the bombing. He set up an office in a builder's hut and went on a four-month world tour to raise funds. After five years, in 1964, the finely restored building was reconsecrated.

After retiring from St Mary-le-Bow in 1979, McCulloch lived his last years as a recluse in Westminster. He had been given to expressing his disillusion with traditional concepts of the ministry. "My experience as a clergyman has been the long process of discovering the extent and nature of the intolerable imprisonment of Christian priesthood."

If he could live his life again he said, he would enter Holy

Orders only on condition that he could earn his own bread and serve the Church outside the parochial system.

Joseph McCulloch's wife, Betty, predeceased him. He is survived by a son and two daughters.

March 5, 1990

The Very Reverend
H. C. N. "Bill" Williams

The Very Reverend H. C. N. "Bill" Williams, the former Provost of Coventry who has died aged 75, was a dynamic leader during the 1960s and 1970s, when he made the Cathedral an international symbol of reconciliation and of the Church's willingness to address itself to the modern era.

He was appointed Provost while the new Cathedral was being rebuilt after wartime bombing. By the time of its completion in 1962 he had a clear plan of the shape of its future ministry and a gifted Chapter and staff to enable him to carry it out.

As he contemplated the ruins of the old building, Williams conceived the idea of the Cathedral as a "phoenix rising from the ashes" to engage in a mission of reconciliation, initially between wartime enemies in Britain and Germany, but later to all areas of human conflict – racial, economic and political.

Imaginative use was made of a "Cross of Nails", contrived from three nails rescued from the ruins, which Williams took with him on teaching and lecturing tours in Germany, America and other parts of the world, and which led to the establishment of Cross of Nails centres where people sought to become agents of reconciliation in society.

Soon after the completion of the main building of the Cathedral, he arranged for a party of young Germans to come over to Coventry to help rebuild both the old vestries, which their fathers had destroyed, and an international youth centre later dedicated to the memory of J. F. Kennedy by Bishop Otto Dibelius of Berlin. A group of young people from Coventry also went to Dresden to share in the rebuilding of that city.

Williams drew much of his inspiration from the concept of a Benedictine community concerned with the whole of life, and after the spectacular consecration of the cathedral, which was seen by millions on television, he found the world flocking to its doors.

Long queues formed to enter the building and the money provided by their offerings and purchases at the gift shop and restaurant enabled him to build up a staff of more than 120, employed on a wide range of religious and social projects.

The influence of Coventry soon spread to other cathedrals and it is not too much to say that the vigorous life and warmth of welcome experienced, uniquely, in most English cathedrals today is due to the pioneering ministry of Bill Williams.

The international dimension of this ministry made it difficult, however, for Coventry Cathedral to relate effectively to its immediate city and diocesan communities, both of which often complained of being neglected.

Neither was Williams easy to work with. Like many visionary prophets, there was a paranoid element in his personality which made him excessively jealous of the Cathedral's reputation and liable to explode in anger at the slightest hint of criticism. His long absences from Coventry were occasionally regarded as something of a relief.

It is fortunate that Cuthbert Bardsley, who was Bishop of Coventry at the time, understood and admired him, and was able to exercise his own notable ministry of reconciliation between Williams and those who served with him.

Later Williams became critical of Basil Spence's design for the Cathedral, claiming that it was a difficult building to use and describing Graham Sutherland's great tapestry as "like a poster".

Harold Claude Noel Williams was born at Grahamstown, South Africa, on December 6, 1914 and educated at Graeme College, before coming to England to read Theology and prepare for ordination at Hatfield College, Durham. He often said that he felt cramped in England after the open spaces of Africa and that he needed a worldwide ministry.

After three years as a curate in Winchester, he returned to South Africa in 1941 as chaplain of St Matthew's College, becoming principal of the college in 1943.

In 1950 he was back in Winchester as Vicar of Hyde, and four years later was appointed Rector of St Mary's Southampton. The ancient parish church and many other churches in central Southampton had been destroyed by wartime bombing and Williams was entrusted with the formidable task of rebuilding St Mary's and leading the reorganisation and renewal of church life in the city centre.

Not everything he achieved during the next four years has stood the test of time but it was on the strength of his energetic ministry at Southampton and his capacity for inspiring others that he was appointed, in 1958, to the key post at Coventry.

He once described the Cathedral as "a laboratory of experiment" and had no difficulty in declining an invitation to become a Suffragan Bishop in the north of England. Before his retirement in 1981, he wrote a number of books, mainly about cathedral life and the reform of the church, and also a book about African folk songs.

Bill Williams's love of mountain-climbing fitted his life and personality well – he said that he always sang the *Te Deum* when he reached a peak.

He married, in 1940, Pamela Taylor; they had two sons and three daughters (one of whom predeceased him).

April 11, 1990

The Reverend Roy Trevivian

The Reverend Roy Trevivian, who has died aged 69, was a brilliant BBC radio producer of religious programmes whose nine years at Broadcasting House were full of incident and ended disastrously.

His most famous programme was *Speakeasy* on Radio 1, in which Jimmy Savile combined entertainment and edification in a unique way. The religious content of the programme was not always obvious, but the programme attracted large audiences and prime ministers were more than ready to be interviewed on it.

Trevivian was also responsible for starting *Five To Ten*, in which ordinary people were brought into a studio to speak about personal concerns.

His gift was to bring the common touch to programmes without the slightest hint of condescension, and he was fascinated by showbusiness. He was less successful in judging what was acceptable on Radio 4, and this led to his downfall.

In 1971 Trevivian was the producer of a *Thought for the Day* broadcast in which the speaker was allowed to launch a sharp attack on the Heath administration's handling of the Northern Ireland problem. This was regarded as a serious error and, added to a number of other problems, brought about his speedy departure from the BBC.

The speaker, Dr Colin Morris, was rather more fortunate: he was later appointed Head of Religious Broadcasting and is now Controller of BBC Northern Ireland. The remainder of Trevivian's life was tinged with tragedy.

Roy Trevivian was born in 1921 and brought up in harsh surroundings in Stockport. He rejoiced in his northern origins, but was constantly struggling to cope with the serious psychological damage inflicted on him in his youth.

Methodism came to the rescue and, after serving in the RAF in India and training at Richmond Theological College, he was ordained into the Methodist ministry.

Trevivian was a popular minister in Surrey in the early 1950s, then decided to seek ordination in the Church of England. He spent a year at Lichfield Theological College; had a short curacy at Burgh Heath, near Tadworth; then became vicar of a new housing area parish in Guildford.

He was in his element in a sphere where he was not required to bow to the conventional and in 1964 the then Bishop of Guildford, George Reindorp, who had noted his gift as a popular communicator, recommended him to the BBC.

The work of a producer-cum-performer perfectly fitted one side of his character, but left the damaged side of him cruelly exposed. The years of total abstinence required of him by Methodism were more than made up for in Broadcasting House bars.

Trevivian's marriage foundered, his language was too colourful for a clergyman; and, like some others in the entertainment world, he was at times afflicted with deep melancholy. He could be impossible to work with.

After leaving the BBC he was for the next few years under medical care and incapable of taking another appointment, but he wrote a paperback *So You're Lonely*, which was widely read at the time.

He then became chaplain of the Mayflower Family Centre in Canning Town, where he found an accepting community and did sterling work among young people and adults who were miles removed from conventional church life.

In 1981, though, Trevivian had a severe stroke which deprived him of his speech and left him badly disabled for the rest of his life, which he spent in the Royal Star and Garter Home at Richmond and then in a Cheshire Home in Cornwall.

Shining through the darkness of so much of his life there was, however, a bright light of goodness, love and courage, and to those who knew him well it was a miracle that he accomplished so much. When, in 1988, a course of addresses on 20th century saints was given in Westminster Abbey, Roy Trevivian was numbered among them. The choice caused some eyebrows to be raised but it was by no means an inappropriate one.

He is survived by his wife Yvonne, and by a son and a daughter.

May 12, 1990

Chancellor the Reverend E. Garth Moore

Chancellor the Reverend E. Garth Moore, who has died aged 84, was one of the foremost ecclesiastical lawyers of his day, serving as Chancellor, Vicar-General and Official Principal of the dioceses of Southwark, Durham and Gloucester and also as chairman of the General Synod's Legal Advisory Commission.

He was a substantial contributor to the ecclesiastical section of the third edition of *Halsbury's Laws of England*.

Moore's attachment to the letter of the law and his uncompromising, sometimes tyrranous attitude in the Consistory Court over which he presided had, however, the effect of making a large number of clergy and laity question the validity of the ecclesiastical law in a community based on faith and love – and even drove some to regard Chancellors as the successors of the Jewish lawyers who had secured Christ's crucifixion.

He was disappointed to miss appointment as Dean of the Arches – the highest office in the ecclesiastical courts.

A crisis point was reached in Southwark in 1964 when, after a spectacular clash between the Bishop, Mervyn Stockwood, and the Chancellor, the Bishop decided to preside over his own Consistory Court and so reduce Moore's influence.

The clergy of the diocese had come to feel that Moore was intolerant and unsympathetic when faculties for change were required. Matters came to a head when he questioned the demolition of a church in Peckham which, owing to serious building faults, had been declared unsafe.

Some years earlier Stockwood had been advised by Moore to undertake the public deposition of a sexually delinquent clergyman which had caused much adverse publicity and which Stockwood later believed to have been a serious mistake. Moore returned to the Southwark Consistory Court after Stockwood's retirement in 1980.

Of his knowledge of ecclesiastical law there could be no doubt, and he was frequently consulted by archbishops' bishops and others faced with knotty legal problems. He firmly believed – and this may have been the source of some of the difficulties – that the Church's law derived its authority ultimately from religious beliefs about the creation of the universe.

He also had strong views on the relationship between church law and statute law. Thus he decreed that since confession in the presence of a priest is prescribed by the Book of Common Prayer, which has the authority of the 1662 Act of Uniformity, a priest is not only protected against a demand to disclose what he has heard in the confessional but is actually prohibited from making such a disclosure.

Fortunately Moore's pronouncements were not entirely devoid of humour. On the question of the rights of a clergyman to graze his cattle in the churchyard, he said that while "cattle" need not be confined to cows, but could include horses, goats and geese, it excluded elephants and giraffes since "they are not cattle".

He also opined that "a choir of women resplendent in floppy caps and purple, like so many bishopesses, is neither enjoined nor forbidden by the law". But for him the ordination of women to the priesthood was most certainly forbidden by both law and theology.

A devout man, he was himself ordained to the priesthood at the age of 56 and as he grew older he mellowed somewhat, finding great satisfaction in his work as vicar of the Guild Church of St Mary Abchurch in the City of London where, as in Cambridge, he helped many people with personal problems.

A judge's son, Evelyn Garth Moore was born on February 6, 1906, and educated at Durham School and Trinity College, Cambridge, where he read law. He was called to the Bar by Gray's Inn in 1928 and practised, mainly in criminal cases, on the South-Eastern Circuit until the outbreak of the Second World War, when he was commissioned in the Royal Artillery.

His legal expertise was however required by the Judge Advocate-General's Department, and he spent the greater part of the war presiding, as a major, over courts martial in Britain, Greece and the Middle East.

Soon after demobilisation he was elected a Fellow of Corpus Christi College, Cambridge, whose "high and dry" tradition was much to his taste, and served as lecturer and director of studies in Law from 1947 to 1972.

He also became deputy chairman of the Huntingdonshire Quarter Sessions, and in 1959 added the Cambridgeshire Quarter Sessions to his responsibilities. He was High Bailiff of Ely Cathedral from 1961 to 1986.

Moore's teaching gifts were recognised by his appointments as lecturer in criminal procedure and evidence by the Council of Legal Education, and he was a tutor at Gray's Inn. He was a member of the Bar Council and also sat as an assessor on the disciplinary committee of the Royal College of Veterinary Surgeons.

Moore took a keen interest in psychic phenomena and was enlisted as president of the Churches' Fellowship for Psychical and Spiritual Studies. His publications included *Believe it or Not: Christianity and Psychical Research*, *The Church's Ministry of Healing*, and *An Introduction to English Canon Law*.

Among his enthusiasms were architecture, furniture, untipped cigarettes and gin martini cocktails.

He was unmarried.

June 6, 1990

The Right Reverend Launcelot Fleming

The Right Reverend Launcelot Fleming, who has died aged 82, was one of the most interesting and highly regarded Church of England bishops this century.

Between 1949 and 1971 he occupied the bishoprics of Portsmouth and Norwich, and he spent the final years of his ecclesiastical career as Dean of Windsor.

In the 1930s, as a young Fellow of Trinity Hall, Cambridge, Fleming had accompanied the three-year British Graham Land

Expedition to the Antarctic. After an eventful time as a naval chaplain during the 1939–45 War, he became director of the Scott Polar Research Institute at Cambridge.

A humble, rather shy man, he nonetheless made abiding friendships wherever he went, and it is said that at one Christmas during his Norwich years he received some 3,000 greetings cards.

William Launcelot Scott Fleming was born on August 7, 1907 in Edinburgh, where his father was a notable physician. He was educated at Rugby and Trinity Hall, where he took a first in Natural Sciences, before spending two years studying geology at Yale.

On his return to England, Fleming decided to enter Holy Orders. During his time as a student at Westcott House he took part, as a geologist, in an expedition to Iceland. A week after his ordination as Chaplain and Fellow of Trinity Hall in 1933 he was off again, this time as chief scientist on an expedition to the north of Spitzbergen.

The next year he became Dean of Trinity Hall, and almost immediately was invited to go to the Antarctic as geologist and chaplain of a major British expedition to Graham Land.

Some important discoveries were made during the next three years, and Fleming made a considerable impression on his companions. All the expedition members were later decorated with the Polar Medal by King George VI.

From 1937 to 1940 Fleming was fully occupied with his academic duties in Cambridge, where he played a full part in the life of the Hall and proved a highly successful rowing coach. He also became secretary of the Conference of Schoolmasters and College Tutors, a post he held until 1949.

In 1940 he enlisted as a Royal Navy chaplain, and later that year was appointed to the battleship *Queen Elizabeth*. The ship saw a good deal of service in the Eastern Mediterranean and was frequently under attack, especially in the closing stages of the Battle of Crete.

On November 24, 1941, having by this time become the flagship of the Mediterranean Fleet, the vessel left Alexandria with the battleships *Barham* and *Valiant* and eight destroyers. The next day the *Barham*, sailing close to the *Queen Elizabeth*, was struck by three enemy torpedoes.

The ship turned on its side, blew up and was sunk within minutes, leaving about 45 survivors in the water and more than 850 officers and ratings – including the captain – dead. All this was witnessed from the *Queen Elizabeth*. Amid the chaos Fleming obtained permission to say prayers for the dead and for the Fleet over his ship's loudspeaker system.

Just over three weeks later the *Queen Elizabeth* was herself hit by a torpedo while in harbour at Alexandria and badly damaged. Repairs and refitting occupied more than 18 months, and in August 1943 Fleming was appointed senior chaplain of HMS *Ganges*, a training establishment at Shotley.

He remained there until December 1944, when he was released from the Royal Navy to become director of service ordination candidates – which entailed the supervision of the selection procedure for some 3,000 servicemen who had indicated an interest in ordination at the end of the war.

In 1946 Fleming returned to Trinity Hall, and combined his duties there with the directorship of the Scott Polar Research Institute – at a time when the Institute's activities were expanding considerably.

Offers of the principalship of Westcott House and of the bishopric of Edinburgh were declined; but in the summer of 1949 he became Bishop of Portsmouth, his reluctance to become a bishop overcome by the chance of renewed contact with the Royal Navy.

Portsmouth, one of the smaller dioceses, was a good choice for a man who, although vastly experienced in human relationships, had never worked in a parish and had little knowledge of how the Church of England actually worked. Fleming quickly learned the ropes, but much preferred pastoral work among the clergy to the chairmanship of diocesan committees – most of which he delegated to the archdeacons.

Neither did Fleming care for the Church Assembly, though his interest in young people led him to accept the chairmanship of the Church of England Youth Council.

As always, he drove himself too hard and his car too fast, but he took time off to play hockey and squash, and in 1953 spent 11 days with the British North Greenland Expedition. His maiden speech in the House of Lords, in 1956, was concerned with cruelty to whales.

At the beginning of 1960 Fleming was translated to Norwich – geographically the second largest diocese in the Church of England. Once more he concentrated on the pastoral care of the clergy, and he soon came to see that the Church's work in remote rural areas with declining populations could continue only if the tiny parishes – often with huge churches – were grouped together and served by teams of clergy.

By the time he was due to leave Norwich 18 per cent of the clergy were working in teams and a report had been published on the future of the many churches in the city of Norwich. Fleming also played a significant part in the development of the new University of East Anglia.

Although preaching and public speaking never came easily to him, he began to speak much more frequently in the House of Lords, generally on environmental and conservation issues.

By 1971 Fleming had been a diocesan bishop for more than 20 years and when he was invited to become Dean of Windsor and Domestic Chaplain to the Queen he accepted, believing that freedom from the exhausting work of a diocese would let him continue his ministry until he was 70.

This he achieved, and he also carried out important work at St George's House, the conference centre in Windsor Castle. But sharp divisions of opinion among the canons made it virtually impossible for the Dean to exercise decisive leadership in the affairs of the Chapel, and this caused him much unhappiness.

Fleming was appointed KCVO on his retirement in 1976, after which he spent many useful years ministering in and from Dorset, where he lived in a house lovingly converted from an old stone barn; and he still greatly enjoyed his visits to schools and colleges.

He is survived by his wife, Jane, whom he married in 1965.

August 1, 1990

John Harriott

John Harriott, the former Jesuit priest and writer on Catholic and ecumenical affairs, who has died aged 57, contributed a consistently trenchant column to *The Tablet*.

Early last month, for example, he predicted that "it will not be long before Mrs Thatcher jumps or is shot from her blazing saddle".

Just to be sure he fired off a few more salvoes: "She and her faction," Harriott declared, "have turned her party into something almost resembling the East European parties now utterly discredited, where conformity and time-serving are the only road to preferment, and dissent a capital offence."

This aroused predictable indignation – as it was meant to. Harriott sounded like a raging radical, characterised by what a reviewer of his latest book, *The Empire of the Heart*, called "Holy Asperity".

But his aim was to "speak the truth in charity", and his fierceness was always mitigated by humour.

His background was impeccably conservative. The son of the bandmaster in the East Surrey Regiment, John Harriott was born on January 2, 1933, and educated at Wimbledon College (which came second only to Stonyhurst in the number of its VCs).

Young John might well have joined the Army himself. Instead, at the age of 16, he entered the Society of Jesus, which for many people in the late 1940s had the "spit and polish" of a Guards regiment.

He read English at Campion Hall, Oxford, and Philosophy and Theology at Heythrop College in Oxfordshire, where sheep safely grazed, threatened only by a mis-hit golf ball. A stylish opening bat and useful off-break bowler, he displayed leadership qualities as captain of the cricket team.

Ordained priest in 1965, he devoted himself to preaching and retreat-giving until 1968, when he was derailed by *Humanae Vitae*, the Papal encyclical banning artificial birth control.

Together with 54 other Catholic priests Harriott signed a

public letter of protest and was treated as a moral leper. Eventually he was allowed to make a carefully controlled return to public life as assistant editor of the Jesuit magazine, *The Month*.

Before long he was reporting further instances of Vatican skulduggery in the treatment meted out to its delegation at the UN World Population Conference in Bucharest in 1974. Though still much appreciated by the Jesuit superiors in Rome, those in England thought Harriott a rather reckless liberal.

When he began to live at the Catholic Institute of International Relations, then by Regent's Park, they issued an ultimatum: return to the Jesuit fold or leave it. This made up Harriott's mind.

In 1978 he left the Jesuits in body if not in spirit; married Shirley du Boulay, a BBC television producer; and began to work at the Independent Broadcasting Authority.

Harriott was familiar with the world of television, having written a report on broadcasting for the Social Morality Council. His main work was to negotiate the renewal of franchises for the regional companies.

But he was an unhappy commuter, and resigned in 1986 to devote himself to writing.

His columns in *The Tablet* were called "Periscopes". This implied both an all-round survey and a restricted perspective. As a columnist he illuminated and infuriated in equal proportions – but he was always immensely readable.

He excelled in lateral thinking. In his penultimate column he recounted how, as he lurked in the back corridors of the Vatican, a sheet of vellum was thrust into his hand by a mysterious stranger: it was a plan for the commercial sponsorship of the Vatican. The jokes flowed thick and fast thereafter.

In another column he inveighed against the idea that "you have to be dumb to be religious, and that to be religious is today a lost cause".

His readers began to grasp that there was a strong element of nostalgia in his radicalism, and that he had the "conservatism" of G. K. Chesterton, his avowed master: he drew back on the edge of the precipice.

"To abandon religion," he wrote, "may be honest and honourable, but it is not exactly leaping a prison wall, more like jumping into the dustbin; not a grand illumination, more a putting out of lights."

Like Chesterton, Harriott managed to combine the utmost intellectual rigour with the utmost personal kindness.

December 28, 1990

1991

The Reverend Dr Werner Simonson

The Reverend Dr Werner Simonson, who has died aged 101, was a high court judge in Nazi Germany but in 1939 fled to Britain, where he became a priest in the Church of England.

He ministered quietly and faithfully in three London parishes, in all of which he was greatly loved, and in retirement took services and preached at St John's, Stanmore, until just a few weeks before his death.

Werner Siegmund Moritz Simonson was born into an aristocratic Prussian legal family at Luckenwalde near Berlin on November 25, 1889.

His grandparents were Jewish, but his parents converted to the Lutheran faith and Simonson was brought up in this tradition, though it was not until later in life that his upbringing bore fruit.

Simonson's childhood years were spent in an atmosphere of high culture, and he learnt early to appreciate music and painting.

He liked to recall, too, that he had been dandled on Bismarck's knee.

His law studies at Leipzig University were interrupted by the First World War, in which he served in the army.

Captured on the Western Front, he was then sent to a prisoner-of-war camp in France.

Simonson returned to university after the war and acquired his doctorate in 1921. He then embarked on a brilliant career which took him to the judicial bench.

But in the 1930s he was quick to realise that liberal life and culture were dangerously menaced by the rise of Nazism.

His association with those at the Confessing Lutheran Church who were opposed to Hitler, together with his Jewish background, made him a marked man.

He was dismissed from the judiciary and by 1938 knew that it would only be a matter of time before he was arrested. Both his mother and his sister later died in concentration camps.

With the help of Bishop George Bell of Chichester and a few other friends Simonson left Germany early in 1939 and arrived penniless in England. A few months later he was interned as an enemy alien and despatched to a camp in the Isle of Man.

Simonson was not detained for long and on his release he felt called to use his experience to work for the Church.

He was at first discouraged from this on grounds of his age but he persisted and eventually secured a place at Ridley Hall, Cambridge, to train for the ministry of the Church of England.

He was ordained in St Paul's Cathedral in 1942 and, although he was offered a senior judicial appointment in post-war Germany, he spent the next seven years as a curate at Christ Church, Fulham.

This was followed by another seven-year stint as Vicar of St Mark's, Dalston, and he completed his full-time Ministry with nine years as Vicar of St Luke's, West Hampstead.

Dr Simonson left a deep impression of saintliness wherever he went.

Throughout his ecclesiastical career he retained not only a marked German accent but also quite a lot of the content of his former Lutheran allegiance, though he was never rigid in his views.

The overall impression he gave was of a humble, self-effacing man who had learned much from his experiences. He was diligent in his pastoral care of parishioners and for some years acted as a chaplain to visitors in Westminster Abbey.

He retired from parish work in 1965 and four years later published a fascinating and inspiring autobiography entitled *The Last Judgment*.

His wife, Leonie, who also came from a distinguished German legal family, was unable to leave Germany with him and in 1945 found herself at Dresden in the Russian occupied zone.

Once again Bishop Bell came to the rescue, and she was the first German civilian to reach England after the war.

She proved to be remarkably unruffled on finding the husband she had last known as a judge transformed into a parson and soon settled into English life. She died in 1986.

Simonson is survived by his only son, Juergen, who escaped

from a German labour force in France in 1944, was also ordained and until his recent retirement was Rector of St Mary's, Barnes, and an honorary Canon of Southwark Cathedral.

February 8, 1991

The Reverend Elsie Chamberlain

The Reverend Elsie Chamberlain, who has died aged 81, was a pioneering Congregationalist minister and a superb leader of worship for the radio.

She chaired the Congregational Union of England and Wales from 1956 to 1957, and was President of the Congregational Federation from 1973 to 1974.

She was best known, however, for her work at the BBC, which she joined in 1954. For some years she was in charge of the early morning programme, *Lift Up Your Hearts*.

Elsie Dorothea Chamberlain was born into a devoutly Christian family in London on March 3, 1910, and educated at King's College, London, where she read divinity.

She became a minister after preparation at St Paul's House, Liverpool, under one of the earliest women ministers, the Revd Muriel Paulden, and in 1941 she took up a post at Christ Church, Friern Barnet.

She remained there until 1946, when she became the first woman to be appointed chaplain to the forces. She served in the Women's Auxiliary Air Force at Cranwell. Here she met and married, in 1947, a High Church Anglican priest, the Reverend John L. St C. Garrington.

The two formed an unusual but remarkably happy partnership, which gave scope for both ministries, though Elsie suspected that her non-conformist commitments cast something of a blight on his career.

She was working at Vineyard Congregational Church, Richmond, when she was offered the job in the religious broadcasting department at the BBC.

She remained there until 1967, when she left somewhat reluctantly after *Lift Up Your Hearts* was marked for secularisation.

Despite her success on the radio Elsie Chamberlain was not tempted by television: she felt that the inevitable visual promotion of the speaker would detract from the message.

During the 1970s her independence became increasingly apparent. Always present at ecumenical gatherings, she could not support the Union of Congregationalists and Presbyterians in the United Reformed Church of 1973, and helped to form the Congregational Federation.

Throughout her life Elsie Chamberlain was a vehement supporter of a female ministry. There was a period, for instance, before the Methodist Church ordained women, when she would not write or speak on its behalf because she felt it discriminated against its deaconesses.

She was not a theologian and was impatient of the niceties of theological debate. She contemptuously dismissed as "hooey" the arguments against women priests which were advanced by some Anglicans.

From 1984 to 1985 she was President of the National Free Church Women's Council, and she lived to see many of her hopes for women in the church realised.

When her husband was vicar of Greenstead, Essex, she looked after the chapel at neighbouring Hutton. After his death in 1978 she ministered at Taunton and then at the Congregational Centre at Nottingham.

April 16, 1991

Canon David Rutter

Canon David Rutter, the Precentor of Lincoln Cathedral who has died aged 65, was a staunch Prayer Book Anglican of the old school and spent the last 20 years of his life resisting pressure to move with the times.

He moved to Lincoln in 1965 and was due to retire at the end of this month. Previously he spent 10 years as a minor canon of St Paul's Cathedral, where he had considerable responsibility for the music and the ordering of services. It was on the strength of his performance there that he was preferred to the more senior post at Lincoln.

Unfortunately, his arrival coincided with the introduction of some of the new Anglican services, to which Rutter was, and remained, resolutely opposed. He was quite unwilling to compromise in liturgical matters, believing that the new services represented a lowering of the standards which cathedrals existed to uphold, and that forsaking the Book of Common Prayer could lead only to disaster for the Church of England.

One of his shortest and most memorable sermons at Lincoln was preached at Mattins on the day when, somewhat later than in most places, the "Series 2" Communion Service was introduced.

He said simply: "Dean Dunlop, the man of taste, rejected this service. Dean Peck, the man of prayer, rejected this service. It has remained for the present Dean to introduce it. In the name of the Father, and of the Son, and of the Holy Ghost. Amen." This led to considerable conflict with the Dean and the rest of the Chapter.

Rutter was not involved in the recent débâcle at Lincoln, which resulted from the heavy losses sustained after the cathedral's greatest treasure, a copy of Magna Carta, was sent to an exhibition in Australia in 1988.

By this time ill-health had led to his virtual withdrawal from the cathedral's life, and for the last two years he played no active part in the ordering of its services.

In his final sermon he startled the congregation somewhat by reading to them the contents of his will, which included a demand that there should be no funeral or memorial service for him in the Cathedral.

He was for some years involved in the occult and would occasionally describe having shaken hands with some of the great men buried at St Paul's. The choristers at Lincoln were once surprised to learn that the celebrated but long dead church musician, Sir Edward Bairstow, had conducted their most recent rehearsal.

Rutter's uncompromising outlook and marked eccentricities were, however, accompanied by gentleness and compassion. He was an assiduous visitor of the sick and had no fewer than 52 godchildren, with all of whom he kept regularly in touch.

David Carter Rutter was born in 1925 and educated at Bishop Holgate's Grammar School, York, from which he won a scholarship to Exeter College, Oxford. He prepared for Holy Orders at Cuddesdon Theological College and was ordained in 1950 to a curacy at Thornaby-on-Tees.

In 1953 he went as sub-warden to St Deiniol's, Hawarden, the residential and mainly ecclesiastical library founded by Gladstone. Rutter's quiet encouragement there helped many diffident students to produce better results than expected. In 1955 he became a minor canon of St Paul's, with the historic title of Junior Cardinal and Succentor.

When the Prayer Book Society was formed in 1975 and a local branch took root at Lincoln, Rutter offered a room in the cathedral precincts for the inaugural meeting.

His subsequent acceptance of the chairmanship of the society's Lincoln branch did little to ingratiate him to his seniors at the Cathedral, but he would not be turned from his path.

Despite by now being almost totally blind from diabetes, he successfully chaired many discussions and acted as a congenial host, ensuring everyone was made to feel welcome.

His remarkable memory was invaluable in recalling the events of cathedral life over more than a quarter of a century – although it also made it impossible for him ever to forget what he perceived to have been a slight.

The aftermath of the Magna Carta fiasco greatly saddened

Rutter's last months but when he offered his resignation a few weeks ago he made it clear it was on the grounds of ill-health.

Rutter never married, and lived with his mother in the beautiful Precentory at Lincoln until her death a few years ago.

June 19, 1991

The Very Reverend Lord MacLeod of Fuinary

The Very Reverend Lord MacLeod of Fuinary, a former Moderator of the Church of Scotland,was a preacher given to burning jeremiads in the manner of an Old Testament prophet; but the central achievement of his life was the creation of a community on Iona to be a spiritual forcing-house amid the religious indifference of the modern world.

MacLeod claimed that St Columba's purpose in founding the original monastery on Iona in the sixth century had been "ecstatically active". If the brotherhood had occasionally been found in retreat on the island, this was only so that they might sally forth refreshed for their essential missionary purpose.

A similar philosophy lay behind the community MacLeod founded there in 1938. "We have had enough books to declare the superiority of the Kingdom of God over Fascism and Communism," he declared. "What men begin to want is a little more evidence that we believe in the efficacy of that Kingdom with something of the forthright intensity that these lesser creeds might seem able to command."

MacLeod's experiences among the unemployed in 1930s Glasgow had made him sharply aware that the Church of Scotland was in crisis, quite out of touch with the new industrialised society. The first aim of the Iona Community was to recruit ministers for pastoral work in the new housing estates of Scotland.

The original scheme provided for 20 probationer-ministers to visit Iona during the summer months; they would then work in the crowded industrial cities for the remainder of their two-year contract.

The summer community also included unemployed masons, carpenters and other craftsmen from the mainland, who helped restore the ruined Benedictine monastery.

MacLeod hoped that on Iona the ministers should be "corporately separate" from the 20th century; but he also intended that they might learn, through the experience of living with the craftsmen, how removed they were from their flocks.

This was the core of the community. But every year pilgrims came from all over the world to make retreats on the island, and hundreds of young people arrived to join in the work of the community, and so the project took on the character of an ecumenical movement within the Church.

MacLeod himself was far from being a blinkered Presbyterian. When he was elected as Moderator of the General Assembly in 1957 an objector expressed his disgust at the new Moderator's "episcopal emphasis".

Indeed, though the mere mention of "bishop" smacked of popery among his co-religionists, MacLeod did favour some reconciliation of the episcopal, presbyterian and congregational principles of ecclesiastical organisation.

His political views, though, were much more dogmatic; nor did he hesitate to identify them with true Christianity. Proud to declare himself a socialist, he showed himself fiercely opposed to those who believed that religion was simply a matter between a man and his Maker, independent of any social obligation.

Those who thought of religion only in terms of worship, MacLeod argued, were unlikely to hear the voice of God. Equally, "whether we are to go to hell or heaven is dependent on what we do about people's bodies, not their spiritual welfare".

MacLeod regarded well-intentioned capitalists in the same way as Tolstoy did: "I sit on a man's back, choking him and making him carry me, and yet assure myself and others that I am sorry for him and wish to lighten his load by all possible means – *except by getting off his back.*"

When he published the Cunningham lectures he had given at Edinburgh University in 1954 he chose the significant title *Only One Way Left*.

A preacher in the great Scottish tradition, whose impassioned eloquence swept through the congregation like a rushing mighty wind, MacLeod never hesitated to denounce the evils of this world. His later utterances were haunted by the apocalyptic nightmare of racial war; and he feared that the time might come when one would pray to be delivered from being born white.

As for the power of international finance: "This new Moloch devours our young," he thundered. And MacLeod was sure that God would regard the Common Market beef and butter mountain as "sin".

Another target was "the gross impurities of secular science", a phrase which chiefly related to research on chemical warfare. Notably valiant as a soldier in the First World War, MacLeod afterwards became a dedicated pacifist, in contrast to the vast majority of Christians, whom he dubbed "passivist: they have neither the gumption to be pacifist nor the guts to be participant."

By the 1950s MacLeod believed that the British people had learned the lesson of interdependence, that the Welfare State was an application of Christianity to society, and that Christian Socialism would alone save humanity. The coming of Mrs Thatcher, far from undermining this faith, left him all the more convinced that it was securely founded.

George Fielden MacLeod was born on June 17, 1895 into a family which had already given notable service to the Church of Scotland – both his great-grandfather and grandfather had been Moderators of the General Assembly.

His father, John MacLeod, an accountant, was Conservative MP first for the Central, and then for the Kelvingrove division of Glasgow, and was created a baronet in 1924.

Young George was educated at Winchester and Oriel College, Oxford. In the First World War he served in Salonica and France, mostly with the Argyll and Sutherland Highlanders, of which he was adjutant for three years; his gallantry was recognised by the award of an MC and the *Croix de Guerre* with palms.

Upon his return from the war he took his degree at Oxford, and passed through the Divinity Hall at Edinburgh. In 1921 he obtained the Scottish nomination to the Union Theological Seminary in New York, and then undertook missionary work at the Arrow Lakes Lumber Camps in British Columbia.

Those who take to the straight and narrow path in adulthood are inclined to dwell somewhat exaggeratedly upon the sins of their youth; before he "surrendered his life to Christ" MacLeod had been given to drinking and gambling and had smoked 50 cigarettes a day.

In the early days of ministry, when he was an assistant at St Giles's, Edinburgh, he would arrive dashingly at the cathedral door in an open-topped sports car, before proceeding to stir the consciences of the rich and the hearts of the women in the congregation.

The genteel church-goers of Edinburgh decided that here, indeed, was a preacher for the Jazz Age.

Already, though, a transformation was bubbling up through the yeast of his spirit – born partly, perhaps, of his experiences in the trenches, and partly of a steadily growing rage for social justice. In the mid-1920s he was ordained as chaplain to Toc H in Glasgow.

From 1926 to 1930 MacLeod was Collegiate Minister at St Cuthbert's in Edinburgh, where he won golden opinions for his work among the young, "for whom he seemed to have a magnetic attraction"; and then from 1930 to 1938 he was minister of Govan Parish Church in the depressed shipyards of Glasgow.

In the Second World War MacLeod appeared on Hitler's list for liquidation – the Nazi "roll of honour" as Humphrey Bogart described it in *Casablanca*. At the same time, thanks to his pacifism, the British would not allow him to broadcast.

In 1963 MacLeod was made president and chairman of the Council of International Fellowship of Reconciliation, in 1989 he received the Templeton Prize for progress in religion. His books included *We Shall Rebuild* (1944), in which he outlined the principles of Iona community.

MacLeod inherited the family baronetcy from his nephew in 1944, and in 1967 was created a life peer as Baron MacLeod of Fuinary. He married, in 1948, Lorna, daughter of the Rev Donald Macleod, who died in 1984; they had two sons and a daughter.

The elder son, John Maxwell Norman MacLeod, born in 1952, now succeeds to the baronetcy.

June 28, 1991

The Right Reverend Horace Donegan

The Right Reverend Horace Donegan, the former Anglican Bishop of New York who has died aged 91, was outspoken in his denunciation of what he saw as the pernicious racism at the heart of American society.

But his close identification with the Civil Rights Movement did not always reflect the aspirations of his flock. In 1965 various individuals and parishes withdrew pledges of two million dollars contributed for the completion of New York's Cathedral of St John the Divine.

Donegan's reaction was clear-cut: "I can only hope that the cathedral's very unfinished quality will stand as a memorial to a diocese which in the 20th century tried to do what it believed to be right."

Nevertheless, the next year he and the cathedral's trustees approved a $25 million scheme to complete the building. But after the race riots in the summer of 1967 Donegan announced that the project was to be abandoned.

"There will be no fund-raising drive so long as I am Bishop," he declared, "until there is greater evidence that the anguish and despair of our unfavoured people has been relieved. The scaffolding will remain on the unfinished cathedral as a symbol of the anguish of the surrounding slums."

Earlier, in the 1950s, Donegan had been a staunch opponent of Senator McCarthy's Communist witch-hunts, which he considered to have been motivated by "a spurious patriotism" and to have "imperilled liberties which are part of our American life".

Donegan's liberalism was no less evident in Church affairs. He once proposed that Lent should be reduced from 40 to seven days, because "what was acceptable in the 17th century has become unrealistic for men and women catching commuter trains".

In 1977 he was among the bishops who took part in the first official ordination of a woman priest.

A doctor's son, Horace William Baden Donegan was born on May 17, 1900 at Matlock, Derbyshire, though the family migrated to Baltimore while he was still a child.

Young Horace showed some talent as an actor and decided to train for the stage, but this plan was torpedoed when he fell in love with his landlady's daughter. So alarmed was the landlady at the prospect of an actor as her son-in-law that Donegan decided to train for Holy Orders instead – though in the event he never married.

He studied at Harvard Divinity School, spent some time in Oxford reading theology, and finished his training in 1927 at the Episcopal Theological School in Cambridge, Massachusetts.

For two years he was a curate at All Saints Church, Worcester, Massachusetts, before becoming Rector of Christ Church, Baltimore, where he stayed until 1933.

Donegan's appointment as Rector of St James's Church, New York, began a metropolitan ministry that was to extend over almost 40 years, and a love affair with the city that endured for the rest of his life.

As Rector of a busy Manhattan parish, and later as Bishop, he found ample scope for exercising the dramatic gifts which, but for the intervention of the landlady's daughter, might have made him a great actor. He was a born orator, with a perfect sense of timing and a remarkable ability for combining the humourous with the serious.

Donegan was elected Suffragan Bishop of New York in 1947, and when, two years later, it became known that the Diocesan Bishop would shortly retire, he was chosen as successor by acclamation – the first time in the history of the diocese that an episcopal appointment had been made in this manner.

Donegan's pastoral skill was as pronounced as his oratorical abilities, and as a bishop he presided over a special committee concerned with the rehabilitation of American clergymen who found themselves in trouble of one kind or another.

His skill as an administrator took him to the presidency of many of the Episcopal Church's national boards and committees, and he was always in demand for charitable causes.

Among the numerous honorary degrees and awards that came Donegan's way were the Medal of the City of New York, the Legion of Honour of France and the Silver Medal of the Red Cross of Japan. He was vice-president of the Pilgrims.

His English roots meant a great deal to him, and he was often in London, where he did much in the 1950s to foster relations between the diocese of New York and London, and where the catholicity of his taste was reflected by his membership of both the Athenaeum and Kennel Clubs.

He was appointed honorary CBE in 1957.

November 18, 1991

1992

The Reverend Florence Tim Oi Li

The Reverend Florence Tim Oi Li, who has died in Toronto, Canada, aged 85, was the first woman ever to become an Anglican priest.

Of Chinese extraction, in 1944 she found herself at the centre of an international controversy after her irregular ordination to the Anglican priesthood by the then Bishop of Hong Kong, R. O. Hall.

Bishop Hall, although not generally in favour of the ordination of women, acted unilaterally to meet a desperate wartime situation in China. His action was condemned by the Archbishop of Canterbury and by the Lambeth Conference of Bishops, and for some years Tim Oi Li was persuaded not to function as a priest.

But persecution came as much from within her native country as from outside. Between 1958 and 1974 she was forced by the Communist authorities to work, first on a chicken farm and subsequently as a manual worker in various factories in Canton.

Initially she and some fellow Christians were free to meet early in the morning for prayers and Bible study, but after the Cultural Revolution in 1968 all outward expressions of religious belief were forbidden and she maintained her faith secretly.

By 1979, when freedom of religious belief and worship were again permitted, Tim Oi Li was already past retirement age, but she soon became associated with a reopened Chinese church. After emigrating to Canada in 1981, she ministered for another decade at an Anglican church in Toronto, which was shared by English-speaking and Chinese congregations.

In 1984, by which time women had been officially ordained to the priesthood in several parts of the Anglican Communion, Tim Oi Li attended a service in Westminster Abbey to mark the 40th anniversary of her ordination. During the service a message from Dr Robert Runcie, the Archbishop of Canterbury, was read:

"Sometimes you have suffered from misunderstandings about your ministry. You have never been eager to promote yourself, but only to build up the life of the Church and serve its mission in places of desperate human need. Your selfless ministry is an example to us all."

Tim Oi Li was a tiny woman, humble and down to earth, yet recognisably holy, with immense resources of faith and courage.

She was born in Hong Kong on May 5, 1907. Her father trained as a doctor but gave up medicine to become headmaster of a local school. Although a Christian, he had two wives: Tim Oi Li was a child of the second. She adopted the name of Florence as a teenager, in honour of her heroine Florence Nightingale.

She attended her father's school near Kowloon until she was 14, when she was obliged to leave and take care of the rest of the large family.

Seven years later Florence enrolled at the Belilios Public School for Girls, training as a teacher in the evenings. Her education was not completed until she was 27, when she began to teach in a fishing village on the island of Ap Li Chall.

Meanwhile she had become a member of St Paul's Anglican Church in Hong Kong. After a short time in teaching she went to the Union Theological College in Canton to prepare for full-time lay work in the Church.

This occupied her for almost four years, during which Canton was frequently bombed by the Japanese; nevertheless she took her degree with honours.

From 1938 to 1940 Tim Oi Li was on the staff of All Saints' Church, Kowloon, dealing mainly with refugees from China. She then moved to the Portuguese colony of Macao, where after six months she was ordained deacon.

Macao was within the rules of the Church at the time, but after the Japanese occupation of Hong Kong in 1941 the colony was flooded with refugees, on their way to "free" China.

Tim Oi Li found herself leading the Church's mission single-handed. In the absence of a resident priest, she was allowed to take baptisms, weddings and funerals; she also undertook some medical and missionary work. But because she was not a priest, she could not celebrate Holy Communion, nor, in wartime conditions, were there any visiting priests to fill the gap.

In these exceptional circumstances, Tim Oi Li was given permission as a deacon to celebrate Holy Communion. After she had been doing this for some two years Bishop Hall decided that it would be best to regularise the situation by making her a priest.

When the war ended, Tim Oi Li was driven by pressure from the Chinese House of Bishops and from Lambeth to resign from her priestly ministry.

Her next move, in 1947, was to Hoppo, near the Vietnamese border, where she functioned only as a deacon and succeeded in revitalising a weak local church. After two years she resumed work as a priest but in the early part of 1951 the church was closed by the new Communist rulers.

Next year she went to do further theological study at Yeaching College, Peking, and in 1953 joined the staff of the Union Theological College in Canton.

There she taught English Church history and the principles of a new "Three-Self" movement, which was designed to bring autonomy to every area of China's life, including its religious organisations.

This appointment lasted four years, until the Communists drove her to harsh work and a clandestine religious life.

Although 21 years were to pass before she was free to minister again in any form, her faith remained strong, and she lived long enough to see the Anglican Communion with more than 1,000 women priests in its ranks.

Tim Oi Li never married.

March 2, 1992

Canon Maurice Brunsden

Canon Maurice Brunsden, who has died aged 71, had a brief moment of unwelcome fame in 1977 when he was arrested, detained and then expelled from South Africa after spending 23 years as Rector of Heidelberg – a "Coloured" parish in Cape Province.

The reason for Brunsden's expulsion was never entirely clear, for while he was steadfastly opposed to apartheid – and in particular to the injustices of the Group Areas Act – he was in no sense a political priest. His attitude to his parishioners was unfashionably paternalistic.

A suggestion made at the time of his arrest, that guns were being stored in the church tower, seemed ludicrous – yet there was a naive element in Brunsden's character that could be exploited, and he may perhaps have been used by others.

Equally, his extreme expression of Anglo-Catholicism did not endear him to his fanatical Calvinist neighbours, and his outspoken comments on the effects of government policies on the life of the Church made him some enemies in high places. Later, he always spoke bitterly of his ill-treatment at the hands of the South African police.

Maurice Calthorpe Brunsden was born at Reading in 1921. He attended Holy Trinity Church, a leading Anglo-Catholic centre, where he felt drawn to the priesthood.

After serving in the RAF during the Second World War, he went to South Africa, where he prepared for Holy Orders at St Paul's College, Grahamstown.

In 1952 he became Rector of Calvinia in the Western Cape, and two years later he moved to Heidelberg, east of Cape Town.

On arrival in the parish he found a plain church of concrete construction, but although money was short he furnished it in a style more familiar to pre-Vatican II Roman Catholicism than to anything in the Anglican tradition. Although undoubtedly exotic, the furnishings were of great beauty, for Brunsden had flair and an amateur knowledge of church robes and ornaments.

He made a mitre for each of the South African bishops, and any friends who became Canons were advised of their correct vesture – which was very splendid and sometimes led to their being confused with Roman Cardinals.

His own Canonry of Madrid was appropriately outlandish, having being conferred upon him by the Bishop of the Spanish Reformed Episcopal Church.

Beneath these externals there was, however, a holy man and a devoted priest who cared deeply for his people and who was greatly loved by the Coloured community in Heidelberg.

It was a tragedy for him as well as for them when the area was re-zoned as "White" and they were obliged to move away from St Barnabas Church, which became a focal point in their lives. On his return to England, Brunsden served briefly as a curate in Cornwall before returning to his native Reading in 1978 as Vicar of St Bartholomew's Church, Earley. This proved to be an unhappy appointment for him and for the parish.

His heart remained in South Africa, his health never recovered from his ordeal at the hands of the South African police, and a style of churchmanship acceptable in the unusual circumstances of the Eastern Cape could not be translated to a suburb of Reading.

In 1985 he suffered a stroke and retired. Two years later he was sufficiently recovered to be able to assist at Holy Trinity, the church of his boyhood.

Maurice Brunsden maintained contact with a multitude of friends whom he regaled with a fund of personal stories, some of which owed as much to his vivid imagination as to his powers of recollection.

He was unmarried.

September 1, 1992

Canon David Diamond

Canon David Diamond, who has died aged 57, became Rector of St Paul's Church, Deptford, in 1968, and for nearly a quarter of a century served the entire community with a rare combination of zeal, flair and godliness; the local newspaper will commemorate his death with a special edition.

Diamond's approach was in some ways an unfashionable one, and in theory it should not have worked. His heroes were the great Anglo-Catholic slum priests of the 19th century, and he adopted their paternalistic style and and method. Colourful services in the high church tradition were accompanied by intense pastoral work on the streets, with a special concern for the poor and the delinquent.

Seriousness, though, did not preclude festivity and fun, and the strengthening of community bonds was a vital part of his policy.

Diamond mixed easily with people of all ages and backgrounds, and developed a special rapport with the criminal classes.

He spoke up for them in the courts, visited them in prison and cared for their families while they were away – even though his Rectory was burgled on 40 occasions.

The success of his approach owed much to his engaging personality and unceasing toil, and the Church of England has a place in Deptford without parallel in any other British inner-city.

David John Diamond was born at Streatham in 1935, and during his early years was deeply influenced by St Peter's Church there – a well-known centre of Anglo-Catholicism.

After taking a degree at Leeds University, he prepared for ordination at St Stephen's House, Oxford, a college for which he retained an affection and on whose governing body he later served.

Diamond's first appointment was as curate in the large parish of Tue Brook in Liverpool from 1962 to 1968. His impact was immediate and, although he related well to the whole community, young people in particular were drawn to him.

In 1968 Mervyn Stockwood, who was then Bishop of

Southwark and had become aware of Diamond's gifts, invited him to take charge of St Paul's, Deptford. This was a heavy responsibility for a 33-year-old priest, but he proved an inspired choice.

The flamboyant baroque architecture of the church provided the perfect setting for the man and the method. The worship became extravagant, but was arranged with great sensitivity and care, so that all who took part in it were made aware of life's deeper, spiritual dimension.

It offered warmth without superficial mateyness and spoke powerfully to many who had previously been beyond the Church's range of influence – not least at baptisms, weddings and funerals.

Celebration within the church soon spread to the streets of the parish, in the form of an annual Deptford Festival, of which Diamond was the founder and chief impresario.

This carnival includes a wide variety of parties and festivities which engage virtually the entire population of the area, and has been visited by both the Queen and Queen Elizabeth the Queen Mother – as well as more frequently by Princess Margaret, who took a special interest in his work and gave him much encouragement.

Solemn celebrations of Mass are an integral part of the programme, for Diamond saw the whole of life in sacramental terms.

The heavy demands and sheer pace of such a ministry took their toll of Diamond's health. He suffered a heart attack and a slight stroke 10 years ago, but made a good recovery and was soon in action again. In 1973 he had been made an honorary canon of Southwark Cathedral, and he spent a great deal of time on the training of his curates.

In the end it all proved too much for so devoted a priest to carry, and Diamond died suddenly in Glasgow, soon after arriving on the night sleeper for a brief holiday.

He was unmarried.

September 7, 1992

Canon Hugh Murphy

Canon Hugh Murphy, a Roman Catholic priest and a tireless worker for peace in Northern Ireland, who has died in Belfast aged 73, found himself much in the news in 1978 when he was kidnapped by "loyalist" Protestant gunmen.

The Ulster Freedom Fighters carried out the kidnapping to avenge the IRA's kidnapping of a policeman, Constable William Turbitt, after an ambush in South Armagh which had left one colleague dead.

Early one morning Father Murphy was woken by a knock at the door of his house at Ahoghill, Co. Antrim. He looked out and saw a man who said he was in trouble. On going down he found two hooded men carrying handguns, who told him that if he went with them he could help to save someone's life.

Frogmarched down the street and bundled into a car, he was driven to a derelict barn where he was held, his hands and feet bound and his head covered with a coal sack. His kidnappers told him that if any harm came to the policeman, he would meet a similar fate. He was certain he would be killed. But 12 hours later, after appeals by church leaders and politicians, including the Reverend Ian Paisley, he was released. He was still wearing his pyjamas.

"It is not the nicest experience to be hooded and tied all day long," Father Murphy said afterwards, "but it helped me to say my prayers."

Having learned from his captors that it was Ian Paisley's appeal which had saved his life, he remarked that he would have to "vote for Dr Paisley from now on".

After a joyful reunion with his nonagenarian mother, Father Murphy appealed to the IRA to show compassion – but to no avail. Constable Turbitt was found shot dead hours later.

An RUC man was subsequently jailed for his role in the abduction of Father Murphy. The experience left him shocked, and he suffered greatly with his nerves for years afterwards.

A publican's son, Hugh Patrick Murphy was born at

Holywood, Co. Down, on April 6, 1919. He was educated at St Malachy's College and Queen's University, Belfast.

He studied for the priesthood at Maynooth, Co. Kildare. Ordained in 1944, he was appointed chaplain for Gibraltarian evacuees at Clough, Co. Down.

During nearly half a century as a priest, he served throughout the diocese of Down and Connor. In 1967, after a heart attack, he was moved to the seaside town of Portrush.

In 1972 he became parish priest at Ahoghill, and later served at Coleraine. His last appointment was at Whitehouse, Belfast.

As the Troubles worsened in the 1970s Father Murphy was at the forefront of efforts to promote understanding between the two communities and vigorously condemned the IRA.

Father Murphy was a religious adviser to Ulster Television and a member of the BBC Religious Committee. He was Royal Navy Chaplain (Reserve) at the port of Belfast and was appointed OBE in 1974.

An accomplished cook, he loved to prepare lavish feasts for his friends.

October 27, 1992

The Reverend Bryan Houghton

The Reverend Bryan Houghton, who has died in France aged 81, was a singular and exceptional parish priest of Bury St Edmunds and Slough.

In 1969 he publicly resigned his 11-year custody of Bury St Edmunds, unwilling to accept the vernacular English Mass imposed by the reforms of Vatican II.

His resignation, attended by national media, took effect on November 23, the Feast Day of St Edmund in that year, a week before the Latin Tridentine Mass was banned in England and Wales. At a time when many priests had abandoned both parish and priesthood for very different reasons, Houghton was an exception in saying: " I remain . . . a loyal priest of Holy Church."

He became a loyal rebel, treading the tightrope between the enthusiasms of the reformers – against which he campaigned with some success, culminating in the restoration of the Latin Mass by Interdict of the late Cardinal Heenan – and the outright Latinist rebellion of Archbishop Lefebre, which he was never inclined to join.

Earlier this week, on the 23rd anniversary of his resignation, Houghton's funeral took place in the cathedral at Viviers sur Rhone, in the diocese of Avignon, where the bishop had given him permission to say Mass in the old rite. Thanks in large part to his efforts, it is now available to those who request it.

Bryan Houghton was a convert, with a late vocation to the priesthood. Born in 1911, he was educated at Stowe and Christ Church, Oxford, where he read history and won a fencing Blue.

He then joined the Paris office of Barclays Overseas for a career in banking. He ascribed his conversion to events in post-revolutionary Russia in the late 1920s.

Houghton arrived at Bury St Edmunds in 1958, after 18 years in Slough, where he had founded the parish of St Anthony's during the Second World War and built up a herd of goats, to supply the parish dances he organised for the young troops at Windsor with unrationed goat's milk ice cream. They are still remembered there as the "Holy Goats".

At Bury he applied this aptitude for unorthodox organisation to a fleet of ancient buses he purchased and restored, and drove round the Suffolk villages every weekend to rope in isolated, carless and lapsed Catholics for Mass.

Although a natural fund raiser, Houghton also had recourse to a private income, which he "used and re-used" to further his parish building in the immediate post-war years when grants were minimal or non-existent.

His Anglican background enabled him to build bridges to the Church of England at a time when ecumenism was in its wary infancy – although he nearly overturned this applecart when he established the provenance of the bones of St Edmund, in the custody of the Duke of Norfolk at Arundel since the beginning of the century.

They had been returned to England by the French hierarchy, intended for a shrine in the new Westminster Cathedral, which caused a fierce row at the time with Anglican orthodoxy at Cambridge, and with local clergy at Bury in the 1950s, when Houghton diplomatically withdrew his hopes of bringing them back to the town.

The now formidable and successful expansion of Catholic education around Bury is seen as his monument, together with the towering campanile of St Anthony's alongside Slough Trading Estate.

November 29, 1992

The Reverend Alan Ecclestone

The Reverend Alan Ecclestone, who has died aged 88, was possessed of a brilliant mind and endowed with outstanding pastoral gifts. But he took the teaching of Christ too seriously – some would say he understood it too naively – to be preferred to high office in the Church. Not even a modest honorary canonry came his way.

The danger signal, for those in authority, shone clearly in 1948, when Ecclestone, not long after his appointment as vicar of a large parish in the poorest part of Sheffield, joined the Communist Party.

The local branch of the party began to meet in the vicarage, and during the course of the next 20 years he stood six times as a Communist candidate in local elections, coming last on every occasion.

He and his wife (who also became a Communist) travelled widely, speaking on Communist platforms, and he attended

Communist-organised peace conferences in Paris and Warsaw after the Second World War.

Ecclestone always made it clear that while he believed Marx's economic analysis to be accurate, he could not accept the philosophical basis of Marxism, neither had he any sympathy with the ways in which Communism was being applied at that time in the Soviet Union and other parts of Eastern Europe.

Yet he was convinced that love of one's neighbour required a society based on the maxim "From each according to his ability, to each according to his need", and believed that Communism was the only political movement that sought to achieve this.

In spite of these qualifications and explanations, Ecclestone's activities caused considerable alarm in Church circles, even Leslie Hunter, his bishop, who was one of the most open-minded and socially concerned Church leaders of the 20th century and a great admirer of Ecclestone's parish work, thought that he had gone too far.

As a result, Ecclestone spent the rest of his parochial ministry in Sheffield where he was greatly loved and where a long, sustained experiment in lay involvement in the local church aroused considerable interest in other parts of the Church of England. Then, following his retirement, he embarked on what turned out to be a second ministry of conducting retreats and writing books on prayer, which placed him among the most highly regarded and influential teachers on the spiritual life.

Alan Ecclestone was born in Stoke-on-Trent in 1904 and went up to Cambridge as a scholar of St Catharine's College, where he took firsts in History and English. During vacations he worshipped at the church at Sneyd in Burslem, where he came under the influence of its vicar Father Jim Wilson (brother of Edward Wilson of the Arctic).

Wilson was a member of the socialist Catholic Crusade and after services would take the Cross of St George and the Red Flag into the market place and preach Christian Socialism.

On coming down from Cambridge Ecclestone was appointed a lecturer in English at Durham University and began an association with the Workers' Educational Association which continued for the next 40 years.

In 1930 he felt drawn to Holy Orders and, after spending a year at Wells Theological College, became curate of a parish in Carlisle. Thus began a lifelong love of Cumbria and the Lake District.

Another curacy, at St John's, Barrow-in-Furness, was followed in 1936 by appointment as vicar of Frizington, an iron ore parish, where most of the men were unemployed and living in deep poverty. This experience fuelled his already firmly-established socialist ideals. In addition to intensive pastoral work he began to experiment with a participatory parish meeting, which he was to develop further when he moved to Sheffield in 1942.

Holy Trinity, Darnall, was then one of the toughest of Sheffield's tough parishes, with an entirely working-class population of 15,000 which had suffered greatly during the wartime bombing.

For the next 27 years Ecclestone − a widely cultivated man who tried to read the whole of Shakespeare's works every year − identified himself completely with this parish. He was assiduous in his concern for the sick, the poor and anyone in trouble, and he sought to introduce an element of gaiety into the community by means of colourful services in the parish church.

The parish meeting, for which he became more widely known, was an expression of his belief, shared with those of the Congregationalist tradition, that the local church consists of all its members who ought to meet regularly, not only for worship but also for experience of Christian community life and the planning of the Christian mission in the neighbourhood. At Darnall this included the sending of delegates to meetings at the City Hall to ask questions about social policy.

A weekly church meeting was a tall order for hard-working people who were not accustomed to attending decision-making assemblies, and the number participating was never huge. But the idea spread to other parishes by means of a monthly leaflet, the *Leap*, until overtaken by the process of synodical government in the Church of England – which Ecclestone insisted was not the same thing, for it was elective rather than fully participatory and concerned almost exclusively with ecclesiastical matters

In 1969 Ecclestone retired to a small, whitewashed cottage in Cumbria, where, surrounded by his 12,000 books, he began to share with a wider audience the deep spirituality which had informed and sustained his ministry in Sheffield. *Yes to God* (1975) was a best-seller, won the Collins Religious Book Award and was said to have "taken prayer on to the streets".

This was followed by *A Staircase for Silence* (1977), which drew heavily on the French poet, mystic and visionary Charles Peguy; *The Night Sky of the Lord* (1980) and *Scaffolding of the Spirit* (1987). In all these he related the life of the spirit to the challenges of the modern world.

In old age Alan Ecclestone ceased to be a member of the Communist Party although he retained Communist ideals. His reforming spirit led him to complain that the Church of England had not included Shakespeare, Milton, Keats, Wordsworth and Blake in its official list of saints and teachers.

His wife, Delia, died in 1984, and his son Giles, a former House of Commons Clerk, secretary of the General Synod Board for Social Responsibility and parish priest, died in 1990.

Another son, Jake, is deputy general secretary of the National Union of Journalists.

December 16, 1992

1993

The Reverend Dr Arthur Tindal Hart

The Reverend Dr Arthur Tindal Hart, who has died aged 84, was the foremost historian of the English clergy and an exemplar of all the traditional virtues of the country parson.

In many ways he belonged to another age, as was symbolised by his persistence in driving ancient motor-cars. He was among the last of a generation of Church of England clergymen whose responsibilities in country parishes left them with the leisure to pursue scholarly or other interests.

Tindal Hart's output of historical studies was prodigious. His special gift lay in the unearthing of contemporary accounts of the clergy – many of them highly entertaining – and in relating them to the broader movement of events in the Church.

It was perhaps his demotic approach, not always as meticulous as modern historical methods require, that denied him the fellowship of a Cambridge college, which he greatly yearned for at one time.

Nevertheless, his first two books – biographies of early 18th-century bishops – were sound enough to earn him a Cambridge DD, and in the end he derived immense satisfaction from his work as a parish priest.

Arthur Tindal Hart was born in Hertfordshire in 1908 and educated at Emmanuel College, Cambridge, where he took a first in history. Having decided on Holy Orders, he went to Ripon Hall, Oxford, then the main centre of liberal modernist theology, and was ordained in 1932 by Archbishop Cosmo Gordon Lang to a curacy at Herne Bay.

After three years he moved to Lydd, on Romney Marsh, but in 1937 EW Barnes, the liberal Bishop of Birmingham, appointed him Vicar of St Paul's Church, Bordesley Green.

In this large, urban parish – where he was also Chaplain of Birmingham City Sanatorium – Tindal Hart found much scope for his pastoral gifts but little time for his scholarly concerns. So he was pleased to be appointed, in 1946, Rector of the Northamptonshire country parish of Blatherwycke and also Rector of nearby King's Cliffe.

Tindal Hart's gifts as an historian and writer now began to blossom. *The Life and Times of John Sharp, Archbishop of York* (1949) was soon followed by *William Lloyd, Bishop and Prophet* (1952). Then came *The Nineteenth-Century Country Parson* (1954), a joint work with Edward Carpenter, which marked the beginning of a series of books on the clergy in each of the post-Reformation centuries. *The Curate's Lot* (1970) was especially illuminating, a subtle mixture of humour and sadness.

His sympathy was always with his subjects and although he made much of the eccentricities of the clergy he was quick to point out that the overwhelming majority of them in every period exercised quiet, diligent ministries which were an influence for good in English society.

Tindal Hart's view of bishops was less charitable, though. He believed fervently in the independence of the parish clergy and greatly deplored the movement, which began in the 1960s, for grouping parishes and deploying priests in teams. By this time he had become Rector of Appleton, near Abingdon, where he remained until 1966. His final appointment was to the Sussex parish of Selmeston.

Tindal Hart contributed to the official histories of St Paul's Cathedral and Westminster Abbey. He also composed humorous verse, and he was always a lively conversationalist.

When he retired in 1973 to a college for elderly clergy at Lingfield, Surrey, he gave several series of lectures which attracted much local interest and were later published under arresting titles, such as *Murder and the Monarchy* and *Murder in the Church of England*.

His wife predeceased him, and there were no children.

February 11, 1993

Cardinal Francesco Carpino

Cardinal Francesco Carpino, who has died in Rome aged 88, caused a sensation in 1970 when he resigned as Archbishop of Palermo after only three years in the post.

No one could understand why he did so – including Pope Paul VI, who is said to have asked the tall and taciturn Carpino his reasons, but did not receive an answer.

Carpino had claimed that Palermo's difficult problems required "a young bishop with abundant energy". Commentators wondered whether he had received threats from the Mafia, had clashed with the diocesan clergy or was irritated that he had not been appointed head of one of the Congregations (which correspond to a ministry in a civil government in the Roman Catholic Church's central administration).

Francesco Carpino was born at Syracuse, Sicily, on May 18, 1905 and studied at the Lateran University in Rome. He was ordained in 1927 and taught at the seminary in Noto, Sicily. In 1929 he was appointed to the Chair of Sacramental Theology at the Lateran University, where he remained until 1951.

He helped persecuted Italian Jews during the Second World War and refugees immediately afterwards.

In 1951 Carpino returned to Sicily as coadjutor archbishop, then as Archbishop of Monreale. In 1961 he went back to Rome as No 2 in the congregation for the appointment of bishops.

This meant that he was automatically secretary of the Conclave which elected Paul VI, but he was not a "kingmaker". In April 1967 he was made pro-Prefect of the Congregation of Sacraments and four months later Cardinal Archbishop of Palermo.

He succeeded Cardinal Russini, a conservative who had been close to the Christian Democratic Party. Unlike his predecessor, Carpino did not deny the Mafia's existence, and he disliked the identification of the Church with the Christian Democratic Party.

He divided the Palermo diocese into pastoral zones and instituted many new parishes. After his abrupt and mysterious resignation he returned to Rome, where he participated in the work of the Council for the Public Affairs of the Church, the Congregation for the Clergy, the Causes of Saints, and the Curial Supreme Court.

But he was not made head of a curial office and led a reserved life, devoting much of his time to study.

October 28, 1993

Canon Robin Lamburn

Canon Robin Lamburn, who has died in the village of Kindwiti, Tanzania, aged 89, was sometimes likened to St Paul. Small, bald, opinionated and bad tempered, he was, however, devoted to the care of others and to the spreading of the Christian faith.

In 1961, when Tanganyika was about to become independent, Lamburn had completed more than 30 years of missionary service in that country and might well have retired with honour to England.

Instead he moved 300 miles north of Masasi to the notoriously unhealthy and almost solidly Muslim area of the Refuzi delta. There was no Christian church or mission in the district, and he began by building himself a hut in Kindwiti and by caring for 100 leprosy patients.

When Lamburn arrived the village was gloomy and despondent. The leprosy sufferers were outcasts from their own villages, with little hope of cure. All of them were living off charity and many were alcoholics.

Lamburn spent the rest of his long life in this community, continuing to live in his hut, with no electricity or running water, and giving himself totally to the care of the sick.

He also built a mud church, in which he celebrated Communion every morning, inviting people of all faiths or none.

Medical aid was eventually forthcoming, attitudes were

changed, and Kindwiti became a happy village. Most of the inhabitants now are the healthy relatives of leprosy patients, whole families live together and grow much of their own food, as well as make their own furniture, utensils and footwear.

In 1985 Lamburn was awarded the Albert Schweitzer Prize for Humanities. He had earlier received a medal from Pope John Paul II, and been appointed MBE in 1955.

A relative of Richmal Crompton, author of the Just William books, Roger George Patrick Lamburn (always known as Robin) was born in 1904 and educated at Trinity College, Cambridge, where he read natural sciences.

He went on to St Stephen's House, Oxford, where he found the Anglo-Catholic regime much to his liking. He was a curate at St George's Church, Southall, from 1927 to 1930.

Lamburn then volunteered for the high church Universities' Mission to Central Africa. After six years of missionary work in the diocese of Masasi he was appointed Warden of St Cyprian's Theological College at Tunduru.

There he was responsible for the education of a new generation of African priests, destined to lead their Church. Their training at Lamburn's hands was thorough and disciplined, for he was an uncompromising high churchman – "more Catholic than the Pope" it was said.

Although he became a Tanzanian citizen, Lamburn's view of African potential tended to the cynical: he believed that "witch-craft and hookworm" would always defeat "progress" in rural Africa.

He spoke out against President Nyerere's plan for amalgamat-ing villages and clashed with Trevor Huddleston, the champion of African rights, who became Bishop of Masasi in 1960.

During his time at St Cyprian's, Lamburn became a canon of Masasi Cathedral and in 1949 was appointed Archdeacon of Masasi and Education Secretary. This involved much travel in a vast diocese and, besides the care of the mission stations and their clergy, he was responsible for many schools.

Robin Lamburn was not always the easiest companion. If his

estimate of African capabilities was not high, his attitude to those Europeans he regarded as fools was decidedly intolerant.

Yet his underlying love of people of all races was unbounded, and his ministry to them always deeply sacrificial.

He was unmarried.

October 30, 1993

Canon Roy McKay

Canon Roy McKay, who has died aged 93, was a pioneering, reforming and often controversial Head of Religious Broadcasting at the BBC from 1955 to 1963.

Indeed, McKay was the first Head of Religious Broadcasting to be identified more closely with the BBC than with the Church.

When he arrived at Broadcasting House, after a ministry spent in parishes and public schools, there was little religious broadcasting on television, and religious radio programming consisted almost entirely of church services and edifying talks.

By the time he left such broadcasting had greatly expanded to the now familiar pattern of acts of worship augmented by documentaries, magazine programmes, social comment, and discussions and debates involving both believers and unbelievers. It was during his tenure that *Songs of Praise* was launched.

As the new approach developed, McKay often found himself in conflict with church leaders and on one occasion his policy was denounced by the Church Assembly. But he was quite unrepentant and said that religious broadcasting would only win large audiences and serve its true purpose if it moved from the sanctuary to the market-place.

He was equally tough in fighting within the BBC for air-time for religious broadcasts on weekdays as well as Sundays.

Roy McKay was born on November 4, 1900 and educated at

Marlborough and Magdalen College, Oxford, where he read jurisprudence. After a brief spell as a solicitor's articled clerk he abandoned the legal profession to enter Ripon Hall, Oxford, where he prepared for Holy Orders.

He was ordained in Southwark Cathedral in 1926 and – after a number of parochial appointments and a short period as chaplain at Santa Cruz, Tenerife – he was appointed chaplain of Alleyn's College, Dulwich, in 1937.

He remained in the school for six years and was then appointed by Bishop George Bell of Chichester as vicar of Goring-by-Sea. Parish life was not, however, his real metier, and in 1943 he returned to the public school world as chaplain of Canford School in Dorset.

It was from this post, and without any significant experience of broadcasting, that he moved to the BBC and carried out what was tantamount to a revolution in religious communication.

He fitted into the style of the BBC with remarkable ease, proved to be a good administrator and an excellent leader of a growing team of talented producers.

When he left the Corporation in 1963 he was unemployed for a time, and he took the opportunity to write a small book, *Take Care of the Sense*, in which he outlined his philosophy of religious broadcasting and gave some account of what he had achieved.

Eventually the Dean and Chapter of St Paul's came to the rescue and appointed McKay as rector of the tiny parish of St James, Garlickhythe, in the City of London, where he served from 1965 to 1970.

When his full-time ministry ended he continued to live in the Barbican for several years and wrote a biography of the celebrated Bishop Leonard Wilson of Singapore and Birmingham before moving to Stamford, Lincolnshire.

McKay became an honorary canon of Chichester in 1957 and was Preacher to Lincoln's Inn from 1958 to 1959.

He married, in 1927, Mary Fraser; they had a son (who predeceased him) and a daughter.

November 9, 1993

The Right Reverend Kenneth Bevan

The Right Reverend Kenneth Bevan, who has died aged 95, spent 25 years as a missionary in China and was Bishop of Eastern Szechwan from 1940 to 1950.

Firmly placed in the evangelical tradition of the Church of England, he offered for service with the China Inland Mission in 1925 and exercised a heroic ministry in West China.

Many small congregations, scattered across the region, were accessible only by taking a boat along the Yangtze or by trekking across the mountains.

This was a hazardous undertaking, since robbers frequently lay in wait for unsuspecting travellers; on several occasions Bevan lost his clothes and personal possessions. In the end he took to travelling as light as possible and used to boast that he could manage with only his Bible and a toothbrush.

The conflict between the National and the Red armies was another source of danger. Mission houses were often commandeered by the army, and then left a few months later stripped of all furniture and belongings.

When Japan entered the Second World War and occupied large areas of China, Szechwan remained free, but missionary work could be carried out only with the greatest difficulty.

Bevan and his wife, Jocelyn, herself a missionary, continued to preach the Christian faith to people who had not previously heard of it, sustained by a deep sense of vocation. During the war the Japanese interned their three daughters at Chefoo, in North-East China.

Bevan gave himself unstintingly to personal ministry and to leading his church. When foreigners were finally expelled from China, the work of the church was able to continue thanks to the number of Chinese Christians he had trained and ordained.

Kenneth Graham Bevan was born at Great Yarmouth on September 27, 1898. His father, who had captained the first Welsh Rugby XV to play England in 1881, was Vicar of St George's Church, Great Yarmouth, and young Kenneth was the sixth son in a family of 10 children – all six sons were eventually ordained.

After attending the local grammar school, he went to the London College of Divinity, at that time a leading institution for the training of evangelical clergymen. From 1923 to 1925, before sailing for China, he was a curate at Holy Trinity Church, Tunbridge Wells.

When he returned to England at the end of 1950 Bevan became Vicar of Woolhope with Checkly, a small country parish in Herefordshire; two years later the even smaller parish of Putley was added to his responsibilities.

In 1955 he was appointed Rural Dean of Hereford South and in the next year became a Prebendary of Hereford Cathedral. Besides his local pastoral work, which he carried out with the same diligence and dedication that had characterised his years in China, he was frequently called upon to exercise his ministry as a bishop.

In 1966, Bevan moved north to become Master of Archbishop Holgate's Hospital at Hemsworth, near Pontefract. Care of this ancient almshouse was only a retirement job, but he served also as an Assistant Bishop in Wakefield diocese and was very active in the parishes until he retired, aged 79, to York.

By this time Bevan had become very conscious of the special needs of the retired clergy and was instrumental in setting up the Retired Clergy Association, which soon attracted a large membership, and of which he was the first chairman.

He married, in 1927, Jocelyn Barber, who died in 1992; they had three daughters.

December 16, 1993

1994

The Reverend Professor
Frederick Copleston

The Reverend Professor Frederick Copleston, SJ, who has died aged 86, was the author of a seminal nine-volume history of philosophy and had a remarkable impact on the teaching of philosophy in Roman Catholic institutions.

Before Copleston the Catholic study of philosophy had been largely a disguised form of religious apologetic. As a result of his approach to philosophical scholarship from the Pre-Socratics to Sartre the Church developed a greater respect for the discipline in its own right.

From 1940 Freddie Copleston had been teaching scholastics (students for the priesthood) at the Jesuit college then located at Heythrop, Oxfordshire.

He wanted to produce for them a manual to demonstrate there was such a thing as the "perennial philosophy" best exemplified in the writings of St Thomas Aquinas. The first volume (which Copleston considered the least successful and wanted to revise) was written from that standpoint. In his later volumes, much praised for their lucidity and objectivity, he abandoned this apologetic approach.

He had his own firm favourites (Hegel and Karl Jaspers among them) and also his dislikes, notably logical positivism, though he became a friend of its leading exponent, Freddie Ayer. In 1949 the two of them debated logical positivism on the wireless.

The text was not published – though a transcript of his discussion with Bertrand Russell on the existence of God (broadcast a year earlier) later appeared in that philosopher's *Why I Am Not a Christian* (1957). Copleston considered the debate with Ayer to have been the more intellectually demanding.

Frederick Charles Copleston was born on April 10, 1907, to a staunchly Anglican family; two of his uncles were bishops. His father had been Chief Justice of Burma, though he retired to Devon before Freddie's birth.

In 1925, while still at Marlborough, he became a Roman Catholic. His family was distressed by his conversion, but remained welcoming when he was expelled from school. He went on to St John's College, Oxford, where he read Greats.

Only in his fourth year did he develop a particular interest in philosophy. After leaving Oxford he thought first of becoming a diocesan priest, and spent a year in the seminary of the Archdiocese of Birmingham.

In 1930, though, he entered the Society of Jesus, and the next decade was taken up by studies for the priesthood. He had an uncomfortable final year of Jesuit training in Germany, which he left shortly before war broke out.

Copleston felt patriotically obliged to volunteer as a Chaplain to the Forces, but his superiors thought otherwise, and he was sent to teach at Heythrop. After the war he was a frequent visitor to Germany, where he lectured under the aegis of the Control Commission.

From 1952 he was required to spend one semester in Rome, teaching what was described as metaphysics, and a second at Heythrop, lecturing in the history of philosophy.

Despite this heavy work load he was a prolific author. His first book, on Nietzsche, appeared in 1942; his second, on Schopenhauer, in the same year as the first volume of the *History*. He produced a one-volume study of medieval philosophy, and a textbook on Thomas Aquinas.

In 1970 Heythrop became a constituent college of London University, and Copleston became its first principal; the university awarded him a professorship in 1972.

For the first time in his life he had the services of a secretary and, during the vacations at least, considerable leisure. He used both to produce a substantial volume on *Philosophy in Russia*, though it did not appear until 1986. There was also a slimmer spin-off two years later on Russian religious thought.

Much of his time after retirement from Heythrop was spent teaching in the United States: he particularly enjoyed Santa Clara University. A semester in Hawaii inspired both *Philosophies and*

Cultures in 1980 and, two years afterwards, his Gifford Lectures, *Religion and the One: Philosophies East and West.* He also published a collection of essays, *On the History of Philosophy.*

Copleston was an outstanding teacher and a lucid and witty lecturer, who inspired affection among his students.

He was awarded numerous honorary doctorates in philosophy and one, much to his surprise, in theology. He was appointed CBE last year.

February 10, 1994

The Reverend Geoffrey Harding

The Reverend Geoffrey Harding, who has died aged 84, was a pioneer of holistic therapy for the sick and director from 1959 to 1973 of the Churches' Council for Healing.

The Council brought together doctors, clergy and counsellors to consider the relationship between their different approaches. Harding was drawn to this task, which became a lifelong concern, through his own experience of an emotional breakdown as a young curate in London in the 1930s, when he discovered a therapeutic combination of relaxation and prayer.

Some of his methods could be startling. When he left the Council to become Vicar of St Mary Woolnoth in the City of London he inaugurated lunchtime sessions for those who were feeling the strains and stresses of their jobs.

Bankers, stockbrokers, insurance underwriters and others who came to the church were commanded to lie on the floor and, under Harding's guidance, to find complete relaxation before returning to their offices. The large numbers who attended these sessions testified to their value, and Harding believed such exercises were a safeguard against stress-related illness.

Regarding himself as something of a prophet – which the growth of a fine, flowing beard in his later years helped confirm in the public eye – Harding was far from relaxed in his relationship with the Church.

He was convinced that its failure to meet what he perceived to be the real needs of people was nothing short of a disaster. He believed that people were in need of health and healing, and that the Church, instead of promoting these, chose to fritter its energies on secondary matters.

Geoffrey Clarence Harding was born in London on October 4, 1909, and educated at St John's College, Oxford, where he read Greats and theology.

After preparing for Holy Orders at Bishops' College, Cheshunt, in 1932 he became a curate at St John's Smith Square, which before its wartime bombing was a large and flourishing Westminster parish. Two years later he moved to another fashionable church – St Mark's, North Audley Street, Mayfair.

It was during those years that Harding experienced stress-related breakdown, and it was not until 1940 that he was able to undertake much pastoral responsibility.

From 1940 to 1943 he was Vicar of St Erkenwald's Church in Southend, and then joined the RAF as a chaplain. Shortly before D-Day he was detached from the RAF to serve an Army unit, and on D-Day itself was with a landing party. He won the MC for his care of the wounded and dying on Omaha beach – a unique distinction for an RAF chaplain.

On demobilisation in 1946, with the support of an ever-increasing circle of friends, Harding established at Milton Abbey, Dorset, a small centre for the treatment of ex-Servicemen suffering from the psychological traumas of war. Relaxation and prayer were vital parts of this treatment, but Harding was always ready to recognise the need for conventional medicine and psychiatry.

In 1951 he returned to the parish ministry as Rector of Inkpen, near Newbury, and after three years moved to become Vicar of Kilmeston with Beauworth in Hampshire. In both places he made full use of his experience of healing and, as interest in the subject began to grow, found himself in demand at meetings and conferences all over England.

Harding encouraged the establishment of more residential healing centres on the lines of his own experiment at Milton Abbey and wrote many pamphlets advocating a holistic approach to disease and providing instruction in his method of relaxation. He was founding president of the Relaxation Society.

When the newly-established Churches' Council for Healing required a director in 1959, Archbishop Geoffrey Fisher nominated Harding.

It proved an inspired choice, and over the next 14 years, Harding won increasing support from churches as well as the confidence of the British Medical Association and the Royal Colleges.

During those years he also formed a lasting friendship with the chairman of the Council, David Jenkins, who later became Bishop of Durham.

Feeling the need of a base for his work, Harding joined the staff of St Mary Woolnoth as St Antholin Lecturer, and was for a time a curate of St Michael's, Cornhill. He also travelled widely, and was involved in the work of the Guild of Health and the Institute for Religion and Medicine, of which he was a founder member.

Inevitably, he became something of a guru. Possessed of a certain charisma, he had only to step into a room to announce his presence, and he had an encyclopaedic knowledge, not always carefully ordered, of facts, references and opinions on almost every subject. But his feet were always firmly on the ground. His book *Lying Down in Church* was published in 1990.

Shortly before his retirement from St Mary Woolnoth he became a liveryman of the Guild of Air Pilots and Navigators and also chaplain of the Guild. He continued his association with the church as an honorary curate until 1987, when he moved to Devon.

His wife predeceased him; they had two sons.

April 5, 1994

The Right Reverend Ted Wickham

The Right Reverend Ted Wickham, who has died aged 82, was Suffragan Bishop of Middleton from 1959 to 1982 and before that the pioneering leader of the Sheffield Industrial Mission.

In the latter post he was internationally celebrated for his attempt to engage the Church in the life of an increasingly secularised industrial society.

During his years in Sheffield (from 1944 to 1959) he formed a large team of industrial chaplains who worked in the iron, steel and engineering works of South Yorkshire, undertaking some pastoral work but mainly holding group meetings during breaks and between shifts to discuss the relationship between faith and the issues arising in the workplace.

Weekend gatherings dealt with these subjects in greater depth, and at one point every large industrial concern in Sheffield and Rotherham was sending members of its staff to the conferences.

Wickham's work in Britain coincided with the activities of the priest-worker movement in France, but he was strongly opposed to the employment of ordained men in secular work and also to the Church identifying itself only with shop-floor workers.

"Industrial mission," he said, "must relate to all men, to the weak of this world as well as the strong – and both are present in industry in vast numbers."

Not long after Wickham's removal to Middleton in 1959, Dr Leslie Hunter, the then Bishop of Sheffield, who had been his strongest supporter, retired and the new bishop, unsympathetic to the aims and methods of the Industrial Mission, initiated changes which altered the character and scale of its activities.

By that time, however, the Wickham model had been copied around the world, from Detroit, Michigan, to Port Harcourt, Nigeria.

Edward Ralph Wickham was born in London on November 3, 1911 and never lost his Cockney style. He left school at 15 and worked in a thermoplastics factory for several years. During the

1930s he was unemployed for a time, and later used to claim to be the only Anglican bishop to have been on the dole.

With ordination in mind, he taught himself Latin, Greek and Hebrew, and in 1937 obtained a London University external BD. He then spent a few terms at St Stephen's House, Oxford, and in 1938 was ordained to a curacy in the poor Tyneside parish of Shieldfield.

There he became aware of the extent to which the Church was out of touch with the working class, and began to consider how the problem might be tackled.

But the parish was flattened by a single night's wartime bombing, and in 1941 he was appointed chaplain of the Royal Ordnance Factory at Swynnerton, Staffordshire, the largest ordnance factory in the country, employing 25,000 workers. There Wickham experimented with some of the chaplaincy methods he would later develop in Sheffield.

From 1951 to 1959 he was a residentiary canon of Sheffield Cathedral, as well as senior chaplain of the Industrial Mission, and from 1955 to 1957 he held the Sir Henry Stephenson Fellowship at Sheffield University. This enabled him to write *Church and People in an Industrial City* – a study of church life in Sheffield which remains a standard work on the Christian mission in an industrial society.

Wickham's appointment in 1959 to the suffragan bishopric of Middleton in the Manchester diocese occasioned surprise, as his style was not that of a typical Anglican bishop and he had often criticised the parochial clergy.

It was commonly believed that he had been "kicked upstairs" in the cause of ecclesiastical politics, and his early years in Manchester were not easy. Nevertheless, he learned how to minister effectively to clergy and people in inner-city parishes and found ways of expressing his belief that a suffragan bishop should serve local institutions.

He was deeply involved in the development of the new Salford University and served as chairman of the Council and Pro-Chancellor from 1975 to 1983.

Wickham was also chairman of the World Council of Churches committee for urban and industrial mission and vice-chairman of the Church of England industrial council. On his retirement in 1982 he became an assistant bishop in the Manchester diocese.

His later books were *Encounters with Modern Society* (1964), *Growth & Inflation* (1975) and *Growth, Justice and Work* (1985).

He married, in 1944, Helen Neville Moss; they had a son and two daughters.

October 1, 1994

1995

The Right Reverend Mervyn Stockwood

The Right Reverend Mervyn Stockwood, who has died aged 81, was one of the century's most controversial Church of England bishops.

He was Bishop of Southwark from 1959 to 1980 and before that a notable vicar of the university church at Cambridge. An avowed socialist, he enjoyed the friendship of Clement Attlee, Sir Stafford Cripps and Aneurin Bevan during the years of the post-war Labour government.

Stockwood was a reformer in moral and ecclesiastical matters and often expressed his opinions in vivid language which brought widespread publicity. He seemed to enjoy this. At his final service in Southwark Cathedral he was presented with a jeroboam of champagne, which he acknowledged to be an appropriate gift: "I have attempted to bring a little fizz into the diocese."

He had a complex personality. He craved affection, but could be a demanding, even ruthless friend. He made much of his egalitarian ideals, but kept a liveried servant and would tolerate only a cordon bleu cook. He had a genuine concern for the poor, but was more often in the company of the titled rich, among whom he was pleased to number at one time the Duke and Duchess of Windsor. He hated fascism but was a close friend of the late Sir Oswald Mosley.

In Church matters he was the *enfant terrible* of the Establishment, but in his personal faith he was traditional and sometimes exhibited the less attractive aspects of prelacy.

A solicitor's son, Arthur Mervyn Stockwood was born on May 27, 1913 at Bridgend. After the death of his father on the Somme in 1916 the family moved to Bristol. Young Mervyn was educated at Kelly College, Tavistock.

Much influenced by the Anglo-Catholicism of All Saints, Clifton, he decided to seek ordination.

Some indication of Stockwood's character may be gained from a story he told of being rebuked as a little boy at All Saints by a "ferocious looking man called a sacristan" for failing to remove his cap. Fifty years later he returned to the church as a bishop declaring triumphantly that "that little boy is now standing in this pulpit, and today he is allowed to wear a hat in church".

Before ordination, however, he had to finance a university education, so he taught at Shrewsbury for two years before going to Christ's College, Cambridge, and thence to Westcott House.

In 1936 he was ordained as a curate of St Matthew's, Moorfields – a large parish in the east end of Bristol – where he remained for 19 years, becoming its vicar in 1941.

He exercised a remarkable ministry there, not least during wartime, when the parish was heavily bombed and the church damaged by fire. The local MP was then Sir Stafford Cripps, later to become Chancellor of the Exchequer, and it was through him that Stockwood joined the Labour Party. He used to say that his Lenten penance was to wear the tie of the Cambridge University Conservative Association, to which he had belonged in his sinful youth.

In 1946 Stockwood was elected to Bristol City Council and became chairman of its health committee, causing some controversy by setting up a birth control clinic in one of the poorer areas of the city.

During his Bristol years he was elected to the Convocation of Canterbury and also served on the British Council of Churches and the Central Religious Advisory Committee of the BBC, often staying when in London at No. 11 Downing Street with Sir Stafford Cripps. He became an honorary canon of Bristol Cathedral in 1952.

Three years later he became vicar of Great St Mary's, the university church in Cambridge. It proved an inspired appointment, and although Stockwood held the post for only four years he made a great impact on both the university and the town. Average Sunday congregations rose from 200 to 1,000 and famous, and sometimes infamous, preachers and speakers occupied the pulpit.

In 1960 he became Bishop of Southwark, on the nomination of Harold Macmillan, and began an episcopal ministry of considerable style and vigour. Soon after his consecration he fiercely attacked a magistrate for sending a young mother to prison, a few days later the magistrate died of a heart attack.

After Stockwood spoke on the radio in favour of birth control clinics, the Roman Catholic Apostolic Delegate refused to sit next to him at a charity lunch at the Savoy Hotel. A priest of the diocese who declined to use the Book of Common Prayer was forced to resign.

"You are doing a great job," Geoffrey Fisher, the Archbishop of Canterbury, wrote to him, "though very often in the wrong way."

Much later Stockwood fell out with Fisher after refusing Freemasons the use of a church.

In an attempt to revive the Christian mission in south London, Stockwood brought into the diocese a number of able young priests, many of whom he had known at Cambridge and most of whom were enthusiastic supporters of the reforming movement of the 1960s. The most prominent of these was John Robinson, the Dean of Clare College, who had been Stockwood's curate in Bristol and became Bishop of Woolwich.

The publication of Robinson's book *Honest To God* in 1963, combined with the activities of the other reformers, led to the coining of the phrase "South Bank Religion".

In fact, Stockwood was no theologian and felt no personal need of Robinson's questioning approach, but he was ready for one of his suffragan bishops to break new ground and supported him strongly in the face of a storm of public criticism.

One project on which the two bishops collaborated and which was to have lasting significance was the Southwark Ordination Course – a scheme designed for men (and later women) who could not undertake full-time study.

Stockwood was often in the House of Lords and spoke frequently about housing, unemployment, Rhodesia, apartheid and homosexuality.

In one debate on Rhodesia, held shortly before Christmas, he suggested that those peers who supported the Smith regime should take tins of whitewash and change the colour of the black and yellow kings at the Christmas crib.

He generally voted with Labour, whether in government or opposition, though in the 1970s he became disenchanted with the Wilson administration.

During his time at Southwark he made a number of overseas tours, visiting the Pope on two occasions and accompanying a Parliamentary delegation to the Soviet Union.

In 1978 he wrote an article praising the achievements of Nicolae Ceausescu in Romania, particularly maintaining churches and building new ones.

Stockwood's last five years at Southwark were spent, as he put it, "immersed in depths of despairing gloom", plagued by boils and eczema, with "less and less interest in organised religion". He had a special antipathy to the development of a synodical government in the Church of England.

Twenty-one years in a demanding and often discouraging diocese had been too long for a man of his temperament, and he might well have benefited from translation to another See, although it would not have been easy to place him elsewhere.

After his retirement to Bath in 1980 he recovered some of his earlier zest and took part in the ordination of an Englishwoman to the priesthood in the United States. He also wrote an autobiography, *Chanctonbury Ring*.

He was unmarried.

January 14, 1995

Canon John Hayter

Canon John Hayter, who has died aged 80, was priest-in-charge of Kuala Lumpur at the time of the Japanese invasion of Malaya in December 1941.

He was recalled to Singapore, where he had been assistant chaplain of St Andrew's Cathedral, and during the siege of the city in February 1942 ministered unstintingly to the people of Singapore. From March 1943 until May 1944 Hayter was interned in Changi jail, in company with his bishop, the renowned Leonard Wilson.

Unlike Wilson, Hayter was not tortured; but from October 1943 the regime in Changi jail was a harsh one. Holy Communion that Christmas had to be celebrated secretly in a cell, and Hayter played an important part in maintaining the morale of his fellow prisoners, who eventually numbered more than 3,000.

John Charles Edwin Hayter was born on March 25, 1915 at Southampton, where his father taught at the King Edward VI School. While at Lancing he was greatly influenced by a sermon in the college chapel, and determined to be ordained and work overseas.

At St Edmund's Hall, Oxford, he displayed no great intellectual prowess but went on to Westcott House Cambridge, to prepare for Holy Orders. In 1938 he became a curate at the Hampshire market town of Romsey.

Three years later he sailed for Singapore in a Dutch cargo boat – a voyage that lasted eight weeks, one week being lost when the vessel scraped a shingle bank and had to return to Liverpool for repairs. Soon after taking up his appointment at Singapore, Leonard Wilson, who had been dean of Hong Kong, also arrived as the new bishop and the two men became close friends.

As the Japanese advanced on Singapore in January 1942, Hayter was employed by the government in dealing with the many homeless refugees who were surging on to the island, he also helped to evacuate women and children by sea. He served as chaplain to the Civil Defence Services and when the air raids began ministered to the many casualties.

During the siege the cathedral became a hospital, though services continued to be conducted in those parts of the building not occupied by beds. As the number of casualties increased it became necessary for the victims to be buried in mass graves and Hayter was involved in conducting many funerals and in comforting the bereaved.

After the surrender to the Japanese the Church enjoyed 13 months of relative freedom. For some reason, never fully understood, the authorities appointed a devout Japanese Anglican, Lieutenant Andrew Ogawa, as director of religious affairs in Singapore and he, at some risk to himself, allowed the churches to function more or less as they chose, provided they confined their activities to religious matters.

Hayter, who became a lifelong friend of Ogawa, was made priest-in-charge of St Hilda's church, Katong, to which he cycled daily from the cathedral and where he built up a flourishing congregation. He also assisted the bishop and visited some of the PoW camps.

All this ended on March 29, 1943 when, at 48 hours' notice, Hayter and Bishop Wilson were sent to Changi. With 27 other ministers who had been interned, they found it possible to conduct services and give Christian instruction until the crackdown in October of that year.

In May 1944 he was transferred from Changi to Sime Road camp, where he lived in very crowded conditions and was employed in digging and in felling trees.

After his release at the beginning of September 1945 Hayter spent a little more than a month in Singapore before returning to England for extended leave. He then went back to Malaya as vicar of South Perak.

In 1949 Hayter returned to England, still bearing the psychological scars of his experiences and needing a time of recovery before accepting much new responsibility. He served as a curate at Solihull, Warwickshire until 1952, then had two years as a curate in Winchester, and then was chaplain of the Royal Free Hospital, London.

He was next appointed vicar of Boldre on the edge of the New Forest, where he remained for 27 years, until his retirement in 1982. He was a exemplary parish priest, greatly loved, and particularly helpful to people in trouble.

He became an honorary canon of Winchester Cathedral in 1979 and it gave him special satisfaction that a short anthem, *Spirit*

of mercy, truth and love, composed by Denis Soul for use in Changi
jail, was sung last month in Winchester Cathedral and in Romsey
Abbey as part of the VJ Day services

His wife, whom he had met in Malaya, predeceased him; there
were no children.

September 21, 1995

The Reverend Christopher Neil-Smith

The Reverend Christopher Neil-Smith, who has died aged 75,
spent more than 30 years as vicar of St Saviour's, Hampstead, and
for much of this time was a leading authority and practitioner in
the mysterious realm of exorcism.

Neil-Smith carried out many thousands of exorcisms and
claimed to have cast out a great variety of evil spirits – or "forces",
as he preferred to call them – from those who appeared to be possessed.

One of his most difficult cases involved the high priestess of a
witches' coven. After Neil-Smith had laid hands upon her head
before the church altar, she fell unconscious and had to be revived
with holy water.

Sometimes Neil-Smith was thrown across the floor of the
church in the course of an exorcism, and it was not uncommon
for the church furnishings to vibrate.

When the prison authorities turned to Neil-Smith for help with
a violent "Hell's Angel", he performed an exorcism in the prison
chapel. The young man was subdued, and afterwards mended his
ways.

On another occasion Neil-Smith explained to a juvenile court in
Essex that a 13-year-old boy had set fire to his school while under
the influence of an evil spirit. The court learned that the incendi-
arist spirit had fled in response to Neil-Smith's admonitory prayer.

Broadcasting House also claimed Neil-Smith's attention when he demonstrated for the benefit of a radio audience the exorcising of a man who had appeared in court on a charge of grievous bodily harm. Listeners heard the sound of the accused wrestling with the spirit.

Ghosts and the paranormal phenomena encountered in haunted houses were frequently brought to heel by Neil-Smith, and his services were in demand far beyond the bounds of his Hampstead parish. But for the most part he led the comparatively uneventful life of a conscientious parish priest.

A priest's son, John Christopher Neil-Smith was born on November 11, 1920. He was educated in Scotland and at Pembroke College, Cambridge, where he read theology. He then prepared for Holy Orders at Westcott House, Cambridge.

From 1944 to 1946 Neil-Smith served a curacy at Bishopwearmouth. He was then on the staff at St Stephen's, Rochester Row, Westminster, before becoming a curate at the church of Christ the Saviour, Ealing.

After six happy years in Ealing, he was appointed vicar of the north London parish of Ponders End in 1953. Six years later he moved to Hampstead.

Neil-Smith recalled that his first experience of the power of concentrated evil was in 1963 when in the course of laying his hands on a man for healing he felt himself to have been "invaded by a spirit".

The man turned out to be an unfrocked priest who had been dabbling in black magic. Neil-Smith sought the advice of a highly-regarded exorcist-priest of that time, Gilbert Shaw, who detected in him psychic sensitivity.

During the next few years Shaw trained Neil-Smith as an exorcist. In due course he was licensed by the Bishop of London to act in this capacity in the diocese of London. He also won the approval of the Archbishop of Canterbury.

It was never Neil-Smith's intention to invite publicity for his work, which he regarded as a part of his normal pastoral ministry. He belonged to the Anglo–Catholic wing of his Church, linked exorcism with the sacramental life and recognised that those liberated from the forces of evil required continuing pastoral care.

But the publication of his book *The Exorcist and the Possessed* chanced to coincide with interest in the sensational American film *The Exorcist* (1973). In the public mind there arose some confusion about the authorship of the film and the book.

Within a year, Neil-Smith had carried out 1,000 exorcisms and become a minor celebrity. The media emphasised the more dramatic elements in his ministry, and encouraged him to some extravagances which he later regretted.

He was in fact far removed from the charismatic healers and exorcists who claim public attention from time to time. A deeply thoughtful priest, he was a trusted confessor and counsellor to people of all ages.

Neil-Smith's own parish was less appreciative of his capacities. But he bore this stoically until, broken in health, he retired to Ealing where once again he found great happiness.

He was married, and had two sons.

November 18, 1995

The Reverend Harold Duncan

The Reverend Harold Duncan, who has died aged 92, was a perfect exemplar of what used to be known as "muscular Christianity".

Standing 6ft 4in tall and weighing over 17st, he was a formidable rugby player, who turned out at various times for the Bath, Bristol and Blackheath clubs, and also a boxer of some distinction. He combined these pursuits with a fervent evangelical faith which took him to northern Canada as a pioneer missionary to the Eskimos of Baffinland and later to the headship of the Cambridge University Mission in Bermondsey.

Duncan went to Pond Inlet in Baffinland with a companion in 1929, having been ordained deacon by the Bishop of Ontario. Their missionary work included a certain degree of exploration in uncharted territory and it was understood that they would have no contact with the outside world until a ship returned the next year. It proved to be a taxing venture and Duncan was left on his own when his companion was killed in a gun accident.

None the less, Duncan quickly won the respect and affection of the Eskimos. On one occasion they brought to him a boy who had been severely mauled by a husky. Duncan had no medical training, but in response to the entreaties of the parents, he attempted to sew up the boy's lacerations. The operation was not successful and the boy died; but his parents were grateful for the attempt to save him.

Duncan was an austere man imbued with a strong sense of duty. Although he seemed like a giant to those whom he sought to convert, he had a warm personality and was unfailingly kind. He established a number of churches.

Artefacts from his days in Baffinland are now on permanent exhibition at the Scott Polar Institute at Cambridge.

A publisher's son, Harold Norton Duncan was born in London on November 17, 1903. He went to Monkton Combe Junior School, Bath, then to Kingsland Grange, Shrewsbury, where he won a scholarship to King Edward VI School, Sheffield.

From 1920 to 1923 he taught at Birkdale Preparatory School in Sheffield and took some external examinations of Trinity College, Dublin and London University. He then spent five years on the teaching staff of Monkton Combe.

In 1928, having felt drawn to missionary work, Duncan entered the Bible Churchmen's College, Bristol.

The next year he embarked upon his short but eventful mission to the Eskimos. When he returned to England at the end of 1934, Duncan was ordained priest in Southwark Cathedral and became general superintendent of Mr Fegen's Homes for orphan children and also head of the Cambridge Mission at Bermondsey.

After five years, he decided to return to teaching, first at

Monkton Combe Senior School then as Senior Master of its Junior School.

But a subordinate position was not to his liking, for he had strong views about education. He was one of the early exponents of the holistic approach, placing a strong emphasis on the spiritual and the physical as well as on the intellectual elements.

From 1948 to 1966, he was able to put his beliefs into practice as headmaster of Cloverley Hall School at Whitchurch in Shropshire. Rugby, boxing and other sports were prominent in the curriculum and the school had a strict orderly regime, but Duncan was a fine teacher and displayed a concern and a fondness for his pupils and staff which they reciprocated.

In 1966 he sought a more relaxed ministry as rector of the rural parishes of Easton and Letheringham in Suffolk where his evangelical approach included the compilation of religious poems, which some of his parishioners found helpful.

Before long he was seeking another challenge, which came with a vengeance in the form of the superintendency of the Protestant Irish Church Missions in Dublin. His ministry among the poorer sections of the Dublin community occupied him from 1972 to 1974, and he spent the next seven years, until his retirement, as the Mission's Deputation Secretary for the South of England – addressing meetings and raising money.

Duncan was unmarried.

December 20, 1995

1996

Canon Douglas Rhymes

Canon Douglas Rhymes, who has died aged 81, was one of the leading figures in the radical, reforming movement, centred on the diocese of Southwark in the 1960s, which came to be known as "South Bank religion".

While Bishop John Robinson was concerned with theological issues in his best-selling *Honest to God*, and others were dealing with the parochial system, Rhymes pleaded for the liberalisation of Christian morality.

In a course of sermons given in Southwark Cathedral in March 1963, later developed into the book *No New Morality*, Rhymes said that the Church must always choose the path of love rather than of law, of compassion rather than convention.

This, he argued, would lead to a willingness to remarry the divorced and to accept the validity of homosexual relationships.

His liberal views prompted a storm of protest in Church circles, and Rhymes was accused of undermining Christian morality.

But 30 years later, when he repeated the argument in a partly autobiographical volume, *Time Past to Time Future*, no-one noticed; by that time he was the rather elderly Lecturer in Ethics at the conservative Chichester Theological College.

His outstanding pastoral ministry was exercised in a variety of parishes, from the poorest parts of inner London to the rich stock-broker belt of Surrey. In all these places he practised what he preached about love and compassion.

Douglas Alfred Rhymes was born in Devon on March 26, 1914. His father, a schoolmaster, moved to Birmingham after serving in the First World War and young Douglas attended King Edward VI School.

He then spent a few years selling insurance but, after attending one of Birmingham's leading Anglo-Catholic churches, felt drawn to the priesthood.

He took a Second in Philosophy at Birmingham University and then became part of a coterie including W. H. Auden and Stephen Spender which met weekly in a pub to discuss politics. He was briefly a member of the Communist Party, believing this to be the only effective antidote to Fascism.

It had been his intention to go to Oriel College, Oxford, to read Theology but the outbreak of war in 1939 put paid to that, and after spending a year at the ultra-liberal Ripon Hall, Oxford, Rhymes was ordained to a curacy at Dovercourt, on the east coast of Essex. This was very much a front-line parish in the early 1940s, and when his curacy came to an end in 1943, he enlisted as an Army chaplain.

Posted to the Westminster Dragoons, Rhymes was with the 30th Armoured Brigade when it landed in France soon after D-Day; the brigade used its flail tanks to blow up mines in advance of infantry attacks.

Rhymes later said that the experience of working alongside men in hazardous conditions had made him specially sensitive to human need and distrustful of ready-made moral precepts. He was one of the chaplains who conducted mass burials at Belsen.

On leaving the Army in 1946 Rhymes spent three years as a curate of Romford parish church, where he was responsible for two daughter churches, including one on a rapidly expanding council estate.

He then spent a year in another new area in Chelmsford before moving to Southwark Cathedral as a priest-vicar, with particular responsibility for All Hallows, Southwark. This backstreet parish behind Borough Station had lost its church in the Blitz, and was one of the most deprived areas in London.

Rhymes devoted himself to endless visiting of the people in their homes and became a much-loved figure in the parish. He became sacrist of Southwark Cathedral in 1952.

In 1954 he was appointed vicar of All Saints Church, Eltham, a thriving Surrey parish with a team of curates, and began to convene study groups to consider, in a religious context, some of the problems of the secular world.

The success of this approach led to his appointment in 1962 as director of lay training in the diocese and as a canon residentiary and librarian of Southwark Cathedral.

Rhymes soon became involved in the movement for reform. He organised weekend courses for lay people at Wychcroft, the diocesan training centre, and was the joint author of *Layman's Church* (1963). Another book, *Prayer in the Secular City* (1967), argued that prayer should be related to daily life and not simply be a matter of "saying prayers".

By now Rhymes was a notable, if not notorious, figure in the Church, and was seen by some as the most dangerous of all the reformers. He was a vocal member of the Church Assembly, to which he had been elected in 1959.

But in 1968 he stepped off the national stage to become vicar of St Giles Church in Camberwell – a tough inner-city parish with every conceivable social problem. The church crypt offered shelter and counselling for alcoholics and drug addicts. Rhymes threw himself into all this with his customary verve and found time to write another book, *Through Prayer to Reality* (1974), which powerfully expressed his own spirituality.

After eight years he was appointed vicar of the salubrious Surrey parish of Woldingham. Here his pastoral gifts were again fully employed and he founded the Woldingham Business and Professional Group, which met every Sunday to discuss work-related issues.

In 1984 Rhymes retired to Sussex, but remained very active for many more years, assisting in the parishes, serving on the Chichester Council for Pastoral Care, teaching in the theological college, and helping to found an Institute for the Study of Religion and Sexuality.

He never married.

January 6, 1996

The Venerable Peter Eliot

The Venerable Peter Eliot, who has died aged 85, was Archdeacon of Worcester from 1961 to 1975.

Before his ordination, in his mid-forties, Eliot was a partner in a City of London law firm- he also had a distinguished military career. This varied background, combined with his deep concern for people, enabled him to become the trusted pastor of the 120 parish clergy in his archdeaconry and a highly regarded figure throughout Worcestershire.

Peter Charles Eliot was born on October 30, 1910, and educated at Wellington and Magdalene College, Cambridge. In 1934 he was admitted as a solicitor, and later that year commissioned in a territorial battalion of the Kent Yeomanry, in which he went on to serve throughout the Second World War.

Eliot went to France with the BEF in late 1939. After Dunkirk in 1940 he was posted to Iraq, and later saw action in North Africa, including Alamein, and Italy.

In 1945 he was appointed MBE and awarded the TD. After the war he returned to legal practice, but remained in the Territorials and, as a lieutenant-colonel, commanded the Kent Yeomanry from 1949 to 1952.

At about this time Eliot came under the influence of Mervyn Charles-Edwards, vicar of St Martin-in-the-Fields, and decided to seek Holy Orders. After a year at Westcott House, Cambridge, he returned to St Martin's as a curate and remained there, taking a full part in the church's social work, until 1957.

During a fishing holiday in Cumberland that year one of Eliot's companions chanced to be the Bishop of Carlisle, who invited him to become vicar of Cockermouth and Workington.

Four happy parochial years followed, including a spell as rural dean. But by 1961 Charles-Edwards had become Bishop of Worcester and enticed Eliot to join him as an archdeacon.

From 1961 to 1965 Eliot was also vicar of the small parish of Cropthorne with Charlton, near Pershore, and he then became a canon residentiary of Worcester Cathedral. This proved an excellent move: he took the duties of the archdeaconry and the canonry with equal seriousness and became a bridgebuilder between the diocese and its cathedral.

Eliot's somewhat patrician style suited the beautiful house in the cathedral close which he shared with his wife, Lady Alethea, the daughter of the 1st and last Lord Buxton.

No. 12 College Green became a centre of generous hospitality and a place of fun, as the archdeacon had, since the 1930s been a member of the Old Stagers Amateur Theatrical Society (founded by his grandfather) and both he and Lady Alethea found the stage a valuable antidote to ecclesiastical solemnity.

When he retired to Herefordshire in 1975 Eliot still had 20 years of enthusiastic and energetic ministry ahead of him. This was exercised in the parish of Kingsland, near Leominster, where he was content to be an honorary curate and, as always, became involved in the life of the whole community.

He and his wife revived the Kingsland Flower Show (he was its president for several years), and founded the Kingsland Amateur Dramatic Society. Both gave acclaimed performances in the 1994 Christmas pantomime and the former archdeacon's interpretation of the role of the Wizard of Oz will long be remembered.

January 25, 1996

The Right Reverend Vernon Nicholls

The Right Reverend Vernon Nicholls, who has died aged 78, was Bishop of Sodor and Man from 1974 to 1983, during which time he both reorganised parishes and supported the use of the birch.

Nicholls was ideally suited to this second oldest and smallest of the Church of England's 43 dioceses. A man of warm personality, he mixed easily and enjoyed good company and good wine. He liked to tell the story of a Liverpool station porter who called to a colleague: "Hey, Bert, come and help me with this luggage for the Bishop of Sodom and Gomorrah."

His administrative skills proved useful in a diocese in need of reorganisation, while his conservative outlook on social matters was perfectly attuned to the Isle of Man. In 1977 he used his position in the Upper House of the Manx Parliament to vote against a Bill designed to curb birching.

The next year he appealed to the Manx people to register their disapproval of the condemnation of birching by the European Court of Human Rights. Nicholls believed that fear of the birch made it safer for the aged and the infirm to walk the streets by night.

Nicholls's ex-officio position on the Legislative Council enabled him to serve on the Manx Boards of Education, Social Security and Health Services. He was also a Justice of the Peace, and founded a council on alcoholism.

He amalgamated parishes to cope with the shortage of clerical manpower and money. The church of St German became the cathedral of the diocese, with the Bishop as its Dean, the ancient cathedral having been virtually a ruin since the 18th century. Nicholls also strengthened the calibre of the clergy by filling key posts with priests imported from the mainland.

Vernon Sampson Nicholls, a Cornishman, was born on September 3, 1917. From Truro School he went to Durham University, where he came under Evangelical influence, and subsequently moved to Clifton Theological College, Bristol, to prepare for Holy Orders.

From 1941 to 1942 he was a curate at St Oswald's church, Bedminster Down, Bristol, then returned to Cornwall as a curate at Liskeard.

Two years later he enlisted as an Army chaplain. In 1946 he returned to parish work as vicar of Meopham in Kent. For the next 10 years he exercised a vigorous ministry embracing the whole of community life. He became rural dean of Cobham and was a member of Strood rural district council from 1948 to 1956.

Nicholls then moved to very different pastures as vicar and rural dean of Walsall – a tough assignment in the West Midlands where the churches often seemed ill-equipped for their task. Sharing of resources and re-drawing of parish boundaries were necessary and Nicholls – who had a good head for money – succeeded in restoring confidence.

He was chaplain of Walsall General Hospital and in 1961 became a prebendary of Lichfield Cathedral.

On the strength of his performance at Walsall Nicholls was appointed Archdeacon of Birmingham in 1967. This was another demanding post in a city with small congregations and too many churches.

He became diocesan planning officer and, in order to increase parochial income, co-ordinating officer for Christian stewardship.

The building of churches and schools for areas of new housing was another of his concerns and he fought hard to ensure that priests and buildings were in place once housing estates were started.

When the bishopric of Sodor and Man fell vacant in 1974, a strong administrator was required. Although Nicholls had by now spent nearly 20 years in the industrial Midlands, his skill and personality made him first choice.

He made an immediate impact by announcing that he did not propose to live in Bishop's Court – the historic home of the bishop, with its 12 bedrooms, three kitchens and four cottages on an eight-acre estate. This provoked a public outcry, but objectors were told brusquely, "History and sentiment don't pay bills." A more modest property was bought.

Nicholls was efficient, and clergy accustomed to long episcopal delay were astonished to receive replies to their letters by return of post. Rapid decision-making could, however, be regarded as impetuosity on an island not generally in a hurry. Some mistakes were made. But he cared for his people and widespread regret was expressed when he retired in 1983.

His retirement was spent at Stratford-upon-Avon where he became an Honorary Assistant Bishop in the Coventry diocese.

From 1984 to 1990 he was a member of the South Warwickshire Drug Advisory Committee. He was also Grand Master of the Warwickshire Province of Freemasons.

His tranquillity was disturbed in 1990, when it was revealed that in 1982 he had removed a personal deposit of £100,000 from the Savings and Investment Bank in the Isle of Man shortly before it crashed. Thousands of small investors suffered losses totalling £42 million.

A Manx MP wondered if the Bishop had received "divine guidance" or simply a tip-off from privileged sources. Nicholls denied any foreknowledge and said it was pure coincidence that he had withdrawn his money to buy a retirement home.

Nicholls married, in 1943, Phyllis Potter; they had a son and a daughter.

February 6, 1996

Prebendary Newell Wallbank

Prebendary Newell Wallbank, who has died aged 81, was appointed in 1937 to a curacy at the Priory Church of St Bartholomew the Great, Smithfield, the City of London's oldest church. In 1945 he succeeded his godfather as rector of St Bartholomew's, and he remained there until his retirement in 1979, thus spending the whole of his ministry in one parish.

The combination of a magnificent Norman building, a sparsely populated parish, and, for most of his time there, an above-average income, suited Wallbank well, for he was at heart a musician and a scholar.

A Doctor of Music at the age of 22, he composed a great deal of what is believed to be very fine music, but he allowed none of it to be heard in public. For relaxation he took a London University degree in Philosophy, a Diploma in Public Administration, and in 1956 completed a second PhD.

He had little interest in theology and ecclesiastical affairs.

Newell Eddius Wallbank, whose parents were both musicians, was born on June 30, 1914. He won a scholarship to Queens' College, Cambridge, where he read music and stayed on to take a MusB. His doctorate in music was awarded by Trinity College, Dublin, in 1936.

He then decided to prepare for Holy Orders at Ripon Hall, Oxford — at that time a centre of liberal modernism — and at the behest of his godfather, Canon E. S. Savage, was ordained to St Bartholomew's.

His succession to the rectory in 1945 did not go unchallenged. The then Bishop of London, Dr Geoffrey Fisher (later Archbishop of Canterbury) believed that Wallbank, at only 33, was much too young for one of the City's richest livings — and the proposal too close to nepotism to be acceptable.

Wallbank responded with a masterly letter in which he told Fisher that he agreed with what he had written and desired earnestly to comply with his wishes, but that unfortunately he had made a solemn oath to his godfather that he would succeed him, and his conscience would not permit him to break it.

Wallbank's love for St Bartholomew's was enhanced by the knowledge that the church had been founded in 1123 by Rahere, a court minstrel of King Henry I; and he established a fine musical tradition there which continues today.

He became deeply involved in the life of St Bartholomew's Hospital, and from 1968 to 1979 was chaplain of the Imperial Society of Knights Bachelor, which uses the church as its official chapel. He raised more than £100,000 for the restoration of the church in 1972; at his instigation the patronage was transferred to Westminster Abbey.

A quick-witted, good-natured man and a faultless mimic, Wallbank had the style of a layman, not a priest, and it was with some reluctance that he served as rural dean of the City of London from 1958 to 1963. He became a prebendary of St Paul's Cathedral in 1964.

In retirement Wallbank taught music for a time at Eton.

It was to his beloved St Bartholomew's that he returned to die. While taking part in a service there he had a heart attack. Fully robed, he expired at once.

Newell Wallbank is survived by his wife, Phyllis, and by two sons and a daughter.

March 7, 1996

The Reverend David Nicholls

The Reverend David Nicholls, who has died aged 60, became in 1978 vicar of Littlemore, Oxford, a parish celebrated for its connection with John Henry Newman.

He exercised a notable pastoral ministry in the large, working-class parish, but was more widely known as one of the most learned and acute religious commentators on the political and economic scene.

Nicholls belonged to the small Anglo-Catholic tradition of the Church of England, which sees an inseparable connection between a deep sacramental theology and an organic understanding of society, in which equality and justice are the controlling factors.

His comments on issues of current political concern were, consequently, always profoundly theological, and much more than a mere combination of liberal thinking and religious aspiration.

There was a distinctive other-worldliness in his outlook, and a constant emphasis on worship and contemplation. His evaluation of people and events was directly related to what he understood to be divine revelation; this ensured that his critique of society was always radical.

But his withering criticism was directed at politicians of both Right and Left. He was equally demanding with Church leaders who ventured to comment on social and political matters. Even

Archbishop William Temple, generally regarded as the 20th century's leading Anglican social reformer, was considered by Nicholls to have been fatally compromised with the Establishment of his day.

It was perhaps a failure to formulate an adequate theology of power in a civil society that caused Nicholls to be less constructive and influential than he might otherwise have been. He had a marvellous ability to locate the weaknesses in social and political policies and to puncture the pretensions of some of those who proposed them, but it was never easy to discern what alternative policies and persons he would have preferred.

Thus Nicholls declared himself a Socialist and was a member of the Labour party, but sometimes spoke the language of radical Conservatism.

"As our descendants look back to the 20th century," he suggested, "they will surely wonder at the uncritical support given by almost all Christian Churches to the growing power and scope of the coercive state, and to the tragically mistaken policy of getting the state to do for us things that we should be doing for ourselves.

"Social action does not necessarily mean state action, and we are disastrously wrong in rendering to Caesar the things that are God's." His distrust of the state was so great that he sometimes seemed to favour anarchism.

David Gwyn Nicholls was born at Woking on June 3, 1936. He went from the local grammar school to the LSE where he took a First in Economics. He then went to King's College, Cambridge to undertake research on the social thinking of J. Neville Figgis, an Anglican monk whose combination of theology and political theory aroused much interest during the early 1900s.

Having completed a PhD and taken a Master of Theology at Yale, Nicholls prepared for Holy Orders at Cuddesdon Theological College. This was followed by a curacy at St George's Church, Bloomsbury, combined from 1962 to 1966 with membership of the Anglican chaplaincy team at London University.

He was then appointed lecturer in government at the University of the West Indies in Trinidad where he remained until 1973. During this time he developed a special interest in the social and political development of the Caribbean region, especially Haiti, which he came to know well.

He later wrote a history of *Haiti from Dessalines to Duvalier* (1979) which has now run to three editions and is regarded as a classic, and also *Haiti in Caribbean Context: ethnicity, economy and revolt* (1985).

On his return to England Nicholls became chaplain, lecturer and fellow of Exeter College, Oxford. This was a five-year appointment during which, besides his effective chaplaincy work, he completed his major work on Haiti and published two other books, *Three Varieties of Pluralism* (1974) and *The Pluralist State* (1975).

There being no other academic appointment open to him in England, he went – by no means happily – to take charge of the parish of Littlemore.

Here he remained for the next 18 years, busy in the parish which had grown much larger than in Newman's day, but also still active in teaching and writing. He gave the Hulsean lectures at Cambridge in 1985 which formed the basis of two important books, *Deity and Domination* (1989) and *God and Government in an Age of Reason* (1995).

He also helped to found the Jubilee Group, which seeks to encourage radical social thinking in Anglo-Catholic circles, and edited 10 small volumes to mark the 150th anniversary of the Oxford Movement in 1983. He co-edited in 1991 a collection of critical essays on Cardinal Newman, designed to counter the growing pressure for his canonisation.

Nicholls was involved in the work of Oxfam and the Institute for Race Relations and from 1992 to 1995 was president of the Society for Caribbean Studies in the United Kingdom.

A constant stream of overseas visitors found their way to his hospitable vicarage where they were entertained not only by an engaging vicar and his wife, but also by a colourful macaw which originated from Trinidad and was named after a notable 18th century latitudinarian theologian – Archdeacon Paley. The bird and its owner died within a few days of each other.

Nicholls is survived by his wife, Gillian, there were no children.

June 25, 1996

The Right Reverend George Sessford

The Right Reverend George Sessford, who has died aged 67, was Bishop of Moray, Ross and Caithness from 1970 to 1993.

He had intended to remain in office until 1995 and complete 25 years as bishop of the largest diocese territorially in the British Isles, but the decision of the Scottish Episcopal Church to ordain women to the priesthood led him to retire on his 65th birthday.

A man of strong theological opinions, Sessford found himself battling against change on a number of other fronts. He was unhappy about his Church's decision to permit the remarriage of people who had been divorced. Although he was greatly in favour of co-operation between different Churches, he was not ready to compromise on matters which he believed to threaten Catholic order.

Yet it was not difficult for those of a less conservative outlook to work with him. He had a strong pastoral sense and a deep commitment to mission, but above all an unbending loyalty to the Anglican tradition as expressed in the Scottish Church. Thus, having lost his fight against the remarriage of the divorced, he was ready to back the necessary new legislation provided it left bishops free to judge particular cases in the light of their own theology of marriage.

George Minshull Sessford was born at Aintree, Liverpool, on November 7, 1928. After attending Oulton High and Liverpool Collegiate schools, he did his National Service in the Royal Army Service Corps.

After taking an Arts degree at St Andrews, he spent two years at Lincoln Theological College.

From 1953 to 1955 he was a curate of St Mary's Cathedral, Glasgow. He then became an effective chaplain to Anglican students at Glasgow University. In 1958 he was appointed priest-in-charge of the Church of the Holy Name, in Cumbernauld New Town. There he established a strong new congregation in the rapidly developing town, finding time also to be a lecturer at Jordanhill College of Education, until 1962. During this period he played a leading part in a movement called To Serve Thee Better, which aimed to renew the missionary life of the Church.

In 1966, for family health reasons, he moved to Moray to be rector of Forres. Four years later, at the age of 41, he was elected bishop of the diocese, which covers almost the whole of northern Scotland and is roughly the size of Wales. Inevitably, he was involved in a great deal of travelling from his home in Inverness to keep in contact with widely scattered parishes and missions.

He also had a particular concern for the Church's ministry to holidaymakers in the Highlands.

Soon after becoming a bishop, Sessford was elected president of Truth and Unity – an organisation founded to defend traditional faith and practice against what were seen as liberalising tendencies spreading from south of the border.

Spiritually, as well as physically, Sessford was a big man, and he occupied his minority position in a changing Church with dignity and grace.

He was a keen sailor on Loch Ness, in his little boat *The Piskie*, had a passion for Lanchester motor cars, and in his earlier years was the only bishop known to be a breeder of donkeys.

His first wife, Norah, died in 1985 and he is survived by his second wife, Joan, and by three daughters of his first marriage.

July 29, 1996

The Reverend Christopher Gray

The Reverend Christopher Gray, who has been murdered outside his vicarage in Liverpool aged 32, was described by the Bishop of Liverpool as "one of the brightest hopes of his generation".

Intellectually, Gray was of the highest calibre. At Oxford he took a congratulatory First in Mods and Greats, and a rare B Phil on Aristotle's conception of substance. Professor Adrian Hastings of Leeds University, where Gray took a First in Theology, described him as "quite the most brilliant student I have had the pleasure of teaching." Gray spoke nine languages.

As a priest, Gray devoted himself to the service of the poorest of the poor in Liverpool, first as a curate of St Jude's Church, Knowsley, and from 1995 as priest-in-charge of St Margaret's Church, Anfield.

In both places his outstanding intellectual gifts proved no obstacle to his leadership and deeply sensitive pastoral care for all his parishioners, whether they attended his church or not. He inspired affection as well as great respect. Yet Gray's motivation was not to be confused with that of the social worker.

He drew his strength and commitment from beliefs in the nature of God, the Incarnation, the Church and the Sacraments which have exerted a powerful influence on the Anglo-Catholic movement in the Church of England since the 19th century and have inspired some outstandingly able priests to heroic work in the slums of the great cities.

Although martyrdom in Liverpool seemed unlikely, Gray appears to have considered the possibility. In a contribution to the book *The Fire and the Clay* (1993) he wrote: "The supreme act of the shepherd is to lay down his life for the sheep . . . Priests are called to be people who grow to be like Christ in their faithful service of their flocks, even to the point of sacrificing their own lives."

Christopher John Gray was born on January 2, 1964 at Gosport, Hampshire. From the local grammar school he won a county scholarship to Winchester, and from there a scholarship to University College, Oxford.

During his time at Oxford he came under the influence of Pusey House (the Anglo-Catholic centre) and felt drawn to the priesthood. Before going to Mirfield Theological College he spent six months with the L'Arche community, in Paris, working with people who had learning difficulties.

This was followed by six months in a parish at Walton, Liverpool, where he used his considerable musical gifts in the leadership of the choir, and also taught in the Church school. It was this experience that drew him back to Liverpool where he was ordained in 1992.

At Mirfield he was very much at home in the tradition of the Community of the Resurrection, which has produced some of the towering figures of the Church of England, including Archbishop Trevor Huddleston. For them, and for Gray, there was no division between sacred and secular or between sacraments and society. The priesthood provided the vital link, and required the highest degree of spiritual dedication and commitment.

Christopher Gray was unmarried.

August 17, 1996

1997

The Reverend W. Awdry

The Reverend W. Awdrey, who has died aged 85, was the creator of Thomas the Tank Engine, Gordon the Grumpy Express, the Fat Controller and the whole group of human-faced rolling stock whose adventures celebrated the golden sunset of steam railways.

Their stories – recounted in some 30 books which led to television series and numerous commercial spinoffs – began in 1944 when Awdry's three-year-old son Christopher was ill with measles.

Nursery rhymes had palled with repetition. So Awdry, although no artist, drew some engines with faces to illustrate the lines, "Early in the morning, down at the station,/All the little engines standing in a row." To go with them he wove a few tales which the child, long after he had recovered, insisted be repeated word for word.

The first engine Awdry named Edward ("it was the first name that came into my head"), and he jotted the stories down on the backs of old circulars. He saw little value in the stories, but at his wife's suggestion they were sent to Edmund Ward, a fine art printer in Birmingham, who paid £40 for the copyright and commissioned an indifferent illustrator.

The Three Railway Engines was published in 1945, it sold remarkably well, and over the next year was reprinted four times. *Thomas the Tank Engine* appeared in 1946, and a steady flow of additions appeared every autumn for the next two years. By then Awdry found the task of coming up with new stories too onerous, and handed over to Christopher.

One part of the Awdry books' success was that they came out in small, easy to handle volumes; another was the fine work of the later illustrators whose bright, brochure-style pictures showed a world of well-kept stations, neatly dressed passengers and overalled workmen.

They also appealed for the way the narrative was crafted to trip off parental lips with the rhythm of rolling stock. James the Red Engine puffs, "Come along, come along," as he struggles up a steep hill, while his coaches say encouragingly, "You're pulling us well, you're pulling us well." As Gordon is made to haul some trucks, he complains, "A goods train, a goods train" in disgust.

For all their simplicity, each of the stories was based on a real incident, such as the loss of some trucks, a derailment, or a fish found in an engine's boiler.

Sometimes Awdry's readers questioned the likelihood of such events. In one story, Percy is forced down a gradient by his loaded trucks and collides with the rear of a stationary train at the bottom, ending up perched precariously on top of a wagon.

Railway enthusiasts by the score wrote to Awdry claiming that such an event or anything like it was quite impossible. "My reply", said Awdry, "is that it actually did happen on April 13 1876, on the London, Chatham & Dover Railway, and that a photograph of the accident is to be found on page 31 of Volume XXXIV of *Model Railway News*."

Wilbert Vere Awdry was born on June 15, 1911 at Ampfield, Hampshire, where his father, a railway enthusiast, was vicar.

Every Wednesday afternoon, young Wilbert went for a walk with his father which ended with them climbing an embankment to see the engines of the London and South East Railway pass on the way from Romsey to Eastleigh.

If it was raining they were admitted to the platelayers' cabin, where there was always talk of steam-engines and their ways.

Awdry went to Dauntsey's School, Devizes, and St Peter's Hall, Oxford, before completing his training at Wycliffe Hall, Oxford. He spent three years teaching at St George's School, Jerusalem, before being ordained at Winchester Cathedral in 1936.

He first took a curacy at Odiham, Hampshire, and then moved to West Lavington in the same county. During the Second World War his pacifism led the notorious Bishop Barnes to appoint him Vicar of the large parish of King's Norton, Birmingham. He next became vicar of Elsworth with Knapwell in Cambridgeshire, where he proved a diligent pastor in the moderate evangelical tradition, and was a great favourite with the children of the parish.

In 1951 Awdry became Rural Dean of Bourn. Two years later

he moved to the larger parish of Emneth near Wisbech, where he ministered faithfully for another 12 years before retiring to Stroud, Gloucestershire, to give part-time assistance in local parishes.

Inevitably problems ensued as the stories became international bestsellers. Pressing inquiries from eager children were fielded by placing his railway on the mythical island of Sodor, located somewhere between the Isle of Man and Barrow-in-Furness. For Sodor Awdry designed, with the help of his children, an entire fictional landscape criss-crossed by a network of railway lines.

Awdry halted the first television series in 1959 because the BBC wrote in a scene that he believed inauthentic. Thirty years later he was pleased by a new animated production put out by Central Television, using the voice of Ringo Starr. But he was exasperated when Central started to write their own story-lines.

In 1951, Awdry published *Our Child Begins to Pray*. Besides his children's books, he edited *Industrial Archaeology in Gloucestershire* (1973), which ran to three editions, and was joint editor of *A Guide to Steam Railways in Great Britain* (1979). In 1987 he was joint author of a history of the Birmingham and Gloucester Railway.

In his last years, Awdry looked back philosophically on his two callings. "Railways and the Church have their critics," he would say. "But both are the best ways of getting man to his ultimate destination."

He married, in 1938, Margaret Vale, who died in 1989; they had a son and two daughters.

March 22, 1997

Canon "Johnnie" Johnston

Canon "Johnnie" Johnston, who has died aged 90, made an unusual career change, from being a reporter and gaining a scoop on the divorce of Wallis Simpson, to being Vicar of the parish of Dedham, Essex, renowned for its beauty and artistic connections.

Johnston was Vicar of Dedham for 25 years, and became one of the Church of England's outstanding priests. He combined a traditional faith with a broad interest in human life, a delight in the unexpected and considerable flair as a communicator.

This flair was demonstrated before his ordination and in a very different context when, as a young journalist working for an American news agency, he went to Ipswich Assizes on October 27, 1936 to cover a divorce case, Simpson W. *v* Simpson E. A.

The town was thronged with journalists, mainly Americans, who were aware of the petitioner's involvement with King Edward VIII. But when the judge went into early recess and the rest of the hacks went off for lunch Johnston stayed behind. He was rewarded by the sight of Mrs Simpson arriving at the court, accompanied by Sir Norman Birkett, her lawyer, and within a matter of minutes the divorce had been granted. With the aid of a telephone in a nearby dairy, the diligent young reporter conveyed the news to New York and secured a world exclusive.

Earlier that year, in January, Johnston had received advance intimation of the imminent death of King George V. He chanced to be lodging with the village carpenter at Sandringham, who took him into his workshop to see a special coffin he was making. This would, he predicted, soon be needed.

Nothing in Johnston's long ministry at Dedham could quite match this for excitement, but he succeeded in filling the large parish church (painted by Constable), with a thriving congregation.

He also played a leading part in the life of the community, most notably in a local and national outcry that saved Dedham Vale from despoliation by developers who planned to use part of it for London overspill housing. He was among the protest group that delivered a petition with 20,000 signatures to the Minister of Housing, Richard Crossman in 1965.

Albert Richard Johnston was born at Canning Town on September 16, 1906. He left a local school early to become a messenger for a cable company and this led to his brief career as a journalist with news agencies and on the *New York Times*.

When he was 22 he felt drawn to Holy Orders, but his poor Latin caused him to fail the entrance exam to King's College, London.

Not long after his world scoop, by which time he was a lay reader, he tried again, successfully, but problems of a different kind arose over a conflict between his studies and his involvement in wartime journalism – necessary for the payment of his college fees and the support of a wife and two small children.

In the end he left without a degree, but was immediately taken up by the Bishop of Chelmsford, Henry Wilson, who was short of clergy and needed a curate for a parish in the Tilbury Docks area of Essex (a prime target for German bombers).

Johnston was there from 1941 to 1943 and then joined the RAF as a chaplain, serving with Fighter, Bomber and Coastal Commands before being posted to India in the build-up for the planned invasion of Japan.

While serving in the Orkney islands he flew with the crew of an aircraft engaged in a particularly dangerous mission over Norway. This was quite contrary to official regulations, but he sensed that the crew needed moral support. After the successful operation the crew were decorated with DFCs and DFMs, and Johnston was mentioned in despatches. He also made his mark by representing the RAF at football – a lifelong enthusiasm.

On demobilisation in 1946 he became Rector of St Leonard's, Colchester. This was a rundown Essex parish which the Bishop was on the point of suppressing, but he decided to give it a last chance under Johnston's leadership. Within a year it was responding with a new life and by 1948 it was one of Colchester's liveliest and best-supported churches. The fabric was put in order, the interior was redecorated, the bells were pealing again and a large choir was leading the worship.

When the parish of Dedham became vacant in 1950 Johnston was one of 36 nominees for the post of vicar, and his appointment occasioned some surprise. Once again a major work of renewal was needed, for his predecessor had been in office for 44 years and the congregation was at a low ebb.

Within months the attendances at Matins and Evensong had increased considerably and at festivals the church was filled to overflowing.

The Harvest Festival, which extended over two Sundays and included five afternoon services, attracted hundreds of people from far and wide, and large-scale Nativity and Passion plays involved the whole village.

The Royal Philharmonic Orchestra and the choir of the Temple Church gave performances in the church, and over the course of a quarter of a century the church was completely restored and its interior beautifully renewed.

Johnston was fortunate to have a good deal of local talent at his disposal, for his parishioners included the painter Sir Alfred Munnings, the classical architect Raymond Erith and his pupil Quinlan Terry, and General Freddie Birch, who administered the church's finances.

They responded to his outstanding leadership, which was informed by a deep spirituality and a compassion for individuals, as well as a vigorous desire to get things done. He was Rural Dean of Dedham from 1953 to 1974 and became an Honorary Canon of Chelmsford Cathedral in 1964.

In 1971 he retired early because of sudden ill health, but he looked after the beautiful Suffolk parish of Kersey on a voluntary basis for five years before retiring to Bury St Edmunds.

He is survived by his wife, Dorothy, and a son and a daughter.

May 23, 1997

The Reverend J. R. "Mad Jack" Stacey

The Reverend J. R. "Mad Jack" Stacey, who has died aged 64, was a priest of the Church in Wales; his eccentricities, combined with a deep pastoral sensitivity, endeared him to his parishioners and, during a spell as an Army chaplain, attracted both admiration and exasperation.

The Northumberland Fusiliers, "The Fighting Fifth", gave him the nickname Mad Jack during their involvement in the Aden crisis. Stacey, cowed by nothing, insisted on staying with his men under enemy fire. The commanding officer, unable to control this "turbulent padre", sent him for small-arms training so that he might protect himself in emergency.

The CO was later astonished to find Stacey ministering to wounded enemy. This earned him the name "Nazarini" among the Arabs. He was mentioned in despatches.

John Roderick Stacey was born in Bristol on April 14, 1933. His father, a painter and decorator, soon moved to Newport, Monmouthshire, where at the local high school Jack was described as having "a precocious intelligence".

He went to Bristol University, where he read English and Philosophy, and then prepared for Holy Orders at St David's College, Lampeter. From 1956 to 1958 he was a curate at Bedwellty; this was followed by four years at Monmouth parish church.

Stacey was then appointed Vicar of New Tredegar, but after four years surprised his bishop by announcing he was going to become an Army chaplain. His first posting was to the Argyll and Sutherland Highlanders, then serving in Germany. From there he joined the Northumberland Fusiliers in Aden.

Leaving the Army in 1970, Stacey became a team vicar in Ebbw Vale where he joined a handful of parishioners in the building of a church tower. He became a senior chaplain in the Territorial Army, a district commissioner in the Scout movement and was also a prominent Freemason.

From 1973 onwards Stacey ministered in rural parishes in Monmouthshire, first as Vicar of Mamhilad and Llanfihangel

Pontymoile, then as Vicar of Pontnewynydd, and since 1985 as Rector of Bettws Newydd group of parishes.

At one moment he might be found baptising nonchurchgoing farmers in their milking sheds, and at another grinding astronomical telescope mirrors.

Stacey always cared for anyone in trouble; during his final illness he would hobble around the hospital ward handing out packets of contraband cigarettes to his fellow cancer victims.

He is survived by his wife, Diana; they had a son and two daughters.

June 5, 1997

Canon Brian Matthews

Canon Brian Matthews, who has died aged 83, spent almost 40 years ministering to English-speaking people living or holiday-making on the French Riviera.

He was chaplain of St Paul's, Monte Carlo, from 1958 to 1983, and on his official retirement moved a few miles along the coast to Beaulieu-sur-Mer, where he served as chaplain until shortly before his death.

The work of a priest in surroundings of such ostentatious wealth could never be easy, but Matthews had just the right gifts for the special ministry to which he became deeply committed. He lived simply – spartanly in the eyes of his neighbours – but his capacity for drinking whisky enabled him to mix easily with the varied, sometimes exotic, personalities who formed his congregation or belonged to the wider Monegasque community.

On one occasion he sought to enter the Casino in an open-neck shirt but was refused entry. Returning in a clerical collar, he was warmly welcomed. He got on well with Prince Rainier and other members of the Grimaldi family, who much appreciated his contribution to the life of the principality.

But Matthews was also alert to the plight of expatriate widows who had fallen on hard times and who struggled to eke out a respectable existence in a world of conspicuous affluence. His Christmas lunch, held especially for them, was always a poignant occasion, replete with fascinating reminiscences of Monte Carlo's social life in the 1930s.

The rapid expansion of tourism in the 1960s greatly increased Matthews's workload, and in 1976 he was also appointed Archdeacon of the Riviera, with oversight of all the Anglican chaplaincies on the French and Italian rivieras, as well as in Andorra.

Brian Benjamin Matthews was born at Chignall Smealy, Essex, on March 13, 1914. From Haileybury he went to Hertford College, Oxford where he read Modern History. He then prepared for Holy Orders at Chichester Theological College.

From 1937 to 1941 he was a curate at Aldershot, but he then entered the wartime Royal Navy as a chaplain. In 1942 he was posted to San Francisco to join the cruiser *Orion*, which was undergoing repairs after suffering severe damage during the evacuation of soldiers from Crete in May 1941.

He remained in this ship for the rest of the war, and was present at the shelling of the Normandy beaches on D-Day. He recounted that he was reading *The Daily Telegraph* in the bar when *Orion* was once again damaged by enemy fire.

After demobilisation in 1946, Matthews spent two years as a curate at Tewkesbury Abbey. He then became chaplain of Denstone College, where he also served as a housemaster and taught religious studies. He took a great deal of trouble over the ordering of worship in the chapel, and his pastoral ministry among the boys was long remembered.

During summer holidays Matthews often undertook locum chaplaincies in Europe, and it was after a ministry of this kind in Monte Carlo that he was appointed to full-time work there in 1958.

It was a strange inheritance. Reverence for the Queen and

devotion to the Union Flag often seemed to be accorded higher priority than the normal purposes and symbols of a Christian church. The absence of hymn boards was explained by an occurrence some years earlier when a visitor to the church noted the displayed hymn numbers, used them in the Casino and won a fortune. The chaplain of that time thought it wise to remove such a temptation.

Matthews took all this in his stride, and his own conservative approach to worship – he would use only the Book of Common Prayer – enabled him to win the confidence of the congregation and introduce it to his own moderate Catholic outlook.

Remaining in Monte Carlo for 25 years also helped to establish a tradition less coloured by nationalism, and Matthews forged strong links with the local Roman Catholic and Reformed churches.

He became a Canon of St Paul's Cathedral, Malta, in 1973, and in the same year was appointed OBE.

In 1975, on the occasion of the Golden Jubilee of the foundation of the English Church in Monte Carlo, Prince Rainier appointed him a Chevalier of the Order of St Charles.

Matthews was unmarried.

July 1, 1997

The Reverend Professor Ulrich Simon

The Reverend Professor Ulrich Simon, who has died aged 83, was one of the most sensitive and creative Church of England theologians of the 20th century, though his gifts were not always recognised and his message went largely unheeded.

Simon taught at King's College, London, for 35 years, and was Professor of Christian Literature from 1972 to 1980, serving as Dean of King's for his final two years.

He was a refugee from Hitler's Germany, where his father, a non-practising Jew, was murdered at Auschwitz. His brother later met a similar fate in the Soviet Union

When he came to England in 1933 he was already badly bruised by his experience of a disintegrated German culture, and was grateful to find what seemed to him at the time to be a safe haven in the historic Church of England.

But the marks of his youth, and reflection on the events of his adult life, brought to his teaching and writing a strong note of despair, and like the prophets of the Old Testament, by whom he was also much influenced, his hope was grounded in the mysterious providence of God, rather than in any human achievement.

Simon was especially fearful of liberal trends in theology and ethics, seeing these as opening the door to totalitarianism, so he was greatly troubled by developments in the churches during the 1960s and 1970s.

He described Bishop John Robinson's *Honest to God* as "a mean little book", and was especially critical of liturgical reformers who, he declared, "located the strength of Christian convictions in the citadel of worship, and hence trained their guns on the sanctuary and the priesthood; if they could secularise the Eucharist they would have chased their honest God out of the mystery of life."

He greatly approved of Karl Barth, the Swiss theologian, both for his opposition to Hitler and for his theological insights.

Ulrich Ernst Simon was born in Berlin on September 21, 1913. He remembered wounded soldiers returning to their homes at the end of the First World War and the acute social problems of Germany in the 1920s.

He attended the Grünewald Gymnasium where Dietrich Bonhoeffer, also destined to be a theologian and to be hanged for his involvement in a plot against Hitler, was a fellow pupil. His father was a professional musician and the home was the meeting place of famous German musicians and intellectuals.

During his late teens Simon was attracted by Communism, but he discerned the danger when Hitler rose to power, and fled to England. He was astonished by the freedom and tranquillity he found here and obtained employment in a City of London bank, using, he said, Shakespeare as a guide to English life.

Soon however, he was drawn by despair about the world to the study of theology, and enrolled as a student at King's College, London in 1935.

After taking the London BD he went to Lincoln Theological College to complete his preparation for ordination, and in 1939 he became a curate on the vast new housing estate at St Helier in south London.

Here he experienced the fears and pains of war at first hand, and recalled how, when attending a tutorial for his Master's degree at Sion College on the Thames Embankment, his teacher was quite undistracted by the fact that the college roof had been set on fire by incendiary bombs.

In 1943 he moved to another curacy at Upton, near Slough, but when the theological department of King's College returned to London at the end of the war he joined its teaching staff as a lecturer in the Old Testament, and in 1959 was awarded a London DD and appointed Reader in Theology.

Simon was a brilliant teacher whose stimulating lectures and tutorials left several generations of students in his debt. But his concern for the prophetic, rather than the technical, approach to the Bible and doctrine told against him when he applied for professorial chairs in other universities, and he had some disappointments.

In the end he was appointed to a newly created chair of Christian Literature at King's, where his profound knowledge of European literature, particularly that of the 20th century, enabled him to make a unique contribution to theological study in Britain.

He wrote more than a dozen books, of which *A Theology of Auschwitz* (1967) attracted the most attention. Others included *Theology of Salvation* (1953), *Heaven in the Christian Tradition* (1958), and the semi-autobiographical *Sitting in Judgment* (1978).

Disenchantment with late 20th-century culture brought sadness to his closing years and he turned increasingly to the music of Beethoven and Haydn for consolation. He was an accomplished violinist.

Ulrich Simon is survived by his wife, Joan, who was the daughter of a minor canon of Westminster Abbey; they had two sons and a daughter.

August 6, 1997

The Reverend Peter Gamble

The Reverend Peter Gamble, who has died aged 77, was a colourful priest-schoolmaster who admitted in retirement that his homosexuality had been the mainspring of his personal life.

His brief experiment in running an Anglo-American school in Oxfordshire in the 1960s ended disastrously through a combination of drug-taking by pupils and financial insolvency. He was obliged to spend the last years of his teaching career at Harrow School.

Earlier he had been chaplain and housemaster at Milton Abbey School, which he left after a row with the headmaster. This was followed by eight years as chaplain and tutor at Millfield School, where his brother, Brian, was also a teacher.

His gifts as a teacher were considerable, as was his appreciation of beautiful boys. Though his autobiography *The More We Are Together* (1993), subtitled "Memoirs of a Wayward Life", indicate he often sailed close to the wind in his relationships with boys, the physical element was limited and never created scandal.

The Anglo-American school project, whose blameless patrons included Sir John Gielgud, Dame Rebecca West, Douglas Fairbanks Junior, Sir George Thomson and T. E. Utley, was never sufficiently thought through and always lacked adequate financial backing. It was unfortunate for Gamble and those associated with him that when it started in 1967 the extent of the developing drugs problem among older schoolchildren was not widely recognised and there was little experience of dealing with it.

Gamble took a very tough line. During the first year of the school's life four of its 42 pupils (all in the 16–18 age range) were expelled and another two suspended. A member of the teaching staff was dismissed for spending a weekend with a girl pupil. Matters were further complicated when Sir John Tilley, in whose home the school was housed, accused Gamble of being too rigid, and gave him notice to leave the house at the end of the academic year.

New premises were soon found at Barcote Manor, on the Berkshire–Oxfordshire border, and a bank loan financed the purchase. A language school for foreigners wishing to learn English was also established at Carfax, Oxford, enabling Gamble to continue to use an Oxford address. For a time all was well. Pupils came from America and other parts of the world, as well as from Britain, and the regime was unfashionably strict. Academic results were encouraging.

But by 1970 the drugs squad was making enquiries about the extra-curricular activities of some pupils, and Gamble once again employed draconian measures – expelling four pupils, easing out another six, and placing four more on strict probation. This was reassuring to the parents of the innocent, but reduced the school roll to a point where the enterprise was barely viable financially.

September 1971 saw another fall in enrolment and the school went into voluntary liquidation. Gamble, with the then Bishop of Portsmouth, John Phillips, making kindly noises at his side, met the angry creditors who accused him of gross irresponsibility. But eventually Barcote Manor was sold at a favourable price and all were paid in full.

Several months passed before the erstwhile headmaster joined the teaching staff at Harrow, where he was given responsibility for A-level English and Latin. "There were", he later recorded, "many good-looking boys amid my pupils, but it was for Alec that I fell."

Peter John Gamble was born at Streatham Hill, in south London, in 1920. He attended two local private schools and left when he was 16 without any academic qualifications. His first job was in Fleet Street as an office boy with a monthly magazine *The Review*.

Before long he was not only making the tea but also writing some of the book reviews. This was not enough to satisfy the proprietor, who soon dispensed with his services. He then joined *Readers' News*, the organ of the Readers' Union, and after a spell of answering readers' letters he became deputy editor.

In 1940, however, the Readers' Union moved out of London to avoid the wartime bombing and it was decided that the deputy editor's services were no longer required. This left him with a number of problems besides that of immediate employment. He had joined the Peace Pledge Union and was totally opposed to the war, and he had also had some dealings with the British Union of Fascists, which made him the subject of a police investigation.

Having cleared himself of Nazi sympathies – "I only wrote a letter to Hitler" – and registered as a conscientious objector, he was taken on as a teacher at a boys' private school in Wimbledon. His teaching skills at this stage were undeveloped but he got on well with the boys and fell in love with Julien from Belgium. Their close relationship ended when Julien was old enough to join the Belgian navy.

Gamble himself moved on to Belvedere Lodge School at Esher, Surrey, but his contribution to the educational life of the nation was not deemed essential and, on appearing before a Conscientious Objectors' Board, he was ordered to join the Westminster Civil Defence, then struggling with the Blitz.

The importance of this task failed to inspire him and he contrived during his off-duty hours to return to the Readers' Union as head of editorial. This brought him into contact with a number of leading figures in London, with time to spare for patronage of the capital's private clubs for homosexuals.

All this came to a sudden end when he was posted to East Devon to join a regional civil defence column then engaged in the relief of bomb-torn Plymouth. Dissatisfied with his lot, Gamble went absent without leave and when traced was sentenced to a month in Exeter prison.

On his release he declined to wear Civil Defence uniform and was jailed for another month. An attempt to make him serve with hard labour was thwarted when his lawyer discovered that such a sentence could not be imposed on a conscientious objector.

By this time the Civil Defence authorities believed they could manage without him and he was sent to work in a coal mine at Bolsover in Derbyshire. This occupied him for just over a year, and then a local tribunal, having decided that he had done his best in the circumstances, released him from the colliery in September 1945 in order to teach at Kingsholme School.

After a good start with English and Latin, Gamble found himself in trouble with the headmaster for kissing a boy. Although this was smoothed over, he left soon after for another preparatory school – Yaltons at Banstead. While there he discovered that his war service entitled him to a government further education grant and he secured admission to St Catherine's Society to read English.

Accommodation in the university and the city being severely limited, he lodged at Ripon Hall, the Church of England's liberal modernist theological college, and while there was encouraged to seek holy Orders. His protestation that he knew no theology and believed very little of the Christian faith was swept aside and, after acceptance by a church selection conference and a few months at another theological college, he was ordained by the ultra-modernist Bishop of Birmingham, E. W. Barnes, to a curacy at Erdington.

This occupied him from 1952 to 1954 and, finding no vacancies for school chaplains, he went to Paris as assistant chaplain at the Embassy Church. This involved conducting services at Anglican centres in Belgium, Holland and France. After just over a year he returned to England to resume his chequered career in education and to renew his contacts with the homosexual clubs of Soho.

That he was not cut out for parochial ministry was demonstrated when, following his retirement from Harrow, he filled in as a curate. A Remembrance Day sermon in which he condemned the Western powers' reliance on nuclear weapons led to a protest meeting of colonels and other members of the congregation in the churchyard after the service. Other sermons on theological matters were no less controversial.

October 3, 1997

The Right Reverend Douglas Feaver

The Right Reverend Douglas Feaver, who has died aged 83, was Bishop of Peterborough from 1972 to 1984.

Eric Abbott, a notably wise and generous Dean of Westminster, described Feaver as "the rudest man in the Church of England". There was ample evidence to support this verdict.

"Women members of the General Synod," Feaver once declared, "have seething bosoms but nothing above." During a Confirmation Service he asked some boy candidates, "Do you know the sort of girl you would like to marry?" Then, pointing his crozier in the direction of three elderly women candidates, he added: "Mind you, there's not much of a choice here tonight." After the wedding of one of his junior clergy he announced: "I prefer funerals."

This caustic sense of humour disguised a shy man of complex personality. After a brilliant career at Oxford, Feaver never fully matured, and quite failed to realise how hurtful his flippant comments could be. One explanation is that as a young wartime RAF chaplain serving in Egypt he had become critically ill and heard his grave being dug outside the hospital ward where he was lying.

Feaver belonged to an era in the life of the Church of England that was fading by the time he became a bishop. His spirituality was founded on the Authorised Version, which he described as "the one memorable version of the Bible", and on the Book of

Common Prayer. Those drawn to the Alternative Service Book should, he advised: "Taste it and spit it out."

Douglas Russell Feaver was born at Bristol on May 22, 1914. He went to Bristol Grammar School, then became a scholar of Keble College, Oxford, where he carried all before him, taking Firsts in Modern History and Theology, and winning the coveted Liddon Studentship.

Scorning the suggestion of an academic career, he went to Wells Theological College to prepare for Holy Orders and in 1938 became a curate of St Albans Abbey. The high standard of cathedral worship suited him, for he had been brought up at St Mary Redcliffe, Bristol, and thereafter was a stickler for disciplined church services.

Four happy years at St Albans ended when he volunteered for the wartime RAF. He served on a number of stations at home and overseas.

But on his demobilisation St Albans reclaimed him and he returned to become, at the early age of 32, Canon and Sub-Dean. The Abbey, with its large, intelligent congregation, provided just the right sphere for his preaching, and those who could not cope with his personality had other members of the Chapter to whom they could turn for pastoral consolation.

During the next 12 years he became more widely known in the Church and gained considerable influence as chief book reviewer for the *Church Times*. He was an editor's dream contributor: his high intellectual capacity enabled him to get to the heart of a big book quickly; his lucid, elegant prose of exact length required no correction; and he never failed to meet a deadline.

Feaver's rudeness and lack of easy social graces – he was rarely willing to shake hands – stood in the way of his appointment to an expected Deanery and, for some years, seemed even more of a problem when bishoprics were discussed.

But when Feaver's time at St Albans was up in 1958, Bishop F. R. Barry of Southwell, who appreciated his intellect, appointed him Vicar of St Mary's, the ancient parish church of Nottingham.

With this went an Honorary Canonry of Southwell Minster and the responsibilities of Rural Dean of Nottingham.

This proved to be a success – up to a point. Nottingham soon became aware of its new Vicar, and the services at St Mary's attracted many who valued traditional Anglicanism at its best. Always an autocrat, Feaver never hesitated to rig Church Council meetings and it was a brave, or foolish parishioner who opposed him.

A long sequence of courageous curates were given a first-class training, and Feaver was a good pastor to those who needed him. He served as a governor of Nottingham Bluecoat School and was chairman of a boys' probation hostel, but he was not the kind of priest to become involved in a wide range of community activity.

Relations with the liberal Bishop Barry eventually became strained and there was a never-to-be-forgotten Diocesan Conference at which Feaver stood to speak and the bishop, who was very deaf, inquired of a neighbour on the platform: "Is that Feaver speaking?" On being told it was he ostentatiously switched off his antiquated hearing aid and said in a loud voice: "Tell me when he's finished."

Feaver was no lover of conferences and synods. Of the General Synod, on which he served from 1970 to 1972, and then compulsorily during his 12 years as a bishop, he said: "I wonder when I am sitting there why church people should be asked for money to pay to keep this cuckoo growing." At the end of the 1978 Lambeth Conference he told his diocese: "Nothing much came of it, but then nothing much was put in."

He deplored most of the proposals for change in the life of the Church, ranging from the modification of patronage to the ordination of women, insisting that "newness consists in renewal, not in novelty, and experiment must go hand in hand with experience".

Feaver's appointment to the bishopric of Peterborough in 1972 came as a surprise, not least to himself. At his first Diocesan Synod he announced: "I have no intention of moving again; the undertakers can be my next removers and the Church Commissioners can pay."

The tall, stooping figure of Feaver, crowned by a fine head of silver hair, suggested a distinguished bishop and scholar, and certainly he cared for the Church of England. He was sensible enough to trust his clergy to lead their parishes without overmuch episcopal interference. Those who knew him best admired him most, and he was an entertaining raconteur with a gift for mimicry.

His first wife Katherine, who was the daughter of the Reverend W. T. Stubbs, an Anglican clergyman, died in 1987. The next year he married Miss Clare Harvey, a family friend and recently retired headmistress of a girls' school, who survives him. He is also survived by a son and two daughters of his first marriage.

November 11, 1997

1998

The Reverend Kenneth Hayes

The Reverend Kenneth Hayes, who has died aged 67, was a Baptist minister who comforted the families of the 144 people killed in the Aberfan disaster in 1966, among whom was his own son.

At a quarter past nine on the morning of October 21, 1966, Pantglas Junior School was engulfed by an avalanche of three million tons of coal slurry. One of the gigantic, rain-sodden waste heaps piled on the Glamorganshire hillside above Aberfan had slipped; 116 children and 28 adults were killed in the ensuing catastrophe.

Hayes was first alerted by hearing shouts in the village. "I went up the road and turned the bend," he recalled. "I could see nothing but a mountain of black waste."

As the villagers dug frantically at the mound, Hayes visited the parents and friends of those who had been found dead or who were still missing, offering words of comfort and sympathy throughout the night.

Although his own nine-year-old son, Dyfrig, had been trapped by the tip, Hayes never let his own fears show. His son's body was found the next evening; his other son, Gwillym, had been ill and had stayed at home that Friday.

On Sunday, 12 hours after his son's body had been found, Hayes kept faith with his chapel, substituting for his normal act of worship a simple service of prayers and hymns at his Zion Baptist Church. Only those villagers who were too old or too young to dig came; the bulk of the congregation consisted of journalists and television reporters, many of whom cried throughout the service.

In his address, Hayes appealed to the Coal Board to abandon its policy of tipping and then urged that there be no bitterness: "Let us thank God that things are not worse". As the congregation broke into the hymn "Safe in the Arms of Jesus", Hayes sat down in his chair on the dais and wept.

Kenneth James Hayes was born at Risca, Glamorganshire, in 1930. His father was a railwayman and Hayes worked on the railways himself before being ordained as a Baptist minister in 1953.

For the next three years he was pastor of the churches of Ramah and Hephzibah, Erwood, and Seion, Sennybridge. He was then minister of Presteigne and Stansbatch from 1956 to 1964 before taking over the Zion English Baptist chapel at Merthyr Vale, near Aberfan.

After the disaster, Hayes acted as a rallying point for the bereaved, who much admired his faith and strength. The fact that he too had lost a son helped him to understand the emotions of the villagers, and the need for action prevented him from brooding.

Hayes's wife, Mona, took charge of the distribution of toys sent, at the urging of Princess Margaret, to the young relatives of those who had died.

Hayes spoke with conviction, authority and sincerity, and he became chairman of the bereaved parents' association, asking that they should be allowed to come to terms with their loss without the intrusion of public attention. The psychological scars took many years to heal; those children who had survived the disaster were forbidden to play in the street lest it upset the parents of those who had died.

Hayes also helped to lead the campaign against the practice of waste tipping, and attended every session of the inquiry into the catastrophe, which found nine employees of the Coal Board to blame for the landslide. Hayes characteristically offered to help any of the men if they came to him.

He became a trustee of several of the memorial funds set up in the wake of the disaster. The principal appeal received £175 million in donations. Hayes was also a trustee of the Aberfan educational trust and of the foundation that cared for the cemetery on the hillside where the victims were buried.

Hayes vigorously demanded the return of £150,000 taken from the appeal-fund by the government of Harold Wilson and used to pay for the removal of local waste tips. He was gratified when the present Government announced earlier this year that the sum would be repaid and used to maintain the Aberfan cemetery.

In the mid-1970s, Hayes persuaded two other local Baptist churches to join with his congregation, and thereafter led one unified Baptist chapel in Merthyr Vale.

Despite ill health he continued to preach even after he had retired to Rhoose, South Glamorgan.

January 1, 1998

The Reverend Harry Bagnall

The Reverend Harry Bagnall, who has died aged 67, was Rector of Christ Church Cathedral, Port Stanley, at the time of the Falklands War in 1982.

At the end of the conflict he was appointed OBE for what the Governor of the Islands, Sir Rex Hunt described as "sterling service and selfless bravery".

The Governor was deported by the invaders and it fell to Bagnall and his Roman Catholic colleague in Port Stanley, Monsignor Daniel Spraggon, to represent the islanders to the Argentine generals. The two priests made a formidable duo and became conspicuous figures in streets dominated by military uniforms.

At first, the Military Governor, General Menendez, tried to win their support. Bagnall was summoned to the official residence to be assured, over tea served in china bearing the Queen's insignia, that freedom of worship would continue. But the Rector was uncooperative and challenged the military authorities on several issues – successfully

He rejected Argentine attempts to dig trenches in the Cathedral grounds, and would not allow them to stockpile weapons there. He stored away the flagpole to prevent the Argentine flag from being raised and insisted that ensigns hanging in the Cathedral be left untouched. These included that of the Falklands Islands Defence Force and one from the cruiser *Achilles*, flown during the Battle of the River Plate in 1939

The first weekend of the invasion included Palm Sunday and Bagnall used a Falklands shrub, known as "diddle-dee", to make Palm Sunday crosses, which he and many islanders wore throughout the occupation as a symbol of unity. Crowded Cathedral congregations continued to sing the National Anthem.

The prospect of a visit from the Anglican Bishop of Argentina, who lived in Buenos Aires, alarmed Bagnall; he believed that any contact with Argentina would be compromising, and the Archbishop of Canterbury, Robert Runcie, advised the Bishop to keep away.

None of which was anywhere near Bagnall's mind when he applied for the post at the most southerly cathedral in the world. His wife spotted the advertisement which intrigued them – "We are looking for an exceptional, adventurous man, married, for the Falkland Islands. Must be physically fit, able to drive and de-bog a Land Rover; butcher own beef and mutton, keep vegetable garden, ducks and hens; dig, dry and burn peat."

Few Church of England clergymen could have met these requirements, but prior to his ordination, Bagnall had been in the Army and the police, and had also worked in the meat trade. So when his wife said: "Harry perhaps it's you they're looking for", he felt the hand of Providence guiding him.

Later, in a book describing his Falklands experiences, *Faith Under Fire*, he said that this had been the fulfilment of a lifelong desire to serve God abroad. His faith, he said, had never before been put to such practical use. The experience made him less fussy in his church duties and more sensitive to what needed to be done. "This became so exciting," he said, "that I would leave my house in the morning, throw my hands in the air and say 'Well, Lord where are we going today?'".

Often enough, during the war, it was to comfort the sick and elderly and give reassurance.

His practical gifts were complemented by a strong pastoral sense and, although he and his wife could have been taken back to Britain at the opening of hostilities, they were convinced that they must remain with those who would bear the burden of the war.

Harry Bagnall was born on August 23, 1930, in the West Yorkshire village of Fitzwilliam. After a variety of jobs he felt called to Holy Orders and was ordained in Sheffield Cathedral in 1967.

He spent the next three years as a curate at Goole. After two more years as a curate, at the church of St Leonard and St Jude, Doncaster, he was given responsibility for the Church's work in the Doncaster new housing areas of New Cantley, and it was after seven years there that he responded to the challenge of the Falklands.

On his return to England in 1986, he went back to his native Yorkshire and for nine years exercised a greatly valued ministry as Vicar of Hook with Airmyn, near Goole.

He is survived by his wife and two sons.

February 12, 1998

The Reverend Sir James Roll, Bt

The Reverend Sir James Roll, Bt, who has died aged 85, was a 26-year-old curate in Bethnal Green when he succeeded to the baronetcy created for his grandfather at the end of his term of office as Lord Mayor of London in 1921; with the baronetcy went a share, with two brothers, in an estate valued in 1939 at £465,000 – something more than £9 million in today's values.

But neither the title nor the money made a scrap of difference to the way of life embraced by a young man who, from the age of 16, had felt called to Holy Orders and to work among the poor. He spent the Second World War years as a curate in the most heavily bombed areas of east London, and when eventually he was persuaded to become a vicar he went to a tough parish in Dagenham, where he remained until his retirement 25 years later.

In this parish, where there was no official vicarage, he lived in a small rented house similar to the council houses occupied by his parishioners, most of whom had been moved to Dagenham from the slums of east London. He was a greatly loved priest who could be seen every morning and in the late afternoon, at precisely the same times, walking to church to conduct the daily worship.

The rest of the day was spent by this kindly, humble, self-effacing pastor in caring for the sick, the elderly, the housebound and anyone in trouble. Children were his special delight and, besides his substantial financial support of children's charities, he established a holiday home at Westcliff-on-Sea for Sunday school pupils from his own and other Dagenham parishes. He was also a strong supporter of the Society for the Protection of the Unborn Child.

Roll's other great love was animals. Never without his own dog, he was one of the pioneers of services of thanksgiving for animals, held every year in October near the feast day of St Francis of Assisi. Hundreds of people brought their pets to his churches where they were encouraged to treat them with reverence and care. He gave large sums to animal charities.

James William Cecil Roll was born in Essex on June 1, 1912. From Chigwell School he went up to Pembroke College, Oxford, but left without taking a degree and completed his training for Holy Orders at Chichester Theological College.

Inspired by the example of earlier Anglo-Catholic slum priests, he became a curate at the church of St James the Greater, Bethnal Green, in 1937. When he inherited the baronetcy and the fortune created by his grandfather, who had been chairman of the Pearl Assurance Company, he was asked if he intended to continue his work for the Church.

"Why not?" was his response, "I came here 18 months ago and I was a priest before I became a baronet. It isn't my fault that I happened to become a baronet as well as a curate. There is important work to be done here in Bethnal Green and I have found more kind hearts in these East End streets than I ever did before."

When his brothers attracted some publicity by buying horses so that they could compete against each other in the Grand National, he commented: "I know nothing about racehorses but my brothers are entitled to live and spend their money as they please. I have chosen my way and I am happy in it."

His happiness was undiminished by the onset of the German blitz on London, by which time he had moved to St Matthew's, Victoria Docks. Day and night found him on the streets ministering to casualties and to distraught families who had lost their homes as well as relatives and friends. He took time off only to serve as chairman of a children's home at West Rasen, Lincolnshire, which was opened in 1941 to provide special care for war orphans. Most of the money for this came from him, as was that needed for an East End hostel for boys on probation which he established.

In 1944 he became a curate at East Ham parish church where he remained for 14 years, content to exercise a pastoral ministry in an area with many people living in poverty. He was charged at Grays in 1955 with permitting a boy under 17 to drive his car and allowing him to use it without insurance. He told the magistrates that he had handed over the keys because the boy had said that his father wanted to borrow the car. Both charges were dismissed.

During his 21 years as a curate Roll accepted no stipend. On his appointment as Vicar of St John's, Dagenham, in 1958, he explained to his East Ham parishioners: "This doesn't mean I have gone broke. It is just that I feel it would be good for me and for the parish to have a change."

The press made Dagenham aware of his wealth, but without this and the evidence of his great generosity, no one would have guessed that their priest was rich. He spent next to nothing on himself and sometimes needed to be reminded that his shoes would benefit from repair.

Most of his time was spent wearing them out on the streets of the parish, and his heavy responsibilities increased when three huge blocks of flats were built on a green belt site. He was also a compelling preacher.

At the age of 70, he retired to Leigh-on-Sea, where, for another 15 years, he continued to minister – at St Clement's church and neighbouring parishes – and to administer his holiday home for children at Westcliff.

He was unmarried and died largely unknown in the wider Church of England.

February 25, 1998

Monsignor Alfred Gilbey

Monsignor Alfred Gilbey, the former Chaplain to the Roman Catholic undergraduates of Cambridge University, who has died aged 96, was an unusual ecclesiastical figure – well known in Cambridge, London clubs and country houses, but very easy to caricature and misunderstand.

For generations of Cambridge men, non-Catholic as well as Catholic, Alfred Gilbey was the University dignitary who had made the most impact on them and for whom they felt the greatest affection and respect.

His extraordinary influence as Chaplain, from 1932 to 1965, was due in part to his piety, his rock-like faith and his ability to explain Catholic beliefs in clear and simple terms; and partly to his kindliness and friendliness, his sympathy, his courtesy and charm.

At Fisher House, the Catholic Chaplaincy in Guildhall Street, all comers were given a warm welcome – and also sherry or port if the hour was appropriate. Having some private means (though not nearly as much as was supposed) enabled him to be generous with his hospitality: luncheon parties at the Pitt Club, the Lion or the Bath, dinner parties in his panelled dining-room hung with Stuart portraits, Sunday teas at which any member of his flock could turn up.

At this former inn of 17th-century origin, Gilbey created a

civilised country-house atmosphere and built up a library which eventually boasted a fine collection of books and pamphlets about Cambridge.

He was himself an authority on the history of Cambridge and its lore. To this and to his many other intellectual interests, which included architecture, he had a very scholarly approach; though he would mention his pass degree as evidence that he was no academic.

His anecdotes were entertaining and he would tell them succinctly and with precision; in his distinctive but not always distinct voice he had an uncanny facility for the *mot juste*.

But what, more than anything else, made his company so delightful was the air of serenity which came partly from his religious faith and partly from his intense interest in people and things.

His enjoyment of life was particularly infectious when out with the Trinity Foot Beagles, of which he was a regular and enthusiastic follower, having been a foxhunter in his youth.

Inevitably myths were woven around Alfred Gilbey. Because as Chaplain he instructed many converts, he was believed to be an active proselytiser; but in truth most of his converts had never met him until they came to him for instruction.

The non-Catholic undergraduates with whom he associated tended to be sporting young men not much given to religious discussion; many of them became his lifelong friends while never having any leanings to Catholicism.

His patrician manner and his sartorial elegance – the frock coat, the broad-brimmed or tall hat, the cassock trimmed with the purple of a Domestic Prelate to the Pope, which he became in 1950, and of the superior dignity of Protonotary Apostolic, to which he was elevated in 1963 – caused some people to imagine him to be more socially exalted than he was.

He never aspired to move in high society; his friends were drawn from all stations in life. He would say that men are not equal in the sight of God – some saints being greater than others. But he did not pretend to divine powers of discrimination himself.

Yet, when in the 1960s the University became increasingly

class-conscious, it began to be felt, in certain quarters, that Gilbey was unsuited to be Chaplain to the new type of undergraduate; it was even suggested that some young men would be intimidated by the sight of the volumes of the Peerage on his bookshelves.

The more immediate cause of his departure from Cambridge in 1965 was his refusal to open his Chaplaincy to women undergraduates (who up until then had had a separate Chaplaincy of their own); his reason was that he considered it important that his Chaplaincy should retain the quasi-monastic atmosphere of the traditional men's colleges.

This gave rise to the myth that he disliked women; in fact he welcomed women to Fisher House as guests, and numbered many women among his dearest friends. He was delighted to officiate at the weddings of former members of his flock and he would afterwards take the same fatherly interest in the wives as he did in the husbands.

Alfred Newman Gilbey was born on July 13, 1901– he used to say how glad he was not to have been born a day earlier or later, on Orange Day or Bastille Day. His middle name did not derive from Cardinal Newman; he was the youngest of the seven children of Newman Gilbey of Mark Hall Essex, and Maria Victorina de Ysasi. His grandfather and namesake was one of the founders of the family wine business.

Both his father and his uncle William Gilbey brought back Spanish brides and Catholicism from Jerez as well as sherry; William's grandson, Dom Gabriel Gilbey, who inherited the Barony of Vaux of Harrowden, was the first Benedictine to sit in the House of Lords since the Reformation.

Alfred Gilbey looked Spanish, loved Spain and used to say that Spanish mothers were the best in the world. At the same time he was English to the core, devoted to hunting and to the countryside of East Anglia.

He was a staunch upholder of the customs, conventions and traditions of Englishmen of his generation and background; for instance he was always punctilious in doffing his hat when he passed the Cenotaph.

Influenced by the writings of Monsignor R. H. Benson, the brother of A. C. and E. F. Benson, Gilbey decided at an early age that he wanted to be a priest.

But his father insisted that he should first enjoy himself in the world, which he proceeded to do with gusto: going from Beaumont to spend four blissful years at Trinity College, Cambridge, ending with only a pass degree but with his priestly vocation stronger than ever.

So he went to study at the Beda College in Rome and was ordained priest in the family chapel at Mark Hall, in the diocese of Brentwood, in 1929. He was ordained in his own patrimony; that is, he retained responsibility for his own maintenance instead of being sponsored by a bishop and incardinated into a diocese.

He served as the Bishop of Brentwood's private secretary until he went to Cambridge as Chaplain three years later.

Alfred Gilbey's retirement was spent mostly in London at the Travellers' Club, where he had a permanent bedroom and a tiny oratory in the former boot room. He would declare that he felt entirely at home at the Travellers' – more so than at his other clubs, the Athenaeum and Buck's, which he considered to be above him: the one intellectually, the other socially.

As an octogenarian, he felt greatly touched at being unexpectedly invited to become an honorary member of Pratt's; he was no less gratified at being invited to join the Old Brotherhood, a dining club of the Catholic secular clergy. Two other distinctions came to him when he was in his eighties – he was made a Canon of Brentwood and a Grand Cross Conventual Chaplain *ad honorem* in the Order of Malta, of which he had been a member since 1947.

In his retirement his days were almost fuller than they had been in Cambridge; in London he was more accessible to his friends, who could never have enough of his company. He kept all his faculties into his nineties and enjoyed amazingly good health, which he attributed to his going about as much as possible on foot.

On his visits to Cambridge, even in his late eighties, he never missed an opportunity of going out with the Trinity Foot Beagles;

and he went to Northumberland every September to hunt with them there.

He did become very bent of stature and, when he was 94, he gave up catching a bus each morning, after a benefactor insisted on sending a car instead to take him to Brompton Oratory, where he said his Mass – in the Tridentine rite, which, in conformity to Canon Law, his age entitled him to use.

As yet another interest for his youthful old age, the course of instruction which he gave his converts was, on the initiative of one of them, published as a book entitled *We Believe* (1983). It was widely acclaimed and its sales exceeded all expectations.

The volume's underlying theme, that Catholicism entails an acceptance of the teaching authority of the Church, was the bedrock of Alfred Gilbey's own life and ministry. He was resolute in refusing to construct a Church of his own devising, in accordance with personal preferences.

Once, in 1968, at the time of the controversy over the Church's attitude to birth control, a woman sitting next to him at dinner said to him brightly: "Do tell me, Monsignor, what do you think of the Pill?"

"I don't" was his reply.

David Watkin writes: Alfred Gilbey once observed to Monsignor Ronald Knox, "Dear Ronnie, I have the sort of mind that turned the Last Supper into a Pontifical High Mass." This was when they were both staying at Downside Abbey and Knox observed with mild amazement Gilbey's slow and ritualised process of packing a suitcase, gradually building up a three-dimensional mosaic in which every object had its allotted space.

Gilbey's comment well conveys his humour, self-knowledge and unswerving devotion to the forms of pre-Vatican II Catholicism.

Packing, moreover, was to play a large role in his life, especially in the years following his retirement as Catholic Chaplain at Cambridge. He constantly travelled about Britain and the Continent to perform weddings, baptisms and requiem Masses for his vast flock which, though centred on his Cambridge undergraduates, continued to expand.

He was also one of the most sought-after spiritual advisers of his time, giving unstintingly of counsel which was rooted in his life of prayer. What gave unique power to his advice to those trying to be Catholics in the modern Church was his own ability to combine spiritual devotion with enjoyment of temporal goods.

He moved between the two with disconcerting rapidity. The Travellers' Club in Pall Mall might seem a surprisingly worldly home for a Catholic prelate, yet he created a chapel at the top of the back staircase where he could retreat from the guests on whom he lavished unceasing hospitality in the public rooms of the club.

Cardinal Heenan gave him a licence to reserve the Blessed Sacrament in this chapel, and also permission to say the Tridentine Mass on all occasions, whether public or private. This privilege made him much in demand from the many Catholics who found the post-Vatican II liturgy intolerable. He contrived to serve them without becoming a renegade like Archbishop Lefebvre.

It would be impossible to exaggerate the influence on Alfred Gilbey of his upbringing at Mark Hall, Essex, where he was born into a world which unusually combined traditional Edwardian country-house life with the Spanish Catholic piety of his mother who had come from Spain to marry his father.

As a gilded, amusing, clever, generous and attractive under-graduate at Trinity, he kept from many of his friends his inner life and his ambition to become a priest.

As Catholic chaplain at Cambridge he received an extraordinary number of young men into the Church, though he achieved this without any direct proselytisation. He ran Fisher House, the Catholic chaplaincy, as an open house, like a free London club.

Catholic undergraduates would bring their non-Catholic friends who, falling under Gilbey's magnetic spell, would remain for instruction in the faith. He was persuaded to publish these instructions as a book, *We Believe*, based on a tape-recording made by a Peterhouse undergraduate whom he was instructing in his room at the Travellers'.

We Believe was the subject of an admiring article in *The Times* by Roger Scruton, while Auberon Waugh wrote a preface to the American edition, and A. N. Wilson interviewed Gilbey for *Harper's*.

The Beda College, where he had studied, moved to new and unattractive premises, and Mark Hall had been burned down by landgirls, thus sparing it, as Gilbey wryly observed, from the worse fate of becoming the community centre of Harlow New Town.

The external fabric of much of his life was destroyed, but his faith remained so utterly intact that to his thousands of friends and admirers he seemed to embody the notion of sanctity in the modern world.

March 27, 1998

The Right Reverend William Stewart

The Right Reverend William Stewart, who has died aged 54, was appointed Suffragan Bishop of Taunton only last June; although he was at that time apparently in the best of health, cancer was diagnosed in November and chemotherapy failed to save him.

During his short time in the diocese of Bath and Wells, however, Will Stewart made a considerable impact. Standing 6ft 7in tall, he was an imposing figure. He possessed outstanding pastoral gifts.

Even more influential was his courageous response to the grim medical tidings. Writing in the diocesan magazine in January, he said: "I do not want to leave this world, especially since God has just called me to a new and exciting ministry. I wept at the prospect of losing it all. But few, if any, of us will journey through 1998 without some kind of adversity, and the text from Isaiah, 'Do not be afraid, for I am your God' has attained a new meaning in recent weeks."

Earlier this month, announcing that he was withdrawing from

public ministry for a time to undergo treatment, he thanked the people of the diocese for their love, support and prayer and said he believed that in the providence of God "everything works together for good".

William Allen Stewart was born on September 19, 1943. From Uppingham he went up to Trinity College, Cambridge, where he read History. Feeling called to Holy Orders, he went to Cranmer Hall, Durham, and secured the Diploma in Theology.

From 1968 to 1974 he was a curate, first at Eccleshall, in Sheffield, then at Cheltenham. From 1974 to 1980 he was Vicar of St James's, Gloucester, and, for his last two years there, was also responsible for the adjoining parish of All Saints.

In both places his capacity for listening to people was soon recognised, as was the care that informed his pastoral advice. He had a great sense of fun, and his sermons were marked by a rare combination of scholarship and passion.

Stewart exercised a similarly impressive ministry at Upton, near Torquay, from 1980 to 1985. He was then ready for wider responsibility as Vicar of St Mark's, Oulton Broad, Suffolk. In this parish of 14,000 people, embracing part of Lowestoft, he raised £250,000 to re-roof the nave and to build a new church centre. Once again, he became a much-loved pastor, admired by all.

In 1992 he was appointed Rural Dean of Lothingland, covering the whole of Lowestoft and its surrounding villages, and in 1994 was made an Honorary Canon of Norwich Cathedral.

A keen sportsman, he played cricket with the Norwich Diocesan Clergy XI and with the Bath and Wells XI.

He is survived by his wife Janet (a priest) and by their two sons and two daughters.

April 3, 1998

The Most Reverend Trevor Huddleston

The Most Reverend Trevor Huddleston, who has died aged 84, was a notable bishop in three different parts of the Anglican Communion – Tanzania, Stepney and Mauritius.

But he will be best remembered as Father Huddleston the monk of the Community of the Resurrection, who during the Forties ministered in the black township of Sophiatown, in South Africa, and became one of the leading figures in the international effort to end apartheid.

His book *Naught for Your Comfort*, published in 1956, soon after he had been withdrawn from South Africa by his Community, was an international bestseller. It opened the eyes of many to the effects of apartheid on black individuals and communities.

Huddleston was far removed from the popular image of an agitator. A gentle person, of a deeply religious nature, he exuded warmth, joy and friendship, and was perhaps happiest when in the company of children – who adored him.

Yet beneath all this, and often finding dramatic expression, was immense strength and moral courage and an absolute unwillingness to compromise with what he regarded as evil, especially when this caused suffering to the weak.

"The Christian," he once said, "is always an agitator if he is true to his calling." In *Naught for Your Comfort* he likened apartheid to the racialism of Nazi Germany and to slavery. "Hell is not a bad description of South Africa," he concluded.

Towards the end of Huddleston's time at Sophiatown, a government official had told him: "You deserve to be drummed out of the country or strung up from the nearest lamp-post as a renegade." Such reactions were the best possible evidence of the power of his message.

Ernest Urban Trevor Huddleston was born at Bedford on June 15, 1913. His father, Captain Sir Ernest Huddleston, became Director of the Royal Indian Marine. Among his ancestors was Father John Huddleston who helped King Charles II to escape after the Battle of Worcester, and received the King into the Roman Catholic church on his deathbed.

Trevor Huddleston was encouraged to attend church as a boy, and went from Lancing up to Christ Church, Oxford, where he read history. During vacations he went on hop-picking missions in Kent and became interested in the Christian Socialist Movement, particularly the work of Anglo-Catholic priests in slum parishes.

Having decided on ordination, he first spent a year studying mission work in India and Ceylon, then went to Wells Theological College. He was ordained in 1936 to a curacy at Swindon, where he got on very well with the railwaymen.

In 1939 he went to test his vocation at the Anglican Community of the Resurrection at Mirfield, in Yorkshire. He was professed as a monk in 1941. Two years later he was sent to be priest in charge of the community's mission in Sophiatown and Orlando, near Johannesburg, where he remained until 1949.

Archbishop Desmond Tutu has recalled how, as a boy, he was standing with his mother outside a hostel where she was the cleaner. A white priest, in cassock and large black hat, swept by and, to the great astonishment of the young Tutu, doffed his hat to the black lady.

The priest was Father Huddleston, and his action was characteristic of a ministry of care and compassion for people of every race, nurtured by the disciplined life of a monk and the sacramental life of the church of Christ the King which was his base in Sophiatown. From 1949 onwards he was in charge of all his community's work in South Africa.

Huddleston came to international notice soon after the accession to power of the National Party in 1948, when he protested vehemently against the forcible removal of the blacks from their houses in Sophiatown. After the implementation of the Bantu Education Act, he refused to hand over to the government St Peter's School ("the Black Eton of South Africa") and instead closed it down.

He argued then, as he continued to do for the rest of his life, that since apartheid was fundamentally evil it could not be reformed or collaborated with. He was among the first to advocate a sports and cultural boycott of South Africa, and the application of economic sanctions by the rest of the world.

Then, in 1956, came the mysterious order that Huddleston should leave South Africa and return to Mirfield as Guardian of the Novices. There was a widespread belief that the community had been put under pressure by the Pretoria government.

The publication of *Naught for Your Comfort* more or less coincided with his return and, besides looking after a handful of novices, he undertook a good deal of preaching, public speaking and writing.

Huddleston's public work was facilitated by his move to London, in 1958, as Prior of his community's house in Holland Park. Two years later, though, he was elected Bishop of Masasi, in South Eastern Tanganyika, soon to become Tanzania.

The next eight years were spent helping both the Church and the nation to respond to the challenge of independence. There was great poverty in the countryside, and Huddleston worked closely with President Julius Nyerere, who became a firm friend. In 1968 he handed over the diocese of Masasi to its first African bishop.

In 1963 Huddleston conducted a mission at Oxford University, publishing his addresses as *The True and Living God*.

From 1968 to 1978 he was suffragan bishop of Stepney. This post enabled him to become involved in the problems of poverty and racism in London's East End, while leaving him some freedom to pursue his vocation as a national and international spokesman for the oppressed.

He quickly won the hearts of the East Enders, arranged for some local men to be trained for the priesthood so that the area might have the beginnings of an indigenous ministry, and helped to establish the Huddleston Centre for the Handicapped.

In 1978, to the surprise of many, including himself, Huddleston was elected Bishop of Mauritius and Archbishop of the Indian Ocean – a far-flung province that takes in Seychelles and the Malagasy Republic. In Mauritius he found that the Christians were heavily out-numbered by Muslims and Hindus, and that there were many fewer Anglicans than Roman Catholics.

The experience deepened Huddleston's appreciation of the positive elements in the non-Christian faiths. He became a strong advocate of multi-faith collaboration in the battles against racism and poverty.

At various times, and particularly after his retirement in 1983, he travelled widely to address mass meetings and to plead with governments for firm action against the white rulers of South Africa. In 1982 the UN awarded him its Gold Medal.

Huddleston retired with the intention of devoting his remaining years to the struggle against apartheid. He lived at the rectory of St James's, Piccadilly, and did everything he could to increase awareness of the deepening tragedy in South Africa and to raise money to help the victims of its rulers.

The ending of apartheid and the election in 1994 of a multi-racial government under Nelson Mandela answered Huddleston's prayers and gave him unbridled joy. In 1995 he decided to return to South Africa in order to help the building of a new, reconciled nation.

But after a few months in Cape Town he found he could not settle. The rapid pace of change left him confused. Largely unrecognised by the younger generation of African leaders, he became very unhappy and decided to return to England. "Apartheid still lives," he declared in an interview at Johannesburg airport.

Trevor Huddleston spent his final years with the Community of the Resurrection at Mirfield.

Earlier this year he was appointed KCMG.

April 21, 1998

The Reverend Michael Vasey

The Reverend Michael Vasey, who has died aged 52, achieved considerable notoriety in 1995 when he argued in his book *Strangers and Friends* that the Bible does not condemn homosexuality and that homosexual relationships are not incompatible with Christian belief and membership of the Church.

The book occasioned great surprise and some offence in Evangelical circles. Vasey was a respected Evangelical scholar, a member of General Synod and considered, up to that point, a champion of the Evangelical viewpoint.

The Church Pastoral Aid Society forbade its patronage secretary, who had originally commissioned the book, to endorse it; the Evangelical Alliance, having accused Vasey of "simply baptising the prevailing culture", mounted a campaign to discredit it.

Vasey's chief contribution to the life of the Church of England was, however, as a liturgical scholar who recognised the importance of language and imagery in worship. Generations of students at St John's College, Durham, where Vasey became a tutor in 1975, learned that the Book of Common Prayer was not the only way in which Evangelicals might worship, but were also discouraged from supposing that slap-dash informality was an adequate substitute for traditional liturgy.

As a member of the Liturgical Commission, which he joined in 1986, Vasey played a leading part in the revision of the Alternative Service Book (1980) which is now producing services with more evocative language and stronger imagery. He had a gift for drafting new prayers, a number of which, widely admired, are to be found in the revised Baptism service.

Michael Richard Vasey the son of a diplomat, was born on January 23, 1946. His mother was Jewish, and in regard for his background, Vasey always wore the Star of David. His concern for minorities and his doggedness in the face of opposition owed much to his upbringing.

From Shrewsbury, Vasey went up to Balliol College, Oxford, and then prepared for Holy Orders at Wycliffe Hall. Recognised as an Evangelical of unusual ability, after a four-year curacy at Tonbridge parish church he joined the teaching staff of St John's College, Durham, where he would exercise the remainder of his ministry.

He had a sharp mind and, while his teaching style was not always appreciated by the less able, he was a considerate tutor and kept in touch with students long after they had left St John's.

As a scholar, Vasey was well equipped to handle the theology and history of liturgy, but his interest was primarily pastoral and he believed strongly that forms of service should be judged by their ability to encourage uplifting worship, not by technical "correctness".

Besides the Liturgical Commission, he was a member of the Joint Liturgical Group, concerned with coordinating the efforts of all the British churches in this field; and he was the Church of England Observer on the Pastoral Liturgy Committee of the Roman Catholic Bishops' Conference of England and Wales.

In 1990, Vasey and a number of fellow-liturgists founded Praxis, an organisation to encourage greater understanding of the nature and practice of worship. As secretary, Vasey organised conferences and meetings, and also wrote several widely circulated booklets on liturgical subjects.

Although he had not attempted to conceal his homosexuality, the experience of being robbed by two youths in a gay bar in 1989 led Vasey to "come out" formally. In 1991, he published a pamphlet, *Evangelical Christians and Gay Rights*, in which he expressed his belief that Jesus would have felt very much at home in a gay bar, and that the inability of many Christians to learn from gay culture was a sign of their own alienation from biblical tradition.

His broad position, presented more fully in his book *Strangers and Friends*, was that Jesus spoke no word against homosexuals, and that the few biblical texts believed to outlaw homosexual practice were no more binding on Christians than other texts which in the past were used to uphold slavery and anti-semitism.

He went on to lament the fact that the Church was a "hostile institution" for homosexuals, and in 1996 he successfully persuaded the General Synod to accept a disciplinary reform that would enable bishops to shield homosexual clergy against malicious complaints about their behaviour.

He was expecting to attend the General Synod meeting at York this weekend, but died suddenly of a heart attack.

July 3, 1998

The Right Reverend Howell Witt

The Right Reverend Howell Witt, who has died aged 78, began life as the son of a Welsh docker, and became one of the most colourful figures in the Anglican Church in Australia between 1965 and 1981.

It was a post he took up with some reservations. "When the good Lord made me," he once said, "he made me a clown. And a clown he called to the Priesthood. But to the episcopate? That surely was another matter."

The North West see – covering 720,000 square miles, or nearly a quarter of the Australian continent – was the largest diocese by land area in the Anglican communion. In consequence, Witt spent seven months of the year travelling, while his wife and children remained at the Bishop's Palace, formerly a boarding house at Geraldtown, 250 miles north of Perth.

The bishop not only learned to fly an aeroplane; he became expert in such arts as sheep-dipping, catching crayfish and rounding up wild goats.

In the absence of proper church buildings he would improvise places of worship in dance halls, railway sidings and shearing sheds. He liked to recall the occasion when he was visited in the back of beyond by Prince Philip, who found himself reading the lesson from the witness box of the local police court.

For Witt, the long hours of travel afforded the best time for his devotions, as he put it he prayed in transit rather than in transept, bellowing Anglican hymns and passages from the Book of Common Prayer into the passing wilderness.

He remembered arriving in the port of Dampier, then under construction, and officiating in a mess where the all-male congregation was drawn from 65 nationalities. They thrust forward to shake his hand; clasped him to their bosoms and kissed both cheeks; knelt at his feet and kissed his ring. "I don't think that they're all Anglican," the local priest whispered.

Howell Arthur John Witt was born on July 12, 1920 near the docks at Newport, Monmouthshire, where his grandfather as well as his father had worked. His father, a Methodist, was a man of saintly character, his mother taught in Sunday School.

Early in life Howell Witt felt himself called to the ministry. This never prevented him, however, from developing his comic streak and indulging his flair for the stage. And though he used to describe himself as a midget, he was big enough to play rugby for the London Welsh.

He took a degree at Leeds University, and then prepared for Holy Orders at the College of Resurrection, Mirfield. He was ordained in 1944 and served as a curate first at Usk and then at Camberwell, south London. In 1949 he became Anglican chaplain at the Woomera rocket range in the deserts of South Australia.

This afforded Witt an introduction to the arts of improvisation. He conducted his first Sunday service at Woomera in a spare room used by the barber. Having lost his luggage, he called for a bottle of port and a slice of bread and made do with a pewter beer mug as a chalice, and a cheese dish as paten. A sheet served as altar cloth and blankets as kneelers.

Later he was to open the Woomera fete dressed as Deborah, Dowager Duchess of Dingo Creek, complete with hooped skirt, tiara and false bosom. That was only after a drama involving two camels, their Aboriginal minders and much dashing about the desert in costume. The Dowager Duchess also opened a fete at St Peter's College, the leading boys' school in Adelaide.

In 1954 Witt went to St Mary Magdalene in Adelaide, but after three years volunteered for the post of priest in charge of Elizabeth, a new satellite town largely peopled by British migrants where social work seemed to make more immediate claims than spiritual care. Witt complained that he spent more time standing up to hire purchase companies than on his knees.

He remembered answering a call from a woman who said she was about to put her head in a gas oven. It was not until he was halfway to her house that he remembered that Elizabeth was an all electric town.

Witt put his church, St Theodore's, to a multitude of uses, as youth club, theatre, pensioners' club and gymnasium. His energy seemed inexhaustible. He built two churches; coached a junior rugby side; scripted and took part in programmes for the South Australian Christian Television Association; acted with the Adelaide repertory theatre; and wrote columns for two newspapers.

When he became a bishop he took with him a firm idea of the parish as the centre of the Church's operations, and saw his main espiscopal duty as simply sharing in parish life.

Witt's reminiscences, *Bush Bishop* (1979), reflect his dynamic and popular preaching style. In 1981 he left the North West diocese to become Bishop of Bathurst in New South Wales; though badly hurt in an accident, he stayed in this post until 1989. When he died he was listening to his favourite hymn, *Cwm Rhondda*.

Howell Witt married, in 1949, Doreen Edwards, who died in 1983; they had three sons and two daughters.

July 22, 1998

The Reverend Edward Carpenter

The Reverend Edward Carpenter, KCVO, who has died aged 87, was one of the most erudite and engaging Deans ever to preside over England's national shrine of Westminster Abbey.

He was Dean of Westminster from 1974 to 1985, and altogether served Westminster Abbey for 34 years, having been appointed a Canon in 1951. With the possible exception of the eminent Victorian Dean Stanley, he effected more changes than any of his predecessors in the Abbey's day to day life.

During his time most of the old formalities that gave the impression of stuffiness were dispensed with. Visitors, whether attending a great service or simply passing through in the course of a packaged tour, were much more warmly welcomed, and a great variety of organisations was encouraged to hold services there.

Carpenter also made a special effort, largely successful, to strengthen the links between the Abbey and the Commonwealth. High Commissioners were invited to read Lessons at Evensong on the anniversaries of their nation's independence, and at the annual Commonwealth Day Observance, one of the highlights of Carpenter's year, the many faiths of Commonwealth citizens found expression in the worship.

All this was accomplished in a little over a decade by a Dean who was essentially a scholar and a thinker. It certainly delayed the completion and publication of the long-awaited biography of Archbishop Geoffrey Fisher, to which he set his hand as long ago as 1972 and which did not see the light of day until 1991. But at least some of the delay was caused by the author's reluctance to end what had become for him a fascinating labour of love.

His admiration for Fisher was in no way lessened by the discovery of a letter from the Archbishop to the Prime Minister in which he advised that under no circumstances should Canon Edward Carpenter be offered a bishopric since "he is interested in far too many things and ought to become a professor of History".

During the earlier stages of his life Carpenter was certainly well qualified for a university post. He took a First in History at

London, followed by an MA with distinction, then a PhD. He wrote a number of biographies of 17th- and 18th-century bishops, as well as a comprehensive survey of all the Archbishops of Canterbury. To most subjects he applied the mind of an historian.

But he was equally interested in the ethical aspects of the Christian faith. He not only wrote a book, *Common Sense about Christian Ethics* (1961), but also sought to practise what he preached by actively supporting many campaigns for social reform. Thus he was in the thick of the battle to end capital punishment, he marched in the campaigns against nuclear weapons (being a life-long pacifist), he was prominent in the United Nations Association, he was a keen supporter of the animal welfare societies and, perhaps needless to say, he was a vegetarian and travelled about London on a bicycle.

Carpenter was a liberal theologian of a breed that came to the fore in the 1920s and 1930s in the activities of the Modern Churchmens Union, and then rapidly declined after the Second World War. Its scepticism about the Bible was matched by its optimism about human nature and the perfectibility of human society.

Thus Carpenter, who was a fine if somewhat prolix preacher, rarely referred to the Bible in his sermons, but often selected a text from Cicero or Plato and illustrated his points with copious quotations from his beloved Shelley or the almost equal!y revered Dr Johnson. On more than one occasion he prefaced his reading of a Lesson by suggesting that St Paul had got things wrong. He was closely involved with the Council of Christians and Jews, and the World Congress of Faiths.

Edward Frederick Carpenter was born on November 27, 1910. His father was a local builder of modest means and sent his son to Strodes School, Egham. From there he went to King's College, London, to study history. It was while he was completing his work for a Master's degree that he came under the influence of the liberal movement in theology and decided to seek ordination. He was ordained at St Paul's in 1935 to a curacy at Holy Trinity,

Marylebone, where he stayed for six years. He then moved to St Mary's, Harrow, and in 1945 became Rector of Great Stanmore, Middlesex.

The next six years were a time of great happiness for Carpenter, who revelled in the pastoral opportunities of parish life and made a considerable impact on the life of Stanmore. Among those who were impressed by his work was C R Attlee, then Prime Minister, who had a house in Stanmore. In 1951 Attlee appointed Carpenter a Canon of Westminster. This caused considerable consternation in the Abbey cloisters, for not only was the new canon the product of a red-brick university but he was also being imposed, against ecclesiastical advice, by a Labour Prime Minister.

Carpenter was given a cool reception and was for a time very unhappy, but gradually he found his feet and came to value both the history enshrined in the stones of the Abbey and the freedom which a canonry gave him to pursue his studies and his many other interests.

Carpenter took part in the Coronation in 1953, carrying the orb to the high altar. In 1959 he became Treasurer of the Abbey – which post, despite his complete lack of interest in money, he held until he became Dean in 1974. He was Archdeacon of Westminster from 1963 to 1974.

By the time he was appointed to the Deanery he was almost 64 and there was nothing about Westminster Abbey that he did not know. Earlier he had been disappointed when he was passed over for the Deanery of St Paul's (he was the joint-author of a history of the cathedral). He did not consider the offer of the Deanery of Manchester a proper consolation prize, but he was "made" for Westminster Abbey and for a London ministry.

When he became Dean he shed none of his existing interests, and packed into a 20-hour day (for he required little sleep) an extraordinary range of work. He was for many years chairman of the governing body of the Camden School for Girls as well as of Westminster School, and found it impossible to decline an invitation to speak at a dinner, which he usually did brilliantly, or to preach in a tiny village church.

The combination of intellectual brilliance, simplicity and sheer goodness will cause many to believe that they are unlikely to see his like again. And those who witnessed his entertainment of the Dalai Lama at Westminster, and his inadvertent downing of the Queen Mother's gin and tonic while proposing her 80th birthday health will be certain that as a churchman he is irreplaceable.

He was appointed KCVO on his retirement and earlier received an honorary DD from London University and a Lambeth DD from the Archbishop of Canterbury. But these honours meant much less to him than the infrequent successes of Chelsea Football Club, of which he was a passionate supporter.

He married Lilian Wright when he was a curate in Marylebone; they had three sons and a daughter.

August 27, 1998

The Reverend Donald Pateman

The Reverend Donald Pateman, who has died aged 83, was perhaps the most "politically incorrect" clergyman in the Church of England.

He devoted his 50-year ministry to the East End of London. Last month, after 42 years as vicar of St Mark's, Dalston, ill health forced him to retire.

A man of surprising and strong views, which he was not afraid to voice, he was reported in 1977 to the then Race Relations Board and to the Archbishop of Canterbury for comments on immigrants in the parish magazine.

He described Britain as a scroungers' paradise. "Money is handed out," he said, "on a lavish scale. As soon as you arrive from Zambia or Botswana or Timbuctoo your first question is: 'Where's the nearest Social Security Office?' Arrived there, you receive your first handout, the first of many hundred. There are a million abusers in this country, a million cuts waiting to be made, a million scroungers to be given the proverbial kick in the backside."

No action was taken against Pateman, who in any case had appointed one of his curates to welcome West Indians settling in the parish in large numbers. Pateman not only succeeded in attracting many of them to his church, but also retained their staunch allegiance.

Among others who incurred his wrath were youths who misbehaved, and those whom he believed encouraged them by abandoning corporal punishment. In 1965 he called the Home Secretary, Roy Jenkins, a "purring old tabby" for closing down Britain's largest approved school and phasing out corporal punishment.

Pateman returned to this subject in 1978, when he accused local councillors of wasting ratepayers' money on a "cosy home for nasty little female muggers". He wanted the law changed so that those found guilty of mugging, football hooliganism or robbery with violence could be flogged. He conducted a referendum among 5,000 of his parishioners and won overwhelming approval.

Yet Pateman was fond of children. Irrespective of race or religious background, he encouraged them to use the vicarage for their games. When, in 1962, the choristers asked if they might wear Eton suits, including the traditional collars, he advertised for secondhand items, and a local store supplied six complete outfits.

The choristers were not exempt from corporal punishment if they stepped out of line, and this was administered by the Vicar, who claimed that parents thanked him for taking their errant sons in hand.

The punishment for brides arriving late for their weddings was different. In 1992 he introduced a sliding scale, details of which were handed to couples at wedding rehearsals. Ten minutes late meant the cutting of one of the hymns, 20 minutes the loss of two hymns and the dismissal from church of the photographer, 25 minutes to the dropping of all hymns and the dismissal of the choir, and 30 minutes late would cause the wedding to be cancelled.

Twenty years earlier when postmen were on strike, Pateman had announced that any seeking marriage in his church would be given a "work-to-rule ceremony" – no choir, no bells, no heating, no lighting, no music, no photographs, no confetti. He added: "Postmen earn the same money as me. I spent three years at university and I am expected to live on £21 a week. Why can't they?"

Donald Herbert Pateman was born at Kirby Muxloe, Leicestershire, on February 22, 1915. He had a strict Victorian upbringing. He worked in commerce and served in the RAF in the Second World War.

At this time he felt drawn to Holy Orders and to the service of the poor. On demobilisation, he went to the London College of Divinity, where the Principal was Donald Coggan, later Archbishop of Canterbury. There Pateman secured a theological diploma.

From 1948 to 1951 he was curate of St James-the-Less, Bethnal Green, and then of All Hallows, Bromley-by-Bow. He also took on the honorary secretaryship of the Society for Relief of Distress – a charity for the East End poor. In 1956 he was appointed vicar of St Mark's.

This was a heavy responsibility. The cathedral-like church was not then well attended and, as a listed building, would need constant expensive work. Being of the conservative Evangelical tradition, he decided the task required the combination of the Book of Common Prayer, the King James Bible, and intensive pastoral work in the streets of his parish.

Over the next 42 years Pateman never deviated. His sermons were short and down to earth; he hated pomposity. The congregation grew, and large sums were raised to maintain the building. He was delighted to be exempt from a regulation requiring clergy to retire at 70. When, finally, ill health gave him no choice, 1,000 people of all races and faiths attended a service of farewell and thanksgiving for his ministry.

He never married.

October 20, 1998

The Reverend Daniel Zindo

The Right Reverend Daniel Zindo who has died aged 54 in a motor accident near Kampala, Uganda, was the Acting Archbishop of the Anglican Church in the Sudan.

Zindo had contributed a great deal to the survival of the Church in a country devastated by civil war and famine, and ruled by an oppressive Muslim government. Much more was expected of him. A tall, well built man, who had been Bishop of Yambio since 1984, he was intellectually able and had great vitality, which enabled him to get things done in situations of permanent crisis.

In November last year, his wife and one of his daughters were murdered by his deranged son-in-law. His only brother died a week later and two of his nieces shortly afterwards, leaving him with 21 dependant relatives. Yet his warm, open personality was unaffected, his engaging sense of humour was undiminished and he was left with the burning conviction that the remainder of his own life must be dedicated to the strengthening and uniting of the Church and of the Sudanese nation.

In August this year he made a considerable impact on the Lambeth conference of Anglican bishops held in Canterbury. After the terrorist attacks on the British and American embassies in Khartoum, which provoked an American bombing reprisal, he appealed to all parties to find a peaceful solution.

Daniel Zindo was born into a Sudanese Christian family in 1944. He trained for Holy Orders at Bishop Hannington College and Bishop Tucker College, Uganda. When his leadership potential was recognised he was sent to Oak Hill College in north London where he took a London University degree.

He was ordained in 1972, and after five years of parish and mission work became Secretary of Yambio diocese. In 1982 he was appointed vice-principal of Bishop Gwynne Theological College, Juba, and two years later was elected Bishop of Yambio. He was a good listener who shared in the acute suffering of his people but radiated hope.

When Archbishop Benjamina Yugusuk retired from the see of

Juba earlier this year, it proved impossible to elect a successor, since tribal difficulties precluded the assembly of all the bishops. Zindo, Dean of the Province since 1988, was therefore appointed Acting Archbishop. A formal election would have to wait indefinitely for a cessation of hostilities.

The location of his diocese, in south-western Sudan close to the border with Zaire, could hardly have been worse for access to the rest of the largest country in Africa. Zindo, who confessed that he had been looking forward to a sabbatical, with an opportunity to rest, read and think, soon found himself confronted by several apparently intractable problems.

Because of the fighting in Sudan, the Sudanese bishops found it easier to hold their meetings and conduct some administration outside the country. Zindo was killed when travelling to Kampala to open an office there. Nonetheless, the Archbishop was eager to establish a base in Khartoum, the capital of Sudan, even though this involved frequent travel through the war zone. The Archbishop of Canterbury, Dr George Carey, promised Zindo that the Anglican Communion would finance the establishment of such a base.

The main Cathedral for the Anglican province of Sudan is at Juba, 700 miles south of Khartoum. The theological college and church offices are also there, and can only be reached when the government permits the Archbishop to travel on military aircraft. Zindo had no personal transport; he did not even own a typewriter.

Zindo was about to initiate a five-year plan for the Church to help to relieve the famine in Sudan and aid reconstruction afterwards. He was encouraged by the ceasefire that has recently made it possible for aid to reach the worst hit famine areas.

He also saw the urgent need to heal divisions in the Church created by bitter tribal feuds. In 1994 he was elected Chairman of the Sudan Council of Churches. Recent years have seen a huge influx of converts to all the Sudanese churches and increasingly close collaboration between Anglicans and Roman Catholics – something to which Zindo was deeply committed.

October 23, 1998

The Reverend Douglas Wollen

The Reverend Douglas Wollen, a Methodist minister who has died aged 89, was a socialist and pacifist, and never failed to declare his principles.

He believed this was the way of Charles Wesley for today – and had an altercation on the subject with Margaret Thatcher when showing her around Wesley's House, City Road, in 1981.

Douglas Wollen was born on June 22, 1909 at Chigwell, Essex. After school he had hoped for a place at Oxford, but abandoned the idea when his father died. He became a teacher, took a History degree as an external student at London, and then an MA in education.

Wollen joined the Methodist Temperance and Social Welfare Department and entered the ministry, with no formal theological training, in 1939. He "travelled" in nine circuits, from Camborne to Chesterfield. He retired from Poplar in 1979, but became honorary historian at Wesley's house.

He feared Methodism becoming hierarchical, opposed separation of District Chairmen from circuits, and frowned on any who accepted the office. He wrote on art, and established a collection of 20th-century Methodist art, now at Westminster College, Oxford.

Douglas Wollen married, in 1937, Winifrid Waterman, who died in 1987. They had two sons and a daughter.

November 25, 1998

The Reverend Lord Soper

The Reverend Lord Soper, who has died aged 95, was the best known Methodist of his time; throughout his life a soapbox preacher of Christian socialism and campaigner for radical causes, he was Superintendent of the West London Mission at Kingsway Hall from 1936 to 1978.

"I have said it before and I will say it again," Soper announced at Speakers' Corner on his 90th birthday, "it is impossible to reconcile capitalism with the message of Christianity".

This simple proposition, repeated in his sonorous voice ardently and often – he was regularly at Tower Hill from 1927 and Speakers' Corner from 1942 – was at the heart of his message.

Even before the Second World War he was regarded as one of the three outstanding Methodist ministers in central London. It was said of Dr William Sangster that he loved God, of Dr Leslie Weatherhead that he loved sinners, and of Dr Donald Soper that he loved an argument.

An outspoken republican, Soper seemed to relish unpopular causes. He provoked outrage with his opposition to any kind of militarism – from the Second World War to the Gulf War. Throughout the Cold War he offered friendship to Russia, and was an enthusiastic supporter of the Campaign for Nuclear Disarmament.

When he spoke at Tower Hill and Speakers' Corner, there would invariably be hecklers waiting for him. Soper welcomed them, for he thought they gave life to his meetings. He did not hesitate to answer back in kind, or to dismiss them as "fathead" or "rascal". He himself, it seemed, never suffered from any apprehension that he might be mistaken.

Soper appeared frequently on wireless and television. He was a regular guest on *Any Questions?* and on various television chat shows, including, on several occasions, *Wogan*.

Staunchly socialist, Soper maintained that Tories made poor Christians. But he was inclined to forgive trespasses, and allowed in 1993 that the former Prime Minister Edward Heath had "become a lot wiser in 20 years".

By that time Soper was scarcely more enamoured of the Labour Party. Created a life peer by Harold Wilson in 1965 for his work with down-and-outs in London, Soper took the party whip throughout his years in the House of Lords. But in later years he berated the Labour Party for having abandoned its radical aims.

His ultimate hope, however, was always placed in the hereafter. "I have a simple faith," he said. "I believe things that are eternally true and good will be in abundance beyond the grave, and so I can prepare myself to some degree by aspiring to those things now, before I take up my residence there."

Donald Oliver Soper was born on January 31, 1903 in Wandsworth, south London. His parents were convinced Wesleyan Methodists: his father worked as an insurance adjuster, but devoted himself to campaigning for teetotalism.

Soper later reflected that this strand of Methodism could entail a "very narrow, pietistic and very largely middle-class attitude". He lost his faith briefly as an undergraduate and later came to value Primitive Methodism, with its roots among the labouring classes.

Donald was educated at Aske's School, Hatcham, and St Catharine's College, Cambridge. At school he found most things – "from Greek to the trombone" – easy. He captained the teams for soccer, boxing and cricket. In later life he took up golf and became an avid exponent of surfing.

Soper's passion for cricket, however, was blighted at the age of 18 when a batsman was killed by a quick delivery he had bowled.

After taking his degree, Soper decided to enter the ministry of the Wesleyan Methodist Church, and remained in Cambridge to study theology at the newly-opened Wesley House. He subsequently took a PhD at the London School of Economics.

Soper's ministry was spent entirely in London. In 1926 he started to serve in the South London Mission on the Old Kent Road; he was ordained the next year. The misery that he witnessed at the beginning of the Depression in this already poor area, had a profound effect on him.

He moved to Islington in 1929 and stayed there until 1936. But it was his long superintendency of the West London Mission that established Soper's reputation in the public mind. Between 1931 and 1936 he recorded several series of talks for the BBC which, according to *Bystander* magazine, "brought showers of questions to Broadcasting House".

Soper was by then a convinced pacifist and during the Second World War became increasingly vocal in his opposition to the conflict. His views led to his being banned by the BBC in 1941. During the war his open-air gatherings were regularly monitored by a government observer, armed with a notebook.

Passive resistance to Hitlerism proved a tough line to sustain and Soper was obliged to exercise tact: "I learnt many years ago not to insult people," he said. "I remember in 1940 when I was speaking about the war, a man disagreed with me. He started shouting and I put him in his place. Afterwards, he told me his son had been killed in the Army."

But he was not put off his stride, and on one occasion continued to preach at Tower Hill even as a V 1 flying bomb droned low overhead; and the crowd stayed to listen.

After the war Soper became a noted anti-nuclear campaigner, as chairman of the National Hydrogen-bomb Campaign Committee, then in the Campaign for Nuclear Disarmament. He took part often in Aldermaston marches.

He was President of the Methodist Conference in 1953. His presidency was marked by characteristic blasts against inequity and privilege – the two were kissing cousins in his mind.

He urged British withdrawal from the Suez Canal Zone and from Kenya, and played a leading role, with Tony Benn and Fenner Brockway, in the formation of the Movement for Colonial Freedom.

Soper also inveighed against the Queen for encouraging gambling by attending races, and against Prince Philip for playing polo on a Sunday – though, in the storm which followed, Soper denied being a hardline Sabbatarian.

Despite protestations that he abhorred godless totalitarianism Soper caused a stir when, at the height of the Cold War, he declared that he "would rather see the world overrun by Communism than plunge into a Third World War".

He returned to the theme in the mid-1960s when confronting the decadence he found inherent in the new youth culture. "If Beatlemania typifies Western society," he said, "then, with all their faults, give me the Soviets . . . It is nothing short of comic to hear musicians talking about the novelty of the 'Liverpool Sound'. What balderdash!"

Soper's success in publicising his message reinforced the sales of a steady stream of books, many concerned with the relationship between politics and religion. Perhaps his best, though, was a devotional work, *All His Grace*, published in 1957 as the Methodist Church's Lent Book. He also published a volume of autobiography in 1984, *Calling for Action*.

In 1965 Soper resigned his post as an alderman of the Greater London Council to take his seat in the House of Lords. He continued to hold his post at the West London Mission for a further 13 years. For the territorial designation of his peerage he chose Kingsway in honour of the Mission's headquarters at Kingsway Hall.

Soper had his own ideas about the Peerage. "If you want the Lords to be useful," he declared at Speakers' Corner, "you must get rid of the effete hereditary peers who are no use at all. I have been a 'Reverend' for some 40 years. This is an even more euphonious and spiritual title than 'Lord'. This is a decline for me."

He was a regular attender and speaker at the House of Lords, where he combined his strong views on such subjects as abortion and euthanasia with firm stances on such traditional Methodist concerns as gambling and drinking.

A vegetarian "with occasional lapses" (sometimes on his doctor's advice), Soper became President of the League Against Cruel Sports in 1967, a post which he held for more than 20 years.

In 1980 he was again outspoken in his criticism of the sporting activities of the Royal Family, on this occasion attacking Prince Charles and Princess Anne for taking part in fox hunting.

From 1974 to 1978 Soper was chairman of the campaign group for the homeless, Shelter. In 1981 he was awarded the World Methodist Council's Peace Award.

He was elected an honorary fellow of St Catharine's in 1966, and received an honorary doctorate from Cambridge in 1988.

Despite being a public institution – an instantly recognisable white-haired figure in black cassock atop his open-air soapbox – Soper remained a private man. He often said that he could not face the crowds at Tower Hill or Hyde Park unless he had quietly taken Communion.

A competent pianist himself, Soper loved jazz, especially the music of Jelly Roll Morton. He had a fine collection of the Dixieland and New Orleans recordings. He could not, he said, "contemplate heaven without the music of Bach and Fats Waller".

He married, in 1929, Marie Dean; they had four daughters. In deference to him, his wife, who died in 1994, eschewed alcohol until he retired from his superintendency of the West London Mission in 1978. She then took it up in moderation.

December 23, 1998

1999

Canon Bill Vanstone

Canon Bill Vanstone, who has died aged 75, was perhaps the most academically brilliant Anglican clergyman of his generation.

He took a Double First in Classical Mods and Greats at Oxford, a First in Theology at Cambridge – where Professor Charlie Moule described him as the most gifted pupil he had ever taught – and went on to take a Master's degree at the Union Theological Seminary in New York.

Vanstone then steadfastly refused all offers of academic posts. Instead he devoted 21 years to pastoral ministry on a new housing estate in Rochdale. When ill-health eventually obliged him to give this up, he became a Canon Residentiary of Chester Cathedral.

Although he had an acute and original theological mind, Vanstone related easily and sensitively to people of all sorts, and few of his parishioners knew of his academic record.

As a young man, he had been greatly influenced by the example of a North Country priest who spent 50 years in the same parish, and while always interested in theological issues, Vanstone often asserted that Christianity is not a system but a way of life. This came through clearly in his three books: *Love's Endeavour, Love's Expense* (1979), *The Stature of Waiting* (1982) and *Fare Well in Christ* (1997).

All were quite slim volumes, but combined – powerfully – theological insight and homely illustrations from pastoral experience. A marked degree of radicalism in the first book gave way to mature wisdom in the last, and Vanstone had a large following of readers.

William Hubert Vanstone, the son of a clergyman, was born on May 9, 1923. From school he went straight into the Royal Air Force, where he trained as a pilot and was lucky to survive the crash of his Mosquito fighter.

On demobilisation, he went up to Oxford, as a scholar of Balliol, where he secured his Double First before moving across to Cambridge. There he was greatly influenced by the New

Testament scholarship of Professor Moule, as he was later to be by Paul Tillich's insights into psychology and symbolism when he was in New York.

During his time in Cambridge, Vanstone also prepared for Holy Orders at Westcott House, where he became a close friend of Robert Runcie, the future Archbishop of Canterbury.

On his return from America in 1950, he was ordained to a curacy at St Thomas's, Halliwell, in Bolton, and after five years there was asked to initiate the Church's work on a new housing estate at Kirkholt, in Rochdale.

By this time, he was regularly receiving offers of fellowships at Oxford and Cambridge, but he declined them all, as later he declined numerous offers of senior posts in the Church. His vocation, he said, was simply to serve God and his fellow human beings.

The task at Kirkholt was of the pioneering kind: it involved starting up a parish ministry from scratch and building a new church. Vanstone kept open house at the vicarage, the door of which was never locked, and spent long hours walking the streets of the parish, getting to know those he met.

He became an Examining Chaplain to the Bishop of Manchester in 1959, and an honorary Canon of Manchester Cathedral in 1968. But he never told anyone in the parish of his canonry, preferring to remain "Mr Vanstone".

More than two decades of devoted pastoral work ended in 1976, when Vanstone had a severe heart attack – the only thing, it was said, that would persuade him to leave the parish. The Bishop of Chester, Victor Whitsey, who had been with him at Westcott House, came to the rescue with the provision of a cottage and a light duty post as his theological adviser.

But after a year Vanstone asked to be allowed to become Vicar of Hattersley, another housing estate, but of a different sort, and one with a macabre atmosphere because of its association with the "Moors murders". Although Bishop Whitsey had no one else willing to take on the parish, he at first refused; but eventually he relented and Vanstone moved into the vicarage.

Twelve months, though, was long enough to demonstrate that Vanstone did not have the necessary health and strength. In 1978, he accepted appointment as a Canon Residentiary of Chester Cathedral, and played a full and distinctive part in the life of the cathedral until his retirement in 1990.

He also wrote, conducted retreats at theological colleges and convents, and for several years served on the Church of England's Doctrine Commission. On the whole, though, he had little time for bishops and church dignitaries, once likening the Church to "a swimming pool in which all the noise comes from the shallow end".

Perceiving a lack of theological depth in contemporary liturgical work, Vanstone had a strong attachment to the Book of Common Prayer. In retirement in Gloucestershire he celebrated Holy Communion according to the 1662 rite, and preached a well crafted sermon every Sunday in a tiny country church.

He was unmarried.

March 15, 1999

Cardinal Basil Hume

Cardinal Basil Hume, who has died aged 76, was an outstandingly popular Archbishop of Westminster whose sincerity and expertly judged public pronouncements strengthened both the reputation and the self-confidence of Roman Catholics in England and Wales.

The first Benedictine to hold this office, Hume, though half-French and half-Scottish, came across as essentially English and upper-middle class. This, added to an attractive spirituality, self-deprecating wit and imposing appearance, gave him advantages that had not been granted to his predecessor Cardinal Heenan, the product of an Irish working-class background.

The Queen, though Supreme Governor of the Church of

England, is reputed to have dubbed Basil Hume "My Cardinal". She went to Vespers at his cathedral and chose him to become one of the 24 members of the Order of Merit; he made a great effort to receive the honour from her at Buckingham Palace as his fatal illness grew worse.

By the end of Hume's 23 years in office, English Catholics had moved closer to the centre of the national stage than seemed possible when he was appointed in 1976. His words and tone at a requiem Mass for Diana, Princess of Wales, and a week later for Mother Teresa were noted far beyond the thousands who crowded Westminster Cathedral on those occasions. For millions who saw him on television or heard him on the wireless he conveyed an unfeigned seriousness about spiritual and moral matters that never lost sight of human frailties.

There was broad agreement, too, that it was thanks to the Cardinal that the Catholic Church in England did not split into opposing camps of conservative and liberals. Here he did build, perhaps, on the work of Heenan. But Hume had also developed remarkable diplomatic skills during his period as Abbot of Ampleforth, when, in the aftermath of the Second Vatican Council, he succeeded in reconciling warring factions of ecclesiastically Left- and Right-wing monks.

As Archbishop of Westminster, he appeared to realise that the currency of clerical interventions in public life is swiftly devalued if made too often. Although on most subjects his sympathies lay to the Left, he made sure that his protests on behalf of the Guildford Four, and the traditional family, and, above all, against abortion, occupied a moral high ground far above the party–political crossfire into which some clergy are drawn.

But the greatest test of Hume's diplomacy involved his relations with the Holy See, and it was one he passed with flying colours. During the pontificate of Pope John Paul II, the Cardinal managed to preserve excellent relations with the Vatican. He helped persuade the Pope to come to Britain in 1982, and to ensure that the visit was a public relations triumph for all concerned, Catholic and Anglican.

He was unswervingly loyal to Pope John Paul in public, yet managed to appear significantly less hard-line than the Pope on delicate sexual and moral issues. Faced with harsh statements from the Pope or from Cardinal Joseph Ratzinger, the Vatican guardian of orthodox doctrine, not once did Hume contradict the uncomfortable teachings they contained. Instead, he subtly applied a more acceptable gloss to them which rarely failed to satisfy liberal commentators.

The classic example was Rome's insistence, reiterated during the 1980s and 1990s, that homosexual acts were "objectively wrong". Quite right, said Hume in 1993; but this did not mean that homosexuals should feel guilty about their orientation. On the contrary, they were "precious in the eyes of God". This did not stop him, though, from banning an entry in the *Catholic Directory* for Quest, an association for homosexual Catholics which had refused to declare its acceptance of the Roman teaching.

Nor was Hume unaware of the strong adherence among a minority to the old Latin Mass. Thanks to an arrangement put in place by Cardinal Heenan, the so-called Tridentine Mass could legally be celebrated in England; Hume, while not wishing to encourage any liturgical split within his territory, gave permission for it to be said in three London churches each Sunday.

The point of Hume's tightrope balancing acts was twofold: to take the sting out of unpopular pronouncements, and to ensure that Rome did not feel compelled to root out liberals, as it had in America. That the act succeeded so well irritated some conservative Catholics, who felt that Hume occasionally managed to charm his way out of quite serious errors of judgment – for example, when he failed to act against school textbooks of dubious orthodoxy.

There was also unhappiness in some quarters at the calibre of some of the bishops and diocesan staff who served under Hume. It seemed to some almost as if the Cardinal – a strikingly tall, white-haired figure with what one writer described as "long Plantagenet features" – preferred to further the careers of humourless and unprepossessing liberals.

Certainly, with the partial exception of Archbishop Derek Worlock of Liverpool, no other bishop ever managed to rival Hume's ascendancy over the English and Welsh hierarchy. But this could scarcely be laid at Hume's door, since bishops' appointments were largely made on the recommendation of the Papal Nuncio in London.

If Hume usually tried to display statesmanlike caution, he also possessed an impulsiveness and sense of mischief which would occasionally get the better of him. This was exhibited most clearly in his dealings with the Church of England. He was shocked when, in November 1992, the General Synod voted to ordain women priests. "The point is not whether there should or should not be women priests, but whether the Church of England, which represents 4 per cent of Christianity, can decide something like this on its own," he said.

But when, soon afterwards, he was approached by scores of Anglo-Catholic priests who promised to bring their congregations over to Rome, he seemed to become positively light-headed at the prospect of a realignment of English Christianity. In an interview with *The Tablet* in March 1993, he said: "This could be a big moment of grace, it could be the conversion of England for which we have prayed all these years."

The reaction to this from Lambeth Palace was icy, and Cardinal Hume did not expand on that theme. Indeed, he seemed to change his mind and was soon sending out much less encouraging signals to the disaffected Anglican clergy.

The idea of a "Roman option" – special concessions for Anglo-Catholic converts, such as Anglican-rite; liturgies and a dispensation allowing married priests to run parishes – met a wall of resistance from Hume's fellow English Roman Catholic bishops.

In the event, about 300 Anglican clergy did become Roman Catholics, on Rome's terms. They included Dr Graham Leonard, the former Bishop of London, whom Hume had always admired: he ordained him to the Catholic priesthood conditionally, using a formula which acknowledged that Dr Leonard might already be validly ordained through the Old Catholic succession.

Opinion remained divided as to Hume's role in the drama of the Roman option. Many Anglo-Catholics and some Roman Catholic traditionalists felt that Hume had "dropped the ball" and passed up a wonderful opportunity to supplant the Church of England as the Church of the nation.

Others felt that he was right to distance himself from a group which was perhaps seeking to play off Archbishop's House, Westminster, against Lambeth Palace to see who would offer the better deal. What was undeniably true, though, was that Anglican clergy in Westminster diocese who decided to submit to Rome could rely on generous treatment from Cardinal Hume.

If nothing else, the crisis illustrated Hume's genius for sound-bites. At a press conference in 1993, he was asked if the Elizabethan Settlement might now be at an end. "Could be!" he grinned. He also told would-be converts that "there is no question of becoming Catholic *a la carte*. You have to take the menu – or move to another restaurant."

The Cardinal was born George Hume (he took the name Basil on entering the Benedictines) on March 2, 1923 at Newcastle upon Tyne.

He was the third of five children of a Scottish father, Sir William Hume, a heart consultant and Professor of Medicine at Durham University; he was not a Roman Catholic. His Parisian mother, born Marie Elisabeth Tisseyre, was the daughter of a French colonel and spoke French to her children.

Young George grew up in comfortable circumstances – he had a nurse and learned to ride – which contrasted sharply with the poverty of Tyneside during the Depression. Even as a child, Hume was aware of this: the sight of shoeless children influenced his Leftish political sympathies and also played a part in his decision to become a monk.

Hume spent, off and on, 42 years at Ampleforth, whose preparatory school he joined at the age of 11, and which he only really left to come to Westminster. At school, Hume took imme-diately to the monks' brand of muscular Christianity: he excelled at rugby, though he described himself as only "Division Two" academically.

At 18, he took the difficult decision to join Ampleforth Abbey as a monk – difficult not just because the routine of a junior monk was gruelling, but because – the nation being at war – it meant taking exemption from military service. "It was a terrible choice," he told John Mortimer decades later. "If it happened again, I think I'd have gone into the Army."

The Benedictines sent Hume to their house at Oxford, St Benet's Hall, where he read History. (During the papal conclaves of 1978, the student newspaper Cherwell ran a story with the headline "Benet's Man Next Pope?")

After his solemn vows, he enjoyed many happy years as an Ampleforth housemaster, developing a particular rapport with troublesome pupils. "It's true I like rogues," he said. "You never meet a conceited rogue."

Hume's appointment as Abbot at the age of 40 coincided with the upheavals of Vatican II. His balance of liberal and conservative instincts meant that he was ideally qualified to hold office at such a difficult time: remarkably, only 10 out of 145 monks left the community over the decade.

Socially, too, Basil Hume fitted the bill. As the son of a professional man, he was able to bridge the gap between the upper-class ethos of Ampleforth and the egalitarian mood of the Church in the Sixties. He did, however, feel the strain. A fellow monk described him as "emotionally, physically and spiritually depressed" during his later years at Ampleforth.

When Cardinal Heenan died in November 1975, Basil Hume was mentioned as a possible successor, though the front runner was thought to be Bishop Derek Worlock (then of Portsmouth), a socialist who combined liberal principles with an authoritarian manner. Hume was chosen after the Apostolic Delegate, Bruno Heim, intervened to block Worlock's appointment, supported by lobbying from influential Catholics who felt they did not wish to live with such an abrasive figure.

Hume's subsequent career justified the Establishment's faith in him. He offered reluctant but unequivocal support to the British expeditions in both the Falklands and the Gulf, in the latter case distancing himself from the rather histrionic anti-war statements of Pope John Paul. He condemned nuclear weapons, but refused to support CND.

On those rare occasions when Cardinal Hume took on the British Establishment, he usually won. In 1978, he was convinced by a relative of one of the Guildford Four that they were innocent of the 1975 pub bombing. After visiting them in prison, he began intensive lobbying of both Labour and Conservative government ministers. He hosted meetings at Archbishop's House of a high-powered group of former Home Secretaries and Law Lords who shared his view of the case. It was the beginning of a long process which culminated in the release of the Guildford Four in 1989.

Such were Hume's diplomatic skills and personal holiness that many English felt he would have made an excellent Pope. Whether his name was considered in the first conclave of 1978 remains unclear: some Vatican watchers felt that if he had spoken Italian and had been in office for longer he might have been in the running.

In common with other Christian denominations, church-going among Roman Catholics declined during Hume's years at Westminster. There were new converts too, though, about 600 a year being welcomed during a public service each Lent. Some of the converts were public figures; the Duchess of Kent was received privately by the Cardinal in 1994. He made no fuss over what might have seemed the delicate matter of a member of the Royal Family becoming a Roman Catholic; the first thing the world knew was after the event. He showed his astuteness by not even appearing to think it a feather in his cap. MPs such as Ann Widdecombe and John Gummer were also received into the Roman Catholic Church by clergy at the cathedral.

The diocese had a debt of £6 million when Hume became archbishop, and the debt doubled over the following decade; only by strenuous efforts was it eliminated. One of the institutions at risk from money troubles was the cathedral choir school. A man less attuned to the liturgical value and aesthetic excellence of a well-trained choir might well have let it fail. Hume, with the help of the cathedral administrators, made the choir a priority. His decision was rewarded by its winning several music awards and its choirmaster being snapped up by Westminster Abbey.

Hume was moved by the desperate state of the many homeless people who begged and often slept in the streets around Westminster Cathedral. Some of them were youngsters, and in 1986 he founded the Cardinal Hume Centre for young people at risk. He also encouraged work with young homeless people by the Society of St Vincent de Paul. In the cold December of 1990 he threw open the cathedral hall to rough-sleepers as a night shelter; it was to remain in use for this purpose for two years until a permanent shelter could be set up.

He was even more affected by the sight of starving people in Ethiopia, which he visited during the famine of 1984. As well as seeking support from his flock for the Catholic Fund for Overseas Development he attempted to influence British foreign policy not only to provide emergency aid but also, from as early as 1985, to cancel debts which poor countries could not pay.

Of his books the most successful was *To Be a Pilgrim* (1984). His earliest collection of addresses (to monks) was published in 1977 as *Searching for God*; his last collection of meditations *The Mystery of the Cross* came out in 1998.

Only once did Basil Hume badly miscalculate an intervention in public affairs, when he backed a plan by Left-wing education advisers to close the sixth form of one of London's best comprehensive schools, the Cardinal Vaughan. The plan was to found a sixth form college which would pool the resources of the Cardinal Vaughan and two other less well-known schools. But in the event, he was embarrassingly out-manoeuvred by the parents, who opted out of local authority control.

What upset many Catholics about the Cardinal's stance was that it seemed so out of character. He was, for the most part, an unstuffy man; a lifelong supporter of Newcastle United, he enjoyed watching football and drinking a little beer.

He liked to be addressed as "Father Basil', rather than "Your Eminence"; and he seldom wore a pectoral cross.

June 18, 1999

2000

Father Brocard Sewell

Father Brocard Sewell, the literary biographer who has died aged 87, saved a series of minor figures from permanent obscurity, but brought episcopal wrath down on his head by calling for the resignation of Pope Paul VI.

Sewell was a quietly spoken Carmelite friar whose taste for the calmer byways of literature invariably resulted in better reviews than sales. Then in 1968 he wrote a letter to *The Times* attacking the encyclical *Humanae Vitae*, which had confirmed the Roman Catholic Church's opposition to contraception.

Sewell began by suggesting that such a stance would only intensify the distrust of the papacy which had been felt by the Orthodox Church since the Great Schism; he went on to advocate that Paul VI should follow the example of the 13th-century Pope Celestine V and resign.

In the furore that followed, Sewell was ordered to leave his friary at Aylesford in Kent and was even suspended from preaching and hearing confessions. Seven weeks later, 57 other Roman Catholic priests wrote to the newspaper supporting his stand, and in some cases earned far stronger displeasure from their bishops.

For Sewell, the worst long-term effects were the death of the literary quarterly he had founded, the *Aylesford Review*, and his subsequent exile in Nova Scotia.

The son of a schoolmaster, Michael Seymour Sewell was born in Bangkok on July 30, 1912. He was brought up in Cornwall and educated at Weymouth College, which he had to leave early because his father lost money running a prep school.

Already attracted to Roman Catholicism, Michael became an office boy for both the Distributist League, which argued for the equal division of property, and for the magazine *GK's Weekly*, for which Chesterton wrote a regular column.

After being received into the Church at 20, Sewell tried his vocation with the Dominican Order at Woodchester, Gloucestershire, taking the name Eric in religion, but left after seven months. He next became apprenticed to Hilary Pepler, the printer member of the Guild of St Joseph and St Dominic, the Catholic craftsmen's community modelled on medieval lines

But when Pepler became unpaid secretary of the Distributist League, Sewell found himself back where he had started eight years earlier. However, he enjoyed speaking at meetings for the League, and took particular satisfaction in organising a debate held at Central Hall, Westminster, between the celebrated preacher Father Vincent McNabb, advocating Distribution, and the future Labour cabinet minister, John Strachey, representing Communism.

After the outbreak of war in 1939, Sewell taught in a prep school and helped the printer Rene Hague (Eric Gill's son-in-law) run a small press, before he was called up and spent four years as a clerk in the RAF.

On being demobbed, he joined the Austin Canons of the Lateran at Bodmin, Cornwall. But after completing his novitiate and studying further in Belgium, he transferred to the new English Carmelite province, taking the name Brocard.

Once ordained priest at Aylesford, Sewell undertook occasional parochial work, particularly enjoying celebrating Mass at Maidstone Gaol, where his server was a baronet whom he described with characteristic charity as "having been committed . . . for some piece of financial misjudgment".

He also became the community's librarian, started a small printing press which produced handmade books and began the *Aylesford Review*. This magazine concentrated on matters of Carmelite interest at first, but soon became more concerned with the arts and social issues.

It encouraged such young novelists as Angela Carter and D. M. Thomas, and provided a forum for more established figures such as Elizabeth Jennings, Stevie Smith and Henry Williamson.

The magazine also showed interest in political and social issues, publishing a stinging attack on Lord Denning's report which whitewashed the Establishment's treatment of Stephen Ward, the osteopath convicted of living off prostitution in the Profumo case.

Inevitably, Sewell's efforts attracted trouble. It arrived in the post one morning, prompting the Irish prior of Aylesford to exclaim: "St Anthony! Brocard is in trouble with the Red Hat."

Cardinal Griffin the Archbishop of Westminster, had taken umbrage at an article suggesting that he had declared the hydrogen bomb evil. Soon afterwards there was a public debate between supporters and opponents of the bomb.

When the meeting passed a resolution declaring a nuclear deterrent immoral, Sewell politely wrote to the cardinal suggesting he seek its condemnation in Rome. In the end, the Benedictine Abbot of Ramsgate was instructed to make a visitation to Aylesford; he ruled that Sewell had no charge to answer.

Following the row over *The Times* letter, about which he had failed to consult his superior, Sewell took leave of absence during which he produced a justification for his stand, *The Vatican Oracle* (1970).

He then alleviated his order's embarrassment by going to St Francis Xavier University in Nova Scotia, where he lectured on the writers of the 1890s and started another literary journal, the *Antigonish Review*. This was modelled on the *Aylesford Review*, but after a while it was decided that it should concentrate instead on providing a forum for local writing.

Sewell then moved to his order's Mount Carmel College in Ontario. While he enjoyed his Canadian sojourn, Sewell later reflected that "the average North American boy is a thoroughly likable person; but he has a strong disinclination to learn anything."

Back in Britain by the 1970s, Sewell returned to his biographical work. Nobody could deny his talents. He was a careful, charitable and gently witty writer. But some wondered whether his subjects were worth the effort from a literary viewpoint, or entirely suitable from the religious.

There was G. K. Chesterton's unlovely journalist brother Cecil; the poet Olive Custance, who married Lord Alfred Douglas; and, perhaps most important, Oscar Wilde's friend John Gray, who later became a priest.

There were also accounts of the witchcraft writer Montague Summers (published with rare discretion under the pseudonym

Joseph Jerome) and of Brother Benedict Gardner, an eccentric actor, circus proprietor, educationalist and founder of a non-Catholic religious order.

He published studies of Henry Williamson, the poet Frances Horovitz, a reappraisal of *GK's Weekly* and two autobiographies, including *The Habit of a Lifetime* (1992).

Not the least disconcerting thing about attacking Sewell was that one might be faced by his extraordinary range of sympathies and interests, which embraced both socialism and membership of the British Union of Fascists; while his friends ranged from every variety of writer and would-be writer to Sir Oswald Mosley and Christine Keeler.

Sewell always escaped the severest sanctions because he accepted that he was under discipline and willingly undertook any tasks given him. But there was no denying his comic ability to be out of step with authority. The late Mgr Alfred Gilbey shot no stronger glance than the one he gave Sewell when the friar appeared at the Travellers' Club in mufti, wearing a dark shirt and white kipper tie.

He remained an opponent of papal power, referring to John-Paul II as "the present pontiff", yet was critical of relaxations of monastic discipline. When the Latin liturgy was the accepted liturgical language he was a proponent of the vernacular, but when that situation was reversed he became a keen Latin supporter.

While he always expressed his dissent in the mildest manner, some of his friends felt that the clue to his character was the resemblance which his rubicund features bore to those of Beatrix Potter's rodent character Mr Samuel Whiskers.

April 4, 2000

Monsignor Dilwyn Lewis

Monsignor Dilwyn Lewis, who has died aged 76, welcomed the Pope to Britain in 1982 and was subsequently given charge of the running and restoration of the Basilica of St Mary Major in Rome.

Protocol dictated that as chaplain of Gatwick airport Lewis should receive the Pope as he landed. The visit gave Lewis the scope to employ his boundless energy and charm in persuading the airport authorities and police to provide all services without charge.

He was noticed by Archbishop Bruno Heim, then Apostolic Nuncio, and Cardinal Hume, and eventually they arranged for him to be appointed a Canon of the Papal Basilica of St Mary Major in Rome, a post he took up in 1984. At the time the Italian authorities were threatening to close the 1,600-year-old Basilica because of fire and safety problems.

Among other problems the ancient ceiling, decorated with the first gold which came from the New World and donated by Pope Alexander VI, was sagging and in danger of collapse; water had got behind the 7th-century mosaics which were starting to crumble, and indeed the whole church was shabby and run down.

The new Archpriest of the Basilica, Cardinal Luigi Dadaglio, soon put the general administration and restoration works into the hands of Lewis. He was appointed Vical Capitular of the Basilica and created Protonotary Apostolic, the highest of the ancient Vatican titles for non-episcopal functionaries.

Immediately, centuries of somnolence came to an abrupt end as modern business methods were applied to the day-to-day administration of the Basilica, the sale of property and the tendering of contracts. In addition, Lewis used his linguistic gifts on whirlwind fundraising tours, especially in Germany and America, and, gradually, an immense programme of works was undertaken and paid for.

The fabric of the Basilica and its art treasures were restored completely. It is no exaggeration to say that Lewis was responsible for saving for posterity a church which is in itself both a museum of western art and a living part of the world's cultural heritage.

Amid all the restoration work, Monsignor Lewis did not forget that St Mary Major is part of the daily life of the Catholic Church in Rome. He improved the standards of religious services in the Basilica and contributed much by his own presence and flair to the dignity of celebrations, preaching with Welsh fervour and ringing phrase in the many languages he had mastered.

Nor did he forget contemporary cultural life: choirs from the great cathedrals of England and other parts of the world sang regularly at Mass and gave concerts. For the 400th anniversary of Palestrina, who was once maesro di capella in the Basilica, he organised a live recording of the complete Masses by Peter Phillips and the Tallis Scholars. And he always remembered that he had once been a member of the Church of England: he obtained permission from the Vatican for Anglican priests to celebrate the Eucharist in the Basilica, and in 1998 persuaded the Vatican to lend to Canterbury Cathedral for an exhibition a yellow silk dalmatic which had belonged to St Thomas à Becket.

Dilwyn John David Lewis was born on 28 April 1924 in Bridgend, Glamorgan, and was brought up in an orphanage there. He began studies for the Anglican ministry at Kelham College, near Southwell, but left to join the Roman Catholic Church.

He then worked for some years for a cloth company in Bradford in sales, his gift for design was soon recognised and he eventually set up his own freelance design company and moved to London. He operated out of his flat in Duke Street, Mayfair, and sold his designs across Europe. During these years he discovered an aptitude for languages and eventually became fluent in all the main European languages. During a sales trip to Italy in 1960 he met Cardinal Montini, the future Pope Paul VI, at the time Archbishop of Milan. It was he who first suggested Lewis might become a priest. However, he did not take up the offer. He often remarked that had he done so he would by now be a Cardinal. Instead he concentrated upon building up an extremely successful business in the rag trade.

But after an illness and a spell in hospital he felt an emptiness in his life and approached an old friend, David Cashman, the Bishop of Arundel and Brighton, to offer himself for the Church.

So, at the age of 46, in 1970 he was sent as an ecclesiastical student to the Beda College in Rome, a seminary where later vocations pursue a shorter course of studies. He was ordained a priest at Arundel Cathedral in 1974 being appointed curate at St Clement's in Ewell, Surrey.

After a spell as chaplain for English speakers in Reggio Calabria, during which he also worked on ecumenical relations, he was appointed chaplain to Gatwick Airport. It is often alleged that English Roman Catholic authorities find it hard to cope with anything more than mediocre talent, and Dilwyn Lewis might well have passed the rest of his days in the byways of rural Sussex had it not been for the visit of Pope John Paul II to England.

In character, Dilwyn Lewis was forceful and dramatic with a witty turn of phrase at once amusing and embarrassing, especially as his loud voice – able with ease to fill a Basilica – often gave his indiscretions a larger audience than was intended. His frequent tantrums bore witness to a deep psychological wound going back to his childhood and caused many a rift with friends and colleagues. But he was always generous with his great wealth, especially to the young and impoverished, and invariably entertaining even in his anger.

The years of stressful toil and frequent rage with people less energetic than himself undermined his health and in 1996 he suffered the first of seven heart attacks. A quadruple by-pass operation followed and diabetes was diagnosed. He died suddenly in Ireland, a few days after preaching at the First Mass of a newly ordained priest he had met at the Irish College in Rome.

His body was returned to Rome and a requiem Mass concelebrated by the present Archpriest, Cardinal Furno, and the Chapter of the Basilica, was followed by burial in the crypt of St Mary Major.

July 19, 2000

The Reverend Fred Pratt Green

The Reverend Fred Pratt Green, who has died aged 97, was perhaps the most prolific hymn writer of the 20th century; he composed more than 300, including the one used in churches across Britain to celebrate the Queen's Jubilee in 1977.

The most remarkable aspect of Pratt Green's career as a hymnographer was that he did not begin to write hymns until his late sixties, when he was on the verge of retirement from the Methodist ministry. Indeed, before then he had never particularly liked them.

In 1967, however, he was co-opted onto a committee planning a supplement to *The Methodist Hymn Book*. They soon agreed that hymns on new themes such as Christian unity were needed. The difficulty was finding writers for them, until someone remembered that Pratt Green was also a poet (who had been published by the *New Yorker* and even had a poem, *The Odd Couple*, in Philip Larkin's *Oxford Book of Modern Verse*).

Pratt Green agreed to try his hand, and found that he enjoyed the challenge and (not being precious about such work) that he could hymn on almost any subject, from the 1,300th anniversary of the birth of St Boniface to Christian Aid. He never composed for its own sake, only for commissions, but he was soon in great demand, tackling subjects from school confirmations to the war in Vietnam. The only time he was stumped for inspiration was when asked for a Thanksgiving Day hymn for American Indians.

In 1977, the Church of England turned to Pratt Green after rejecting Sir John Betjeman's proferred contribution to the Jubilee (lambasted by Nicholas Fairbairn as "banal and absolutely pathetic"). Pratt Green was a friend of Betjeman's and observed only that he wished Sir John had called it a song instead, and that perhaps God should not have blue eyes in hymns.

Betjeman had spent three months on his effort; in two hours Pratt Green came up with a replacement, sung to the rhythm of *The Battle Hymn of the Republic* and to a tune by Walford Davies, *Vision*:

It is God who holds the nations in the hollow of his hand;
It is God whose light is shining in the darkness of the land;
It is God who builds his City on the Rock and not on sand;
May the living God be praised!

Pratt Green rejected comparisons with another prolific Methodist hymn writer, Charles Wesley (who composed more than 6,000) – "It's like being hailed as the Fourth Person of the Trinity" – but like him remained indefatigable into old age.

He also retained his strong sense of mischief. On being asked at 90, how a hymn started that he had written for the 50th anniversary of the Methodist Homes for the Aged, he smiled sweetly: "Ooh, I can't tell you that. When you get to my age you forget everything. It's quite wonderful."

Frederick Pratt Green was born at Roby, now in Liverpool, on September 2, 1903; his surname was Green, but he began to use his full name after being ordained, since there was already a minister named F. P. Green. His father, a leather merchant, was also a Wesleyan preacher.

Derick, as he was known in the family, went to Rydal, a Methodist boarding school in Colwyn Bay. He harboured ambitions of becoming an architect, but instead was consigned to his father's business. Then, after hearing a sermon on John Masefield's *The Everlasting Mercy* he offered himself for the Methodist ministry.

His health was delicate and his candidacy was nearly turned down. Having graduated from Didsbury Theological College in 1928, he applied to go as a missionary to Africa, but his principal thought it wiser to send him as chaplain to Hunmanby Hall, a girls' school in Yorkshire. There he met and in 1931 married Marjorie Dowsett, a teacher of French.

By 1939, Pratt Green was a minister on the Ilford circuit and was soon combining spiritual duties with those as an air raid warden. In 1944 he moved to Finsbury Park, where he met an agnostic poet, Fallon Webb, who encouraged him to write poems. Three years later he was transferred to Brighton, where at the Dome concert hall he regularly preached to congregations of 2,000.

Later, in 1957, he was appointed chairman of the York and Hull district of the church. The two areas were not getting on well but, although himself a Lancastrian, his natural gift for reconciliation soon had the Yorkshiremen working harmoniously together.

In the last decade of his life, the success of Pratt Green's hymn writing began to generate substantial royalties, especially in America. Funnelled through a trust, these were put to various ends involving hymnody and church music, including the establishment of a collection of hymn books at Durham University. This now has more than 3,000 volumes, reflecting changes in taste, theology and liturgy since the 18th century.

Among the trust's more unusual grants was paying the copyright fees to enable the first Roman Catholic hymn book to be published in Latvia after the demise of Communism.

Its most recent achievement was one close to Pratt Green's heart, the issue of a CD-ROM, *Hymnquest*, which contains the entire British corpus of hymns – more than 15,000 of them – as well as 12,000 tunes. It can also be searched for any of 3,000 themes used by hymn writers over the centuries.

While knowing his own mind, all his life Pratt Green had a willingness to entertain new ideas. A liberal in matters of faith, he believed that one's own church could be fallible, and that there was much to be learned from other religions ("My wife used to say I was really a Taoist"). He kept a copy of Marcus Aurelius's *Meditations* by his bed and consulted it every night.

He was an extremely competent businessman, and one who even in his eighties could work 14 hours a day, wearing out colleagues many decades his junior. He made a point of answering every letter on the same day that he received it.

Fred Pratt Green was appointed MBE in 1995. He was awarded an honorary doctorate by Emory University, Atlanta, in 1982.

His wife predeceased him in 1993. There were no children, but they raised Elizabeth Shepherd, the daughter of a missionary who had died of leprosy in India.

October 25, 2000

2001

The Very Reverend Jack Shearer

The Very Reverend Jack Shearer, who has died aged 74, became Dean of St Anne's Church of Ireland Cathedral, Belfast, in 1985, having previously spent 15 years as Archdeacon of Dromore.

Shearer combined strong pastoral gifts with those of an administrator, and he had a great flair with money. St Anne's Cathedral's finances were in a parlous state when he became Dean, but he turned the situation round and not only balanced the books but went on to build up substantial reserves.

Shearer was best known, however, in his role as Belfast's "Black Santa". He inherited the role from his predecessor and it was one which, with the aid of lively publicity, he developed into an important fundraising effort for charity.

Every year, for the seven days before Christmas, he sat, dressed in black clerical cloak and balaclava, outside the door of the cathedral, with a large empty whiskey barrel in which he collected gifts, mainly for a multitude of Belfast charities but also for Christian Aid and other overseas agencies.

Donations ranged from 50p to several thousands of pounds and the amount placed in the barrel last month amounted to a total of £400,000. This gave Shearer enormous satisfaction, as it had been advertised as his last appearance as "Black Santa" before his retirement at the end of March. In all, he raised more than £2 million in this way during his years as Dean.

Another significant piece of work he accomplished was the development of the cathedral as an "open" church, one to which Belfast people of different religious persuasions or none come to mark occasions of sorrow and joy in the life of the city and the province. Two years ago this ecumenical initiative was extended to embrace close collaboration with St Peter's Roman Catholic Cathedral in what is now known as the Belfast Cathedrals' Partnership – an unthinkable development until quite recently and now a valuable contribution to the Peace Process.

John Shearer, always known as Jack, was born on December 30, 1926 into humble circumstances in the Protestant Shankill Road area of west Belfast.

His father kept a market stall and when Jack was doing badly at the local school he was set to work on the stall with the threat that this would be his lifetime fate unless he took school more seriously.

With no further encouragement, he at once buckled down to meet the demands of Belfast Technical School and in the end won a place at Trinity College, Dublin.

After graduating, he prepared for Holy Orders at the college's Divinity School and in 1950 became curate of Maralin in Lurgan. He then spent seven years as curate of St Patrick's, Ballymacarrett, in Belfast – the largest parish in the Church of Ireland – where he completed a postgraduate degree in Theology and eventually became the senior of six curates.

Subsequently, he was Rector of Ballynahinch, a market town in Co. Down, from 1954 to 1964, and then Rector of Seagoe, Co. Armagh. While at Ballynahinch, he published a book, *Stewardship Step by Step* (1961).

He was at that period an active Orangeman and Freemason, but as Northern Ireland's troubles became more and more serious he recognised the need for reconciliation and mobilised local opposition to the activities of the Protestant paramilitaries. This marked the beginning of his commitment to the fostering of friendship between members of the rival communities.

In 1970, he was given the extra responsibilities of Archdeacon of Dromore. He was a popular figure among the clergy and the laity who valued his gifts as a communicator as well as his readiness to offer expert advice on financial matters of every kind. His ministry to sick people in hospital is still remembered.

He was the obvious candidate for the Deanery of Belfast when this fell vacant in 1985 and, though the cathedral parish has few residents, he built up the life of the congregation and ensured the maintenance and development of the cathedral's strong music tradition.

He became one of Belfast's most admired citizens, and in 1994 he was appointed OBE.

Jack Shearer married, in 1956, Morag Williamson; they had a son and a daughter.

January 17, 2001

The Right Reverend John Taylor

The Right Reverend John Taylor, who has died aged 86, became in 1975 the first priest to be consecrated directly to the see of Winchester since the Middle Ages. He will be chiefly remembered, however, as a missionary leader whose unrivalled knowledge of the Church in Africa enabled him, from the headquarters of the Church Missionary Society in London, to play a vital role in the transfer of authority to the Anglican Church's African dioceses in the 1960s.

His own love of the African people brought a positive response from the political as well as the religious leaders of the newly independent African states. The smooth transfer of Church administration owed a great deal to his vision and sensitive diplomacy. Successive Archbishops of Canterbury relied heavily on his advice, and regarded him as their unofficial Foreign and Commonwealth Secretary.

Taylor's first-hand knowledge of Africa was derived initially from his wardenship, from 1945 to 1954, of Bishop Tucker Memorial College at Mukono, Uganda. There he found himself responsible for the training of a new generation of clergy, many of whom were destined to become the first African bishops in Uganda and Kenya. Indeed, some of them came to Christianity through his influence.

He brought to the task of clergy-training not only a first-class theological mind but also the ability to relate Christian insight to a wide range of 20th-century issues.

Later, during Taylor's 11 years as General Secretary of the Church Missionary Society, the CMS Newsletter, which Taylor wrote with great skill and to a consistently high standard, was essential reading for church leaders of every tradition, and highly influential throughout the Anglican Communion.

Despite a continually heavy burden of administration, Taylor also wrote several books, two of which, *The Primal Vision* (1963), an evaluation of the central features of African religion, and *The Go-Between God* (1972), an interpretation of the work of the Holy Spirit, became classics.

In comparison with all that had gone before his consecration, his term as Bishop of Winchester, from 1975 to 1985, was in some ways less remarkable. But he was a first-rate chairman of the Church's Doctrine Commission, and it was of the greatest value to the Church to have a man of Taylor's prophetic vision on the bench of bishops for a decade.

John Vernon Taylor was born on September 11, 1914 in Cambridge, where his father, later to become Bishop of Sodor and Man, was Vice-Principal of Ridley Hall.

Nurtured in the Evangelical tradition of the Church of England, John was educated at St Lawrence College, Ramsgate, and then as an exhibitioner of Trinity College, Cambridge, where he read English and History.

Having decided to prepare for Holy Orders, he went to Wycliffe Hall, Oxford, and also enrolled at St Catherine's College, Oxford, to read for a degree in Theology. He was ordained in St Paul's Cathedral in 1938 and spent the next two years at the West End church of All Souls', Langham Place.

He then moved north to be curate in charge of a church at St Helens, Lancashire, where he stayed until 1943. At this point he felt drawn to missionary work overseas; but as a long distance sea voyage was all but ruled out while the war lasted, he instead went to the London University Institute of Education to obtain a teaching qualification.

On the return of peace, he was at once sent to Uganda as Warden of Bishop Tucker College, and here began his heartfelt and fruitful association with East Africa – where his work is still remembered with gratitude. In 1955 he joined the staff of the International Missionary Council in Geneva as a research worker. The purpose of this appointment was to enable him to reflect on his African experience and to make his insights more widely available to the World Church. His books *Christianity and Politics in Africa* (1957), *The Growth of the Church in Buganda* (1958) and *African Passion* (1958) were published during the Geneva years.

In 1959 he was called back to London to be Africa Secretary of the Church Missionary Society. Under the powerful leadership of the General Secretary, Canon Max Warren, Taylor continued to develop his powers, and when Warren retired in 1963 Taylor was the natural successor. That year he was also appointed as an honorary Canon of Namirembe Cathedral, Uganda.

While always bearing the mark of the Evangelical conviction which had led him to offer for missionary service in the first place, Taylor became, as the years went by, much more understanding and accepting of other traditions, including those of other faiths.

He was an inspiring preacher who sought to persuade by the sheer reasonableness of his thinking and, while never straying far from Biblical categories of thought, he became a liberal theologian whom no one dared to accuse of diluting the revealed faith.

He also had considerable gifts as an actor, and during his time at Winchester wrote and produced a Passion Play for presentation in the cathedral. This was subsequently broadcast on television and received much praise.

Towards the end of his life, a poetic gift began to flower. This surprised no one, for not far below the surface of the missionary statesman and bishop was the soul of a mystic and artist.

His book of meditations *Weep Not For Me* (1986) and his collection *Christmas Sequence and Other Poems* (1989), reveal a man who knew as much about suffering as he did about success, and one whose greatest gifts were gentleness and humility.

He married, in 1940, Margaret Wright; they had a son and two daughters.

February 1, 2001

Canon Susan Cole-King

Canon Susan Cole-King, who has died aged 66, spent two decades caring for the poorest of the poor, mainly in Africa, before becoming an Anglican priest in America, where she worked among the homeless in New York; she was also the first honorary Canon of Christ Church, Oxford.

The daughter of a bishop, Susan Cole-King was well known in ecclesiastical circles for her support for the cause of women's ordination. Having urged the Church of England to accept women for the ministry, in the early 1990s she herself took charge of a parish at Drayton, in Berkshire.

Canon Cole-King was born Susan Mary Wilson on April 23, 1934 at Eighton Banks, County Durham, where her father, Leonard Wilson, was the vicar. Soon afterwards the family moved to Sunderland and then, in 1938, to Hong Kong, where her father had been appointed Dean of the Cathedral.

But when war broke out the next year, and the situation in the Far East began to look threatening, the dean's family was among those evacuated to Australia. They stayed there until he became Bishop of Singapore in 1941.

When the city was occupied by the Japanese a few months later, Susan, her mother and her brother were again sent to Australia. Bishop Wilson, however, elected to stay behind with his people. He was subsequently incarcerated and tortured in Changi prison.

The family was reunited at the end of the war, and in 1948 returned to England when Leonard Wilson became Dean of Manchester. Five years later, he was appointed Bishop of Birmingham. Susan Wilson, meanwhile, had enrolled as a student nurse at St Thomas's Hospital, London.

Soon, however, she was accepted for training as a doctor and, having qualified in 1962, went to Malawi to undertake primary healthcare in rural villages. In 1971 she took a diploma in Tropical Public Health and later studied Third World Development at Sussex University.

She then had a spell on the staff of the World Health Organisation in Geneva, but found the experience less satisfying than work in the field. But in 1981 she was appointed chief health adviser to Unicef, a post well suited to her talents and experience. Based in New York, she travelled extensively, advising on health care as an integral part of social and economic development.

It was during this time that she came to recognise the importance of the spiritual dimension of healing, and felt called to be a priest.

Ordination was now possible for women in the Anglican Church in America, so she spent two years at the General Theological Seminary in New York before joining the staff of the Church of All Angels on 80th Street, off Broadway, in 1986. Again, the attraction for her was the opportunity to work among the poor, and her medical skills as well as her spiritual insights made an invaluable contribution to this church's ministry to the homeless.

Three years later, having attended a service of celebration for women's ministry in Canterbury Cathedral, she decided to return to England to join those women struggling to be accepted as priests. From 1989 to 1992 she served at Dorchester Abbey, in Oxfordshire, and then spent two years as deacon-in-charge of St Peter's, Drayton.

Although a priest, she accepted this role recognising that it was undesirable for her to celebrate the Eucharist in England until the Church had made up its mind about this issue. This involved disappointing the more militant elements in the movement for the ordination of women, who often urged her to break the rules.

Her work in the parish was greatly valued, and she also conducted retreats and addressed meetings. Her deep spirituality was expressed in her becoming an oblate of the Society of the Sacred Cross at its convent at Tymawr, near Monmouth.

Following the authorisation of women priests in 1994, Susan Cole-King was able to enter more fully into the life of the Church. Such was the esteem in which she was held in Oxford diocese that in 1995 she came top of the poll in the election for the General Synod.

Her experience soon led to her being appointed vice-chairman of the Board of Special Responsibility's international and development committee. She also became an honorary Canon of Christ Church.

She officially retired in 1997, but her concern for the poor and suffering often drew her back to Malawi, whose leaders she tried to persuade to tackle Aids more effectively. In 1998, at the Lambeth Conference, she preached a memorable sermon on suffering.

She married, in 1955 (dissolved 1980), Paul Cole-King. She is survived by three sons and a daughter.

April 9, 2001

Monsignor Patrick Carroll-Abbing

Monsignor Patrick Carroll-Abbing, who has died aged 88, was known as the "Pied Piper of Rome" for his work with street children in Italy.

Carroll-Abbing, who was originally from Ireland, was an official at the Vatican during the Second World War when he started a boys' refuge, known as the "Shoeshine Hotel", in Rome for children orphaned or made homeless by the fighting.

Within two decades he had founded nine "Boys' Towns", a "Girls' Town" and numerous day-care centres throughout Italy, providing homes and education for more than 7,000 children.

John Patrick Carroll-Abbing was born on August 11, 1912 in Co. Dublin into a fervently Roman Catholic family. His three brothers all died young and his rather solitary childhood was spent reading Thackeray, Dickens, Jane Austen, Canon Sheehan and Mrs Henry Wood.

He trained for the priesthood at the English College of the Pontifical University in Rome. After his ordination in 1936, he wanted to go to the diocese of Menevia in predominantly Methodist Wales, but the Vatican authorities decided to keep him in Rome as secretary to Cardinal Pizardo, head of the Holy Office, the central bureau of the Curia.

When war broke out, Carroll-Abbing became voluntary chaplain of the Knights of Malta military hospital in Rome, where he ministered to wounded Italian soldiers. As fighting between the Allies and the German occupiers intensified, he became increasingly concerned about civilian casualties. In February 1944, he created Medical Aid for the Battle Areas, which set up hospitals, provided food and supplies and helped with evacuations.

After the liberation of Italy, Carroll-Abbing was put in charge of all medical supplies sent by American Relief for Italy and was instrumental in setting up clinics and distributing vital foodstuffs across the country. The citizens of Nazi-occupied Rome had been subject to appalling privations, but he was most struck by the thousands of orphaned and homeless children.

"They pushed forward along the road," he recalled in his book *But for the Grace of God* (1966), "barefooted and half-naked, under-nourished and sickly, exposed to every physical and moral danger. I was amazed not by the temptations to which they had succumbed, but by the virtues which they had preserved."

With the approval of Pope Pius XII, Carroll-Abbing opened feeding and clothing centres in cities such as Rome, Palermo, Bari and Naples. He came to know many of the children by name and found places for most of the younger boys in orphanages. The older boys – who had become streetwise, making money by begging, stealing and shining shoes – proved harder to place. "Their illicit activities," he wrote later, "had solved their immediate needs for food, drink and cigarettes. They had grown accustomed to the hardships of the vagabond life."

Carroll-Abbing decided to set up a refuge for the sciuscia (shoeshine boys) in the basement of a bombed-out school near the railway station in Rome. On the first night 30 boys spent the night there and soon it was providing shelter for 100.

Inspired by the Boys' Town founded in America by Father Edward Flanagan, Carroll-Abbing then began to plan a "real town, with streets and houses, workshops and schools" at Tor Marangone on the coast north of Rome.

During the late 1940s, he built up what he described as an industrial village, a sea village and an agricultural village at Tor Marangone, forming the Boys' Republic of Civitavecchia, a democratic community complete with its own elected officials, assembly, courts and even a post office.

By 1957 there were nine Boys' Towns, 40 nurseries and day schools for the children of working mothers, and a Girls' Town at a villa on the outskirts of Rome. Over the next 10 years he established communities in Rome, Palermo, Lucca, Pozzuoli, Chieti and elsewhere, all of which are still in existence.

Carroll-Abbing's other books included *A Chance to Live* (1952), an account of his wartime experiences, and a novel, *Journey to Somewhere* (1955. He was awarded an honorary doctorate from St John's University, New York, the Italian Grand Cross of the Order of Merit and the Gold Medal of the City of Rome.

On the day that Rome was liberated by the Allies, he was awarded the Silver Medal for Valour on the Field of Battle. The citation commended him for rising "up with the fervour of an apostle in defence of humanity tortured and crushed by an oppressor".

July 13, 2001

Brian Brindley

Brian Brindley, who has died aged 69, was a flamboyant Anglo-Catholic canon whose extravagant tastes would have been more easily accommodated in Renaissance Rome than in the postwar Church of England.

Learned, witty and vain, he was for many years one of the great adornments of the General Synod. Indeed, he was probably the most extraordinary-looking clergyman of modern times. He wore his grey curly hair in a style resembling a periwig and dressed in lavish Roman monsignoral attire, including buckled shoes with four-inch heels, which he had painted red.

In another man, such idiosyncrasies would have ensured a career well away from the centres of ecclesiastical power, and it is true that Brindley's parochial ministry never advanced beyond Holy Trinity, Reading, a small Victorian church in one of the least attractive parts of that town.

But he was too cultivated and forceful a character for the Church authorities to ignore, and in the 1980s he became one of the Synod's most effective and popular business managers. He was made an honorary canon of Christ Church, Oxford, in 1986.

There was sadness, therefore, when in the summer of 1989 Brindley's career came to a painfully abrupt end. The *News of the World* printed a front page story based on secretly tape-recorded conversations in which the Canon fantasised about young men. The content was not especially shocking, but he was forced to resign his living after two evangelicals on the Synod circulated photocopies of the tabloid to all 500-odd of their fellow members.

Brian Dominic Frederick Titus Brindley (the second and fourth names were added by himself) was born in London on August 3, 1931 and educated at Stowe, where he developed a life-long love of country houses and an equally strong dislike of Low Church worship.

After National Service in Germany, he read Modern History at Exeter College, Oxford, where he seemed destined for a more sparkling career than he ultimately enjoyed. When the young Princess Margaret visited Oxford she watched a masque in 17th-century style which was written by Brindley and entitled *Porci ante Margeritam* (or "Swine before a Pearl"). Many thought him quite as brilliant as his friends Ned Sherrin and Alan Bennett.

After reading for the Bar in a half-hearted fashion, he settled on the Church and was ordained a priest in 1963 after studying at Ely

Theological College. Some of his friends were surprised at his choice of profession, for Brindley, while fascinated by rubric and liturgy, candidly admitted that he was "not a pious person" and throughout his life he rarely talked about God. He did, however, have an absolutely secure faith in the truth of the Christian religion.

A colour portrait of Brindley which appeared in *Tatler* in 1985 captured the portly cleric at the height of his magnificence, arrayed in a gold Louis XIV chasuble in front of the Pugin screen he rescued from a Birmingham scrapheap.

This, along with the splendid pulpit of All Saints', Oxford, and innumerable candlesticks and reliquaries, transformed Holy Trinity from an undistinguished Gothic box into the boldest and gaudiest of Anglo-Catholic shrines. Fogeyish young men from all over the country made pilgrimages there to peer through the incense at what were arguably the "highest" ceremonies in Anglican history.

Unlike many Anglo-Catholic luminaries, however, Brindley refused to pull up a drawbridge and ignore the rest of the Church of England. As an adviser to the Synod's liturgical commission, he was responsible for changes to the Alternative Service Book ensuring that at least one of its eucharistic prayers was virtually identical to its Roman Catholic equivalent.

Brindley reacted to the sudden ruin of his career with a stoicism and lack of self-pity which deeply impressed his friends. He retired to Brighton, where, after the Church of England voted for women priests, he became a Roman Catholic, taking the name "Leo" as a confirmation name after the Pope who declared Anglican orders null and void. "I felt as if I had been a commercial traveller who had been selling vacuum cleaners for 30 years, only to discover suddenly that they didn't work," he said.

As memories of the scandal faded, he was able to reinvent himself as a writer. He was an inspired chief book reviewer of the *Catholic Herald* and contributed a fortnightly essay to the paper entitled "Charterhouse Chronicles". He also provided calorific recipes for a cookery column in the *Church Times*.

The range of subjects on which Brindley could hold forth authoritatively was breathtaking. They included heraldry, typography, English detective fiction, the architecture of Florence, the gardens of Gertrude Jekyll, the music of Rossini and the prose of Thomas Cranmer (which he thought over-rated). He was also an excellent old-fashioned cook, though some of his guests were intimidated by the heaviness of the cuisine: Brindley was incapable of enjoying even a simple quiche without smothering it in double cream "to make it less rich".

His house in Brighton was, if anything, even more sumptuously decorated than the Royal Pavilion, on which it was partly modelled (and on whose owner he partly modelled himself, Brindley spent vast sums of money reproducing the Pavilion's exquisite chinoiserie, and commissioned a splendid panoramic mural of the building extending over three drawing room walls.

He died surrounded by a dozen of his closest friends, celebrating his 70th birthday at a seven-course dinner at the Athenaeum, he suffered a heart attack between the dressed crab and the boeuf en croute.

August 6, 2001

2002

The Reverend W. A. Criswell

The Reverend W. A. Criswell, who has died aged 92, was a Bible-thumping American preacher revered as the "pope" of the Southern Baptists; the Reverend Billy Graham once described him as "the best preacher I ever heard anywhere".

Criswell, a pastor for 50 years at the First Baptist Church of Dallas, Texas, taught that the Bible is the literal truth and was credited with launching a conservative revolution among evangelical Christians. He wrote 54 books (including *Why I Preach the Bible Is Literally True*) and founded a theological college – Criswell College – as well as four Christian radio stations. He also revived the tradition of the verse-by-verse preaching of the Bible – in the early stages of his ministry, he took 17 years of Sunday sermons to get through the entire Bible.

From his pulpit in Dallas, the white haired, white-suited Criswell fulminated against Darwinists, humanists, liberals, Democrats and anyone who seemed to him to question the historical truth of the Bible. He laughed, he wept, he became enraged one moment and gentle the next, alternating his voice from a whisper to a bellow as the spirit moved him: "On a clear day," he would say, "you can hear me five miles away."

Without notes, but with an open Bible in his hand, Criswell preached about the fires of hell and about the love of God. To make his point he was known to tear out pages while he repeated the mantra: "They say this part isn't true. So let's just throw it away."

Finally, having ripped out the Creation, the Flood, the Virgin birth, the Resurrection and dozens of other stories, he would hold up the few scraps that were left to demonstrate why the Bible was nothing unless people believed every word.

Criswell went to great lengths to prove the literal truth of God's word, even revisiting the 18th-century debate about the origin of fossils – a controversy that paved the way for modern theories of evolution – or "evilution" as Criswell preferred to call it. The alleged discovery of several trilobites in the fossilised sandalled footprint of a man, was proof he claimed, that trilobites had not, as scientists believed, become extinct 230 million years before the appearance of man. "Evilution," he taught, strips mankind of his dignity: "Should we be surprised that children act like animals when they're taught they come from animals?"

Under his leadership the Southern Baptists campaigned to prevent Darwinism being taught in schools and supported a boycott of Disney, criticising some of its films and condemning its practice of offering benefits to same-sex partners of employees. They also enraged American feminists by calling for women to submit graciously to their husbands.

The biblical injunction about rendering unto Caesar the things which are Caesar's, however, seemed to have passed Criswell by. "The notion of separation between church and state was the figment of some infidel's imagination," he said in a CBS television interview in 1984. And he himself had no hesitation about getting involved in politics. For many years he campaigned actively for the Republicans. He led the benediction at the Republican Convention in 1984, calling on God to "bless us as we march to victory and a greater destiny". He fought vigorously to keep John F. Kennedy out of the White House, predicting that his election would lead to "the death of a free church and a free state".

But liberal theologians were his chief target: "Liberals today call themselves moderate," he once observed. "A skunk by any other name still stinks."

He would, he averred, "be more comfortable praying with a Catholic priest who believes in the Virgin Birth, the blood of atonement, and the deity of Christ, than with a liberal Protestant that doesn't." He was, though, capable of changing his mind. For many years, he had opposed having black members in the church, describing black people who had applied to join as "infidels" and integrationism as "heresy". He altered his opinion in 1969, however, telling his deacons: "I came to the profound conclusion that to separate by coercion the body of Christ on the basis of skin pigmentation is unthinkable, un-Christian and unacceptable to God."

Wallie Amos Criswell was born on December 19 1909, at Eldorado, Oklahoma. While he was still a boy, his family moved to Texline, Texas, where his father opened a barber's shop. Wallie had a religious conversion when he was 10, and gave his first sermon during a funeral service for his pet dog.

He graduated from Amarillo High School in 1927, and in the same year was licensed to preach at the First Baptist Church in the town. He went on to Baylor University, where he proved himself an accomplished debater. He briefly considered becoming an actor before studying for six years at the Southern Baptist Theological Seminary at Louisville, Kentucky, where he took a master's degree in Theology and a doctorate in Philosophy.

While still studying, Criswell served as a pastor in small churches in Kentucky, in one of which he met his future wife, Betty Marie Harrie, a schoolteacher and church pianist. After leaving the seminary, he became a full-time pastor at Chiclkasha, Oklahoma, later to move on to the First Church of Muskogee, Oklahoma.

In 1944, aged 34, he was the surprise choice to take over the pulpit at the First Baptist Church of Dallas, succeeding the highly influential George W Truett, who had led the congregation from 1897.

In his first sermon, Criswell set out his vision: "We'll go on and up," he promised. "We'll give to missions more money then ever before. We'll have Sunday School with 5,000 in attendance every Sunday and the services in the church will be in the eye of God."

He was as good as his word. Over the next 50 years, his congregation grew from 6,000 to a peak of 28,000, with 21 missions across the city and annual donations exceeding $12 million. In his mission to save souls for God, nothing was too much for Criswell, who dressed up as a rabbit to hand out Easter eggs to children, and donned a cowboy outfit and 10-gallon hat for the church's annual barbecue.

By the 1960s, Criswell had become the most powerful leader among Southern Baptists, and he served twice as president of the

Southern Baptist Convention, the world's largest Protestant denomination. He preached and conducted evangelising crusades around the world and was a guest of Pope Paul VI in Rome.

Criswell became Senior Pastor at his church in 1991 and Pastor Emeritus in 1995.

His immediate successor departed less than two years after being appointed, accusing Criswell of being unwilling to let go of the reins. The struggle for power inspired David Rambo's play *God's Man in Texas*.

W. A. Criswell is survived by his wife and their daughter.

January 12, 2002

The Reverend Joseph Fahey

The Reverend Joseph Fahey, who has died aged 65, played blackjack "for the greater glory of God", donating his winnings to the Jesuit order.

Fahey was considered a mathematical prodigy and played the blackjack tables from Atlantic City to Las Vegas. Among the sequins, gilt and glitz, he struck an incongruous figure in his shabby blue suit, but he always managed to beat the odds. Blackjack – his chosen game – offers the best odds of any in a casino, but is nonetheless one of the highest earners for casino owners. Fahey, unlike most customers, exploited its possibilities to the full.

Ever true to his vow of poverty, Fahey donated tens of thousands of dollars to Jesuit missions and, as president of Boston College High School from 1988 to 1998, boosted the school's endowment by 500 per cent, financing an athletics centre, library and computer laboratory.

Fahey's view that God and Mammon were perfectly compatible was not one shared by the casinos, which eventually blacklisted him. Card-counting, although not illegal and well beyond the capacity of most casino customers, significantly alters the odds in the punter's favour.

But despite the casinos' hostility, Fahey refused to be beaten and at the end of each term he would give his students a lesson on card counting and how to beat the odds at blackjack. The class was always well attended. As one of his colleagues observed, Fahey understood and affirmed "the Catholic mission of Loyola with its Jesuit emphasis on academic rigour and the integration of learning".

Joseph Fahey was born in 1936. After studying economics at Boston College, he received a doctorate in economics at the Massachusetts Institute of Technology with a thesis on how a local income tax or sales tax would affect Boston's economy. He studied divinity at the Weston Jesuit School of Theology and was ordained priest in 1968.

Fahey taught economics at Holy Cross College, Worcester, Massachusetts, from 1968, becoming dean of academics from 1971 to 1981. Fahey also taught at Boston College, serving as academic vice-president and dean of faculties.

He was president of Boston College High School from 1988 to 1998 and became a member of the boards of trustees of the Catholic Schools Foundation.

Fahey was a trustee of several Jesuit institutions, including the Loyola University of Chicago, and served on the Commission on Institutions of Higher Education for the New England Association of Schools and Colleges.

At the time of his death, Fahey was provincial assistant for finance of the New England Province for the Jesuit order.

January 26, 2002

Praise for *Naked Came the Florida Man*

"Can it still be hurricane season? Must be, because here come Serge A. Storms and his perpetually stoned bro, Coleman, in Tim Dorsey's gonzo crime caper *Naked Came the Florida Man*."
—*The New York Times Book Review*

"Dorsey's latest in the humorous crime fiction category highlights that outrageous brand of Florida humor. With chaos always at his side, Serge A. Storms is back, and this time, he's on a cemetery tour across the state, investigating an urban myth that just might be real and causing mayhem along the way."
—*Parade*

"Upping the ante has always been the strategy for Tim Dorsey's books, which are built on a peculiarly Floridian brand of outrageousness. So it's no surprise that in his latest, *Naked Came the Florida Man,* Dorsey reaches a new high."
—*Newsday*

"Readers with an appetite for gallows humor will be sated."
—*Publishers Weekly* (starred review)

"The newest laugh-out-loud adventure of vigilante Serge A. Storms and his partner in crime, Coleman, on the hunt for justice in the Sunshine State. This time, the pair sets out to investigate an urban legend—with hilarious and rollicking results."
—*Newsweek*

"What more can I say about Tim Dorsey, whose capacity to churn out rollicking, ribald, comic crime thrillers shows no sign of waning in his latest Serge A. Storms effort, *Naked Came the Florida Man. . . .* Packed with verve and vibrancy. Along, of course, with laugh-out-loud, side-splitting fun."
—BookTrib

NAKED CAME THE
Florida Man

NAKED CAME THE
Florida Man

Tim Dorsey

wm

WILLIAM MORROW
An Imprint of HarperCollins*Publishers*

NAKED CAME THE FLORIDA MAN. Copyright © 2020 by Tim Dorsey. All rights reserved. Printed in the United States of America. No part of this book may be used or reproduced in any manner whatsoever without written permission except in the case of brief quotations embodied in critical articles and reviews. For information, address HarperCollins Publishers, 195 Broadway, New York, NY 10007.

HarperCollins books may be purchased for educational, business, or sales promotional use. For information, please email the Special Markets Department at SPsales@harpercollins.com.

A hardcover edition of this book was published in 2020 by William Morrow, an imprint of HarperCollins Publishers.

FIRST WILLIAM MORROW PAPERBACK EDITION PUBLISHED 2020.

Library of Congress Cataloging-in-Publication Data has been applied for.

ISBN 978-0-06-279594-6

20 21 22 23 24   LSC   10 9 8 7 6 5 4 3 2 1

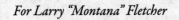

For Larry "Montana" Fletcher

Prologue

2017

Don't shoot guns into the hurricane."

Elsewhere this would go without saying, but Floridians need to be told.

This was an actual warning issued by the Pasco County Sheriff's Office just north of Tampa Bay as a major storm approached. After all, a local man had just been arrested for DUI when he tried to order a taco in a Bank of America drive-through.

The alert was a reaction to people posting plans on the Internet for a party to shoot at the hurricane and make it turn away. The sheriff's notice even included a scientific diagram showing how the vortex of the core could curve bullet paths to come back and hit the shooter.

"Shooting at a hurricane!" said Serge. "That's the most brainless thing I've ever heard!"

Coleman looked out the rear window of their muscle car racing over a bridge. "Why is everyone else driving the other way?"

"Because they're evacuating. It's the smart move."

"Then shouldn't we be evacuating?"

"Absolutely not," said Serge, turning on tactical silicone windshield wipers. "They have to flee because they don't know what they're doing. We're professionals."

"How's that?"

"Everyone else gets ready for storms according to the official instructions." Serge reached under his seat. "Which is fine if you want to survive. But if you're taking it to the next level, all that jazz will just slow you down. Hurricanes are the marrow of Florida history, and my history always goes bone-deep. That's why I prepare for storms with an encyclopedic set of state guidebooks, every conceivable new gadget, and bags of provisions exclusively from the candy and snack aisles. Think about it: Little kids are programmed to thrive and that's the first place they go. That's how a pro has to think."

"I'm still not sure." Coleman flicked a Bic. "We're like the only car heading this direction."

"I've taken every conceivable precaution," said Serge, absentmindedly waving a pistol out the window as Coleman did a bong hit. "What can possibly go wrong?"

1928

The bloated, decaying body rolled into the ditch.

It fell onto its back, cloudy eyes still wide open, creating a frozen expression that bookmarked the last thoughts from a long, brutal life of hardship, hunger, harrow and few complaints. The final thought in those eyes: *What kind of shit* now?

"It creeps me out the way he's staring like that," said a voice at the top of the ditch.

"He's staring at God," said someone else, grabbing a pair of lifeless ankles.

Another body tumbled down the dirt embankment, and another, and so forth. The dead were all African American, just like the dozens of perspiring, shirtless men laboring with shovels.

The shovel gang most likely would have pitched in anyway, out of a sense of community, but this time they didn't have a choice. They occasionally glanced back at the white lawmen with shotguns propped against their shoulders and pools of tobacco spit at their feet.

"What are you looking at—!" The next word was impolite.

It actually should have been quite a nice day in late September. The sky was clear as a dream, and a cooling breeze swept over the fields covered with thousands of tulip-shaped orange wildflowers. The wind made the acres of bright petals sway as one, back and forth, like an immense school of tropical fish. Then the sun rose higher, and the breeze left. The air became stubbornly still, baking in that Central Florida humidity so thick it seemed to have weight. But worst of all:

It stank.

Blame history. It doesn't bother to knock. It doesn't even come in the front door. It's like those newspaper articles about a car that crashes through the wall of a bedroom in the middle of the night. This was before storms had alphabetical names, and it was called the Great Hurricane of 1928. Later it would become the forgotten storm. The victims didn't have money.

It began the afternoon of September 15. All the fancy weather instruments that now give residents a head start on hurricanes had yet to be invented. You'd be chopping carrots for a stew, and then a hurricane was just *there*. But if you were really paying attention over the years, there was one early-warning system. The Seminoles.

Something about pollen and a rapid blooming of the sawgrass. The Indians watched the plants down in the swamp, and when a low haze in front of the setting sun got that weird color, they seemed to know the exact moment to make for high ground. Many scientists have looked into the phenomenon and scoffed at the notion. But the Seminoles were always dependably on the move before each Big Wind, so they'd figured something out.

This time, the tribe had come up out of the Everglades on trails leading to the ramshackle towns of South Bay and Belle Glade, then made a right turn toward West Palm Beach. There was no panic in their march. Simply a parade of native families out for a very long stroll. Some of the townsfolk remembered a similar migration two years earlier, before a lesser hurricane, and decided to follow the Indians out. But most stayed put.

On the morning of September 17, the storm that had peaked at category five made landfall at the Jupiter Inlet lighthouse in northern Palm Beach County. More than a thousand homes were destroyed along the coast before it continued churning inland, unimpressed . . .

Now, a few days later, the digging of massive, macabre pits continued with a sense of urgency. Fear of disease swept the survivors, and in the immediate aftermath the locals were on their own. Many of them were about halfway up the east side of the big lake, which would be Okeechobee, in an empty place that would soon become known for its mass grave, which would be Port Mayaca.

The same frantic scene was replaying itself miles away, in opposite directions, at two other South Florida locations. Even as mass graves go, there wasn't remotely enough room. At least two and a half thousand dead by most accounts. Some said more than three. The nation's worst toll ever, save for the Galveston storm in 1900.

Here was the problem with the hurricane of '28: the storm surge. That's often the case, and almost without exception, the deadly waves come from the ocean. But this time around, death didn't come from the sea; one of the strongest hurricanes in recorded history made a direct hit on the nation's largest fresh-water lake sitting within a state. Who saw that coming? There was no dike, and the storm's rotation easily shoved much of the lake's contents south, in an inescapable ten-to-twenty-foot wall of water that blanketed hundreds of square miles.

In the following hours and days, the water began to recede, and then came the snakes, but that's another story.

As the overwhelming scale of death became clear, they started digging a second grave pit on the other side of the lake in some unknown place called Ortona, and then a third in West Palm Beach, just off Tamarind Avenue. It was back-numbing work for all those residents pressed into service. But here's what really pissed them off: The bodies of black victims filled the pits as fast as they could be thrown in on top of one another. Each white person got their own private pine box.

Then those boxes were loaded onto wagons and taken to the nearby Woodlawn Cemetery for proper burial.

A shotgun man stuck two fingers in his mouth for a shrill whistle that got everyone's attention. Shovels stopped.

"You three! Over there!" The shotgun waved east. "They need more help!"

A trio of drained men trudged toward a separate pile of work, and stared down at a pale corpse.

"Great. The pine boxes," said one of the larger men, named Goat. "I don't mind burying our own, but this is bullshit."

"Just grab him," said a stubby but deceptively strong neighbor. He went by "Stub."

The first worker began lifting the body by the armpits, then suddenly dropped him and jumped back.

"What the hell's gotten into you?" said Stub.

Goat just pointed with a quivering arm. "He's got a bullet hole!"

"Where?"

"In the forehead."

"Jesus, you're right!"

They composed themselves and lifted him into a box, providing a better view. "Wait a minute, I know this guy. It's Mr. Fakakta."

"Who's that?"

"Sugar man," said Goat. "Lived in that big colonial house out past the bend by the ice plant."

"That big place in Pahokee was his?"

"Ain't doing him no good now."

They grabbed the next body, a woman, and just as promptly dropped it.

"She's got a bullet hole, too," said Stub.

"That's his wife," said Goat.

"What on earth is going on?"

The pair quickly scanned nearby bodies. "There's his son. Head almost blown off . . ."

Stub was Catholic, made the sign of the cross. "*Ave Maria*."

Goat glanced back twenty yards and watched a stream of brown juice shoot from between gapped teeth. "Think we should tell the deputy?"

"Definitely," said Goat. "Some monster murdered this whole poor family—"

A shotgun blast went skyward.

Everyone froze.

"Shut up over there and get back to work!" barked the lawman.

The pair nodded respectfully, then began hammering penny nails into the lid of a pine box. "Screw 'em."

Part One

Chapter 1

Help me!" yelled Coleman. "I'm trapped again!"

"Hold on. I've got my own problems." Serge pushed away a piece of plywood and crawled out from under a debris pile of dresser drawers, chunks of ceiling and a toilet lid. He stood to examine all his scratches and bruises, but saw nothing major. He looked around. "Okay, Coleman, where are you?"

"I don't have a clue."

"No, I mean just keep talking and I'll follow your voice."

"Okay," said Coleman. "Hey, Serge, I just realized that 'slow up' and 'slow down' mean the same thing. That's fucked. I'm still stoned."

Serge cleared a path, pushing aside fractured furniture. "Keep talking."

"Have you seen my weed anywhere out there?"

Serge cast aside a torn-down kitchen cabinet and lifted a soaked mattress. "There you are."

Coleman sat up, and his face suddenly reddened as a cord from mangled window blinds tightened around his neck.

Serge flicked open a pocketknife and sliced the thin rope. "Don't you know that's a choking hazard?"

"I didn't have a choice." Coleman rubbed his neck. "It just got me."

Serge stood again and stared thoughtfully at the bright, panoramic view out the front of the building where the wall used to be. "It got everyone."

Coleman checked his own bruises. "Is it over?"

"All over but the shouting," said Serge.

Coleman joined him, looking out across the calm waters of Bogie Channel. "So that was the big Hurricane Irma everyone was talking about?"

Serge would have opened the door, but there wasn't one. He hopped down from the building and walked toward the street. The only sound was the crunch of gravel and broken glass under his sneakers. The air had turned mild and comfortable, nothing to betray what had come before.

Serge placed hands on his hips as he surveyed what had recently been a historic row of quaint old fishing cottages in the backcountry of the Florida Keys. All had been knocked off their foundations, lying helter-skelter practically on top of each other.

Unless you've seen the aftermath of a major hurricane, you wouldn't realize how much of the damage appears to be the result of high explosives. Little pieces of shrapnel everywhere. Slivers and confetti. Most of the other cottages were missing their front walls as well, allowing the wind to go to work inside like sticks of dynamite. Cabin number 7 had no walls at all, just a roof lying on the ground, which had been pushed against the base of a palm tree that neatly cut it open like a jigsaw. The cabin with the least damage, still barely clinging together and listing like a floundering ship off the edge of its concrete slab, was number 5.

Serge looked the other way, toward the landmark two-story clapboard office and bait store at the Old Wooden Bridge Fishing Camp. It had stood apart from the cabins, alone, unprotected, with no trees to shield it on the edge of the channel. Now there was little evidence there had ever been an office, except for the matchbook-size pieces that littered the ground and floated in the water like another bomb had gone off.

Serge wiped his eyes.

"Are you starting to cry?" asked Coleman.

"Why couldn't it have taken out a Starbucks or some shit? We keep losing all our best places." He blew his nose. "I'd bet the bat tower on Sugarloaf is gone, too."

It was.

One of the island's endangered miniature Key deer sprang from the brush and bounded through the debris like an antelope.

"I've never seen one run that fast," said Coleman.

"I'm sure it has a lot on its mind."

Coleman turned back around toward their cottage. "Jesus, we could have been killed! Why did you want to stay here and ride out that hurricane? Didn't you realize it would be this hairy?"

Another doe darted by.

"I knew it would be strong," said Serge. "But these little deer always figure out how to make it through storms, so I figured how hard can it be? Second, I love cabin number five."

"It's your favorite," said Coleman. "You always kiss the number by the door when you first arrive."

"I knew that if God would allow just a single cottage to survive relatively intact, it would be Five. I figured this island would get pretty much torn up, so I wanted to spend a final night in that special place. And last but not least, I seriously miscalculated."

"Wait. Stop," said Coleman. "You mean we really could have been killed? But you promised me I'd be safe."

Serge pulled car keys from his pocket. "What was I thinking?"

"Hey, where are you going?"

They don't call it Big Pine Key for nothing. The day before, Serge had found a spot where he was able to back his car about twenty yards into the woods, surrounded by thick pine trees. The kind of place where the little deer hide.

"It barely has a mark on her," said Coleman. "So we're heading out of here now?"

Serge shook his head and opened the trunk. "It will take a few days for workers to clear the roads, so we'll be camping until then. Help me with this gear."

They pitched a tent with sleeping bags behind the row of battered cabins. A small campfire began to glow in a little pit surrounded by rocks. Bottled water and beer cans bobbed in the melted ice of a cooler. Serge returned to the car for a last item and brought it back to the fire.

"What's that thing?" asked Coleman.

"The beginning of my latest science project." Serge sat down with a clear plastic storage bin in his lap. He opened his pocketknife again and poked a six-inch grid of tiny holes on the end. Then he taped a small, battery-powered fan over it. Then another grid on the opposite end. "This project has an extremely long gestation, and I don't know when it'll come into play, so we might as well use this downtime to get a head start."

Serge grabbed a soggy package from the cooler. He took the lid off the bin and began evenly arranging the bag's contents across the bottom.

"Bacon?" asked Coleman.

"Your universal food group."

"It's the only thing that goes great with everything," said Coleman. "Eggs, pickles, ice cream, Twinkies, other bacon. It's just impossible to go wrong."

"You can with this pack. It seriously spoiled overnight." Serge held out a slimy, uncooked strip. "Unless you dig trichinosis."

"I'll stick to beer," said Coleman. "But why are you putting it in that bin?"

"Read it in a medical journal," Serge said. "In our advanced world of modern medicine, sometimes the best treatment is still low-tech."

"Treatment for what?"

"I'm not treating anything, just using the principle for my experiment," said Serge. "All will be revealed in due time."

Serge finished his task and picked up the bin. He walked over to the edge of the woods, setting it down behind his car . . .

TWO DAYS LATER

Serge listened to the morning news on his emergency radio. He reached inside their small dome tent and began shaking Coleman to no avail. "Come on, wake up! The road's clear. It's time to go."

Serge shook harder and harder until he heard primitive groans. Then Coleman woke up all at once. He had somehow managed to turn himself around in his sleeping bag during the night.

"Help! Help! Something's got me again."

"It's just your sleeping bag. Hold still."

But Coleman had the reasoning ability of someone drowning. "Help! Help!" He thrashed around like a giant caterpillar trying to molt. Then he jumped up and dislodged the tent's poles, and soon he was wrapped up in that, too, rolling left and right.

Serge watched without expression until his pal wore himself out. A piled entanglement of nylon heaved as he panted.

"You finished?" asked Serge. "Because the tent isn't completely wrecked yet."

"Just get me out of this."

Serge extricated his friend and they began breaking camp.

When everything was stowed in the car, Serge walked over to his science project. "Well, I'll be. It worked." He sealed the lid on the storage bin, started the battery-powered fan and stuck the whole business in the back seat.

A gold 1969 Plymouth Satellite emerged from the trees and drove away from the Old Wooden Bridge Fishing Camp. Soon, they were almost out of the Lower Keys, approaching the bridge to Bahia Honda. The debris piles that had been pushed aside by heavy equipment appeared like small mountain ranges down each side of the highway.

"Discussion time. Where were we?"

"When?" asked Coleman.

"I don't know. The hurricane destroyed our train of thought," said Serge. "Which is a plus because a train of thought is just another one of society's cages."

"Why don't we talk about society?" asked Coleman. "Your thoughts?"

"These are dark times." Serge tapped fingers on the steering wheel. "The decline of society can be boiled down to the culture of airline flights."

"I've seen the videos on the Internet."

"You take a couple hundred people from our savagely polarized nation, cram them cheek by jowl in a metal tube and send them up to altitudes where there's no oxygen. Then people read the headlines: 'Wow, I didn't see *that* coming,'" said Serge. "Plane travel used to be glamorous, people getting dressed up, wearing hats. But now it's devolved into a subway in the sky, cursing, shoving, public urination, removing socks from smelly feet."

Coleman popped a can of Schlitz. "Preach."

"It starts before you're even off the ground," said Serge. "Especially if you're in one of those planes where the coach passengers have to walk through first class to get to their seats. It trends Darwin in a serious hurry. First-class passengers watch the coach people walking past them in the aisle and they're like, 'Yeah, you lazy losers, this is what you get for being assholes: inadequate legroom.' . . . Simultaneously, all the coach passengers are checking out the elite in their giant, comfy seats: 'That one clearly doesn't deserve to be up here.' 'What has this guy ever brought to the table?' 'There's another cosmic mistake of seating assignment.' 'Don't even get me started on this prick.' . . . Then on the next flight, for whatever reason, some of the first-class people have to fly coach and vice versa, and they all immediately switch teams: 'God, I hate those fuckers.'"

"Then the plane takes off and the fun really begins," said Coleman.

"Something about flying makes people lose their freaking minds," said Serge. "And I'm not talking about getting grumpy over the food or a kid kicking the back of your seat. I recently spoke with some flight attendants, and the true stories of psychotic breaks at thirty thousand feet would send you screaming for Amtrak. They said the public would be amazed at the number of people who freak out and try to open the doors."

"It's a senseless crime," said Coleman.

"That's why flight crews have to carry so many handcuffs nowadays," said Serge. "One woman was refused alcohol, so she drank liquid soap and bit a stewardess. Two groups of football fans had a brawl from rows seventeen to twenty-eight. During night flights, passengers ask for blankets and then leave spent condoms in seat pockets. Guys take off their shirts, try to light cigarettes, sleep on the floor."

"Sounds like every traffic intersection in Florida."

"And I swear this one's true: Another dude jumped up on the serving cart, dropped his pants and took a dump in the peanut basket. I think you lose frequent flier points for that one."

"It's just not right," said Coleman, pointing out the window at a jet overhead. "There's one now."

"Take a pass on the peanuts."

They were four miles into the Seven Mile Bridge. "Oh man!" said Serge. "Irma whacked Pigeon Key!"

"What's that?"

"Coleman, you've asked the same question the last fifty times we've driven over this bridge!"

"Was I here?"

"Under the old Seven Mile, it's all deep water, except partway across there's a single peculiar little island under the piers, with a steep ramp rolling down to it. Very popular with postcard photographers," said Serge. "Tourists driving down to Key West on the new bridge can't miss it. They all look over and go: 'Aw, how cute.'"

"Like a puppy?"

"Roughly the same level of low-grade gratification. But then puzzlement sets in, especially when they see the ramp. 'What the hell is its deal?'"

"Serge, please tell us."

"I cannot deny the public!" He leaned toward the window for a closer look. "A bunch of Henry Flagler's people lived there when they were working on the oil baron's Overseas Railroad, which opened in 1912 and at one point had four thousand employees toiling under the sun to erect it."

"You said 'erect.'" Coleman giggled. "I see a bunch of wooden buildings that got clobbered."

"Some of the most beautiful examples of old Keys wooden construction. You'll find verandas and gables and tin roofs. Tin is key to my roofing pleasure . . . Damn, it even hit the Honeymoon Cottage."

"They look kind of familiar."

"That's because back in Key West I've dragged you through every art gallery on Duval Street."

"I hate that!"

"I've noticed," said Serge. "Might have something to do with the galleries being sandwiched between the bars."

"So close and yet so far," said Coleman. "I also hate it because whenever we go in galleries it means you're going to get me in a headlock."

"You won't look at the paintings otherwise. You just keep pointing out the door with a trembling arm: '*Beer,*'" said Serge. "Culturing you up requires wrestling moves."

"But then they always throw us out."

"It's so unfair," said Serge. "Doesn't opening a gallery mean they want people to admire art? And that's what we're doing, minding our own business looking at paintings with you in a full nelson. But no, they want us to do it *their* way. I try to explain that the whole concept of art is about individual expression, and I haven't seen any signs that say 'No Wrestling.' They just fixate and respond that all your thrashing to get free is driving away the others."

A burp. "And breaking vases."

"That's on them. They distracted me and your arms got loose."

A fresh can of Schlitz popped. "What were we talking about?"

"The buildings that look familiar to you on Pigeon Key," said Serge. "Before we got eighty-sixed from those galleries of shame, you'd seen dozens of killer paintings depicting quaint pastel cottages with fiery azaleas under vibrant coconut palms. A disproportionate number are from that little island under the bridge, because artists are always setting up easels down there to feel the muse. My favorites are the watercolors. Nothing captures the palette of the Keys like that medium, and I always get pumped visiting Pigeon Key and watching them work. They seem so happy. So I point out that the best art is spawned from a tortured soul, and offer to help. But here's the thing I've learned about these art types: They're highly sensitive, and as a general rule they don't like their easels knocked over when you wrestle."

The Plymouth came off the Seven Mile Bridge into Marathon.

Coleman hung out the window. "Man, there's a whole lot less trash on the sides of the road."

"It's amazing what a difference twenty miles one way or the other makes when the eye comes ashore."

Coleman pulled himself back inside the window and shot-gunned the Schlitz. "Where to now?"

"Where we were going before the hurricane interrupted us," said Serge. "Continuing our cemetery tour of Florida."

"Is that what we were doing?"

"Cemeteries rock! They're portals to our roots with all the obvious history, not to mention upbeat landscaping and bitchin' statuary," said Serge. "The perfect places for a picnic, except I always seem to be the only one with a basket and checkered blanket."

"And playing a kazoo," said Coleman. "Remember the one time they were lowering that guy into the ground?"

"I thought the music would cheer them up."

"Instead they stomped your picnic basket."

"That's the downside of cemeteries," said Serge. "The only occasions most people go is when there's a lot of hysterical crying and they drag a dead body along. I don't have room for that kind of negativity."

The Plymouth crossed a couple of small bridges onto Grassy Key. Serge made a left turn near mile marker 58.

Coleman's head was back out the window, staring at a round, blue-and-yellow sign.

DOLPHIN RESEARCH CENTER.

"This doesn't look like a cemetery."

"It's not *technically* one," said Serge. "But I'm including famous individual grave sites. My tour, my rules."

"So who's buried here?"

Serge parked. "Follow and find out."

Moments later, the pair stood solemnly in a secluded corner of the property near the water, crowded by mangroves and other lush vegetation. In the middle of the plants was a statue. There was a marker below it. Serge knelt with a large sheet of paper and a block of colored wax, making a grave rubbing.

Coleman scratched his head and squinted at the statue of a tail-walking dolphin. "I thought you were taking me to where some scientist or soldier was buried."

Serge continued lightly rubbing. "Back in the day, this majestic creature was arguably the most famous Floridian in the whole country."

Coleman read over Serge's shoulder. "Flipper?"

"The iconic dolphin was introduced to the world in 1963, but few viewers realized the star was actually a female dolphin named Mitzi. And even fewer know that this is her final resting place."

"But why here?"

"Before becoming the research center in 1984, this place opened in 1958 as a roadside attraction named Santini's Porpoise School, and Hollywood came calling. Mitzi trained and resided here until passing away in 1972." Serge stood with his wax rubbing in hand and sniffled.

Coleman put a hand on his shoulder. "You okay, buddy?"

"We're in the presence of gentle greatness," said Serge. "Mitzi was a genius in the industry, able to pop out of the water and make clicking sounds that caused humans to respond: 'What is it, Flipper? You say that an evil research scientist trying to poach rare tropical fish is trapped in his personal submarine near the coral reef surrounded by unexploded mines from World War Two training exercises?'"

"Wow," said Coleman. "Next to that, 'Timmy fell in the well' makes Lassie look like an idiot."

Chapter 2

EIGHT YEARS EARLIER

Just before dawn. The horizon was on fire.

Literally.

Across hundreds of distant acres, bright orange flames whipped violently in the wind.

The sky began to lighten, revealing dozens of columns of black smoke rising hundreds of feet along the rim of the Everglades.

A rusty 1968 Ford pickup truck raced down a lonely dirt road, kicking up a dust plume. The truck was dark red, and the Florida outdoors had made the metal rough like sandpaper. The dirt road stretched through uninhabited miles of open fields. The road was elevated like a causeway, and on each side were canals. Water flowed broadly from Lake Okeechobee down into the Everglades, giving it the nickname River of Grass. The canals had been dug to divert the water and create hundreds of square miles of arable farmland. The canals were deep, and vehicles regularly sank in them. Drownings weren't rare. The pickup truck stayed in the center of the bumpy road, bouncing on old springs. Its bumper was held on by twisted coat hangers and rope. It was doing fifty. The bed of the truck was full of children.

Most of the children held empty canvas sacks and pillowcases. Their clothing was hand-me-down-and-down-again. Striped pullover shirts and ripped denim shorts and even a pair of swim trunks. The ones who had shoes didn't have shoelaces. There was a lot of chatter and laughing in the back of the truck. Bragging. Who had been champions in the past, and who would do even better today. Then the merriment trailed off. They were getting close.

The pickup sped straight toward the nearest fire. It approached upwind, but smoke still wafted over the truck. Some of the kids pulled the necks of their shirts up over their noses and mouths . . .

Palm Beach is the largest of the state's sixty-seven counties, and this was the *other* Palm Beach, the unknown one. Along the Atlantic shore: Worth Avenue, the Breakers Hotel, Rolls-Royce and Mar-a-Lago. On the opposite side, along Lake Okeechobee: boarded-up buildings, empty streets, burglar bars and poverty so corrosive that even the local prison moved out.

The area is now oddly known for only two things: sugar and football players.

These burning fields are where they meet.

From October to April, the harvest is on, and some of the nation's largest sugar growers set fire to their fields in controlled burns that remove leaves and weeds, making way for the mechanical harvesters. The procedure is done with straight lines and right angles. There will be a giant, perfectly square patch of flat, jet-black land where the last burn took place, right next to a thriving green square of waving cane stalks. From the air it looks like a checkerboard. When the fire and smoke start, the children head out, from Pahokee to Belle Glade to South Bay and Harlem.

The '68 pickup skidded to a stop on the dirt road, and the kids in the back hopped out over both sides like troops jumping down from a combat helicopter. They took off running full speed across a black square, their sacks flapping by their sides. Ahead, a wall of cane. The far half of the field was already on fire. They charged into rows of stalks that would soon also be ablaze.

It was a decades-old tradition.

They were hunting rabbits. By hand.

But this wasn't some thrill sport like running with the bulls in Pamplona. It was economic. Each pelt brought a few dollars, and what was left was dinner. Only if you lived around here could you realize how much of a difference that made. From years of experience passed down by word of mouth, even the youngest kids knew how to approach a burning field and head off the rabbits being flushed out.

The kids continued sprinting with all they had, smoke getting thicker. Then they saw them. The first child planted his foot and cut sharply left, diving through a row of stalks and pouncing. A cottontail went into his pillowcase. Then another child cut right, diving on another rabbit. Then another child, and so on as sacks filled.

The cottontails weren't exactly easy to grab, but the jackrabbits were another matter entirely. Almost nobody could lay a hand on them. Almost. Some of those who had accomplished the feat . . . well, everyone knew where they were now.

Amazingly, this short strip of tiny towns along the bottom of Lake Okeechobee has produced more than sixty players in the National Football League. A number so insane that there must be a catch. Word got around, and soon, each fall at high school games, there were almost as many college football scouts in the stands as parents. At first the scouts couldn't believe what they saw. But seeing was believing. These kids were *fast*. Except how was it possible, so many players from such a small area?

The legend began.

Chasing rabbits.

It didn't lead down to Alice's Wonderland, but turned them into professional football players. It even reached a point where ESPN sent journalists down to cover the hunts in the cane fields, reporting how the kids could nimbly cut, change direction and speed up again as the rabbits required. It was a heartwarming myth, but the real reason was more sobering: The kids had been dealt such a cruel hand of hardship at birth that it cultivated a fierce drive to succeed.

And on this particular day, instinct kicked in again. The children knew in their blood exactly when they had pushed it to the last second toward the advancing fire. Then they retreated as fast as they had charged in, regrouping joyously in the safety of the adjacent blackened field, peeking down into their sacks and comparing their hauls. One had four cottontails and proclaimed himself champion of the day, until a heated dispute and a recount. Another sack actually contained a fifth bunny. Hooray!

Then on to the next burning field. Young, lanky boys who had just experienced a growth spurt raced into the cane stalks, dashing and darting with stunning speed. Behind them came the younger kids from grade school, who idolized the older boys and tried to be just like them. They weren't nearly as fast but getting there. They caught the occasional cottontail, but most of the quarry eluded their grasp as they fell facedown in the dirt, and the older boys laughed. Then there was one final youth, the scrawniest of all. Named Chris. But lack of weight didn't affect this child's velocity; in fact it seemed to help. Chris ran on tiptoes. And was surprisingly consistent, nabbing at least one rabbit per field. Then, just as consistently, an older boy would snatch the animal away. "Give me that!" And shove Chris to the ground. "Now go play with your Barbie dolls."

Poverty prevented a lot of things, but not bullying.

They reached the next field and the mad hunt was on again. This time Chris actually came up with *two* rabbits, one in each hand, grinning ear to ear, until getting slammed to the ground again. The critters went in older boys' sacks. Chris just jumped up and took off after another cottontail.

The pickup truck arrived at the last field of the day. This time the haul was so bountiful that the kids pushed the time envelope beyond good judgment. Most were coughing on smoke, feeling the heat of nearby burning stalks, eyes watering as they dove for one more bunny.

Moments later, they burst out of the cane field, initially stunned silent by their own success, then celebrating. As the joy died down and the stinging in their eyes cleared, an odd sensation arrived. Something seemed off. Just a vague gut feeling.

"Is someone not here?"

"Where's Chris?"

"Shit!"

Three of the older boys dashed back into different rows on the edge of the cane field that was rapidly reaching full burn. After only ten yards in, one of the boys found a much younger, skinny kid with a big grin and a bigger jackrabbit.

"Gimme that thing!"

The grin left town. "No! It's mine! I caught him!"

The older boy seized the rabbit by the scruff of the neck, and used his other hand to shove the smaller child down into the dirt and smoke. The child clawed in the soil and fought for breath.

"Now get the fuck up and follow me," said the larger youth. "And don't tell anyone about the jackrabbit or I'll kick your fucking ass! I know where you live!"

The rest of the gang was waiting in the harmless black square, watching nervously as flames grew higher and nearer.

Finally someone pointed. "They're coming out!"

The older boy raised his trophy in triumph.

"Look!"

"James caught a *jack*rabbit!"

"He's going to play college ball for sure!"

On the ride back to Pahokee, the bed of the pickup was much louder than usual. Laughter and tall tales. Everyone had rabbits in their sack. Except one.

Chris just sulked with chin down, the way most of these trips ended.

The others wondered why Chris even bothered to come along. After all, she was a girl.

Chapter 3

THE FLORIDA KEYS

Piles of hurricane debris continued to appear down the sides of the road as if snowplows had been at work. Branches, dresser drawers, broken mirrors, toilets, tires, ceiling fans, cans of food, ripped shirts, rolls of carpet, a deflated basketball and a cuckoo clock.

A Plymouth Satellite raced east.

"Stop the car!" yelled Coleman. "Stop the car!"

Serge screeched the brakes and skidded off the side of the highway.

"Jesus! What is it?"

"Wait here." Coleman jumped out and waddled fifty yards before reaching into the trash. He returned and climbed back in the passenger seat.

Serge pulled back onto the highway. "What have you got there?"

"Check it out!" Coleman thrust his arm an inch from Serge's eyes.

Serge swatted it away. "I'm driving over here."

Coleman cradled his find and brushed off dirt. "It's a squeeze bottle for Florida honey. I remember these from when I was a kid. See? It's a cute smiling alligator from one of those roadside places."

"The old citrus stands," said Serge. "The kind that sold tourists boxes of navel oranges that got crushed by baggage handlers and leaked on the luggage belts, leaving sticky slicks that contaminated other people's suitcases in our state's way of saying, 'Please visit!'"

Coleman twisted off the top and stuck an eyeball in the hole. "I'd been watching the road for something like this."

"You're kidding." Serge looked quickly toward the passenger side. "You were seriously looking for a cool vintage souvenir?"

"Oh, sure. It's just what I wanted."

Serge turned back toward the road and shook his head with a smile. "Well, I'll be. There's hope for you yet . . ."

A half hour later, the gold Satellite sat on the side of the road near mile marker 82 in Islamorada.

Serge glared across the front seat.

"What?" said Coleman.

Serge shook his head again, but with different import. "Hope with you is a fool's errand."

Coleman shrugged and stuck the alligator's head in his mouth, taking a hit from his new honey-bottle bong. He exhaled and pointed. "What's that on the edge of the street? The thing with orange lightbulbs?"

"Temporary highway sign to alert motorists," said Serge. "Don't bother me right now."

"I know it's a road sign," said Coleman. "But they usually say something like 'Detour Ahead.' Why does that one say 'Screw Worm Inspection Station Mile 106'?"

Serge was trying to concentrate on a file folder in his lap. "Because they inspect for screw worms. Probably not now because of the storm. But they'll be back up and running soon."

"I don't even know what a screw worm is," said Coleman. "And why would they need to inspect?"

"It doesn't concern you. Leave me alone." Serge intently flipped through the file.

"I just wanted to know. You're not the only curious one." Then Coleman lapsed into his stoner pastime of playing with the sound of words. "Screw *worm* . . . *screw* worm . . . *screwwwwwwwww* worm . . . screw *wormmmmmmmmm* . . . screw wormy-worm . . ."

Serge slowly raised his reddening face and stared out the windshield.

". . . Screwy-screw worm . . . Worm screwy worm . . ."

"Fuck it!" Serge emitted a deep sigh and closed the file. He grabbed a thermos of coffee and chugged. "Okay, most flies—like houseflies—lay eggs in dead stuff. But there's this nasty other fly from Central American called *Cochliomyia hominivorax*. It needs living flesh and deposits eggs in open animal wounds. To up the gross-out factor, the larvae burrow into the meat as they feed, using a screw-like anchor that is so strong it can penetrate bone. It gets pretty ugly and is often fatal. You don't want to see the photos."

"Maybe," said Coleman. "But what's that got to do with the Keys? Why do we need that sign here if it's in Central America?"

"The United States eradicated screw worm flies in the early 1980s, but somehow they got back in and caused the current out-break that is confined for now to the Florida Keys. That's why they need the signs. Any tourists who bring pets with them on vacation must have them inspected before returning to the mainland."

"They're eating poodles and stuff?"

"Not yet, but the outbreak has already caused much sadness down here." Serge pointed back over his shoulder. "You know those cute little miniature Key deer back on Big Pine that are found nowhere else in the world?"

A pot exhale. "Know 'em and love 'em."

"They seem all sweet and everything, but they're still wild creatures, and during mating season all bets are off. The males have these tiny antlers and they start butting heads for primacy. To watch these little suckers go at it, it's actually kind of funny."

"Kind of like babies fighting."

Serge paused. "When do babies ever fight?"

Coleman puffed and shrugged. "They can't all be nice."

"Whatever. So all this head crashing leaves the tops of the deer's scalps with bunches of antler gashes. That's when the screw worm flies move in, and they work fast! In as little as eight hours, the fleshly laid eggs can hatch and bore down almost an inch. Necrosis follows with equal alacrity, and if immediate care isn't sought, it's game over."

"Cool."

"But here's the freakiest part: Although the host animal is already hopelessly doomed, they're still alive and semi-functioning. That's what happened recently on Big Pine Key. Nobody knew there was an outbreak until they started seeing these zombie-like deer staggering around with parts of their heads gone. They had to euthanize around fifty of the poor fellas. It was the big news down here all season."

"Now I'm sad."

"Maybe this will cheer you up." Serge pulled a photo of a headstone from a manila folder.

Coleman blew another cloud out the window and leaned over. "Whatcha got there?"

"I've begun collecting tombstone rubbings." Fingers flipped through pages. "And the Keys are the best place to start! Whenever launching a new hobby, always pick a starting point that provides immediate success and encourages an obsessive-compulsive lifestyle of more and more hobbies until you retreat from all human contact, subsist on delivered pizza, and remain behind the closed curtains of a house crammed to the eyeballs with comic books, Civil War figures, postage stamp albums, ships in bottles, Coca-Cola signs, prison contraband, display cases of dead moths from across North America, jars of dirt from all fifty states, the world's largest ball of Scotch Tape, and a life-size model made entirely from matchsticks of the Lee Harvey Oswald shooting in the Dallas police basement."

"Never thought of it that way." Puff, puff, puff.

Serge nodded hard as he held up pages. "Take a gander. These are from the Key West Cemetery. The first one is obvious, from the verdigris bronze statue of a sailor overlooking twenty-seven graves of those killed in the 1898 explosion of the USS *Maine* in Havana Harbor . . ." He raised another page. "From there, a severe mood swing to the tombstone of B. P. Robert: 'I told you I was sick,' and Alan Dale Willcox: 'If you're reading this, you desperately need a hobby.'" Serge turned and chuckled. "I fooled him . . . You getting this?"

Coleman exhaled smoke and nodded. "Ball of Scotch Tape."

"The Key West Cemetery is my visual favorite, with aboveground crypts like New Orleans, fantastic statues of angels in various moods and severe tropical landscaping."

"All I know is you woke me up extra early."

"For my Maximum Key West Cemetery Morning Routine: Arise just before dawn and shuffle over to the tiny Five Brothers Cuban grocery on the corner of Southard Street, order pressed cheese toast and café con leche, stick coins in a metal box for a copy of the *Key West Citizen,* then stroll into the cemetery and stretch out on a slab with a great sunrise breakfast while reading an article about a homeless man with no pants arrested for knocking tourists off mopeds with coconuts."

"It doesn't get any better," said Coleman.

"But here's a fun fact to put the perfect coda on that first tour stop. About twenty-five thousand people live in Key West, but there are roughly seventy-five thousand in that cemetery." Serge raised a knowing eyebrow. "Makes you think."

Coleman pointed at the rubbings in Serge's lap. "What's that one?"

"From a cat grave on the grounds of the Hemingway House." He held up another. "And this is from where one of Hemingway's roosters is buried behind Blue Heaven restaurant in the island's Bahama Village section. And finally Mitzi the Dolphin, bringing us up-to-date."

"Was I there?"

"Yes, but pot gives you the short-term memory of a fungus." Serge stowed the file and pulled out fresh pages and wax.

Coleman followed his pal as they left the car behind. "Ever think about what you'd like on your own tombstone?"

Serge tapped his chin. "Maybe something like: 'This is bullshit.'"

"I can dig it." Coleman took another hit. "You know what I'd like?"

"You've stumped me."

"'Dave's not here.'" Giggles.

Serge slowly began nodding. "I like it. On a couple of levels. First, for its simple philosophical truth. Second, as an Easter egg for Cheech and Chong fans who lose their way going into a cemetery."

Serge entered a small, open park and snapped a few photos, then approached a monument and went to work with his wax.

"Wow," said Coleman. "That's the biggest tombstone I've ever seen!"

"Roughly the same shape, but not a tombstone." Rub, rub, rub. "It's the monument to those who lost their lives in the Labor Day hurricane of 1935. The cremated remains of nearly two hundred people are interred just under your feet."

"It looks kind of cool."

"Because it is." Rub, rub, rub. "A giant slab of coral with a bas-relief sculpture of blowing palms. Due to the era, the design is art deco. But it's so subtly placed and presented that most visitors just drive right by without noticing the massive history treasure . . . I don't think I'm going to have enough paper."

Coleman stared down and idly scraped the ground with the toe of a sneaker. "Whew, two hundred."

"Get ready," said Serge. "I have a feeling our next stop is going to be insane."

EIGHT YEARS EARLIER

Boys yelled from all directions.

"I got one!"

"I got one over here, too!"

Chris raced between rows, crashing through cane stalks. She had a bead on another jackrabbit. She began coughing in the thickening smoke, but there was never a thought of giving up. Her technique was to chase rabbits *toward* the fire and confuse them.

More slamming through the cane, scraping her arms up but good. Then she left her feet and stretched out in the air for her pounce.

"Got you!"

She was happily carrying the rabbit out of the field when something collided with her hard from the side, knocking her to the ground. A boy much older and bigger reached down. "Give me that fucking rabbit."

Chris was immediately back on her feet. "He's mine! Give him back!"

But she was just shoved again in the dirt.

This time Chris didn't get right back up. She felt she was about to cry, and she couldn't let that happen. She strained for composure, and dug her fists, clawing, into the rich soil. Then:

"What's this?"

Her left hand felt something strange. She pulled it from the soil and opened her palm. It was a coin. She rubbed the dirt off on her shirt and looked again. A *gold* coin. She read the date.

1907.

From collecting Lincoln pennies, Chris knew about other coins, too. And she still couldn't believe her eyes. It was a Saint-Gaudens twenty-dollar piece, one of the crown jewels of the numismatic world. She knew its value from her guidebooks and always figured she could only dream of having one. This was way better than a rabbit. She found a foot-long marking stake with an orange ribbon and drove it into the ground.

Chris was still studying her find as she came out of the stalks, so distracted she bumped into another of the big boys.

"What do you have in your hand?"

She clenched her fist shut and stuck it behind her back. "Nothing."

"Give it here!"

"No!"

He twisted her arm and pried her fingers open. "Thanks!" Then the final shove to the ground of the day.

Chris went home in a fuming funk and sat outside on a milk crate.

B ells jingled as a door opened in Pahokee.

The pawnshop owner set a jeweler's glass down and looked up. Pawnshops are universally the eyes of the community, and their eclectic brand of commerce tracks the town's secrets: who's gambling, on drugs, getting divorced, quitting the trombone.

Right now, these eyes gazed toward the person entering his shop and told him: *This isn't positive.* It was one of the junior high kids, nothing to buy, nothing to sell. But they were damn fast, and forget trying to catch them once they stole something and made it out the door.

"Stop right there, young man." The owner looked and sounded like James Earl Jones. But his name was Webber. "What's your business here?"

The boy reached in his pocket and held up a yellow circle between his thumb and index finger. "I found a coin."

This was different. A thousand-candlepower smile lit up the shop. "Come on over here, son! Let's see what you've got there."

But the pawnshop owner already knew. Such coins had been dribbling in over the years about one every six months. Always from kids he initially sized up as trouble. They claimed they found them in the cane fields while hunting rabbits, but who knew? Maybe someone's collection was getting poached. The fewer questions the better.

"I found it in a cane field," said an unusually tall fourteen-year-old named Ricky.

"You look like a football player." Webber examined the coin and poked the boy in the shoulder, buttering him up. "I'll bet you're going to win the Muck Bowl for us!"

Ricky bloomed with pride. "I still have a year to go, but Coach says I'm a natural tailback."

"I'm sure you are." Webber set the coin down on a cloth. "Did you take a look at this? Did you read what it says on the back?"

Eager nodding. "Twenty dollars! But it's old, and it's gold!"

"Except you realize that they don't use these coins anymore. They took them out of circulation."

"What does that mean?" asked the youth.

"It means I don't want to give you any bad news. What do you think is a fair price for this coin?"

Ricky pointed. "The back says twenty dollars."

Webber opened his register and pulled out bills to mollify negotiations. "How about fifteen? That's more than I should."

It had the desired effect as the boy stared at the cash and thought: *Shit, yeah. I just snatched it off that sissy girl anyway.*

"Deal."

Thus continued a daisy chain of underhandedness.

They shook hands.

The boy pocketed bills as he headed for the door.

"And bring me any others you find," Webber called out. "I'm good for fifteen dollars each, even though I'm probably losing money. But I can't help it; I'm just a nice guy."

Bells jingled again as the door closed.

Webber had just made his whole month. If melted for just the weight in gold, the coin was worth more than a grand. And a 1907 in this condition could fetch double.

An ebullient moment took a slight, sullen hit. Darn, he would have to notify the police as required under the law for anything of this value.

A beat cop arrived three hours later. Webber had sent the declaration fax of his purchase to police headquarters, and normally it would have stopped at that. But he knew the drill. Word of the coins was slowly getting out.

Bells jingled. The officer entered and twirled his nightstick. "So how many does that make now?"

"How many what?"

"Rare gold coins these kids are finding just laying on the ground."

"I don't know." The pawn owner wiped the lenses of his reading glasses. "A few."

"Seventeen by our count."

"That many?"

"Imagine the odds," said the officer. "Seventeen different kids just walking along and looking down."

"I understand some were under the dirt."

"Whatever you say." The officer walked along the glass display cases and resumed twirling his stick. He stopped and leaned over. "Is that the coin? May I see it?"

The owner sighed and handed him the small plastic protective holder.

"Real pretty," said the officer, turning it over in his hand. "It's just so unbelievable. If I didn't know you better, I'd say you might be fencing coins stolen from some collections."

"Really, they're just kids," said the owner. "You remember the million juke joints we had around here when the town was big? All those workers getting paid and drunk on a Friday night. I'm surprised they didn't drop more of these things stumbling around."

"Okay, I'll go along. And I'm sure you always pay these kids fairly." The officer held up the coin. "How much did this baby set you back?"

Webber stood mute.

"Did I stutter?" asked the officer.

"I-I don't remember."

"Now *you're* stuttering. Come on, it was only a few hours ago."

Webber was a very bad actor as he searched the top of a cluttered desk. "The paperwork's around here somewhere . . ."

"I'm sure it is," said the officer. "By the way, you know my boss's daughter?"

Webber welcomed the change of topic. "Great girl!"

"She's starting high school next fall and wow, is she fantastic in the band. Especially the trombone, except she—"

Webber sighed with renewed resignation as he turned to the shelf. "Just had one come in, real cheap. You probably heard the rumors . . ."

The officer nodded sadly. "Slide McCall. Who would have thought?"

"I just feel for his family," said Webber, handing the instrument across the counter as the daisy chain completed another link.

The officer whistled a merry tune as he headed toward the door with a long piece of brass over his shoulder. "Remember that fencing is a serious offense."

"They're kids. Really."

"Whatever."

Bells jingled.

Chapter 4

THE FLORIDA KEYS

S erge slapped his pal on the shoulder. "Look alive. Next stop."

"Okay." Coleman headed back to the car.

"Where are you going?" asked Serge.

Coleman grabbed a door handle. "Next stop, like you said."

"No, this way."

He led Coleman in the opposite direction, down local roads a couple hundred yards toward the ocean. They arrived in front of an ultra-luxury resort where the first President Bush often stayed during fly-fishing vacations.

"I get it," said Coleman. "We're going to crash another rich place and find a business conference reception with free food and booze. I'm down with that. Let me straighten myself up so we can get through security because this shit is worth it."

"Not necessary," said Serge. "Act however you want."

Coleman wiped his nose on his shirt. "What do you mean?"

"Just be yourself," said Serge. "It is indeed a world-class resort, but we're allowed to cut through the side of the property because the public has the right to access my next stop."

"Be myself? Okay." He pulled a pint of Southern Comfort from his pocket and lifted it to the sun as he guzzled.

"Once again, my words were not chosen with adequate care," said Serge. "Be like *other* people."

"That's different." Coleman stowed the bottle and stumbled after his friend.

They ended up on a sandy beach behind the hotel as waves from the Florida Straits lapped the shore.

"What the hell?" said Coleman.

"Told you it would be cool."

Before them stood a white picket fence surrounding a small cluster of graves and tombstones.

Coleman took a furtive swig from his flask and grabbed the fence for balance. "I never expected a cemetery in the middle of a beach."

"It's not just a cemetery but a *pioneer* cemetery." Serge snapped photos. "You've got three main family plots in there. The Pinders, Russells and Parkers, who settled here back in the 1800s and kicked off what this island is today."

"But how is it allowed on a beach?"

"Because of history lovers!" said Serge. "The die-hard locals knew this stuff here meant a lot, so despite the prevailing wisdom that tombstones are not your first choice for a tourist draw on the beach, they stood firm and dutifully tended the flame of heritage."

"*Whooooaaaaaa.*" Coleman hung on to the top of a picket with one hand, swinging off-balance and bouncing against the fence a few times like a screen door in the wind. "Getting a little funky here."

Serge was lost in the focus of the moment. "But I view the whole tourist-cemetery interface from an optimistic viewpoint that history is the future. A lovely family from Elk Rapids comes down here, and they're like: 'This is paradise. We've got a beautiful sun and sky, our blankets spread out, sodas and baloney sandwiches in the cooler, our kids laughing and splashing in the surf. How can it possibly get any better? . . . Wait, are people buried here?'"

"Where else can they get that?" asked Coleman.

"This is what I keep trying to tell people, but it's always the same closed-mindedness: 'Don't hurt me.'"

"I kind of dig that angel statue in the center."

"Remember the big hurricane monument by the highway? True story: When that storm blew through, it picked up that angel—I'm guessing by the wings—and sent it flying all the way back to the road. I mean, that's a pretty heavy chunk of rock. And it barely got scratched. The local history heroes returned it to its rightful place."

"Must have been a big storm to blow it that far."

"One of the biggest." Serge placed paper to headstone. "And Islamorada was particularly hard hit, with scores of victims. But of course all the people in this cemetery were already dead."

"So they survived?"

Serge stared at Coleman a moment and returned to his rubbing.

Soon they were strolling along the beach, Serge in a straight line, Coleman on a much looser course. His veering became more and more generous until he was offshore.

Serge sternly folded his arms and yelled at the ocean. "Can you please not do that?"

"Sorry." Coleman splashed back toward land. "Having a little trouble coloring inside the lines."

They continued on. Then they stopped and stared down.

"A dead seagull?" said Coleman.

Serge raised his eyes up the shore. "There's another one, and another . . ."

After walking twenty more yards, Serge paused again. "That's weird. Six dead birds, but no clues. No fishing lines or oil or trauma."

"Maybe it was the hurricane," said Coleman.

Serge shook his head. "The bodies are too fresh. Oh, well . . ."

They resumed strolling again and heard a chorus of rambunctious yelling. Three young boys charging down the beach to the water's edge.

"Now that's what I like to see," said Serge. "A footloose childhood like mine spent in the Florida outdoors instead of moving pieces of candy around on cell phones."

"What are they doing?"

"Looks like a bread sack. They're throwing pieces."

"Here come the seagulls." Coleman ducked as they swooped in. "How do they do that? Not a bird around, and then a million."

"Seagulls are the FBI surveillance teams of the animal world. You never know the FBI is there until the shit goes down, and then they're *everywhere*," said Serge. "Likewise, seagulls often don't make their presence known until someone tosses aside the last bite of a hot dog, turning the beach into a Hitchcock movie."

"What are those kids throwing now?" asked Coleman. "It doesn't look like bread anymore."

"What *are* they throwing?" asked Serge, heading off in a trot.

The trio of young boys giggled as they tossed stuff to the frenzy of birds.

"Excuse me," said Serge. "May I see what you're feeding them?"

One of the boys quickly hid something behind his back, and they all stopped laughing.

"Come *onnnnnn,*" said Serge. "I just want in on the fun."

"Then okay," said one of kids. He produced a box of generic Alka-Seltzer.

Serge gasped and grabbed his heart.

From behind: "What the hell are you doing? Get away from those kids!"

It was a voice from someone Serge hadn't noticed on the beach before. He turned and saw a man running down from the palm trees around a resort swimming pool.

He arrived and got between Serge and the boys. "What are you, some kind of pervert?"

"No, but why do you have a video camera in your hand?"

"None of your business! And you're wrecking my shot!"

"I know what you were doing," said Serge. "You told these kids to feed Alka-Seltzer to the birds. And because birds can't burp, they would explode."

"No, I didn't."

"You're lying," said Serge. "And then you were going to film the whole shameful episode with your camera. That level of cruelty is a sickness."

"So what if I was?" He shoved Serge hard in the chest. "What are you going to do about it?" Another shove.

Serge stumbled backward a couple of steps. "Don't you know the whole tale about birds exploding is an urban myth?"

"What are you talking about?"

"They don't explode," said Serge. "They *can* burp, or whatever the avian equivalent is of dealing with the social awkwardness of unpleasant gas that gets looks from the rest of the flock."

"Then what's your problem?"

Serge pointed back up the beach at the half-dozen fallen seagulls that they'd just passed. "While the birds may not explode, you've given them an overdose of aspirin and anhydrous citric acid, the active ingredient in those tablets. A gull that weighs a pound or two can't handle what's meant for an adult human."

"I don't believe you."

"Believe this: The overdose symptoms include high fever, double vision, respiratory distress, cardiac distress, abdominal agony, brain-swelling, seizures. It's such a horrible way to go that those birds probably wished they *had* exploded."

"You—!" The man with the video camera noticed something out in the water and paused. "What's he doing?"

Coleman was up to his belly button in the surf with a strained look on his face.

Serge cupped hands around his mouth. "Coleman! No taking dumps in the ocean! We've talked about this." He turned back around to the man. "Sorry, where were we?"

"You were just about to leave!" Another shove.

"Jesus, there are kids here," said Serge. "What kind of example are you setting as a parent?"

"Ha! I'm not their father. I'm their uncle."

"Well then, by all means, ruin them, Uncle Jack Wagon."

"I've had enough of you!" A final shove, sending Serge down to the sand. "Fuck off!"

"Okay, now you're really being a bad example," said Serge. "Using profanity *and* ending a sentence with a preposition."

Coleman trudged his way back to shore. "What did I miss?" He received his own shove to the chest and toppled over. "Hey, what was that for?"

Serge got up and dusted himself off. "I've really tried to be nice, but now you're being mean to Coleman, which is a broad form of animal cruelty."

The man gritted his teeth in rage and lunged for another shove. This time, Serge quickly slipped aside, grabbed him by the wrist and locked up the man's arm under his armpit.

Now, in fights it's often the bigger combatant who prevails. But sometimes it's the little things. Like the little finger. Bend it back to the breaking point, and people bend to your will.

"Ow! My finger!"

"Tell the kids to go home."

"You mean to the motel room."

Serge rolled his eyes. "Whatever." He bent the finger harder. "Now."

"Boys! Go back to the room!"

"What about the birds?" asked a child.

"Get going!"

The young trio skedaddled.

"Alone at last," said Serge.

"Now will you let go of my finger?"

"Yes." Serge pulled a pistol from under his shirt and stuck it in the man's ribs. "I never got your name."

"Clyde."

"Clyde, start walking."

"Where are we going?"

"Oh, this is going to be a real blast, a regular humdinger," said Serge. "Have you seen the Pioneer Cemetery? . . ."

A little while later, Serge stared down into a car trunk. "Comfy?"

"W-w-what are you going to do—"

The lid slammed shut.

EIGHT YEARS EARLIER

Chris was a weird little kid.

In a good way. Other children take to education like they're being force-fed. But Chris was so naturally curious that she practically became another piece of furniture in the library, spending hours on the computer to look up more data than her course material had to offer.

Then the next day in science class, where they were discussing the basics of our sun, its age, distance. A hand shot up. "I found out that our sun bends time and space. The planets, too. It makes wormholes possible."

"What are you talking about?"

"Einstein. Others proved his theory with a telescope during an eclipse when a star appeared from behind the corona when it shouldn't have."

Then math class and a triangle with equal sides. A hand flew up again.

"The Romans killed Archimedes while he was working on a problem. 'Don't disturb my circles,' he said."

"What?"

Soon, other teachers were showing up out in the hall, pointing through the window of the classroom's door at the odd little kid in the front row with a hand enthusiastically in the air. Still more educators began joining Chris in the library to look up her tidbits, their own curiosity piqued. They glanced over at the young girl sitting a few desks away, leaning farther and farther forward, as if knowledge would pull her right through the computer screen.

Saturday meant no school, but Chris had her own curriculum. She grabbed a notebook, pens, an old compass, some tape and a lunch bag. Chris had grown up alone with her grandmother due to the broken-home epidemic that was going around. The old woman looked up as Chris wheeled her bicycle through the living room of their apartment.

"Where are you going, honey?"

"Treasure hunting."

"Have fun."

The ride was at least a mile, possibly closer to two, but when Chris put her mind to something, get out of the way or prepare to be run over.

Other kids probably didn't remember, but Chris could recall every word of the old schoolyard folklore stories about the evil sugar baron named Fakakta who was found shot to death after the 1928 hurricane. And of course the lost treasure. Kids are allowed to dream.

She was a cute little sight, tiny legs churning as she pedaled her pink bicycle up the side of Hooker Highway. She finally arrived at a cane field from one of her recent rabbit hunts, and turned down a dirt road. Chris had a good memory as she walked her bike through the rows of sugar stalks. She came to a marking stake with an orange ribbon. Then she got out her compass and triangulated her position with a pair of distant power lines. Numbers were jotted in her notebook. Then she commenced digging. It was a scientific sampling grid that only she would have thought of, moving out from the stake. The afternoon wore on under the unfiltered sun, her face filthy from wiping away sweat with dirty hands. She was quickly reaching the logical conclusion: probably just a one-time find. And she didn't have any proof that the bogeyman of the sugar field ever existed. That's when her fingers hit it.

The second coin.

Now Chris had two geometric points to work with. She stood up and aimed her compass, dutifully recording new figures in the notebook. She turned the page and drew a second diagram. The search field had become an elongated oval. Digging continued till she could barely see in the growing darkness, but no more finds. She stuck the coin, compass and notebook in the lunch bag she had brought along, and taped it flat to her stomach under her shirt. No way anyone was going to steal this stuff.

Two boys stopped her a block from the apartment building. "Hey, Milk Crate! What have you got there?"

She hated that nickname. "None of your business!"

"Empty your pockets."

"No!"

"I said empty!"

She turned them inside out. Empty.

"Okay, you can go."

As she put her feet back on the pedals, one of them punched her in the shoulder with an extended knuckle.

"Ow!"

She left laughter behind as she pedaled away . . .

Good thing the next day was a Sunday. Her power of will was locked in, and there was little chance she would have been able to focus in school. She rode her bike back to the cane field again. This time it only took her three hours to find the next coin. The compass and notebook came back out. Coordinates plotted, a new shape diagramed. She stopped and aimed her compass in the direction of Lake Okeechobee, squinting with one eye closed, the tip of her tongue sticking out the corner of her mouth in concentration. Math and science were just intuitive to Chris. Her mind's eye instinctively drew a line from the lake to where she stood, envisioning the shape of the debris field if some treasure chest burst open around here in a storm surge. She decided to load her search southeast of the last coin.

It was only an hour before grimy fingers pulled up the next gold piece. Excitement bubbled. There was a lot of time left before sunset. But that would be it for the day.

Chris pedaled home and ran inside.

"Where have you been?" asked her grandmother.

"Out." She dashed into her bedroom and closed the door. Chris ripped the tape off her stomach and lay on the floor next to her dresser. She stared up as she pulled out the bottom drawer. The two newest coins were taped underneath next to the previous one. She closed the drawer and jumped up just as her grandmother came in.

"Good gracious, child, you're filthy."

Chris dropped into the chair at her small desk and opened the notebook. "I'm fine." A pen clicked open.

"You go wash up right now before you make a mess of the whole place."

"Don't disturb my circles."

"Are you sassing me?"

"No, it's a math joke." She stood from the chair. "I'll go wash up. I love you!"

The next day in school, the teachers had a nagging feeling that something was different in class, but they couldn't quite put their fingers on it. By fourth period, the science teacher figured it out. Chris was unnaturally quiet. She hadn't asked a single question or added something arcane to the discussion, like, "Thomas Edison never slept more than four hours a night." And Chris kept glancing at the clock on the wall. Before this day, she always seemed as though she wanted class to go on forever. Maybe she had the flu.

The bell rang, and the teacher caught her at the door. "Chris, is everything okay?"

"Great! I just got a cool compass that I've been thinking about!" She ran off down the hall.

Weird little kid, the teacher thought. *But in a good way.*

Chris burst through the door of her grandmother's upstairs apartment, rolling in her bike. She ran right for her room. She rifled through papers and magazines and library books on her little desk. It became frantic. She ran out into the living room.

"Grandma, have you seen my green notebook? . . . *Grandma?*"

"In here."

Chris ran to the kitchen. "Grandma, what are you doing reading my notebook?"

"I wouldn't read it if it was your diary because that would be private." The old woman turned the page with sausage fingers. "But you left it open on your desk. All these numbers and complex diagrams, for a child your age no less. So this is how you always get straight A's?" She handed the book back. "I'm very proud of you. Just remember not to care what anyone thinks; you're going to do great things someday."

"Thanks, Grandma." A kiss on the cheek, and then she was off again with her bike.

Today would be a watershed, but it didn't look that way at first, taking two hours to find the next coin. But shortly after, her hands hit something else in the soil. She pulled out a piece of wood. A short thin plank with rusty rails on each end like it had been part of a packing crate. She tossed it aside and began excavating with vigor. The hole was wider than her others, exposing the surface of two more broken planks. She lifted them up and froze. Six more coins in a cluster. There was now no doubt that this wasn't just stray dropped money. The folklore was true. Chris wanted to tell the world, but "I can't tell anybody."

She made all the required documentation in her notebook, then taped everything to her stomach again, and pedaled her bike home like a maniac.

Now she had a problem. An embarrassment of riches, so to speak. If her hunch was correct, she would quickly run out of room under her dresser drawers. And the bag she taped beneath her shirt wasn't going to cut it much longer. She started taping coins inside her shoes, but that just made pedaling too hard. She had a stroke of brilliance.

The next day she raced home from the fields again. Boys stopped her bike at the corner of the apartments. There was a basket on her handlebars with daisies.

"Hey, Milk Crate! What have you got there?"

"None of your business."

The tallest boy looked in the basket. "Textbooks? *Ewww!*" A punch on the shoulder and they let her go.

Chris ran up to her room and removed the rubber strap holding the books together. She opened an old algebra text that she had found discarded behind the school. In the middle of the carved-out pages were her coins for the day.

Next order of business: Improve storage. This would be more difficult. She stared out the window. Then she got down on the floor and began removing tape from under dresser drawers . . .

And so it went. Days, weeks, then months, slowly building her haul. She had depleted all that apparently could be found from that first crate, and there had been a dispiriting lull. But it was followed by the wooden remnants of a second box. Then a hundred yards south, the discovery of the next planks.

A year passed. Then two years. At first it had been pure excitement. Nothing goes together better than kids and buried treasure. But now that she was getting older: "Am I doing something wrong?"

Chris sat at her usual computer in the library the next afternoon. She looked up site after site on salvage laws. She read about how if something sinks in a body of water, under certain circumstances, it's up for grabs. Then she went back to meteorology pages showing detailed computer models and maps of the tidal surge from the 1928 storm. The highest water levels rose twenty feet over the field she'd been working. She sat back and bit her lower lip in thought. "Technically, the treasure *did* sink. And I'm the finder."

Back to work.

More time passed, more trips to the cane fields. But all good things must come to an end. Chris's efforts dwindled in results as she depleted her find, until there was nothing. And she was sure about it, too, because she had dug her scientific sampling holes far and wide in the logical drift directions.

She was happy and sad at the same time. What an adventure it had been. On the other hand, Chris always felt unanchored when she didn't have an obsessive goal to focus her mental energy. She would just have to come up with something else.

It only took a few days. She rode her bike as fast as she could, hyper as hell, down to the high school. She knocked on a door . . .

Chapter 5

The Plymouth Satellite wound its way east on U.S. Highway 1 and crested the bridge out of Key Largo at mile 107. Then it entered what locals call "the Eighteen-Mile Stretch," a no-man's-land of mangroves and wild scrub from the bottom tip of the mainland to the first dribbles of civilization at Florida City. Do not break down, do not run out of gas.

Coleman sucked on his gator bottle and blew smoke out the window. "I never heard about trying to explode birds."

"A sad state of affairs," said Serge. "And not just Alka-Seltzer. Do any kind of Internet search on animal abuse, and it brings up a trail of tears. Pelicans get it especially bad for some reason, and now these ass-heads are filming the brutality and proudly posting it on the web. Rice is another one."

"Rice, like the San Francisco treat?"

Serge nodded. "People feed uncooked rice to birds, waiting for them to burst. It's another myth, and luckily, in that case, the birds aren't poisoned and can fly away. But the intent is still there. I can't get my head around that brand of cowardice."

"But, Serge, there must be another way."

"There is." Serge checked the clip in his pistol and stowed it under the seat. "That's one reason why a lot of people have stopped throwing rice at weddings. Instead they hand out bags of birdseed. Of course they don't realize that the rice is safe, but I'm heartened to see they care enough to err on the side of caution."

"You said it was one reason they stopped throwing rice?"

"The other reason is all the documented slips and falls on the tiny kernels," said Serge. "It dampens the mood when the lovebirds are driving away with tin cans bouncing behind the car and then Grandma Petunia takes a spectacular header in the driveway."

"You know, I admire the way you respect animals," said Coleman.

"Really?"

"Yeah, I like my little nature friends," said Coleman. "Squirrels dig my potato chips."

"You are noble in that way," said Serge. "Although the salt contributes to hypertension. Those tiny fellows are wound way too tight as it is. Especially the flying ones. What is their fucking hurry? I mean, damn, just slow your roll, man."

"What about jelly beans?"

"Diabetes," said Serge.

The Plymouth entered southern Miami on the Dixie Highway. Soon, they passed a church, and Serge craned his neck around as people entered. "Well, I'll be."

Coleman turned. "Someone's getting married?"

"We were just talking about weddings, and one's about to get started," said Serge. "This gives me a chance."

"For what?"

"To restore tradition," said Serge. "Whole generations know not of the rice joy."

"What about Grandma Petunia?"

"My solution is elegantly designed not to break any hips."

Serge drove on until he found what he was looking for. The Plymouth skidded into a parking lot.

An hour later, the pair waited alone in front of the church.

"So we're going to be wedding crashers?" asked Coleman.

"No, that would involve dishonesty," said Serge. "But there's nothing unethical about standing outside a church and rooting for strangers not to get divorced."

"The doors are opening," said Coleman.

"Here they come," said Serge. "Get ready."

Guests poured down the steps and formed crowds on each side of the walkway leading from the church. Finally, the happy newlyweds emerged. They headed down the walkway, showered with cheers and birdseed. They were halfway to their car at the curb when suddenly:

Plop . . . plop, plop, plop . . .

"What on earth?" said the bride.

Plop, plop, plop . . .

The groom looked up in rage. "Who's throwing rice? *Cooked* rice?"

"Me!" Serge raised his hand. "Because I care! There's no way those old geezers over there will crack their noggins."

The groom looked down at his chest. "It's brown! And greasy!"

Serge grinned sheepishly. "It's pork fried rice. Sorry, I got a little hungry and that's my favorite." *Plop, plop . . .*

"My dress!" screamed the bride. "It's ruined!"

"You bastards!"

Serge held out an innocent hand. "What? I'm so happy for you! This is your special day! Don't get divorced!"

"Special day?"

"Yeah," said Serge, "but keep up this kind of gloomy fixation on laundry and tonight you'll be wanking off into a honeymoon suite bathrobe."

"Fuckers!"

"Get 'em!"

"Coleman, time to run again."

Serge easily slipped out of grasp as usual, and just as usual, Coleman was captured. They had him squirming by the arms, and Serge was about to disperse them with a display of the Colt .45 pistol in his waistband. But Coleman was even more effective at the task by jackknifing over and rainbow-vomiting a bouilla-baisse of Southern Comfort and Cool Ranch Doritos across the hems of black tuxedo pants.

"Son of a bitch!"

The Plymouth patched out and raced north on Dixie Highway. They heard a banging sound from the trunk.

"Jesus, can't I get any peace?" Serge slapped the steering wheel while fishing bullets from his pocket. "*I'm* being mellow, but everyone else is rowing against my harmony stream."

O n an overcast afternoon, a gold Satellite sat in the parking lot of a sub-budget motel on Highway A1A. Across the street, a nearly deserted beach in Fort Lauderdale. Purple clouds rolled in over the unstaffed vintage lifeguard stands. The sign above the motel office featured a smiling mermaid, in an attempt to make up for everything else.

Serge and Coleman crashed through the door of room 6.

"This is going to be the best party ever!" said Coleman, dumping a shopping bag on one of the beds and chugging from a bottle of Jack.

"Damn straight," said Serge, emptying his own bag. "We're going old school. And if you're going old school, then go all the way!"

"You don't mean—?"

"That's right!" said Serge. "Kindergarten!"

"Man," said Coleman. "That's off the hook."

"Those were the last of the truly great days," said Serge, pawing through his new stuff on the mattress. "All fun all the time, running around screaming on the playground, crayons and construction paper, those little milk cartons and nap time. No grade-point average yet, no pressure whatsoever except tying your shoes and trying not to spit up."

"But then the janitor could always come with the sawdust," said Coleman.

"It was like watching a miracle," said Serge. "The first time I saw it, I didn't give the sawdust a snowball's chance, but then *damn*! For a while, life was perfect. If there's ever a problem, just throw sawdust on it and everything will be lollipops and unicorns again. And one evening my mom was sitting at the kitchen table, crying over a pile of unpaid bills. She suddenly sits up straight and starts brushing all this stuff out of her hair: 'Serge, what the hell?' I say, 'Sawdust, Mom. Everything's okay now.' But instead I got a time-out in the corner. That was the death of innocence."

"Look at all this cool stuff on the bed!" said Coleman.

"And not a speck of digital." Serge stood. "That's how we lost our way."

"Where are you going?"

"To get the rest of our haul out of the car. I'll need your help."

It had been a whirlwind shopping spree, with stops at quite varied retail outlets until brimming bags filled the car. After several unloading trips, Serge and Coleman were safely ensconced back in the room, enthusiastically sorting their recent purchases on the bed. Paste, safety scissors, pipe cleaners, finger paints, glitter, tinfoil, clothespins, buttons, Play-Doh.

Coleman picked up a couple of the buttons. They were clear, with something round inside that rolled around. "What are these?"

"Eyes you glue on a drawing of a bear or something to make him look wacky."

Coleman held the buttons over his own eyes. "Serge, what do you think?"

"Overkill."

Coleman cast them aside and picked up the scissors. "Remember in kindergarten when you could make a costume out of just a pillowcase?"

"That was the best!" Serge grabbed a sixty-four-count box of Crayolas. "You cut holes for your head and arms and could color whatever your imagination dreamed up. You could be anyone you wanted."

"I was an Indian for Thanksgiving," said Coleman. "What about you?"

"Chief Justice Warren."

"Hey, let's make costumes!"

"Great idea!"

They dashed toward the head of a bed and stripped cases off pillows.

Coleman plopped down at a table and grabbed crayons. "Do you think the motel will mind?"

"We'll just slip them back on the pillows when we're done. They've seen worse."

Coleman leaned over the table, ready to go. "What do you think our costumes should be?"

Serge grabbed a blue crayon. "Superheroes. The pillowcases will imbue us with special powers."

"What hero are you going to be?"

"It's a secret." Serge began coloring furiously. "And don't tell me yours either until you're done."

"I love surprises." Coleman joined in the vigorous scribbling. "So where'd you get this idea for a kindergarten party, anyway?"

Serge intently colored on his own case. "You know how sometimes I like to leave my cell phone in the car and take off on foot?"

"I've been wondering why you do that."

"You take away someone's phone today, and it's like you've cut off their oxygen. They can't survive," said Serge. "But kids used to spend entire childhoods without phones and do just fine. That's why it's essential to leave my phone in the car every so often. My wallet, too. Because I have no money or credit cards, it recalibrates my senses back to grade school, forcing me to appreciate all the free stuff in life, like skipping or rolling around in the grass for no reason. It's about rekindling the lost art of being silly."

"I remember that one time you left your phone and wallet behind, and you were hanging upside down on the monkey bars, making farting sounds with your hands on your mouth."

"And the park officials made us leave just for that? I even explained it was part of my phone-and-wallet-free therapy, like EST, insulin shock or primal scream."

"I think you were freaking everyone out."

"They said it was inappropriate behavior for an adult, which I explained was the exact kind of thinking that now has everyone at each other's throats." Serge grabbed a different color crayon and scribbled. "Anyway, I realized I was severely limiting myself with those brief childlike excursions. I needed to invoke the Total Kindergarten Protocol. But of course society isn't ready, like the monkey-bar fiasco or how they laughed when the Beatles joined that ashram in India. So we need the privacy of a motel room."

"What do you do for this proto— . . . proto— . . ."

"Protocol," said Serge. "In order to cleanse ourselves of the toxicity from the growing-up process, we must revert and do nothing beyond the level of a five-year-old."

"Cool." Coleman grabbed a crayon in one hand and a bottle with the other. Chug, chug, chug.

"Ahem!"

Coleman looked up. "What?"

"I don't think Jack Daniel's is on the lunch menu next to the beanie weenies."

"Oh, judge me for a little snort?" Coleman pointed with a yellow crayon. "I don't remember *that* from childhood."

Serge looked over at a man tied to a motel room chair and gagged with duct tape. He slapped himself in the forehead. "I'd completely forgotten about Clyde."

Coleman scoffed sarcastically. "Did you tie people up in kindergarten?"

Serge walked over to the hostage. "Actually, there was this one incident. It's pretty funny now, but at the time: 'Where the hell did Little Serge get all that rope?'"

The hostage wiggled violently. *"Mmmmm! Mmmmm!"*

Coleman grabbed the bottle of whiskey and resumed coloring. "Sounds like he wants to tell you something." Chug, chug, chug.

Serge rapped knuckles on Clyde's forehead like it was a door. "Is that true?"

Vigorous nodding.

"Promise not to yell?"

More nodding.

Serge quickly ripped off the tape.

"Owwwwwwwwww!"

"I thought you promised?"

"Please don't hurt me!"

"Hurt you?" said Serge, innocently pointing to his own chest. "Oh, *I'm* not going to hurt you."

"Then what are you going to do?"

Serge gestured toward the arts-and-crafts table. "First I need to continue my kindergarten reversion therapy, and then we'll have an after-school party. How about it? . . ." His gleeful expression became a frown. "What? You don't like parties? You're not in a festive mood? . . . Then you leave me no choice . . ."

Serge turned his back to Clyde and bent over a bed.

"No! Please! Whatever you're thinking…"

Serge spun back around. Two buttons were over his eyes. He shook his head back and forth, and the little objects in the buttons rattled around in circles. He removed the buttons. "Pretty wacky, eh?"

Clyde just whimpered.

"Jesus," said Serge. "I give and I give." He tore off another long strip of tape and forcefully wrapped it over Clyde's mouth again. Terrified eyes looked up at him.

"Hold that thought," said Serge. "I'll be back after I'm a superhero . . . But you can't tell anyone my true identity."

There were a number of stray crayon marks on the table, but Coleman was able to get most on the pillowcase.

Serge sat back down. "Wow, you're really going at it!"

"Yep, I dig kindergarten." Scribble, scribble, chug, chug. "And I'm just about done . . . There!" Coleman beamed proudly as he held his case up to Serge.

"It's wonderful! It's . . . It's . . ." Serge didn't want to discourage his buddy. "Absolutely fantastic! . . . Uh, what is it?"

"Can't you tell by the shield on the chest?"

"All I can make out are the letters *B* and *M*," said Serge. "I hope that's not supposed to be bowel—"

"Of course not." Still smiling wide. "Don't you get it? I'm Bong Man!"

"I think it's safe to say that this particular superhero name isn't taken yet." Serge scratched his head. "But you don't have a superpower."

"Oh, I've got a superpower all right." Coleman grabbed the safety scissors. "It's a doozy!"

"What is it?"

"Just go back to your own pillowcase, and by the time you're done, I'll show you."

"If you say so." Serge resumed scribbling, skeptically watching Coleman out of the corner of his eye. *What's that idiot doing?*

Coleman had become a rare blur of industriousness. Construction paper, glue, tape and most of their other supplies came into play.

It was a race to the finish, and it was a tie.

Serge slapped down a crayon. "I'm done."

Coleman tossed an extra clothespin on the table. "Me too." Like poker players: "Show me what you got."

Serge held up a pillowcase with flamingos, rockets, sailfish, race cars, Cinderella's castle, Bok Tower and the lighthouse on Key Biscayne. In the middle, Serge had his own chest shield.

"What does the *CF* stand for?" asked Coleman.

"Captain Florida."

"What's your superpower?"

"I can name the state's sixty-seven counties in under a minute, sometimes." Serge pulled off his T-shirt and tried on the pillowcase. "Your turn. What are you hiding under the table?"

"Close your eyes and promise not to peek."

Serge did. He heard the unmistakable telltale sound of a Bic lighter coming to life. Then a familiar smell of smoke.

"Hey," said Coleman. "I didn't say you could open your eyes yet."

Serge's jaw came unhinged. "Your superpower is that you can make a bong out of ordinary kindergarten craft supplies?"

"Pretty super if you ask me." Puff, puff, puff.

Serge sat back and studied the contraption, held together solely with glue and tape, plus pipe cleaners and clothespins for extremities. Colorful construction paper was bent and rolled and folded like the work of an origami expert. "Coleman, your bong, is that a robot?"

"Robots rule! What do you think?"

"Danger, Will Robinson."

"And I used Play-Doh for the seals." Puff, puff, puff. "Your turn to put up."

Serge took a deep breath before spitting out words rapid-fire like an auctioneer. "Alachua, Baker, Bay, Bradford, Brevard, Broward . . ."

"Mmmmmm! Mmmmmm!"

Serge grabbed a tape dispenser and flung, ricocheting it off Clyde's soon-to-be-bloody nose. "We're trying to be five-year-olds, motherfucker!"

A pot cloud exhaled toward the captive. "Serge, could you hand me those two eye buttons? I want to glue them on my robot to make him wacky."

"Here you go."

"Thanks." Coleman squirted Elmer's Glue. "By the way, what are you planning to do with him?"

Serge reached into a shopping bag. "I've given this one a lot of careful thought." He pulled out a small blue box.

"Alka-Seltzer?" asked Coleman.

"No, a generic brand called Fizzing Circles because I wouldn't want to cast a pall on the good people at Alka-Seltzer."

"That's a weird name."

"Apparently, someone's tightening up trademark infringement laws, because generic names are getting pretty strange in order to keep their legal distance. You need look no further than the cereal aisle. I swear these are all real: Fruit Rings, Square Shaped Corn, Circus Balls, Crispy Hexagons, Pranks instead of Trix, and a knockoff of Life cereal called Live It Up. Children see right through those bowls of bullshit."

"So what's the plan with the tablets?"

"Stalled for now," said Serge. "The first hurdle was how do I get enough tablets in him without them activating before the Big Fizz? I finally found a solution, but the technique was so tediously long that I grew weary of the wit involved. So I went hard the other way . . ."

Serge grabbed a bottle of glue off the table and reached in his grocery sack again. Then he went over to the hostage with the safety scissors and began snipping off his clothes. "Sorry, I know this must be one of your favorite T-shirts because of the slogan on the front: 'I'm Not a Gynecologist, but I'll Take a Look.' Damn, that's funny."

Serge stopped snipping and began smearing glue across Clyde's bare chest. He opened a product from the supermarket and placed the pieces in a careful arrangement. "Now we just wait for the drying process."

Chapter 6

Tequesta, Florida.

The northeastern tip of Palm Beach County on the ocean. Named after the Native American tribe who lived, loved and built shell mounds here for two thousand years until ancestors of the current residents put a stop to that, clearing the way for golf.

It is a quiet, affluent bedroom community with many dockside homes and waterways, making it popular among sportsmen. Most prefer sailing out into the Atlantic under the bright sun for their recreation, but some are nocturnal. Night scuba diving is an exciting change of pace, with all the local reefs. So is night fishing.

On a Tuesday evening, just after eleven o'clock, a twenty-seven-foot Boston Whaler with twin Mercury engines cleared the jetties at Jupiter Inlet and began bouncing across the waves out to sea. The continental shelf off this coast is among the narrowest on the whole U.S. seaboard, sometimes barely a mile wide before precipitously dropping off hundreds of feet, where they call it deep-sea fishing.

The Whaler continued cresting small swells. Four heavy-duty spin-casting rods swayed in their holders like radio antennae. The boat's only occupant, a loner named Remy Skillet, also had two rifles and a shotgun. He was going *shark* fishing. He felt a slight pain in his mouth and thought of missed dental appointments.

A mile out, on the edge of the continental shelf, Remy cut the engine and drifted with the current. All lines went in the water, along with a dumped bucket of bloody chum that spread a grease apron off the stern. Seasoned anglers understand that the sport requires mental stamina, and Remy had the kind of patience of someone who brings guns with him to fish. He began blasting the water with an assault rifle before he realized he was shooting at his own chum slick, now glistening under the moon. He opened another beer. He was so far offshore that the lights of the oceanfront homes formed a single, horizontal thread of light, which was his only indication of where black sky left off and black water began. The ocean wind was more loud than stout, and carried a salty mist from the bow slapping the waves. The salt made Remy reach for another beer. That's when the shark hit the bait.

It was a seven-foot mako, gauging from dorsal to tail, and it began swimming back and forth under the boat, bending one of Remy's thickest rods to the breaking point. This required the shotgun. The water exploded off the port side, then the starboard, then port again. The next blast was decidedly louder than the others, and Remy took a step back and stilled his weapon. "That couldn't have been my gun. What was it?" Then he turned around and recoiled even more. "Holy shit!"

Remy's face glowed in the orange light as a fireball mushroomed into the sky a few hundred yards away. What remained after that was some kind of vessel, at least forty feet long, but it was difficult to determine much else because it had burned practically to the waterline. Remy started up his engine and headed in the direction of the explosion.

Minutes later, Remy idled his boat as it circled the smoldering wreckage. He felt his vessel bump something, and it wasn't the other boat. He looked over the side and couldn't see anything at first, because it was black. Not the water, but the scuba suit that the floating dead guy was wearing. Then he saw a second body in a wet suit, and a third, all bobbing in the waves. The toll ended at four, the last guy wearing jeans and a T-shirt with scorch marks.

Remy scratched his head. "What on God's green earth happened here?"

Then more confusion as one of the previously motionless bodies began to thrash. Remy fell into his captain's chair. "Jumpin' Jesus!"

In all the excitement and beer, Remy had completely forgotten about the shark on his fishing line that he'd dragged over to the scene and that was now devouring the bodies.

"Stop that! Stop that right now!" He racked his twelve-gauge.
Blam! . . . Blam! Blam! Blam! . . . Blam! Blam! . . .

A steadier hand could have accomplished the objective with less ammunition, but Remy was still able to get the situation under control. The last shot sent the shark away from the bodies and diving under the boat . . .

In the days to follow, Remy would be arrested as the prime suspect, mainly because all the victims were presumed to have died from multiple shotgun blasts.

"No, really," Remy told them. "I was trying to preserve the evidence."

"How's that?"

"A shark was eating them."

"You do realize it's now impossible to determine how they died? And we wouldn't even have been able to identify two of them if it weren't for tattoos."

"Am I in trouble? . . ."

But right now, as the bodies were still bobbing around Remy's vessel, he had another question. "Where's that last Schlitz?"

A half mile away, night-vision binoculars watched a sinewy man crouching near the bait wells of a Boston Whaler, then standing up and appearing to drink from a can.

A whisper: "What's going on?"

"I think we just caught a big break."

"But what the hell was all that shooting?"

"That was the big break." The binoculars followed Remy as he headed toward the front of the boat, tripped over something and disappeared from view, then popped back up. "This clown just shot up the evidence."

"Why?"

"He was night-fishing. They use beer."

The three men continued hashing out their predicament in muted tones as they lay on their stomachs across the bow of a six-hundred-horsepower go-fast boat. The boat was as black as their jumpsuits, and all the running lights were off.

They waited silently. The reason was obvious. They were about to slip away from the crime scene, as they say, scot-free. All they had to do was remain dark and quiet until Remy departed without detecting their presence, and pray he didn't lose his navigational bearings and head toward them.

He headed toward them.

"Don't panic," said one of the jumpsuits. "He's still too far off to be on dead reckoning."

They waited.

"He's not veering."

"He'll veer."

Remy's bow light grew brighter.

"He's not veering."

"He'll— . . . Shit!"

The trio vaulted back behind the controls and gave it full

throttle. At the last second, the black void of a large powerboat with its lights off shot out from in front of Remy.

"Whoa!" Remy cut the steering wheel in a classic over-correction, careening for a slalom to port. And because all fishing boats are required to have way more engine than they'll ever need, the centrifugal force flung Remy over the side into the water.

Fortunately, the boat had a "kill switch" in the event the captain went overboard, and the fishing vessel quieted to a stop and settled into the water just a short swim away.

Remy sighed with relief as he floated. "What a night . . ."

Oh, and when the authorities would eventually question Remy, it would be in a hospital room. Because as Remy dog-paddled back to his boat, the shark still on his fishing line came over and bit him.

Chapter 7

FORT LAUDERDALE

Chug, chug, chug. "What are we waiting for?" asked Coleman. "It looks like that stuff on your prisoner is dry now."

Serge glanced out the window. "The weather's still really crappy."

"Is it going to rain?"

"You'd think it would cut loose any second," said Serge. "But it's holding up. Just a full canopy of black clouds. To this day, whenever the weather is crappy like this, I get a joyous sense of childhood déjà vu. Instead of becoming glum, we'd use our imaginations and play endless games indoors."

"You don't mean—"

"To the shopping bags! . . ."

A few minutes later, Serge chased Coleman around the room, running over the tops of beds. "I got you! I got you!"

"You did not!"

"Yes, I did!" Serge blasted his friend in the face.

"Hold on," said Coleman. "I need to refill my squirt gun . . ."

"Mmmmmm! Mmmmmm! . . ."

Minutes later. "Coleman, look! I'm walking the dog! Now I'm doing the cat's cradle. You try."

"Okay." *Zing, clack.* "Ow! My forehead!"

"It's bleeding," said Serge. "Apply pressure."

"I just remembered I hate yo-yos."

"Mmmmmm! Mmmmmm! . . ."

Moments after that: "Coleman, here comes the paper airplane."

"I've never played with paper airplanes like this before."

"It's no fun unless they're on fire . . . Oooh, shit, get it away from the curtains."

"Mmmmmm! Mmmmm! . . ."

More stuff came out of shopping bags. More games ensued. Until finally Serge had his eyes closed tightly as he walked around the room with outstretched arms. "Marco!"

"Polo!"

"Marco!"

"Polo!"

Serge grabbed a face and squeezed a nose. "Is that you, Coleman?"

"No," Coleman yelled from the bathroom doorway. "It's Clyde."

"Sorry."

"Mmmmmm! Mmmmm!"

Serge opened his eyes. "Fun's over."

Coleman took a slow sip of whiskey as he surveyed their room: Hopscotch chalk on the carpet, jump rope wrapped around a broken lamp, a burned smell from a cap-gun battle, a horseshoe sticking out of a wall, pencils stuck in ceiling tiles, scattered marbles, baseball cards, jacks, a pogo stick, a robot bong and a hostage. "This was the best party ever!"

Serge checked the window again. "Looks like the weather's

not going to clear. We'll just have to take our chances and pray there's no cloudburst."

"Cool," said Coleman. "I finally get to see what you have planned for him."

Serge ripped the tape off Clyde's mouth and grinned. "Bet you just can't wait to find out what's in store."

"Y-y-you, you're completely insane!"

"Me?" said Serge, tapping himself in the middle of his pillow-case costume. He reapplied mouth tape. "Coleman, look alive. It's time to get ready and head out."

"Are we going in our pillowcases?"

Serge shook his head and grabbed another shopping bag off the floor. "I've got a better idea." He dumped the sack on a bed. "Let's put these on."

"Where'd you get that stuff?"

"The Party Store has everything!"

Soon they were dressed again.

"Won't this attract extra attention?" asked Coleman.

"Just the opposite," said Serge. "This is like the concept of or-ange vests, clipboards and safety cones. If you're wearing these, the general public simply assumes that you're authorized."

Coleman looked in the mirror as he adjusted his red Afro wig and rubber-ball nose. "Are you sure about this?"

"When have you ever seen anyone question someone dressed like this?" Serge jauntily snapped his polka-dot suspenders. "Peo-ple see clowns and they automatically think you know what you're doing."

Serge freed Clyde from the chair and walked him to the door. He peeked outside to make sure the coast was clear, then hustled Clyde into their car's trunk again and slammed the lid.

They began driving south, pulling up to a red light. Some teenagers in the next car began laughing and pointing. "Look! Clowns!"

Serge flashed a clown badge. "We're authorized."

The light turned green and they sped off.

Coleman sucked on a robot. "Where are we going?"

"To the far end of the beach, just before the port. It's a longer walk from the hotels and usually empty, especially with this kind of overcast weather."

They parked on a secluded corner of a public-access lot. "Coleman, grab that duffel bag at your feet."

A couple came off a walkway over the sea oats from the beach. Serge nodded seriously and respectfully.

"Who are those guys?" the wife asked her husband.

"Couple of clowns."

They drove away, leaving Serge and company alone with unfinished business. He popped the trunk. "Time to rock and roll!"

Serge led Clyde across the sand in the grim weather, poking a pistol in his ribs.

Coleman struggled to keep up alongside, continuously rehitching the duffel's strap over his shoulder. "Serge, I still think the guy looks too weird with all the stuff glued on him. We're bound to get caught."

"And that's where you're wrong." Serge poked the barrel harder for motivation. "We're out in the open with a clear view of any approaching cops. If we do see any, I'll just slice off his wrist bindings and remove the mouth tape. What's he going to say? 'Help! Help! I've been held hostage by two guys who played kindergarten games all day while wearing pillowcases!' He'll come off like designer-drug fiend. Then if the cops question us we say that we just met him in the parking lot, and he must have relapsed after getting off the bus from rehab."

"But what about our clown suits?" asked Coleman. "Won't that make the police suspicious?"

"Again, just the opposite," said Serge. "I'll tell them: 'Look at us. We're professionals. Do we seem like pillowcase guys to you?' Of course the answer's obvious."

"Mmmmmm! Mmmmmm!"

"Where are we taking him?" asked Coleman, trudging through the sand in big, floppy shoes.

"Over there, behind that clutch of palm trees for a little privacy." Serge's own large shoes slapped the beach.

Moments later: "That's far enough." Serge poked a gun in a stomach. "Now sit down and don't give me any trouble or . . . or . . . well, there's really nothing left to hold over your head. Just do it out of politeness."

Clyde sat in the sand, and Serge began going through the bag Coleman had carried. First the rope, tent stakes and hammer. *Wham! Wham! Wham! Wham!* The captive's ankles were secured to the ground. Serge pulled out a bottle of drinking water, the tape and a baggie of pills.

Coleman puffed a robot. "What are those?"

Serge held the baggie to his face. "This was a real bitch to prepare, so I hope it works. Remember the Fizzing Circles I showed you before? And I mentioned a tedious process that caused a mood swing and change of heart? I've since come around on that kind of constipated thinking. I've decided to go for a two-pronged project."

"Dear God," said Coleman.

"That's right," said Serge. "All the most critical pieces of scientific apparatus have redundancy circuits, so why not me?" He tossed the baggie in the sand next to the captive and held up a video camera. "Those babies in that bag might not do the entire trick, but the added visuals will put it over the top. When you commit to a project, you can't just phone it in."

Chug, chug, chug. "I still don't know what those are."

Serge knelt next to Clyde. "It took three whole boxes of Contac. Except not Contac, but the generic called Colored Capsules, because the folks at Contac are good people, too. And since they come in capsules, I twisted them all apart and dumped out the original contents. Then I wiped a bowl down and hit it with a hair dryer to ensure a moisture-free receptacle. I mashed up a whole bunch of the Fizzing Circles until there was just powder in the bowl. Next I carefully spooned it into the empty halves of the previously disassembled capsules and twisted them back together. It took *forever,* but one of the strongest motivational forces in the universe is irony."

Serge reached into Coleman's bag again and pulled out thick plastic goggles. "Clyde, you're going to need these. Safety comes first." He fitted them over the hostage's head with a thick rubber strap.

"Mmmmmm! Mmmmmm!"

"Man, hold your horses," said Serge. "The tape is just about to come off."

Rip.

"Ahhhhh!"

"Keep it down or . . . or . . . just keep it down." Serge uncapped the bottled water and wedged it in the sand. Then he opened the baggie and scooped out a handful. The other hand stuck the pistol in Clyde's cheek. "Are you going to play nice with others? A nod will do."

He nodded.

"Good. Now, as you heard me explain to Coleman, this isn't poison or any addictive prescription, because I just say no to drugs. The ingredients in these capsules are just for upset tummies, and yours must be doing backflips right about now. And in your self-crafted rationale that I observed on that other beach, it's totally moral for me to force you to take them. So open wide and don't chew; the water will be coming right up to wash it down."

The capsules were crammed in his mouth, then the water bottle. It was a struggle at first, but soon Clyde managed to get them swallowed.

"Good student," said Serge, reaching back in the bag. "Just a few more times and I won't bother you in this way again." He repeated the process as needed until the baggie was empty.

"Excellent!" Serge reached in the duffel for more tent stakes and rope. *Wham! Wham! Wham!* The hostage's arms were now stretched out over his head with wrists held fast to the ground.

Serge ripped off yet another strip of duct tape. As he pressed it in place: "You know, I did some Internet research on the subject of cruelty, and the stuff I read brought tears to my eyes. Someone actually crucified a pelican on a wooden light pole. I'll spare you the rest of the ghastly details, but the horrible deaths animals experience in the name of idle entertainment are nothing short of heartbreaking. Not to mention that the tormentors proudly post the videos. What's wrong with people like that?" Serge gestured skyward with the hand holding his own video camera. "I guess I just can't understand the concept of torture."

"Mmmmmm! Mmmmmm!"

Serge grabbed a pocketknife. The blade flipped open and stuck between the captive's lips. "Hold still," said Serge. "I'm going to cut a small slit to give you a little extra air, but I don't know why. I must be going soft or something." Slice. He inserted a drinking straw. "There! You still can't scream, but feel free to go 'toot, toot, toot' like a toy train . . . And now that I've thought about it, I require it. Go ahead."

The captive just stared up with horrified eyes.

"Come on!" said Serge. "Don't make me regret giving you that slit. 'Toot, toot, toot.'"

Clyde was tentative, and it came out more like a question. "Toot, toot, toot?"

The clowns doubled over with laughter. "I don't know why that's so funny," said Serge. "Maybe it's the goggles."

"Or maybe all the corn chips you glued on his chest and legs," said Coleman.

"You might have something there," said Serge. "I'll call him the Bandito."

Puff, puff, chug, chug. "What now?"

"We have to time this perfectly." Serge reached into the

shopping bag a final time. "The capsules in his stomach are just about dissolved."

"He's getting that look on his face like when I have gas," said Coleman.

"Here we go!" Serge reached into a bag of corn chips, and tossed a handful high into the air.

Coleman ducked. "Where'd they come from?"

"FBI surveillance team." Serge tossed another handful toward the sky. Seagulls swarmed and cawed and fought each other for crumbs.

Coleman held out his left arm. "Poop."

"We better back up." Serge looked skyward. "Today's forecast calls for a shitstorm."

"Damn!" Coleman felt the top of his head. "Another one got me. They're following us."

"Because they think we have all the chips." Serge stepped forward and dumped the rest of the bag liberally on the ground. And across Clyde.

"Look at 'em go!" said Coleman. "They're all over him. I think they're accidentally pecking him going for the chips, and he doesn't like it."

"What gives you that idea?"

"Just listen."

"Toot! Toot! Toot! Toot! Toot! . . ."

Serge doubled over again. "I don't know why that's so funny because it shouldn't be."

"I can barely see him anymore because of all the feathers," said Coleman.

Serge raised a video camera. "And for the record, I used non-toxic kindergarten glue. No animals were harmed during the production of this film."

"The tooting stopped," said Coleman.

"There's a good reason for that," said Serge. "Watch."

It began slowly at first, then a growing fountain of white fizz shot up from the tube in the mouth tape.

"You sure gave him a lot to think about," said Coleman.

"It's kind of pretty, like those dancing-water fountains."

"But, Serge, there's one thing I don't get." Coleman tightened the red ball on his nose. "How are birds eating chips off him supposed to teach any lessons?"

"Seagulls are widely misunderstood creatures." He zoomed in with the camera. "We think they're cute little guys nibbling popcorn and tacos. But that's just because they're creatures of opportunity. Did you know that gulls often grab clams, mussels, crabs and even small turtles, then fly to great heights and drop them in parking lots to crack them open for food? Amazingly, that's something they have to learn from scratch each generation because back thousands of years ago when genetic memory was forming their survival instincts, I don't think they had much pavement."

"That's trippy," said Coleman.

"But there's more. We really don't comprehend a seagull's primal nature because all we observe is their behavior around us: 'Let's see. I can bust my ass flying around with this tortoise or, fuck it, I'll just eat these onion rings.' But in the absence of human handouts, they're highly aggressive carnivores, often feasting on rodents, reptiles, amphibians, carrion. Even working in teams on severely injured larger prey that can't escape."

"By the way, what were the safety goggles for?"

"Gulls find the eyes tasty," said Serge. "I have a weak stomach. Another favor I did him, but do I get any thanks?"

"So which do you think will get him first?" asked Coleman. "The circles or the birds?"

"It's neck and neck," said Serge.

"The fizz is shooting higher."

"The circles have the edge."

"Hey, why is that one bird all pink?" asked Coleman.

"I think it nicked his femoral artery," said Serge. "The gulls have retaken the lead."

They stopped talking and watched the spectacle unfold a few more minutes.

Coleman stowed his flask and raised his smoking device. "I have to admit, this is one of your cooler projects."

"Society has become too fast-paced and jaded." Serge looked down at his clown suit, then the robot bong, then a corn-chip-covered hostage spewing fizz and blood through a blizzard of feathers. "But see all the fun you can have if you just leave your cell phone back in the room?"

Chapter 8

The office walls were concrete blocks painted with high-gloss institutional enamel. Framed photos, some decades old, hung sparsely. A couple of felt sports-team pennants. A bookshelf with trophies. The people in the photos wore football helmets.

The desk was standard fare for high school coaches. In other words, junk. Anything nicer, and they'd lose credibility. Behind it, almost overwhelming the desk, sat someone whom the whole town had known and talked about for years. This was the result of both the man's accomplishments and how small the town was.

Back in the day, Lamar Calhoun had been a star running back for the Pahokee Blue Devils, helping claim their first state championship in 1989. He had that rare combination at his age of college-level speed and size. Lamar could cut back in the open field at such mystifying angles that he made the fastest safeties and cornerbacks look foolish. But his specialty was leaping over the defensive line in short-yardage situations. And if one of the linebackers did meet Lamar at the peak of his jump, well, he was just along for the ride, falling backward with Calhoun into the end zone.

College scouts were all over him; cars practically lined up at the curb outside his house as a parade of famous coaches sat in the living room making offers, some quite generous, others NCAA violations. He left for an education in the Midwest. Everyone was certain they'd one day see him on television in an NFL uniform.

Then nothing. It was like he had just vanished. People talked for a while, and there were the typical rumors. But then more high school seasons came and went, more state titles, and even more stars, many of them reaching the pros.

Almost three decades later, when Lamar was all but forgotten, he was suddenly just *back*.

It was minutes before the final bell of the day when he simply strolled in the front entrance of Pahokee High School. Word swept the hallways. People peeked in the widows of the principal's office as faculty and the coaching staff surrounded the towering Lamar, showering praise and recounting glory on the nearby field.

"Appreciate you stopping by."

"Glad you haven't forgotten about us."

"So what brings you through town?"

They all just figured he was a big deal somewhere else and had taken a detour on a business trip to see the school where it all began.

"Actually, I'm not passing through," said Lamar. "I'd like a job."

It got quiet in a hurry. Then stammering from the principal. "Well, uh, sure, I, I mean yeah; it's just so out of the blue."

But it was Lamar after all. The principal said there was an assistant coach opening, running backs, no less, but . . . uh, they were a small-budget school. Would he mind also driving a school bus?

"That's great," said Lamar. "Thanks."

The former gridiron legend smiled and shook hands all around and walked out of the office.

Everyone stretched their necks to watch him leave, thinking: *Who comes back to Pahokee?*

L amar Calhoun sat in his coach's office going over report cards. Player eligibility. Tutoring.

There were some towel-snapping hijinks up the hall in the locker room. Calhoun shouted out the door to knock it off. It was quiet again. He looked back down at grades.

A timid knock at the door and an equally timid voice: "Coach C? Do you have a minute?"

"You again?" He was annoyed but also amused. He made himself smile.

A student walked in. "Have you thought any more about what we discussed?"

"I'm sorry, but it's just impossible," said Lamar.

"Why?" Chris took a seat on the other side of the desk. For the tenth time. Like a bad penny.

"Don't take this wrong, but you're a girl," said the coach. "Why don't you try soccer?"

"Because I want to play football," said Chris. "I've seen stuff in the news. A few girls have actually made boys' teams."

"And all of those were kickers," said the coach. "You want to be a running back."

Chris nodded. "I'm pretty fast."

"Why are you pestering me instead of the head coach?"

"Duh, because you're the running-back coach."

Lamar sighed. "What grade are you in anyway?"

"Junior high. Eighth."

"There you have it," said Lamar, relieved at the conversational escape route. "You've got another year before you should be bothering me again. End of conversation."

He resumed going through report cards.

Chris cleared her throat.

The coach looked up and raised his hands in frustration. "What do you want from me?"

"Make me a manager."

"What?"

"I'll carry water bottles, equipment, help with paperwork, anything. I just want to be around the team."

Lamar was actually smiling inside, but he'd learned that sometimes not being firm wasn't doing anyone favors. "Check back in a year. Now, if you'll excuse me, I have work to do . . ."

V iolent grunting and shouts. Shoulder pads crashed. A running back slammed into the defensive line and purely willed himself for a two-yard gain before the punishment of a gang tackle.

A coach blew a whistle.

Water break.

The teenagers pulled off helmets and gathered round the coolers. Panting, dizzy, sweating, jerseys caked with dirt. They guzzled from paper cups, spitting most out and swallowing the rest. High school football practice was tough enough in the rest of the country, but rarely like out here in what they called The Muck, under the Florida sun in a withering soup of humidity from Lake Okeechobee and surrounding Everglades crop fields.

Another assistant coach sidled up to Lamar Calhoun. "What's going on over there?"

"Where?"

The other coach pointed. With all the players on the sidelines now, the view was clear to the far side of the field. Two rows of truck tires were lined up for high-stepping agility drills. A tiny person was running through them. Or trying to. There was a trip and fall every few tires. The person got right back up for the next several tires and promptly went down again.

"Oh geez," said Calhoun.

"You know who that is?"

Lamar nodded. "Can you take over for me a few minutes?" He headed across the field.

A whistle blew behind him, and the boys lined up again to scrimmage.

Lamar reached the tires. "What are you doing?"

Chris pushed herself up from the vulcanized obstacle course and managed a couple more steps. *Plop*. "I'm practicing, Coach."

Calhoun's voice was more perplexed than angry. "Okay, first, I'm not your coach, and second, you can't be out here."

"Why not?" Huffing and turning around at the end of the tires, then heading back.

Lamar watched as she ran by and fell again. "Because only players are allowed on the field."

"I'm going to be a player."

"Please don't make me throw you out," said Lamar. "It's . . . insurance. Yeah, insurance."

Chris stopped. A resigned "*Allllll* right."

Calhoun watched with conflicted emotions as the young girl slunk off the field. He scratched his head and had no idea what to make of it . . .

Chapter 9

A 1969 Plymouth Satellite sat quietly and alone in the shade of an oak tree. It was lunchtime.

Coleman finished chewing a bite and swallowed. "What are we doing here?"

Serge stuck a fork in his mouth. "Eating pie."

"No, I mean *here*," said Coleman. "This place."

"It's our next stop." Serge chased the bite with more coffee. "The Antioch Cemetery, a few miles east of Micanopy and Cross Creek."

"I'm surprised you picked this one," said Coleman. "It's small and kind of dumpy. Just dirt with some brown grass and weeds."

"That part's a disappointment, but one Floridian buried here makes it more than worthwhile."

"So who is it?"

"Hold on," said Serge, digging in again with his fork. "I'm letting the moment build with pie. This is a celebration of astounding dimensions."

"If it's a celebration, I would have guessed you'd buy a cake."

"I'm done with cake!" said Serge. "Cakes are flashy and get way too much attention compared to pie. All that garish frosting. It's just gratuitous."

Munch, munch. "Why do you say that?"

"Because cakes are the pole dancers of the bakery world, but a pie is the girl you take home to Mom. If cakes had names, they'd be Jazmine, Sunshine, Cinnamon, Duplicity; pie would answer to 'Sarah' and 'Beth.'"

"Never thought of it that way."

"There are defining times in your life when you just have to speak up."

"I can dig it." Coleman took another bite. "And I have to say it's pretty damn good pie. But I've never tasted anything like it."

"It's sour orange pie." A fork scooped.

"Never heard of it." Munch.

"Almost nobody has." Serge chewed and slurped from his coffee mug. "But it's one of our state's most fantastic native dishes ever, made from centuries-old family recipes that are now virtually forgotten. Key lime pie gets all the headlines today. And Key lime's great, don't get me wrong. But sour orange is nirvana. And because it's so unknown, you have to work like the devil to get it. The main ingredient was brought here by the Spanish in the sixteenth century, and now grows wild across the peninsula, characterized by its extra-bumpy and thick skin, like a giant citrus golf ball. Just finding the fruit is a bitch, involving hiking boots and trespassing, or long drives to specialty grocery stores like Cuban bodegas in Miami, where they're sold to make mojo sauce—I like saying 'mojo.' Then boil to a syrup, add eggs and sugar, graham-cracker or saltine-crumb crust, whip more syrup into the meringue, and the crowd goes wild. I found several recipes online, including one in an article for *Gardens and Guns*."

"Is that a real magazine?" asked Coleman.

"I thought it was a joke, too, but it's quite real," said Serge. "I can just see the early organization board meeting to come up with a name: 'We need a concept that appeals to the broadest possible audience covering the entire spectrum, something no other magazine has ever dared! Let's shoot it around the table . . .' Second place was probably *Kittens and Whiskey*."

"I'd buy a subscription to that."

"This pie delivers more than a taste-bud party." Serge yanked the napkin from the neck of his shirt. "Symbolically harkening back to the glorious time and place of the legend laid to rest here. It was out in these sweltering pioneer badlands of Central Florida near Lochloosa Lake, where she had the fruit trees growing off her veranda, and it's a safe bet she baked sour orange pie. Today, a couple of local rustic restaurants in her area are among the few places left where you can still order the real deal."

"So that's why we made that long detour on the way here."

Serge opened the door. "We have rubbing a-callin'."

They strolled across the field until they came upon a slab with no tombstone, just statues of a family of deer, mom, dad, and baby.

"Marjorie Kinnan Rawlings." Serge got down on his knees with an oversize sheet of paper. "Most known for her classic novel *The Yearling,* hence the animals on her grave."

"They look cute."

Rub, rub, rub. "This tour stop is special, and not just for Rawlings. It marks a turning point in our odyssey, where we've picked up the beginning of a long strand of Florida connective tissue that will bring our trip to a fever pitch of heritage, lore and motel antics."

"So where to now?"

"It's amazing how you can jump across the shoulders of Florida giants." Serge stood with his finished page. "By no coincidence, our next stop involves one of Rawlings's writing students . . ."

They call it the Treasure Coast.

Why not?

Florida already had the Gold Coast and the Space Coast, and above that, the First Coast with St. Augustine and all its oldest-everything-in-the-United-States signs.

That left three counties in the middle—Indian River, St. Lucie and Martin—orphaned with no coast of their own. It was hurting business.

Then, in 1961, a group of treasure salvagers made international headlines by discovering wrecks from a silver-and-gold-laden Spanish fleet that disappeared in a hurricane in 1715. A total of eleven ships were lost after departing Havana and ultimately sinking off the Sebastian Inlet near Vero Beach. The local *Press-Journal* newspaper swung into action and coined the term *Treasure Coast*.

Today, there is an annual pirate festival commemorating the 1715 wreck, and souvenir maps are sold everywhere with the locations of the ill-fated ships. Divers still search the well-known and charted sites, occasionally finding an artifact. And after hurricanes, children digging holes in the beach—as they are known to do—are said to unearth a doubloon or two. There are even guidebooks telling metal-detector enthusiasts where to look when visiting the Treasure Coast. And even as late as 2015, a salvage team would rework one of the wrecks thought to be depleted, and recovered another $4 million in gold.

Of the eleven lost ships, three have never been found.

One of the people still looking for them was a crusty salvage operator named Cale Munson, but everybody knew him as

"Captain Crack Nasty." You don't want to know where the nickname came from. Cale tried to shake the moniker for years, then embraced it. He figured it was always good for a seafaring man to have a gritty air of reputation, even if it resulted from personal grooming.

On his business card, Crack wasn't a true treasure salvager, but the regular kind. He operated one of those boat-towing services for when engines blew at sea or a vessel began taking on water. His fees were steep, like all the others in his field, because it was a sellers' market. But the real money came when a boat went down, thanks to state and federal law. The government sought to provide high incentive to rescue unfortunates on the water, as well as mitigate ecological damage from a grounded ship. The statutes so heavily favored salvagers that it meant this: If a boat went down and was raised, the salvager now owned it and could sell it back to its original purchaser.

Captain Crack mulled these codicils as he became increasingly bitter about towing the ultra-wealthy back to shore. He wanted to be wealthy, too, like the owners of the mini-yachts he aided, and especially like the now-famous treasure hunters who pulled up millions in precious metals and gems. He already had scuba equipment from his current gig, which could easily reach a sunken galleon. All he needed was a break. Only one problem: He was lazy. The successful treasure finders did extensive homework, even flying to Spain and spending hours in special libraries poring over parchment ship manifests from the eighteenth century. Crack just put on his scuba suit and dove to scour a site that someone else had already put in the elbow grease to find, like being the second person to discover the *Titanic*. After years of diving, he had exactly one cannonball to show for his efforts.

On a sunny afternoon, Crack was motoring out to a fancy disabled boat that was sitting lower than usual in the waves. The emergency call over the radio said it wasn't a fast leak, but would eventually turn fatal without intervention. From a distance,

Crack could tell it was one of those boats where people didn't fish but sipped champagne. He began thinking about salvage laws again. He pulled back on his throttle. Another call over the radio. *What's the holdup?* Crack answered that everything was under control. He leisurely arrived at the boat to find a bunch of polo and tennis people standing in shin-deep water.

"No problem," said Captain Crack, climbing aboard with an assistant. "Have you out of here in no time." He explained the procedure with the water-pumping machine back on his vessel and the hoses he was sticking down in their bilge. Plus the temporary patch to help the pump outpace the leak.

A half hour later. "We have a problem." He said the patch wasn't holding and the leak was faster than his pump. He didn't tell them that he was running his pump at one-third steam. "Everyone grab your valuables and get on my boat! We don't have much time!"

The theatrics worked. They were actually grateful as they watched their pleasure craft disappear beneath the water. And after bringing the thankful party back to shore, the good captain went back out, strung inflatable bladders under the sunken hull and raised the boat. This time he used a real patch and quickly pumped her dry. Not a bad day's work for $200,000.

From there it was the rhythm of routine. Distress calls came in, and Crack waved off all the other salvagers, saying he was closest. Closest but not fastest. He built in delays and excuses and deliberately incompetent water pumping, until once again: "Everyone on my boat! Hurry!"

And so it went, scuttling vessel after vessel. Captain Crack suddenly had a lot of money. But to him, it wasn't real money. That required treasure. He sat in his dockside office one afternoon, windows open to the cross-breeze, staring at the cannonball on his desk. He got an idea. He wouldn't dive for Spanish wrecks that had already been salvaged. He would go after sites that were *still being worked*. Which was highly illegal because of the claims filed by the rightful discoverers. Which meant cover of night. Crack went down to a government auction and bought on the cheap a sleek black ultra-fast cigarette boat that had been seized from a cocaine cartel. He promptly put her back into criminal service.

T he Treasure Coast officially stops at the Palm Beach County line, where the Gold Coast begins with Tequesta and the surrounding communities. But hurricanes don't take their orders from the chamber of commerce.

A highly professional salvage crew began faithfully showing up at the same spot offshore for two weeks. The descriptions in their claim were deliberately downplayed: just exploring for scant artifacts. But rumors began sweeping the treasure-hunting crowd. Could they have found one of the three missing ships from the 1715 fleet?

Captain Crack anchored a safe distance away and staked them out with a telescope. Divers were making too many trips up to the boat for simple historical excavation. Handing too many baskets of whatever up to a deckhand.

After three days of surveillance, Crack headed out at night with two trusted assistants he had handpicked because of their prison records. They anchored over the site and dove.

Jackpot.

The only pressure was time, and it wasn't how long it took to find the loot, but how fast they could fill their baskets. Gold, silver, rubies, sapphires. It all went up to the cigarette boat.

After the sixth dive, the baskets came aboard. Suddenly: "Uh-oh."

A bright search beam shone in the distance. It came at them fast from the deck of a speeding vessel. Then a megaphone. "What the fuck are you doing on our site?"

Soon they were side by side in the water. Because of the lawlessness of the seas, everyone out there has guns, and now they were all drawn in a standoff.

Captain Crack tried to chill it out with lies. "We had no idea the site was claimed."

"Bullshit! Give us everything you have on your boat!"

"We didn't find anything yet," said Crack.

"Then we're coming aboard!"

"Then we'll kill you," said Crack. "And we'll get away with it under federal piracy laws for illegal boarding at sea."

The professional crew fumed. They were hardened, but not tough enough to get in a gun battle over a fraction of their find. Their leader finally waved his rifle toward shore. "Get out of here and never come back! Or next time we *will* shoot!"

Chapter 10

CENTRAL FLORIDA

The back road ran through God's country.

Town after small town. Little Florida places with names like Weirsdale, Citra, Lochloosa, Waldo, Starke and several more that were so tiny they didn't appear on maps. Volunteer fire departments, hardware stores, barbershops, old movie theaters on Main Street playing only one film, always rated G. Signs at the city limits indicated the Kiwanis and Rotary Club were still at it. Other signs were handmade by Girl Scouts for a spaghetti dinner that Friday. There were antiques stores and ice cream stands, billboards for salvation and speed traps, water towers of all shapes, some celebrating high school championships.

And the churches.

Bright white wooden churches, red-brick churches, and churches in converted farm buildings. Some houses of worship sat crowded together in competition; others alone in cattle pastures.

There were short steeples, tall steeples, and open-sided steeples with big bells. Lutheran, Presbyterian, Pentecostal, and AME Zion. Baptist, Anabaptist, and Primitive Baptist. Some had lighted signs with attempts at humor: ETERNITY: SMOKING OR NONSMOKING? CHOOSE THE BREAD OF LIFE OR YOU ARE TOAST. Some unintentionally so: ACCEPTING APPLICATIONS FOR MISSIONARY POSITION.

The back road was actually several roads, stitched together on an old gas station map the night before by Serge. It would be a long drive to the next tour stop, and he shuddered at the thought of spending all that time on an interstate.

The '69 Plymouth entered Ocklawaha. Soon, a two-story country home with a sweeping front porch came into view. Serge's camera was out the window again. *Click, click, click.*

"It's just an old house," said Coleman.

"And one so historically important that when the land was sold from under it, they barged the whole thing across Lake Weir to this location."

"So what's its deal?"

"Back during the Depression, the infamous Ma Barker Gang terrorized the nation with a spree of bank robberies and kidnappings. In 1935, the FBI finally traced the outfit to Florida and this house, where Ma Barker—also known as Machine Gun Kate—was hiding out under an assumed name with several associates. A gun battle ensued, and the house was sprayed with more than four thousand bullets. Apparently the holes have been patched."

"That's a stone trip," said Coleman.

"It was a different era," said Serge. "They actually laid out the bullet-riddled bodies and sold the photos as postcards to mail back to loved ones: 'Having a great time in Florida, unlike these assholes.'"

Serge stowed the camera and sped north. They passed citrus stands and boiled-peanut stands and someone in overalls walking along the side of the road with a sewing machine in a wheelbarrow. They continued on over hill and dale. One of the countless churches was coming up. Threshing machines worked the field next door. It was a Sunday morning, and the last service had long since let out.

As Serge passed by, he noticed three people on the front steps. A pastor was comforting a distraught couple. The woman cried inconsolably.

"Uh-oh," said Serge. "That's my bat signal."

He made a fishtailing U-turn in the middle of the lonely road and sped back. He ran up to the steps in no time. "Pardon me, but I couldn't help but notice you're upset."

The pastor had an arm around the woman's shoulders. He looked up. "It'll be fine."

"No, it won't!" sobbed the woman.

"Why don't you tell me about it?" said Serge.

"Excuse me," said the preacher. "Who are you?"

"Who are *you*?" said Serge.

"Pastor Donovan, but I—"

"The name's Serge." He shook the preacher's hand. "I roam the countryside, enjoying fresh air, monitoring my hygiene, and helping the downtrodden. Favorite food: pizza. Turnoffs: the word *conflate* and women who think a small dog in a purse is a fashion accessory."

A voice arriving from behind. "I'm Coleman . . ." Trip, splat.

Serge looked down and shook his head, then raised his face again. "Now, how may I be of assistance?"

"I don't think you can," said Donovan.

"Then what have you got to lose?" He turned toward the couple. "And you are . . . ?"

"Buford and Agnes Whorley, of the Nantucket Whorleys," said the man. "We retired here ten years ago."

Agnes broke down again. "And now we have no place to go!"

Serge straightened up with an odd look. "Why not go to where you've been the last ten years?"

Her face was buried in her hands. "We can't! It was stolen from us!"

"This is sounding complicated." Serge turned to address Buford. "Can you back up and explain from the beginning?"

"The house was all bought and paid for, our life savings," said Buford. "But then we began running short on the monthly bills. Who knew we'd live this long, or stuff would get so expensive?"

"What did you do?" asked Serge.

"We thought it was a sign from God," said Agnes. "We began seeing all those ads on TV for reverse mortgages, and it sounded like the answer to our prayers . . ."

Buford nodded. "But then we mentioned it to Tyler from our congregation, and he told us that those reverse things were the biggest racket going. They'd gouge us on the interest rate, then compound it, not to mention hidden up-front costs."

"Let me guess," said Serge. "He offered to help you with a better deal?"

"Told us that a conventional equity loan from an upstanding local bank would accomplish the same goals but on much better terms. He even went and got the loan documents from the bank—"

Serge held up a hand. "I've seen this movie before. Then he asked you to sign some title documents that the bank needed for collateral. And the next thing you knew, the bank called to report a loan problem with the title, and the sheriff was at your door saying your home had been sold and you needed to leave."

"The deputies were so nice," said Agnes. "They told us they had investigated and knew exactly what was going on. But their hands were tied because, while it was totally immoral, it was also totally legal."

Buford nodded again. "And the people who bought the house were another retired couple who used *their* entire life savings. What can you do?"

Serge took a seat on the steps next to them. "This one really breaks my heart. The reverse mortgages on TV are generally legit—it's the lone wolves you have to watch out for. Scams in this department have gone so sky-high in Florida that it's an epidemic waiting to make the press. Worst of all, the predators come to town and weasel their way into positions of trust. The newest trend is joining churches to prey on your virtue and trust in a fellow worshiper. Let me guess: Was this Tyler character in the choir?"

"How'd you know?" asked the pastor.

"And he just joined your congregation?"

"Two months ago," said Donovan. "Seemed like the greatest guy. Explained he had just relocated for employment, and that his wife and children would join him as soon as the school year ended up north. He even showed me their photos."

"Probably came with the wallet," said Serge. "I've heard enough. I assume Tyler has made himself scarce."

"Nobody's seen him since the sheriff knocked," said Buford.

Serge shook his head again. "Anything at all I can go on to track him down?"

"Not really," said Agnes.

But Serge noticed the pastor making a furtive head tilt out of their view. "Serge, I'm sorry there's nothing you can do, but it was kind of you to stop by. Why don't I walk you back to your car?"

"How gracious." Serge looked down. Kick. "Coleman, time to get up."

They all met back at the Plymouth.

"Look, I don't know who you are," said the pastor. "Undercover law enforcement? Private investigator from Tyler's last victim? Bank auditor? But something tells me it's information you can't divulge for professional reasons."

"That would be accurate," said Serge.

"I may be a pastor, but I'm not naive about the world."

"Really?" Serge looked toward the edge of the street. "You had me fooled by your sign."

"What?" Donovan turned. "Whoa. 'Missionary Position.' Slipped right by me."

"Not everyone's an editor."

"What I'm getting at is that I did research on the Internet, and I found out about the angle you were describing," said the preacher. "How these predators are increasingly using churches as their hunting grounds. I rarely curse, but this was more than I could take."

"Understandable."

"I also read how they move on before the locals can figure out their dishonesty, but the land is too fertile in Florida, so they can only go so far."

Serge rested an elbow on the roof of the car. "What are you trying to say?"

"The pastors around these parts keep up with each other. Personally, we're not the Internet types, but our chat rooms have their purpose," said Donovan. "Usually it's positive, like how to pump up congregation attendance. But this time I put out a warning on this Tyler guy so it wouldn't happen to anyone else in the area. I also posted a photo that my secretary was able to grab from the last video of our choir performance."

"I think I see where this is going," said Serge. "Where is he?"

"Goes by 'Nicholas' now." Donovan pointed north up the empty road splitting wild meadows. "Pastor four towns up gave me the word. Joined his church two weeks ago. He's keeping an eye on him so he doesn't pull anything before we can explore our options."

"When is the next service with the choir?" asked Serge.

"Started at noon." The preacher checked his wristwatch. "That gives you forty minutes max to catch him before he leaves."

"How long a drive?"

"Hour."

FOUR YEARS EARLIER

A tiny cork ball rattled around the inside of a small metal enclosure. It had an extension that fit in a coach's mouth. A shrill whistle blew for the hundredth time that afternoon. But this time it was followed by the head coach storming onto the field.

"Dougan! Get over here!"

The player trotted up. "What?"

The coach grabbed a fistful of the wide receiver's jersey between the numbers. "You quit on that play! You were practically walking like my grandmother at the end of your route!"

"But it was a screen to the other side—"

"And now you're arguing with me?"

"No, sir."

"You never, ever quit on a play! You always run through the whistle!" The coach released his grip on the uniform. "Stadium steps! Now!"

The other players winced as Dougan removed his helmet and jogged toward the stacked rows of aluminum benches.

"Helmet on!" the coach yelled after him.

Another collective cringe.

Stadium steps were the worst. The punishment took place where the parents sat for all those Friday-night games under the lights. The punished player ran up the steps all the way to the top row of the viewing stands, then down, then up again, over and over as lactic acid built up in the legs and muscles cramped. But that was no excuse. You kept going without end in sight until the coach mercifully called you back to the field. Then, hopefully, lesson learned.

The exiled receiver's cleats began clanging off the steps. The rest of the players got the message. There would be no more letups before the whistle this day. Play resumed back on the field with noticeably renewed purpose. The blocking harder, pass routes fully run, tackles like car accidents.

It was now taking two or three whistles to stop each play.

Lamar Calhoun was on the sideline, bent forward with hands on his knees, studying the technique of his starting halfback taking a delayed handoff and waiting for the block to open daylight next to the noseguard.

Another assistant coach stepped up next to him, the same one as the day before. Receivers coach named Odom. "Lamar, isn't that you-know-who?"

"What do you mean?"

"Up there." Odom shielded his eyes against the sun. "Just below the press box."

Lamar squinted. "You've got to be kidding me."

Over in the viewing stands, there was now a second set of feet clanging up and down the aluminum steps.

"What's the deal with that kid?" said Odom. "Who the hell runs stadium steps because they *want* to?"

"Good grief," said Calhoun. "Can you take over for me again? . . ."

Lamar arrived at the bottom step just as Chris touched it— "Hey, Coach"—and pivoted to head back up."

"Stop," said Lamar. "What do you think you're doing?"

Heavy breathing. "Getting in condition, Coach."

"Didn't I tell you yesterday that only players were allowed on the field?"

"I'm not on the field, Coach. I'm in the stands."

"And stop calling me Coach."

"Sorry, Coach."

"Sit down." Lamar joined her on the bottom bench. "Maybe I wasn't perfectly clear yesterday, but when I said you couldn't be on the field, I meant the entire grounds, including the stands."

"You didn't say that."

"Now I am."

A pout. But not one of self-pity. Just a moment of frustration until Chris figured out her next move.

"And please don't pout," said Lamar. "Not that."

"Then make me a manager."

"I'll make you a *deal*," said the coach. "Just relax and stop all . . . this . . ."

"This what?"

"All of it. You're driving me nuts," said Lamar. "And when you're a freshman, I think you'd be a great manager."

Chris shook her head. "I'll lose a whole year."

"Of what?"

"Getting better. I want to learn."

She got up and began jogging away. "See you tomorrow, Coach."

"Stop calling me—"

"Sorry . . ."

H ut! Hut! *Hut!*"

The football was snapped. Players violently collided. The quarterback got leveled just after releasing a perfect fade route to the back corner of the end zone. Couldn't blame that one on the defender.

A whistle. The head coach clapped hard a single time. "Now that's what I'm talking about!"

Behind him, two assistant coaches stood next to each other, looking in a different direction.

Odom canted his head and said out the side of his mouth, "Technically she's not on the grounds."

"What do I have to do?"

They continued watching Chris run laps around the outside of the fence.

Odom shook his head, "I don't think she's going to quit."

"You don't have to smile about it."

Practice ended. Everyone headed for the locker room. Almost everyone.

Lamar strolled toward the student parking lot. Chris came dashing around the corner of the fence, head down.

"Sorry, Coach, didn't mean to run into you."

"You win," said Lamar.

"Win what?"

"You can be a manager."

Big grin. "Really?" Jumping up and down now.

"And no jumping when you're manager," said Lamar. "You need to take this seriously. You need to be a help, not a distraction. Meet me in my office before practice tomorrow. And bring your last report card."

"You got it, Coach." She began jumping again.

Lamar turned toward the locker room. "I'm already regretting this."

Chapter 11

CENTRAL FLORIDA

The Plymouth Satellite blazed north through that rural swath of the state where you were never more than five minutes away from the ability to purchase marmalade.

Coleman looked down and found a Cheeto stuck to his shirt. "Ooooh, my lucky day." He popped it in his mouth. *Crunch, crunch.* "Serge, don't take this wrong, but a cemetery tour is kind of dull. Nothing's moving."

"Visiting these final resting places is in large part a pretext." The speedometer needle climbed as the muscle car raced down the orange center line of the two-lane road like a 1970s B-movie starring Steve McQueen. "The graves of people who lived life to the fullest are highly inspirational. They're the perfect place to reflect and remind yourself to never stop chasing your dreams."

"I had a cool dream last night," said Coleman.

"It's not that kind of dream."

"Wait, I want to tell you," said Coleman. "I was sleeping."

"That's usually when you dream."

"No, I mean I was sleeping *in* the dream," said Coleman. "Nothing happened."

Serge turned and stared curiously. Coleman was nodding to himself. "Much better than my nightmares. A few days ago I dreamed that I had a job and had to work all night in the dream and then I woke up tired. I hate that. What about you?"

"Okay, here's the thing I love about dreams." Serge took his hands off the wheel and rubbed them together. "You get to meet famous people throughout history. I've gotten to know Genghis Khan, General Custer, Joan of Arc, Tolstoy—who by the way was really long-winded—Galileo, Gandhi, Gershwin, the Marx Brothers, Richard the Lionhearted. But the high expectations can also lead to major disappointment. For some reason I have this recurring dream that I'm on a passenger train with Jesus, and it begins with him showing me magic tricks, like pulling quarters out of my ear, and I'm like, 'We get it. You're Jesus. Give it a rest.' And every time, before it's over, we somehow end up in a fistfight. But here's the weird part: He's the one who always starts the shit, poking me in the chest with a finger, over and over: 'What are you going to do about it? Huh? Big man? What have you got to say now?' And I tell him, 'Christ, this isn't like you.' And then he sucker-punches me! Who would ever see *that* coming?"

The Satellite sped on down the winding road. Vultures were picking apart an armadillo and took flight. Coleman cracked a can of Pabst. "You're driving pretty fast, even for you."

"Nobody could ever write a better job description for me: Florida, no appointments and a tank of gas," said Serge. "Haven't I mentioned this to you before?"

"Only about a gazillion times."

"Unfortunately, today we have an appointment." He checked his wrist. "And it's going to be close."

Serge gave it more gas, and the red needle in the dashboard climbed higher. Twenty minutes later, they skidded onto the shoulder of the road, next to a barbed-wire fence and bales of hay. Across the street, bells rang in a steeple as congregants poured out the front doors.

"How do you know what he looks like?" asked Coleman.

"I don't." Serge climbed out. "I can narrow it down with choir robes, but then it's just my gut."

They walked against the stream toward the front of the church. Most of the choir people were still up at the altar, stretching out their fellowship time.

"I think I see him," said Serge. "That young guy on the end of the second row."

"How do you know?"

"Most of the others are a bit older. And he just has that entitled shit-grin. It's got to be him."

"What's the plan?"

"Pull the car around back, then wait outside by the entrance."

Ten minutes later, the first of the choir began dribbling out and strolling down the walkway, checking with each other about their next practice time. Serge stood in the grass next to the path. Then, like someone who steps off a curb in front of a bus, he just ambled into the flow.

Crash.

A taller man grabbed Serge by the shoulders for balance. "Are you okay? Sorry, I didn't see you."

Serge had his head down. "No, it was all my fault. I apologize. I just have a lot on my mind." He raised his face and wiped Oscar-winning tears from his eyes.

"Hey, hey, hey, what's the matter?" said the man, holding a folded choir robe.

"It's nothing I need to bother you about." Then Serge covered his face and resumed sobbing. He parted two of his fingers to peek.

"Take as much time as you need." The man placed a hand on Serge's shoulder. "If your life's troubled, you're at the right place. We're all family here. I insist you allow me to help, brother."

Serge finally dropped his hands and sniffled. "It's my mother."

Alarm: "Her health? Is she okay?"

Serge nodded. "It's about money. She might lose her house."

"What? She can't afford the mortgage?"

"No, the house is completely paid for," said Serge. "It's just that between the insurance and all the rising monthly bills, her Social Security doesn't make it anymore. If she can't pay next month's property taxes, the county will seize her house, and she's been there fifty years." He kicked the ground in anger. "I feel so guilty!"

"Why? What did you do?"

"I'm not a good son." Serge wiped his nose on the back of his hand. "I'd pay the taxes myself, but I got laid off, and my own family is behind on everything."

"Then you're in luck."

"Why are you smiling?" asked Serge.

"Because this is my field of expertise. I handle real estate matters all the time." He held out a hand to shake. "My name's Nicholas. Call me Nick."

"Serge."

"Well, Serge, your problems are already behind you," said Nick, extending an arm all the way around his new buddy's shoulders. "I can easily structure something to get more than enough equity out of her house to take care of those taxes. Heck, she'll have so much left over that this time next month, she'll probably be waving bon voyage from a cruise ship."

"But how is that possible?"

"Not only is it possible, it's easy." Nick interlaced his fingers. "But it involves knowledge of how banking and real estate knit together. I'm always amazed at how much needless grief people are going through these days."

"It must have been God who made me bump into you."

"He works in mysterious ways," said Nick.

"You have no idea." Serge's head swiveled as he watched the last of the other people at the church drive away. "How do we do this?"

A hearty laugh. "See? You're already bouncing back . . . The first thing I need to do is take a look at your mother's house to gauge how it will appraise, then check some of her documents to make sure the title isn't clouded. Tell her to get ready to limbo in Cancún." Another laugh.

"I don't know how I can ever repay you," said Serge.

"No need to repay," said Nick. "At this church, it's what we do for each other in His name."

"Okay, when can we start?"

"How about right now? Let's go."

"Fantastic," said Serge.

Nick pointed at the only car in the otherwise empty parking lot. A late-model BMW sports coupe. The vanity plate read: WINNING. "That's mine." He reached in his pocket for a blue-and-white key fob.

"Mine's around back," said Serge.

"I'll follow you out to her place."

"Actually, I'd like to show you something first."

"What is it?"

"When I was going through Mom's papers on the house, I found these other files with financial accounts and securities certificates that I didn't know she had. And I also don't know what they mean. They're in my car. I was hoping maybe you could make heads or tails out of them."

Nick thinking: *Can this get any better?* He stuck the Beemer's keys back in his pocket. "I'd be more than happy to look at those files."

They walked around the rear of the church to the glowing gold Plymouth. Serge stuck a key in the back and popped the lid. Nicholas leaned toward the trunk. "Hmm, I don't see any files."

"Because there aren't any," said Serge.

"Huh? What's going on?"

"I didn't want to embarrass you in front of the others, so I waited until we could have a private little chat back here." Serge held out his hand. "A hundred and fifty thousand dollars, please."

Sincere confusion. "What are you talking about?"

"That's how much you stole from the couple up the road. I'm sure you remember the Whorleys. The Nantucket Whorleys?"

"Oh, now I get it." A smirk. "Yeah, I heard about that. Terrible tragedy. I honestly tried to help them, but they made some bad financial moves. Retirees really have to watch out these days."

Serge's hand remained extended. "I'm still waiting."

"For what?"

"The only mistake they made was trusting you," said Serge.

"Now wait a second," said Nick. "I've tried to be nice, and now you're accusing me? This is all on them. Sorry, but those are the breaks."

"I've seen a lot in my years and didn't think the bar of human behavior could drop any lower, but joining church choirs to exploit people's faith?" said Serge. "There's a little chestnut out there about a special place in hell."

"I've grown weary of you," said Nick. "Okay, say I did it. So what? In fact, now that you've pissed me off, I'm *glad* I did it."

"Then I guess there's nothing more to say."

"Yes, there is," said Nick. "Go fuck yourself!"

"In that case . . ." Serge lunged. "In you go!"

"Ahhhhhh!"

The trunk slammed shut.

FOUR YEARS EARLIER

A bottle of Johnnie Walker sat on a desk next to a cannonball. Captain Crack sat behind the desk drinking Scotch and fingering gold doubloons. He had gotten the taste, and it put the fangs in him. The nerve of those guys! How dare they point guns at *him*?

After much tortured moral gymnastics, Crack decided that it was the guys who'd found the ship who were in the wrong. He made the decision. He looked up at his two associates, sitting in wicker chairs against a wall under an antique harpoon and a stuffed wahoo.

"Suit up," said the captain. "We're going back out tonight."

"But what if they're there?"

Crack stood and grabbed the bottle by the neck. "I'm actually hoping they are . . ."

T he night was moonless, and the wind howled.

A black cigarette boat with all the running lights off skipped across the waves at top speed. There was an element of stealth, but the prime strategy was a blitz attack. Come in dark and fast before they knew it.

From distance surveillance, Crack knew all the divers were in the water, leaving a single hand on deck. And from experience, Crack knew that the person would be monitoring the divers and sonar screens. The black boat circled for a downwind approach to cloak the sound of their engines until the last moment, which was now. The deckhand heard the distinct noise a hundred yards out and lunged for a shotgun.

Seconds later, another standoff.

"It's three to one," said Crack. "Give us your shit."

"Go to hell!"

"Then we're coming aboard!"

"I'll shoot!"

"No, you won't."

Bang!

Crack's eyes widened. He quickly looked down at his chest. No blood. He looked up at the salvage boat. Nobody standing.

Crack peered down into the deck at the still body of the deckhand. Then he shot glances side to side at his henchmen. "Who fired?"

"It was an accident. My finger slipped."

"Fuck it," said Crack. "I'll deal with you later. Let's get aboard and off-load their haul before the divers surface."

The gang efficiently began passing expensive baskets over the gunwales.

Naturally, the divers surfaced. "What the hell's going on? Get off our boat!"

"You're not in a bargaining position," said Crack. "I suggest you just swim away."

"Fuck you!" The first diver started climbing up the swim ladder.

"Screw this!" A henchman dropped his basket and grabbed a rifle. "I'm not going back to prison!"

"What's that mean?" said Crack.

"One dead in a robbery gets you the same as four. No witnesses!"

Bang!

So the others got into the act.

Bang! Bang! Bang! Bang! . . .

When the proverbial smoke cleared, three lifeless wet suits floated and bumped against the hulls of both boats.

"What do we do now?" asked the second henchman.

"What the hell do you think? Finish loading!" Crack went to the inboard motor station of the divers' boat, lifted a hatch and pulled the gas line free, liberally splashing the stern and port.

When they were all back in the cigarette boat and drifting away, Captain Crack pulled out a Zippo and patiently lit an entire roll of toilet paper. It was hurled into the salvage craft. A yellowish fire flickered at first. Then blue flames violently shot out from any vulnerable aperture before a fireball billowed into the sky. Crack threw the cigarette boat in gear and took off.

After a couple hundred yards: "Stop the boat! Stop the boat!"

Crack pulled the throttle all the way back, and the boat settled. "What is it?"

A henchman stretched out an arm. "Someone's coming!"

Crack grabbed night-vision binoculars, and all three crawled out onto the bow on their stomachs.

"What's going on?"

"Shhhhh!" Captain Crack focused the binoculars on a wayward shark fisherman named Remy Skillet as he arrived at the burning boat and poked around, then inexplicably began firing a gun at the already dead. "Unbelievable."

It became even more unbelievable as Remy turned his boat and, instead of motoring off in any number of logical directions, decided to come straight at them.

"Shit!"

The black cigarette boat bolted out of its path at the last moment, and the henchmen turned around just in time to see the physics of the spinning vessel.

"He got thrown overboard . . ."

Crack decided to set a course south, parallel to land, putting distance between his boat and the natural vector out to the murder scene. A few miles later, he cut the engine again and admired the far-off ribbon of lights defining Singer Island.

"Why are we stopping?" asked a henchman.

"To celebrate," said Crack, reaching into a watertight compartment for three glasses and the bottle of Johnnie Walker he had dragged along. "I was planning to celebrate anyway, though I didn't think it would be under these exact circumstances. We had a few bumps, but all in all a successful run tonight."

He handed out the glasses and poured several fingers of the Black Label in each.

"We really appreciate the opportunity," said the first henchman.

"Definitely," said the second, sniffing his drink before sipping.

Crack clinked his glass with theirs. "Congratulations! We're all rich men now."

The first henchmen sipped. "I could seriously get used to this."

Crack turned his back. "Then be quick about it." He faced them again.

One of the henchmen's hands opened, and a glass of Scotch shattered on the deck. "W-w-what's the shotgun for?"

"Do the math," said Crack. "Six dead is the same as four. No witnesses."

"But—"

Blam! Blam!

The henchmen toppled backward into the water.

Captain Crack Nasty set the gun down and picked up a glass. He calmly finished his drink and headed back to shore.

Chapter 12

A Plymouth Satellite raced north along the shore of a formidable river.

"You know what really separates the United States from the rest of the world?" asked Serge.

"Cowbell?"

"Soccer."

"How so?"

"We're the only country that gives such a small shit about it that we deliberately call it by the wrong name."

"I don't know," said Coleman. "I've heard of some pretty scary soccer riots."

"How scary can it be when the rioters are called hooligans?" said Serge. "Visit Philadelphia after any championship game and watch tipped-over police cars burning. And that's when they *win*.

Soccer, on the other hand, has no upside, other than our women's team."

"What do you mean?"

"A little while ago I read where the U.S. national team narrowly defeated the island of Martinique three-to-two," said Serge. "That's like barely beating a Sandals Resort."

"It's just embarrassing." *Belch.* Coleman looked out the window as a swamp gave way to vegetation that thickened and seemed to crowd the road. Pines, oaks, palmettos. Moss hung from branches in a canopy. "Where the hell are we?"

"On the William Bartram Scenic and Historic Highway just southwest of Jacksonville," said Serge. "We're in St. Johns County, named after that big river off to our left. I'll save you the details on Bartram. Okay, I won't. Born in 1739, Bartram was a groundbreaking naturalist known for his colorful drawings of birds and plants. In 1774, he entered Florida and sailed down the river, encountering alligators and Indians and otherwise exploring in a fashion that makes people want to put your name on street signs."

"I see one of the signs now."

"But Bartram is just the aperitif. The main course is still coming up." Serge snapped photos out the window. *Click, click, click.* "Man, I love this highway. The flora is so much different from the southern part of the state, much denser." *Click, click, click.* "Do you realize what's happening again? We're in danger of too much linear thought. We must rage against the machine!"

"I thought soccer was our exit ramp."

"True, true," said Serge. "But now the whole country is into tangents, whether they realize it or not, so we amp up our game!"

"The nation is into tangents?" Coleman's construction-paper robot was starting to fall apart from saliva. He reapplied the wacky eyes and took another double-clutch hit. "How so?"

"Comment threads!" Serge handed Coleman his smartphone. "I've already dialed one up for you. Go to any news site that invites reader comments at the end of stories and start reading. Doesn't matter what the story is about: a new high-altitude diet from the Andes, debt restructuring for the mathematically deranged, royal wedding gaffes in pictures through the years, why Selena Gomez is mum about one sexy topic. The article I just gave you is about a seven-state egg recall for salmonella."

"What am I looking at?"

"Just scroll down. It's like the threads for all the other stories. This one starts with comments about food safety and the FDA and communicating with school cafeterias. But inevitably . . . wait, wait . . . Here it comes! . . . Here it comes! . . ."

Coleman squinted at the tiny screen. "'Food is regulated more than assault rifles! . . . During a robbery do you want to be holding an egg or a gun? . . . It's all the orange president's fault! . . . Lock her up! . . . Snowflakes! . . . Republic-tards!' . . ." Coleman handed the phone back. "I had no idea it was that bad. How did this happen?"

"Technology outpaced our evolution," said Serge. "All of humanity falls along a spectrum of love to hate, and the people bunched up on the shitty end are now defined by too much spare time and keyboards. It happened once before when some pricks got hold of a Gutenberg press—'Bullshit on the Renaissance'—until calmer heads prevailed."

Thud, thud, thud.

Coleman spun around in pot paranoia. "What the hell was that?"

"Relax," said Serge. "Just the guy in the trunk."

"I remember now," said Coleman. "Clyde, who's mean to birdies."

"No, you idiot. We got rid of Clyde back on the beach in Fort Lauderdale," said Serge. "This is the new guy."

"Sorry," said Coleman. "There's so much traffic through your trunk that it's hard for me to keep the players straight."

"Me too," said Serge, pointing up at names written on a row of Post-it notes stuck to the sun visor.

The Plymouth dramatically slowed down as Serge scanned the side of the road.

"What are you doing?" asked Coleman.

"We just passed Cricket Hollow, so it's coming up."

"What is?"

Serge eased off the right side of the road and pointed at an easily missed piece of crooked, weathered wood with carved lettering: BELUTHAHATCHEE.

Coleman sucked his robot. "I still don't know where we are."

"Beluthahatchee is the name of the historic four-acre compound of preeminent Florida folklorist Stetson Kennedy. It's from the Miccosukee tongue, meaning Dark Water. I love it when I find these compounds, like Graceland without amphetamines and sequins."

Serge turned down a dirt road covered with brown leaves. "Stetson is one of my all-time heroes, traveling the state writing books and recording oral histories. He studied writing under Marjorie Kinnan Rawlings, worked on the Federal Writers Project with Zora Neale Hurston, and Woody Guthrie often slept on his couch. Coincidence? You make the call!"

"I say nope."

"Our tour is like the Kevin Bacon game of Florida with lots of dot-connecting that will become more evident as our odyssey continues."

Coleman stared out his window, catching glimpses of water between the trees. "Is there a cemetery around here or something?"

"It's like Mitzi the Dolphin, just a single resting place." Serge slowed as the narrow road curved through an untamed southern jungle. "After Stetson passed away in 2011, they scattered his ashes on the pond next to us, and Woody's son Arlo gave a concert."

Serge finally parked behind the old cedar barn of a home perched on piers over the edge of the water. "I love how Stetson let most of the compound continue to grow wild. But what I love more is that back in the 1950s, he infiltrated the Ku Klux

Klan. He wasn't working with law enforcement or anything, just thought it up and did it all by himself on spec."

"What balls," said Coleman.

"Then he passed what he'd learned over to the authorities and journalists. It was a difficult time in America, and Woody Guthrie was roaming the countryside with an acoustic guitar that had a sticker on it: 'This machine kills fascists.' Woody became quite controversial, and when he needed breaks, he began spending a lot of time at Stetson's to retreat from it all. He was even staying here the night a fire started in the woods and threatened the house, but they put it out. Then they found a note on the front gate from the Klan threatening Kennedy. Mind you, this was after a previous incident when Stetson came home to discover the interior destroyed and all his writings thrown in the water. Anyway, Guthrie was crashing on the couch at Beluthahatchee so much that this is where he finished his memoir, *Seeds of Man,* and composed more than eighty songs, including 'Beluthahatchee Bill,' about Stetson. That resulted in this place being named not once, but twice, as a national literary landmark, for both Woody and Stetson. That's beyond exciting. Think of it, *two times!*"

"I remember when you got all excited after having two orgasms in a row and put that number two NASCAR racing sign on your driver's door."

"It's close, but I think this is bigger." Serge stared wistfully out across the water. "I'm on an urgent quest for the high-water marks of letters in this fine state."

"How come?"

"It's necessary," said Serge. "The state's literary laurels are a needed counterbalance to our recent cultural reputation."

"Which is?"

"Florida Man."

"Oh, yeah," said Coleman. "That maniac who's raising hell all over the place."

"Coleman, it's not just one dude. It's a whole army."

"Really? I thought he was just ambitious."

Serge shook his head. "The entire nation is into the embarrassing craze of Googling 'Florida Man' and seeing what pops up. Last year there was a spike in guys pooping in unpopular locations and contexts. This year they're getting naked."

"Naked?"

Serge pulled out his smartphone again, pressing buttons to enter search terms. "Check out these headlines: 'Naked Florida Man Eats Noodles and Plays Bongos at St. Petersburg Restaurant,' 'Naked Florida Man Rides Bicycle through Interstate 95 Traffic,' 'Naked Florida Man Chases Customers around Chick-Fil-A Parking Lot,' 'Naked Florida Man Continues Gardening Despite Pleas from Neighbors.'"

"But, Serge, how is it possible to fight that?"

"The answer is the written word," said Serge. "Let's just sit here quietly for a moment and take in the tranquillity as Stetson and Woody would have—"

Thud, thud, thud . . .

Serge closed his eyes for a long pause, then opened them. "Wait here."

Coleman turned around to see the trunk open.

Wham, wham, wham . . .

The lid closed and Serge got back in the driver's seat. "Where were we?"

"Tranquillity."

"Right," said Serge. "Here's my favorite impression of this place. When I was here for Stetson's memorial service—"

"Wait a second," said Coleman. "When you mentioned that before, I thought you read it somewhere."

"Nope, here in the flesh," said Serge. "How could anyone living in Florida at the time miss it? But I guess twenty million found some bogus excuse. Moving on: The best moment celebrating

Stetson's life came just before they went down to the pond to spread his ashes, when all those in attendance sang 'This Land Is Your Land.' Can you imagine the emotion?"

"Not me," said Coleman. "Are you about to cry?"

Serge wiped his eyes. "Just a little pollen." He pulled out a tissue and blew his nose. "Okay, I'm busted. It is getting to me a little . . . Mind if we sit until I compose myself—"

Thud, thud, thud . . .

Serge looked down to his lap, then over at Coleman without speaking.

"What?"

Thud, thud, thud . . .

Serge threw up his hands. "I can't live like this. I'm trying to have a private moment of reflection. But no . . ." He pointed back over his shoulder with his thumb. "Some people are so inconsiderate. Do *I* go around bothering people like that?"

"Not from where I'm sitting." Coleman looked down at two handfuls of soggy, falling-apart chunks of construction paper. "My robot's fucked up."

Serge twisted the key in the ignition and the Plymouth came to life.

"Where to now?" asked Coleman. He looked over his shoulder at the trunk. "I mean, I know we're going to have to stop at a motel first, but after that."

"The next visit really is a cemetery." Serge blew his nose a final time and stowed the Kleenex in an anti-litterbug bag hanging from his door. "It's the state's connective tissue I was telling you about. We just picked up the trail with Rawlings back near Cross Creek, now Stetson off Bartram Trail, and the rest of the stops will soon start falling like dominoes, as if actual planning was involved."

Thud, thud, thud . . .

"I forgot what that guy in the trunk did," said Coleman, picking paper off his tongue. "Not that I'm questioning your judgment."

"You were fading in and out back at the church," said Serge. "I'll refresh you on the way to the motel."

"Ready when you are." Coleman was about to toss damp kindergarten paper out the window.

"Stop! Hand it to me for the litter bag."

"Oops, my bad." Coleman passed the trash. "You're always thinking of others."

Thud, thud, thud . . .

"Sometimes even when I don't want to."

Chapter 13

FOUR YEARS EARLIER

Coaches led the team running out of the locker room for another day of torture in the Florida sun. The managers brought up the rear with sacks of balls and tees, ankle tape, first-aid kits. Everyone arrived on the field to find the newest manager already there, sitting quietly on the bench along the sideline, proudly wearing a new Pahokee Blue Devils T-shirt that Coach Calhoun had given her, now the nicest item in her wardrobe. In front of her, coolers of water and Gatorade were already in place. Paper cups arranged neatly in rows. She had kind of arrived early.

An afternoon of athletic violence and exhaustion wore on. Chris was Johnny-on-the-spot, dutifully keeping the paper cups filled, dashing on and off the field with water bottles and towels, and quickly volunteering for any errand. The reaction of the team was varied. Most didn't notice, others didn't care, the rest were amused.

Weeks went by. Chris kept her word. She didn't say a peep, didn't get in the way, just did her job. Players almost started taking it for granted that whenever they needed something from one of the managers, Chris was just right there in front of them, like a mind reader.

On a recent afternoon, the players didn't gather on the field for practice. It was a conditioning day, no pads or helmets. And it involved something else that made the kids from The Muck just that much tougher.

The Herbert Hoover Dike.

The dike was constructed in response to the hurricane of 1928, stretching 143 miles around Lake Okeechobee to contain the water in case of another deadly strike. From the outside, all that could be seen was an earthen berm rising thirty feet.

The players hated that damn dike.

At some forgotten point in the school's history, a coach was driving by the dike and got an idea. It was walking distance from Pahokee High. Make that running distance. And now, this afternoon, players grunted and cursed under their breath as they ran up it and down, fighting for footing, slipping, getting back up.

Chris kept her mouth zipped but kept glancing at Coach Calhoun. He could see her from the corner of his eye, knew what was in her head. Since it wasn't a contact practice, what the heck? He turned. "Go ahead."

"Thanks, Coach." She took off and headed up the dike.

The other players didn't have the luxury to react. They were too busy with the pain in their legs and lungs. But a few did wonder: *Who* wants *to run the dike?*

The receivers coach stepped up next to Calhoun. "She's faster than I thought. Practically keeping up with the boys."

"Told me she chases rabbits."

"Mm-hmm, one of those," said Odom.

Chris raced to the bottom of the dike, touched the ground and began sprinting back up.

The head coach blew a whistle. "Now backward!"

A chorus of quiet groans, then slow backpedaling and more suffering on the berm. A few repetitions of that and another whistle. "Now crab-walk . . ."

Chris got that burning in her calves but didn't quit.

Fifteen minutes later: "All right, bring it in!"

The players staggered down the hill like refugees, and Chris ran around with the water bottles.

The following day's practice was back in the friendly confines of the high school field.

Halfway through, one of the safeties came over to the coolers. Chris recognized him from the rabbit hunts. She held out a paper cup. He stumbled and bumped it, spilling the Gatorade on her T-shirt. *Accidentally.*

Coach Calhoun happened to notice, but it didn't register.

During the next break, the same player trotted off the field to the coolers. In a voice nobody else could hear: "Girls don't run the dike." Then he had another accident, bumping into her hard before running back onto the field. Chris crashed into the table with the paper cups.

This time Calhoun didn't dismiss it. He took a step forward. He felt a hand on his arm. It was Reggie, his first-string halfback. "I got this one, Coach." He put his helmet back on and ran out to the huddle.

Four plays later in the scrimmage, Reggie's number was called and a perfect block off-tackle broke him into the clear. Only one safety to beat. It was open field, which called for a cut, then easily outrunning him for the sideline.

Reggie cut, and the safety reacted. Then something happened that the safety never expected. Reggie cut again, this time the other way, straight *at* the safety.

Reggie caught him running sideways, trying to twist back, and plowed right through him—lifting him off the ground and dropping him on his ribs—before trotting into the end zone. On his way back to the sideline, Reggie bumped into the safety from behind. "Don't mess with Chris."

Practice eventually ended as they all did. Players wrung out beyond what they imagined they could endure. They headed for the locker room.

Chris ran after one of the boys. "Hey, Reggie, thanks!"

"For what?"

"You know, out there."

"I don't know what you're talking about."

"Can I ask you a question?"

"You just did."

"Can you teach me to cut?"

"To what?"

"Cut. You're the best! All-state first team from last year and sure to repeat!"

"Why do you want to learn to cut?"

"I'm going to be a running back."

A chuckle. "Okay, I'll play along. I'll teach you to cut."

"Great!" Chris stopped walking.

Reggie looked at her oddly. "You mean *now*?"

Eager nodding.

"Why not? . . ."

Coach Calhoun finished the day and locked up his office. He grabbed his briefcase and headed out of the locker room for the parking lot. The field was empty. Except for two people in the distance on the far sideline. He stopped and stared. Could it get any stranger?

"Okay, stand here," said Reggie. "You're a cornerback or safety."

"You got it."

"Now, here's the mistake most backs commit." He tucked a ball in the crook of an arm. "They have to make a defender miss an open-field tackle, so they juke or shake-and-bake"—Reggie shuffled his feet quickly in the same spot—"trying to fake him out. The problem is that the runner is waiting to react to how the *defender* will react. That's way too much time."

"So what do you do?"

"Totally commit. You plan your cut ahead of time and take it no matter what the defender does."

"What if he doesn't bite?" asked Chris.

"Then you're tackled."

"Doesn't seem like a good plan."

"It does if you're good at geometry."

"I like math."

"Then you'll understand this. We'll take it in slow motion." Reggie backed up twenty yards and shouted: "We're coming straight at each other." He took a single deliberate step. "So now I begin a slow turn to the right, toward the sideline. And you're going to follow." They each took two steps in unison. "The closer you get, the more I increase my angle until I'm almost running east–west."

"But that gives the defender the angle to run you out of bounds."

"And that's the whole key to selling your fake. You make it too good to be true. You run into their strength, which makes *them* commit." More slow, tandem steps. "Now you're just about on me, and I make my cut . . ." He sped back up and dashed by.

"Cool," said Chris.

"Unreal," said Coach Calhoun in the distance, and he walked to his car.

Coach Calhoun sat in his office going over the playbook for that Friday's game.

Knock knock.

He looked up. "Chris, come on in. Have a seat."

"Thanks, Coach."

"I have to admit, this is working out a lot better than I'd expected. And as for your report card . . ." He leaned back in a creaky chair. "I'll confess that part of the reason I did this was to hold the manager thing over your head to improve your grades, but they're already straight A's. I didn't know you were that smart."

Chris shrugged. "I like school."

"So what can I do for you today?"

"I need a favor. And I hate to ask, because of what you've already done for me . . ."

"Go ahead. You've earned it."

"I kind of need to borrow a football."

"Knowing you, I thought you'd have ten footballs."

"Not really."

"You can't afford a football?"

She looked at the floor. The answer was worse. Certain neighborhood boys always stole them.

The coach got up and went to a bookshelf and grabbed a ball off a stand. He returned and tossed it over his desk to Chris.

She caught it and noticed writing on the side in white letters: Lamar Calhoun, a date from the eighties and 216 Yards. Chris looked up. "I can't accept this."

Lamar just smiled and looked down at his playbook. "Anything else?"

"Uh, actually there is one other thing . . ."

I t was a coaches-only meeting.

Calhoun and Odom arrived early.

The field was empty save for a tiny person at the far end. A ball was kicked. It landed pitifully short and left of the goalposts. The person ran after the ball, then ran back. The process was repeated with the same results.

"Where'd she get a kicking tee?" asked Odom.

"I gave her one."

"So now you're a kicking coach, too?"

"She wants to be a running back."

"How does this lead to that?"

"She said she read articles where a few girls in other parts of the country are now playing on boys' teams," said Calhoun. "I made the mistake of pointing out that those were kickers."

"So she's exploiting a loophole?"

They stared a few more minutes at sheer futile relentlessness. Then they went inside for the meeting. It was a marathon: rosters, films, discussion of college recruitment visits, and most importantly, the game plan for Friday. Their opponent was big on zone defense and double-teaming their best receivers, so they decided to rush between the tackles until it opened up the passing game. The agenda ran so long that it was night when they adjourned.

Calhoun and Odom were chatting about auto maintenance as they headed to the parking lot. They heard something near the far end zone. To them, the sound was unmistakable. A football being kicked.

"She still out there?" said Odom.

"I don't know," said Calhoun. "I can't see her."

"She's kicking in complete darkness."

"Maybe her eyes have adjusted."

They stopped and listened to a few more kicks.

"Something about kids like that," said Odom. "I've only known a few, but they're easy to spot."

"What do you mean?"

Odom faintly watched her tee up again, and miss again, and run after the stray ball again. "There's a big emptiness in there somewhere."

Chapter 14

COCOA BEACH

A gold Plymouth sat in a parking space. The sign on the motel roof was a rocket ship. A broken ice machine stood next to the dumpster.

Serge dragged a chair across the mauve carpet of room number 7.

A belch from the bathroom. Coleman emerged guzzling a bottle of Boone's Farm, then bites of jerky. "What are you doing?"

Serge was sitting with his face a few inches from the TV tube. "Ruining my eyes."

Coleman glanced at the screen. "Another protest march?"

"The new women's movement," said Serge. "I'm forcing it on myself."

"Why?"

"Because I'm embarrassed by my gender." Serge's eyes followed the sign-waving parade. "I'm in total solidarity with everything the protesters stand for. But something has become increasing clear to me: Because I'm a man, I'm not reminded fifty times a day of the shit women are expected to put up with. And I thought I was worldly-wise."

"You're not?"

"Until now, my experience has been limited to witnessing the cliché construction workers catcalling to the fairer sex. But I figured Darwin already had that one covered. I mean, when in the course of human history has that ever worked? Some woman in a business suit is hurrying down the sidewalk, and suddenly a guy in a hard hat starts whistling and making slurping sounds and yelling, 'Give me some of that *pussy*!' . . . And the woman stops in her tracks: 'Hold on a minute. I've got my priorities all screwed up. Forget that big board meeting I'm heading to. Why yes, I will give him pussy.'"

"That's pretty bad," said Coleman. "And you're saying it's even worse?"

"Way worse." Serge inched closer to the TV. "My mistake is that all these years, I've been projecting. In other words, if some notion can't remotely enter my head, I figured other guys were the same. And if it wasn't for newspapers, I never would have imagined that all across the country, men are just pulling out their dicks in unwelcome settings."

"Really?"

"And I'm not talking about Sterno bums or bowery flashers. I'm referring to wealthy, famous, powerful men who are supposedly educated. It's happening in hallways, elevators, during innocuous conversations in hospitality suites."

"It's just not right," said Coleman.

"You'd think this would go without saying, but as a general rule of thumb, if you're chatting with some woman you've just met, your best foot forward isn't to start spanking the monkey."

"That's obvious even to me," said Coleman. "I get embarrassed if there's a cat in the room."

"Speaking of cats in the room . . ."

Serge turned toward yet another motel room chair with a bound and gagged guest, wedged away in the far corner.

"He's been so quiet that I completely forgot about him," said Coleman. He covered his own face with a hand. "I'm so embarrassed."

"Why?"

"When you left me here and went to the store," said Coleman. "I think he saw me."

"Saw you? Doing what? . . . Wait, don't answer that. I think I'm getting the picture."

"I made some noises, too."

"For the love of God, please stop! It's going to be hard enough getting the image out of my head without audio as well." Serge walked over to the hostage. "I think you traumatized him. They may be naming a new syndrome after you."

He ripped duct tape off the mouth. "Sorry about my friend," said Serge. "That should be more than enough punishment for you, but I don't make the rules."

"Please let me go! I did everything you asked!" Whimpering. "I went to the bank with you and got a certified check for those people . . ."

Serge held up a driver's license. "What's wrong with Malcolm Reynolds Greely? Much better than Tyler or Nicholas."

"How many times do I have to say I'm sorry?"

"Yeah, but you don't mean it." Serge tossed the license in the trash and taped the captive's mouth shut again. He grabbed a shopping bag off the dresser.

Coleman came over. "Is that what you bought at the store while I was—"

"Shut up! The image was almost gone." Serge walked over and dumped the bag on the bed.

"What's that stuff?" asked Coleman.

"Everything I need for my next science project."

Coleman picked up each item in turn. "A barber's electric razor, cheese grater, box of small trash bags and . . . I don't recognize this thing."

"It's a time lock." Serge picked up the razor. "A lot like a regular padlock, but you can set the timer to open it at a preordained point in the future."

"This isn't much stuff," said Coleman. "Usually your projects are a lot more complicated."

"It'll be more than enough."

"So what's the timer for anyway?"

"I've fallen into a rut," said Serge. "Different day, same shit. Into the trunk, out of the trunk, into the chair, duct tape, blah, blah, blah . . . But even though this started out predictable, I'm throwing in a twist at the end so nobody can say I was snoozing at the wheel."

"You're just being responsible."

Serge walked over to Malcolm and held up the razor. "A little off the top? . . . Ha! Ha! Ha! . . . Just kidding. Actually a lot off the top."

"Mmmmmmm! Mmmmmmm!"

Serge flicked on the razor and placed it at the back of Malcolm's head just above the neck. He pushed the device upward and deep. Huge clumps of hair fell off the front of the razor as it continued over the top of the captive's scalp, right down the middle, until it reached the edge of his forehead.

Serge turned off the razor. "There you go. I hear reverse mohawks are coming into style." Next he grabbed the cheese grater. "I'd be lying if I said this won't hurt . . . Coleman, grab a towel and come here!" He placed the grater where he'd just shaved and began rubbing.

"Mmmmmm! Mmmmmm!"

"Pipe down," said Serge. "I'm only using the extra-fine side."

Coleman arrived with the towel. "Here you go . . . Jesus, he's bleeding."

"Just a few scrapes." He tossed the grater on one of the beds and applied the towel. "Coleman, hold this in place while I go out to the car."

Serge ran out the door.

Coleman bent down to the captive's face and whispered. "Malcolm, is it? Listen, what you saw earlier? I'd really appreciate it if we could keep that between you and me. If it ever got back to my mom—"

Serge returned. "What are you talking about?"

"Nothin'."

Serge placed a clear rectangle on the bed.

"Hey, I remember that," said Coleman. "It's the storage bin you were putting bacon strips in down on Big Pine Key."

"And it worked. You can let go of the towel."

Coleman joined Serge as they crouched down and peered through the side of the bin.

"It's a bunch of flies."

"*Cochliomyia hominivorax*," said Serge. "Otherwise known as the dreaded screw worm flies that recently plagued the Florida Keys."

"Most of them are dead on the bottom."

"That was inevitable," said Serge. "But there are enough left to do the trick. They have a twenty-day life cycle under ideal conditions."

"How did you know that bacon would lure them into the bin?"

"Read it in a medical journal." Serge ripped open the box of plastic garbage bags. "As I said before, sometimes the best cure is to go low-tech. In the rare cases where screw worms attack humans, doctors use bacon, because the larvae are more attracted to that than human flesh, and the parasites unscrew themselves from their hosts. All completely true: Type 'bacon therapy' into any search engine."

Serge opened one of the trash bags, inflated it with air and fit it over the storage bin. "This is the tricky part. I'll hold the mouth of the bag in place, and you carefully pop the lid and slide it out from underneath."

It went off without a hitch, and Serge shook the bin until enough of the flies took flight into the bag. "Coleman, slide the lid back on."

Serge cinched the mouth of the sack and strolled over to Malcolm.

"Mmmmm?"

"You must be getting pretty confused about now." Serge carefully fit the bag's opening over the top of Malcolm's head. "Coleman! Duct tape!"

"Coming right up."

Several strips were wrapped around Malcolm's forehead, sealing the bag in place. "It's not your fault you don't know what's going on. You simply don't have the scientific background. So I'll tell you a little story . . ."

He did, explaining all about the gruesome infestation in the Keys, right up to: ". . . And I used a cheese grater to mimic lesions when those little deer have antler fights. That's pretty much it."

"Mmmmmmm! Mmmmmmm!"

"Why so glum?" said Serge. "I always give my contestants a bonus round and a chance to survive."

A tap on his shoulder.

"What is it, Coleman?"

"Uh, hate to mention this, but you didn't give the seagull guy a bonus round."

"Of course I did."

Coleman shook his head.

Serge pondered; then: "Damn! . . . I'll just have to make it up to Malcolm to balance my karma account . . . Malcolm, did you hear that? Another jerk's loss is your gain. I'm adjusting the time lock in your favor." He knelt behind the chair. "What you're feeling is me refitting your wrist restraints so the lock will free your hands in, say, three days?"

"Mmmmmm! Mmmmmm!"

"You're going to get pretty hungry, but the key is hydration, so I'll get you some sports bottles and stick the tubes through the tape. Just remember to conserve." Serge hopped and clapped. "And most important of all, when the time lock opens and the bonus round begins, what do you need to do?"

"Mmmmmm! Mmmmmm!"

"That's right!" Serge said with a widening grin. "Find bacon!"

Chapter 15

A stuffed wahoo stared down from the office wall with glassy eyes.

Captain Crack Nasty tilted his head to consider the fish. Then he considered his career position. That shootout on the high seas the previous night wasn't exactly tailored for the long game. He glanced at the bottle of Johnnie Walker on his desk and stuck it in a bottom drawer: *Last time I make business decisions on that stuff.*

Overall, though, Nasty viewed the evening a huge success, even if it was a one-timer. He'd recovered a serious amount of treasure, and he didn't have to split it with anyone. Then there was that ugly violence. Crack hadn't known this about himself before. But he liked it.

Now it was just a matter of tweaking his corporate model. Minimize risk. Captain Crack opened another drawer in his desk and pulled out an empty notebook. He turned on his computer. He had decided to do something quite unnatural to him: homework.

He found a number of wreck sites that weren't exactly inactive. The original salvagers still had valid claims. It was just that they had reached diminishing returns, and the locations were being worked more sporadically. Also, Crack began employing a spotter boat, on the off chance that the claim holders picked the wrong day to come back. He employed more care in selecting his associates, more stable, reliable, less trigger-happy. The bottom line: Take it slow and there could be a long future.

His new crew began doing quite well at five sites from Cape Canaveral to Port Salerno and Hobe Sound, never staying too long, never taking too much at once. Treasure would still be there when they came back, as they did, time after time, until there were only a few items in the bottom of a single dive basket. Then on to the next location.

But there were only so many sites off Florida—even dormant ones—that could produce any decent yield, especially if you had to dart in and out like thieves in the night. That meant even more homework for the good captain. And a funny thing happened. He began to find the research interesting, even enjoyable. The history of maritime trade routes back to the Old World, the life and times of sailors on the galleons, all the unnamed and forgotten hurricanes.

Captain Crack pored over notes he had recently scribbled. Of particular interest was a bit of treasure folklore that didn't have any foundation in the official records. Which meant virgin territory. He was intrigued at the prospect of his first legitimate find . . .

The sun had just gone down when he was interrupted by a knock on his office door. "You wanted to see me?"

"Yes, yes, come in."

It was one of his newest hires, a former marijuana bale loader released from Raiford. Went by Corky.

"What's up?"

"Follow me, Corky." He led him down the dock, making a mental note to hammer down some of the rusty nails that were popping up. They arrived at a black boat. "Climb in. We got work."

"Okay." Corky jumped aboard and looked around. "Where are the other guys?"

"Just us." Crack untied the bowline from a mooring cleat. "No diving. Only recon to GPS a potential wreck with sonar . . ."

Since there wouldn't be any violation of a claimed site, there was no need for speed. Crack motored unhurriedly out to sea, sipping coffee and Scotch. He became quite chatty. It was a new development ever since he'd gotten the research bug, and the crew was getting used to it, in a negative way. They rolled their eyes at all the boring knowledge that Crack now spouted. But only behind his back.

"Corky, you wouldn't believe what I've been researching. Potentially my first legitimate find. It's fascinating!"

"Really?" Corky concealed a sigh. "Tell me about it."

"Our work is inextricably entwined with hurricanes and their storm surges that sent doomed ships down off our coasts." The captain adjusted his course bearing. "Corky, did you know there was a hurricane in 1928 that had a storm surge unlike any other?"

"I can't say that I did."

Crack nodded earnestly. "The surge didn't come from the ocean, but from Lake Okeechobee, producing a tidal wave that wiped out entire neighborhoods of fieldworkers. Then I stumbled upon a wild coincidence. I began hearing about a folktale circulating to this day out at the lake. A treasure was lost in the hurricane! Some sugar baron supposedly squirreled away a fortune. When the storm hit, it took him, his house and whatever he was saving, and decades of farming have since covered up all traces. But to this day, it's said that children playing out in the sugarcane fields occasionally come across an old gold coin. Can you imagine it? An *inland* storm surge producing an *inland* wreck?"

"Wow," Corky said with feigned enthusiasm. "So you're going to go after it?"

Crack sagged slightly. "More homework first. I don't know anything about this sugar baron, which is the key to narrowing the search to a specific location." He cut the engine.

Corky looked over the side as the quiet boat rolled mildly in the swells. "We're here?"

"Yes, we are."

Corky climbed over gear on the deck. "I'll start checking the sonar."

"I've got something I want to show you first."

"What is it?"

"See this tube on the side of the shore radio?" asked Crack.

"Yeah, but I still don't know what I'm looking at."

"It's a pinhole video lens. Covers the whole boat from here on back, kind of like a nanny cam."

"I'm not following," said a bored Corky.

Crack reached down into bow storage and pulled something out. "Now do you follow?"

Corky was no longer bored. He'd had guns pointed at him before, but a twelve-gauge always dials it up to eleven.

"What's going on, Captain?"

"I'm sure you have a pretty damn good idea." Crack gestured with the end of the gun. "That tiny camera was filming every time you stuffed shit in your pockets when we came up from a site. Have I not treated you well? And then you steal from *me*? Don't even try to lie. I could show you the tapes, but I don't care about your opinion."

Corky silently reviewed options.

The captain racked the shotgun with the distinct sound that is a natural stool softener.

"Wait! Wait! Wait!" Corky began babbling. "I just took a little. I was going to give it back. I had car troubles. The electric bill. I was drunk. My girlfriend needed braces—"

Blam!

Corky hit the water and bobbed, well, like a cork.

"That was fun." Crack throttled back up toward land. "Now to do some homework on this sugar baron . . ."

MR. FAKAKTA

Sugarcane is actually a grass.

A grass that changed the march of history in the New World.

It can't entirely be attributed to rum, but that's a good start. During the colonial period, from the Caribbean to the South American coast surrounding French Guyana, farming took off due to the region's conducive blend of climate and rich soil. Bananas, coffee beans, nutmeg, rice, cocoa. But when they started using sugarcane to make molasses, which was shipped north to rum distilleries, sugar took the lead and never looked back.

Jamaica, Trinidad, Barbados, Belize, Cuba, Guadalupe. Plow that other stuff under, boys, and plant that cane. The cash flowed in, but at a price. Brutal conditions in a brutal business, cutthroat competition and politics.

On the island of Hispaniola, in the Dominican Republic, there was a particularly heated rivalry among the four chief growers in the early twentieth century. And it wasn't gentlemanly. Threats, vandalism, workers attacked and maimed. Alliances shifted back and forth like on one of those survival reality-TV shows, until one of the four growers was voted off the island.

Fulgencio Salvador Fakakta drew the short straw. But it was impossible to feel sorry for him. Fakakta was one of those rare comeuppance cases where the bad guy actually lost. He had bribed, cheated, stolen and even murdered his way to wealth and power. And now it had come full circle. In short, the other growers were just tired of this asshole.

Fakakta saw it coming, and it wasn't going to be a polite eviction notice. If he was lucky, they'd burn his plantation home, seize everything he had down to the last penny, and allow him to escape with the shirt on his back. If he was lucky. So Fakakta quietly and quickly liquidated everything into gold, which was all crated up one night and packed onto a chartered ship.

"What's in these crates? Rocks?"

"Shut up and keep loading!"

Fulgencio set sail. The other growers still burned his place to the ground, but at least he had enough for a new start.

Besides the Caribbean, there was one other place where sugarcane had just started to catch hold.

Florida.

It would be years before the crop asserted dominance, so for now, a fugitive sugar baron from the Dominican could affordably buy up bean fields around Lake Okeechobee to plant his stalks.

Fakakta had the experience and ruthlessness to make it work, and soon he was one of the wealthier farmers in the lake region. It wasn't enough. He began stealing from his workers. Docking pay for non-reasons, overcharging for rent on their ridiculous shanties and the food he required that they buy from him as a condition of employment. Then he realized there were far more people looking for work than there were jobs. Can't let that equation go to waste. So he took it up a notch and started not paying some workers entirely. Of course they'd yell and argue and quit. But what else were they going to do? He was white. He'd just hire more guys.

But one particular worker, named Jacob, wouldn't let it go. He kept demanding his money, day after day. Finally, Jacob went out to Fakakta's stately colonial plantation house on the edge of town and pounded on the front door. The next morning he was found hanging from a prominent cypress tree with signs of torture. It was meant to be obvious, unlike the other missing workers, who were never found. The white law didn't care, and everyone else got the message. Fakakta continued amassing his fortune, which he kept in gold. But nobody knew where.

Chapter 16

Malcolm sat quietly in his chair.

Serge and Coleman sat quietly at a table.

Malcolm's eyes stared up at the plastic bag taped to his head. "Mmmmmmm! Mmmmmmm!"

Serge and Coleman wore plain white T-shirts. Open bottles of various colors were scattered across the table. Stains representing the same colors covered their shirts. Coleman leaned over and rubbed feverishly. "I'd completely forgotten about finger painting."

"Finger painting is the best!" Serge made a blue circle with his thumb. "I don't know why society cuts that off after kindergarten. I had dreams of becoming a world-class finger-paint artist. Huge gallery openings in SoHo, the toast of Paris. Then I found out it was just some bullshit to keep us busy until recess. It was the beginning of the counterculture, and that's when I started seeing through all the lies. Finger painting, Vietnam."

"This is excellent when you're high."

Serge looked across the table. "Not bad. You're painting a pumpkin."

"It's a bong," said Coleman. "What are you painting?"

"An egret." Serge chugged a mug of coffee, then stood up and grabbed the page. He taped it to a wall.

"Why are you doing that?"

"Because this motel room has no artwork. We got screwed." He straightened his egret and sat back down. "All motel rooms are supposed to have artwork. But sadly, most guests never notice. You ask ten people what the painting was in the room they stayed in last night, and dollars to doughnuts none will have a clue. Not me! It's the first thing I look for when I open the door!"

"Why?"

"Reminds me of baseball cards, because you never know what you'll get." Serge grabbed a fresh page and resumed work. "I'd buy a pack of cards at the five-and-dime and then sit on the curb out front, gently and affectionately removing each card to reveal surprise after surprise: 'Cool, Carl Yastrzemski. Cookie Rojas, not bad. Do I already have Rollie Fingers? It says on the back of Félix Millán's card that he led the National League in triples. Who the fuck is Buzz Capra?' . . . Same thing with motel paintings, especially budget motels. You go to a fancy *hotel* and get high-quality art that makes sense, following the room's color scheme and local milieu. But the economy joints are the best, especially the kind with old wood paneling. They don't give a shit anymore and buy stuff from art-clearance warehouses that sell paintings by the pound. You're always in for a treat, so when I first arrive at a room, I stop outside and let the anticipation build, like holding that shiny new pack of sports cards. Then I quickly open the door and pump a fist in the air. 'Yes! Sailboats!' I can still see them to this day."

"You remember the sailboats?"

"I remember all the paintings!" said Serge. "The sailboats, a beach scene of three children playing with pails on the sand and each pail was a different primary color, a vase with sunflowers, a cherry pie on a windowsill overlooking corn, magpies on a power line, a train station when they still had baggage porters, a bowl of fruit, a cowboy leaning against a post, a lighthouse in Maine, a terrier, President Coolidge..."

"How do you recall all that?"

"Because I care." Serge dipped a finger in the green bottle while swigging coffee with the other hand. "If people don't watch out, there can be a lot of needless tedium in motel rooms by squandering spare time. But I rarely encounter that problem because I want to squeeze every second out of life. Even if I don't have spare time in a room, I'll *make* time, sitting in a chair staring relentlessly at the wall and metaphysically contemplating all aspects of the painting. What were the headlines of the day when it was created? How many people have straightened it on the wall? Who painted it and why? What about the backstories of the people on the sailboats? I imagine the painting hanging steadily and all-knowing in here since the mid-twentieth century, during poker games, extramarital affairs, kids jumping on beds, someone repeatedly peeking out the window, salesmen with straw hats from a plumbing supply convention, a coroner wheeling out the victim of a heart attack that everyone saw coming. Then I envision a woman at an easel in 1953 who decided to broaden her background of dependable typing skills by taking a mail-order art class, only to have her husband leave her for a Pan Am stewardess, and now she paints just to forget but has never been to the beach. And the little people on one of the sailboats are a family of six from Knoxville who take the same vacation every year to Myrtle Beach, where they always line up the children for an annual photo to document their growth, which after three decades will become the subject of a feel-good magazine article. But what are their political beliefs? How would they view the woman who painted them? Do they even know they're in a painting? These are questions for the ages." He raised his mug. "I'm out of coffee."

Malcolm heard buzzing in the bag taped to his head.

"Mmmmmm! Mmmmmm!"

Serge walked over to the captive. The trash bag had all but deflated on his head, and Serge held it upright and shook, giving the flies renewed space to work. He pointed at a page on the wall. "If you're bored, you can look at my egret and ask metaphysical questions."

He returned to his table and paint.

Coleman leaned toward his friend's new page. "What's this one?"

"Great blue heron." Serge got up and placed it on the wall.

Coleman noticed there was now a long row of overlapping finger paintings along the side of the room. "Serge, what are you doing?"

"Making a mural to compensate for this motel room's lost time without art." Serge aimed a yellow finger at Malcolm. "This science project requires an extended duration of babysitting, so a mural is the only way to go. The room's next guests will seriously get their money's worth."

"Why so long?" asked Coleman. "Can't we just leave him like the others?"

Serge shook his head and drew cattails with a finger. "I'll need to remove the bag and dispose of the remaining flies or I could be responsible for some kind of outbreak from breaching the Keys quarantine. It's the right thing to do."

"What kind of mural?"

"In full disclosure, it's not original." He sat down with another page. "I'm inspired by one of Florida's finest and most enduring works of art. While the state has a wealth of fine galleries, my favorite native painting of all time adorns the lounge of a historic erstwhile grande dame of accommodations in a small town on the southern shore of Lake Okeechobee."

"Mmmmmm! Mmmmmm!"

Coleman packed his alligator honey bottle. Puff, puff. "Even our hostage is into this now. Please tell us more."

"Unlike other swank hotels of bygone eras such as the Breakers or Biltmore, this place is now a bargain. But not because it's hit the skids. Far from it. In another freak of *Freakonomics,* the glory days faded and revenue dropped. But then an interesting thing happened. The place remained just popular enough to create a Goldilocks effect, not overheating or cooling off. Instead, it remains strangely suspended in time as a freeze-frame snapshot of the past. It's so quiet and peaceful that you're often the only person in the opulent period lobby, like staying in a museum."

"But, Serge, what is this fabulous place?"

"The Clewiston Inn, built 1938 by U.S. Sugar in Classic Revival architecture with stately white columns out front, now in the National Register of Historic Sites. It's unexpected to find one of Florida's most impressive hotels in such a modest community, almost nothing but miles of agricultural fields in all directions. The Everglades Bar and Lounge itself remains essentially closed because of lack of traffic, but the management is hospitable enough to open it up upon request for guests to bring their own beverages and food and sit just to enjoy the mural. That gets my five-star rating for dedication to heritage."

"But what about this mural?"

"Commissioned in the early 1940s and painted by J. Clinton Shepherd, director of the Norton Gallery and School of Art over on the coast. I can't tell you how many field trips my classes took to the Norton when I was a kid. And there are countless exquisite features that make the mural stand out from all the pretenders. First, it's not a traditional mural that stretches out straight, but instead wraps three hundred and sixty degrees around the whole lounge.

Also, the mural itself is a panorama of the Everglades, depicting a full menu of its wild inhabitants, from alligators, raccoons, deer and turtles to ibis, ducks and storks. Shepherd prepared for the task by making frequent excursions to the Glades to sketch his wildlife subjects. Then he began painting—and this is the funky part—not on the walls of the bar, but back in his gallery in West Palm Beach. He set up a series of separate, massive canvas panels and, along with his students, went to work with his brushes. When it was complete, they transported it all through empty acres of sugarcane fields until reaching the inn, where they permanently assembled it. But wait! There's more! In the hallway leading to the lounge hangs a row of gold-framed black-and-white photos showing the mural in progress back on the coast. That bonus material alone is so overwhelming that it's easy for visitors to get dizzy and knock over chairs. Actually, that was just me."

"Plus it's a bar," said Coleman.

"Normally I'd smack you, but in this case you're right," said Serge. "No snooty gallery patrons standing back and rubbing their chins in a passive-aggressive jab that you're a Philistine. Just a bunch of regular folk who know what they love."

Coleman crumpled a beer can. "I dig art." A fat finger made a red line on paper.

"Then your big chance is at hand, because the inn's upcoming on our tour." Serge walked over and taped another page to the wall. "Meantime, I'm going to keep working until my paintings encircle this entire room in homage to Shepherd and the hotel."

"But do we have enough time?"

Serge strolled over behind Malcolm. "The time lock says definitely." He raised the drooping bag again over his contestant's head. Buzzing increased.

He rejoined Coleman again at the table. "But I do need to pick up the pace." His index finger mixed red and white paint for a roseate spoonbill. His other hand clicked the television's remote.

"Excellent! I love it when you turn on a motel TV and *Law & Order* is automatically rolling through a marathon! It's like a sign from God."

"Why are you so into that show?"

"Because it's a comedy. Or at least the chase scenes are."

"How's that?"

"The writers apparently spend so much time on the genius of the legal twists that they just backhand the action sequences into the script."

"For instance?"

"If I've seen it once, I've seen it a hundred times: Lenny goes to question a suspect at an automotive garage and flashes his badge at the boss. 'Is Frenchy here?' And the boss turns to some guy repairing a car up on a lift: 'Hey, Frenchy, the cops want to talk to you.' So the guy now has this data: The cops know his name, where he works, and most likely his home address. And what's the logical thing he does every time? Throws a wrench at them and runs out the back. Okay, first, that's a serious uphill explanation to your boss later. Although I don't know the auto repair culture. Maybe everyone's constantly throwing tools and running away, and after lunch they all have a big laugh. Anyway, they always catch Frenchy trying to climb a fence or cornering himself on a rooftop. To mix it up, sometimes it's a loading dock at a shipping company. 'Hey, Three-Fingers Louie, the police are here again.' And they catch Louie every time because he runs into a huge stack of empty cardboard boxes that are placed right where everyone walks."

"How do you know they're empty?"

"The way they fly like they're filled with helium," said Serge. "Let's watch."

They turned toward the TV.

"Hey, Bugsy, the police want to talk . . ."

"There goes the wrench," said Coleman. "He's running . . . damn, cardboard boxes *and* a fence."

"I called it."

Coleman pointed with a purple finger. "Where's the science project at?"

Serge swirled his own finger on a page. "The screws have definitely begun anchoring, just a matter of reaching their depth."

"Mmmmmm! Mmmmmm!"

Serge sat back and sighed. "Am I the only one he's annoying?"

"No. He's getting under my skin, too."

They leaned over the table again and continued painting in silence . . .

The next morning, Serge shook Coleman's shoulder. Bloodshot eyes cracked open as he sat up and bonked his head. "Ow! Where am I?"

"Between the toilet and sink again." Serge checked his watch. "Look alive, we have miles ahead."

They went back into the main room.

"Damn, you really did finish your mural," said Coleman. "There's even a wild turkey. I recognize it from the bottles."

"You had any doubts?"

"Don't take this the wrong way, but sometimes you get super excited and throw yourself into a really long project, and five minutes later you say fuck that and trash everything and take off in the car with your camera."

"You're thinking of the time I wanted to build an exquisitely detailed cardboard model from my own design of the old Orange Bowl during Super Bowl Three in Miami, complete with the Jets and Colts players and each person in the stands. I misjudged the seating capacity."

"What was the seating?"

"Eighty thousand."

"How many seats did you make before you quit?"

"Five. But let's not dwell on setbacks beyond our control." Serge stood behind Malcolm, carefully peeling the tape off his forehead and gathering up the edges of the plastic garbage bag.

At the first glimpse of the captive's head, Serge sprang backward. "Jesus!"

"Mmmmmm! Mmmmmm!"

"Can I see?" asked Coleman.

"It'll give you bad dreams."

Coleman looked anyway. "God-*daaaaaamn*! . . . Man, this is you at your sickest."

"Not my intention. I underestimated the gross-out factor." Serge tied off the plastic trash bag and threw it in a motel garbage can. "Oh, well. I'll just think about that retired couple he tried to swindle and it'll balance the scales . . . Get your luggage."

Coleman grabbed a handle. "He doesn't look like he feels so hot."

Serge opened the motel room door and turned to the hostage one last time. "Remember: Bacon, it's not just for breakfast anymore."

Chapter 17

Friday. Game day.

After school, Coach Calhoun was at his desk finishing up notes on the opponent's defensive line.

A light knock at the door. "You wanted to see me, Coach?"

"Yes, yes, come in."

Chris respectfully took a seat, and Calhoun walked around his desk, leaning casually against its front edge, just as he had during so many other player discussions. Like most of the coaches in The Muck, he knew that football was often the only anchor in these kids' lives. A whistle hanging from your neck meant serving double duty as a priest.

"Chris, other than your report cards, I realize I really don't know anything about you. What's your family like?"

"You mean my grandmother?"

"I mean your whole family."

"It's my grandmother."

"What about your dad?"

"I don't know."

"Mom?"

"I don't know."

"Brothers and sisters?"

She shook her head.

"How old is your grandmother?"

"Old."

"Friends?"

"A few. Mainly boys. All the girls where I live are much older."

"Where do you live?"

She told him. He knew the place. One of those long two-story apartment buildings that looked like a converted motel, because it was. Not a blade of landscaping, just hot dirt and litter. People coming and going at odd hours for wrong reasons.

Calhoun took stock. "You said you had a few friends?"

"Mainly at school. Actually all."

"So what do you do for fun when you're at home?"

"I like to read."

"Like what?"

That got her bubbly. "Oh, wow, I found this great book at the library." She unzipped the backpack in her lap and handed a volume to the coach.

He examined the front cover. "What's this?"

"Astrophysics."

"You're reading about the big bang?"

"It's the foundation for everything. You have to learn that if you're going to study anything else." Chris grew animated with excitement. "Most people don't realize that the bang wasn't an explosion but actually an expansion of space and time, like a balloon inflating, which allowed early matter to exceed the speed of light without violating Einstein's theory."

The coach blinked hard and flipped the book over to the back cover. "You actually understand this stuff?"

"Sure, the author breaks it all down and makes it real easy."

Calhoun handed the book back. "Chris, I know this might be sensitive, but . . . are you okay?"

"What do you mean?"

"Well, I mean, for example, have you ever been bullied?"

Excitement stopped. Chris folded in . . .

I f you've ever had a full handful of sand thrown directly in your eyes at point-blank range, it's something you'll never forget. It's not like you've *got* something in your eyes that you have to get out; you're totally shut down. Disabled in every way. Nose running. The insane pain from the first time you try to raise your eyelids. The only option is to stagger and grope blindly for a place with a water source to flush it out.

It helps if there's someone to guide you. It doesn't help if there's only cruel laughter as you stumble for safety that isn't available. Especially if the nearest water source is a canal full of alligators.

It was one of her earliest recollections. Followed by the sound of a rusty old pickup truck speeding away on a dirt road from another rabbit hunt. Then quiet. Chris felt along with her feet to locate the edge of the road, then down the embankment into the reeds. Fortunately there were no gators today. Chris splashed her face until she could manage to open two red slits and find her way back to town.

The public health clinic gave her prescription ointment for scratched corneas.

"Who did this to you?" asked the nurse.

"I did it to myself."

There were the other times. *All* the other times. It never involved sand again, but you get the picture. Some of the boys actually felt sorry for her and knew it would be the right thing to step in, but they lacked that certain gravitas in the pecking order, and so life went on as it does in the jungle of childhood.

One time that was different. A new mix of boys in the pickup truck. Before long she was facedown again between cane stalks, a large boy pinning her with knees in her back, twisting her right arm almost to the point of a radial fracture. Chris prayed for him to let go, but she never screamed.

Then, suddenly, her arm was free. And the weight was off her back.

"Dammit, Reggie! Why'd you punch me in the head?"

"What's wrong with you? She's half your size."

"Fuck off!" The tormentor ran away.

Chris rolled over in the dirt, and the boy named Reggie helped her up. "Maybe you shouldn't come out here with these guys."

"I want to play football."

That was the last day Reggie was with her group, and then it was back to old routines again. At least she did catch the occasional rabbit, which meant a buck or two toward her football fund. Chris had bought a number of footballs in her short life. Sometimes she was able to play with one for two or three days before it was gone. A football was too precious for Chris to forget and leave somewhere. It was just snatched from her hands. One ball was even stolen as she stepped out of the store where she bought it. She stopped buying footballs and started sitting.

Chris would sit on a milk crate on the balcony outside her grandmother's apartment. Elbows on her knees, chin resting on her fists. She stared out into the empty street with eyes that were lasers of rage. She was one of the happiest kids you'd ever meet, which meant other kids had to make her sad. An hour could easily go by with Chris not moving, eyes locked in that fierce gaze. But it wasn't a gaze of negativity that eats you alive from the inside. It was a look of ferocious, distilled determination. She began sitting out there so often and so long that many adults in the apartment building began subconsciously associating her with that milk crate.

She usually sat on the crate after being run off from whatever the neighborhood boys were having fun doing. The few girls who were around were much older, with their own social castes and more subtle ways of hurting. Chris just kept sitting and glaring with such intensity you'd think she was going to hemorrhage. What was she thinking about all that time?

When Chris wasn't sitting on that crate or getting run off, she spent time in her room, tending curiosity. That meant books from the school library. She loved the science ones. Volcanoes, the planets, how clouds form, photosynthesis. But her all-time favorite was a book about sea creatures. The only thing she knew from Pahokee was Lake Okeechobee and all the bass fishermen, because it was fresh water. But this book brimmed with gripping pictures that filled her imagination with the faraway world of the ocean. Urchins and rays and giant squid. She was particularly fascinated by every detail in the life cycle of the hermit crab. Then there was another book she had purchased, one with holes in it. A collector's book. She would press pennies into the holes according to year, and read voraciously about the mints in Denver and San Francisco, and the wartime pennies made of zinc because artillery shells needed the copper.

But a child like Chris was meant to be outdoors, which meant she was relentless at trying to join in and being run off and sitting on a crate. Here's what she was thinking on that crate: *I'll show them. Someday they'll want to be my friend. They all will . . .* Of course she was just a little kid and only had so much life experience to work with, so she thought: *Yes, something urgent will come up with the boys. Suddenly they'll all need really important information about hermit crabs or Lincoln pennies, and then where will they have to come? That's right, me . . .* She maintained her severe glare of tunnel vision, fantasizing about all the kids in the neighborhood coming up the street in a V formation, led by the biggest and most popular. They'd climb up to her apartment balcony and beg forgiveness, and she'd tell them about crustaceans or loose change or both.

Adults weren't the only ones who observed Chris's devotion to that milk crate. Some of the boys also began to notice. They pointed up at the balcony and laughed. Then it became a running joke. Whenever she tried to hang out and participate in whatever they were doing: "Why don't you go home to your milk crate?"

It began following her around, even when she wasn't trying to join in. She'd be walking down the sidewalk and then shouts from across the street, in a shitty, singsong taunting chant: "Milk *crate* . . . Milk *crate* . . ."

Then they took it further, and it became her nickname. "Where are you going, *Milk Crate*?"

It only made Chris stomp her feet harder on the way home. Ironically, her main source of solace and strength became sitting on that crate. So sit she did. *One day! . . . One day! . . .*

Then one day Chris came home from school and found that someone had stolen her milk crate.

C hris? Chris?" said Coach Calhoun. "Did you hear me? Have you ever been bullied?"

"Huh, what?" She raised her chin from her fists. "I'm sorry. I drifted there for a second."

"I was asking about bullies."

"Oh no. Not really."

"I've never seen a look like that in your eyes before," said Calhoun. "You almost scared me."

"Just tired."

"I heard they call you Milk Crate, not out of affection. And they stole yours."

"No big deal. I got another."

"Okay, if you say so . . . We need to start getting ready for the game."

"You got it, Coach." Chris went to a storage locker for the paper cups.

The game went pretty much as expected, a rout by Pahokee. Reggie was awarded the game ball.

An hour later, the last of the team dribbled out of the locker room in street clothes, laughing and recounting key plays that now loomed larger in their imaginations. Coach Calhoun emerged and headed for his car.

He stopped. The field and stands were empty now, just a single small person at the far end repeatedly trying to kick a football through the uprights.

One of the field maintenance people walked past the coach, opened the main power box and threw a large circuit breaker, turning off the stadium lights. Chris just teed up again and kicked one in the dark.

"Excuse me," Calhoun said to the maintenance guy. "Could you turn the lights back on?"

Chapter 18

THE ATLANTIC COAST

Florida has a lot of cities and towns with *fort* in the name. Given everything else, why not?

Fort Lauderdale, Fort Myers, Fort Meade, Fort Lonesome, Fort White, Fort Walton Beach. Tampa used to be Fort Brooke, and Ocala was Fort King. And there are more than a hundred other well-known actual forts, many still in existence, for which communities are not named. As late as the early twentieth century, the Sunshine State was still frontier country. While people in Manhattan attended operas and Yankee games, many Floridians were, well, Seminoles, the unconquered people, living down in the Glades.

A gold Plymouth Satellite revved south down coastal Highway A1A, through one of the last long, relatively empty and nonberserk stretches of Florida seaside where you can hear yourself think, and that voice is whispering not to take it for granted. Driving by Patrick Air Force Base, through Indialantic, Melbourne Beach, Sebastian Inlet, Wabasso Beach, past the Navy SEAL Museum before turning inland at the jetties.

Into Fort Pierce.

The city is located on the east coast of Florida about sixty miles north of West Palm Beach, named after the army fort built during the Second Seminole War in 1938, which in turn was named for Colonel Benjamin Pierce, brother of the fourteenth president of the United States, for what that's worth. Fort Pierce is the home of the A. E. Backus Gallery, in honor of the famous natural-landscape artist, and birthplace of the Florida Highwaymen painters movement. But in more recent years, as more and more people discover the past, it's developed a growing reputation for something else.

Zora Neale Hurston was a black woman traveling Florida in the 1930s. Not the best time for that combination in the Jim Crow South. Yet she carried it off with such class and dignity that you can only genuflect. She was a novelist, historian, anthropologist and a standout in the Harlem Renaissance scene. Or that's how one avid Floridian put it.

"Stetson Kennedy was often at the wheel of the car," said Serge, at the wheel of the gold Plymouth heading west on Avenue D. "The state's connective tissue I spoke of earlier. Rawlings to Stetson to Zora. She roamed the back roads with him, preserving local history and chronicling her times, kind of like us."

The Plymouth turned north as Serge chugged a travel mug of coffee. "Zora is often associated with Eatonville, one of the first self-governing African American communities, which used to be north of Orlando, and is now engulfed by it. They have a festival for her each year." The car continued a short distance until easing to a stop at 1734 Avenue I. "But Hurston spent her last years here." An arm pointed.

Coleman looked oddly out the window. "That tiny-ass house?"

"Realtors prefer to call it cozy." Serge got out of the car with his mug. "While Zora was well known and respected in literary circles, her body of work never really gained traction with the general public until well after her death in 1960. In fact, Zora lived out her last decade in destitute obscurity. She taught briefly at a local school, wrote a few articles for the local paper, even worked as a motel maid. But her undaunted pride and individual spirit never waned. Near the end she wrote: 'I have made phenomenal growth as a creative artist . . . If I die without money, somebody will bury me.'"

They walked across a tidy lawn toward a modest light blue stucco house with a flat roof. Couldn't be more than five hundred square feet.

"This was her last home." Serge stopped to absorb invisible rays coming off it. "Sometimes history puts the right person at the right place at the right time. Just after Hurston died, a sheriff's deputy named Pat Duval happened to be driving by here when he noticed someone burning trash in a big oil drum. He stopped to inquire, and the man said he was disposing of stuff from the house. Now, the deputy happened to be one of the few people at the time who had read Hurston and knew her worth. He quickly put out the fire, saving invaluable manuscripts and personal papers. Doesn't that spin your derby?"

Coleman was paying attention to something else. "What's with that big sign?"

"Official marker for the house, stop number three of eight on the Hurston Dust Tracks Heritage Trail," said Serge. "The city of Fort Pierce rightfully stepped up to honor Hurston and educate the masses, which I'm totally down with."

"Then why that look on your face?"

Serge finished his coffee in a long swig. "I like to dig up these off-the-path places on my own, and the sign makes it look like I cheated. But I knew about this place before the sign, I swear!" He grabbed Coleman by the front of his shirt. "After I'm gone, you're the only one who can set the record straight!"

"Sure thing," said Coleman. "My shirt . . ."

"Sorry." Serge released him. "Do you think I'm over-reacting?"

"Who am I to judge?"

"I've been thinking of getting a service animal," said Serge. "Or switching to decaf."

"Service animal?" said Coleman. "You're not disabled."

"Oh, how wrong you are," said Serge. "I'm crazy, whack job, nut-bar, basketcase, Looney Tunes, Froot Loops, cuckoo for Cocoa Puffs, screws loose, not playing with a full deck, batshit, bats in the belfry, off my rocker, off the deep end, out where the buses don't run. Stop me when I've made my point."

"No, I get it. I already knew but didn't want to say anything." Coleman whistled. "Wow, you're really admitting that to yourself?"

"Of course. What's the big deal?" Serge got out his camera. "Everyone's a little bit crazy, but my case is state-of-the-art. Usually it's a blessing, endowing me with supernatural powers of free-range thinking: Pavlov's dog, pinecones, softer bath tissue, covalent molecules, Pyrrhic victories, Lou Gehrig, nuance, the induction cooktop, the Yalta Conference, rationalization, pasteurization, Lou Gehrig's *disease,* Lemon Pledge, the number fifty-six, 'Jailhouse Rock,' opening products to void warranty, Hot Pockets, rainfall at the airport, Aztec beating hearts, osmosis, buy-one-get-one, frequent having to go, Netflix original series . . ."

Coleman crushed another beer can. "What about the rest of the time?"

". . . Hydraulic fluid, *Portnoy's Complaint,* the camel's nose under the tent, vote motherfucker! . . . What?"

"The rest of the time?" said Coleman. "When it's not a blessing?"

"Then there's screaming and pointing, and we have to run away again."

"I don't see how a service animal can fix that."

"When you say service animal, most people think of a guide dog leading the blind or performing other essential tasks for the handicapped." Serge handed his camera to Coleman. "But there's a whole other sub-category called 'emotional support animals,' who take the edge off mental conditions. Except that when you're dealing with crazy, you get the kind of animal selections you'd expect. And you wouldn't believe the growing list that is now confounding the transportation industry: from tiny pigs and iguanas to parrots and even boa constrictors, who are said to be able to detect certain seizures in advance and give a little warning squeeze. Other times the squeeze is a different warning—'Get this fucking snake off me!'—so there's an obvious downside. Even some *animals* have support animals. Thoroughbred horse breeders often place a donkey in a stall if one of their studs has a history of spazzing out."

"That's weird."

"I'm thinking of getting a meerkat."

"You mean those cute little guys on nature shows who stand up to look for trouble?"

Serge nodded. "A meerkat could level me out." He walked to the front of the house and smiled. "Take my picture at Zora's. Make sure not to get the sign . . ."

MEANWHILE . . .

In a Cocoa Beach motel room: a ticking sound, then a loud snap.

Malcolm frantically pulled his wrists free from the time lock. He felt the top of his head. *"Ahhhhhhhhh!"*

He ran out of the motel room and into the office.

The jaundiced manager jumped back from the counter. "Ahhhhhhh! What happened to your head? . . ."

Ten minutes later, the motel parking lot swarmed with police vehicles. In the motel office, someone pulled a sheet over a body. The officer in charge looked up. "What the hell happened?"

The motel manager shrugged. "He came in here demanding bacon and then collapsed."

An officer stuck his head in the door. "Lieutenant, I think there's something you need to see."

They rushed up the walkway and entered room number 7. The officer nodded toward a wall.

"Finger paintings?" said the lieutenant.

"I recognize it," said the officer. "The Everglades mural from the Clewiston Inn. The lounge is closed now, but they're really nice about letting guests in. You should go."

The lieutenant glared. "I thought you had some key evidence." He pointed in the general direction of the office. "What's wrong with you? There's a body getting cold back there."

The officer told the lieutenant to take a closer look at one of the paintings.

He did.

It was signed by the artist.

Chapter 19

A faithful stuffed wahoo with glazed eyes stared down from an office wall at a man cradling the receiver of a desk phone between his shoulder and neck. That left his hands free to take vigorous notes.

"Thank you very much for your time." He hung up.

After that final international call to a Dominican Republic historical society, Captain Crack Nasty had everything he could possibly find on one Fulgencio Fakakta, right up until he fled the island in 1921. After that, the years in Florida were still a mystery that phone calls couldn't solve. From here, it was in-person homework.

Time for a road trip.

Crack climbed into the cab of his Dodge Dakota pickup and headed west on Southern Boulevard. He left the outskirts of coastal development, passing the vintage Lion Country Safari roadside attraction, subconsciously thinking, *How old are those animals?* Then onward through Twentymile Bend, all the way out to where the first fumes of development picked up again as he neared the big lake. The road's name changed to Hooker Highway. The schoolkids got a kick out of that.

The captain started at the Pahokee and Belle Glade libraries, looking through special collections of old newspaper microfilms. He drove past the hurricane monument on the way over to the courthouses for records of faded deeds. He cruised the back roads around the addresses he had jotted down. Then he widened his circles of driving out into the nearest sugarcane fields. He picked up a tail. Not law enforcement, but local young men in their twenties. He thought: *What has gone insane in this world when blacks are allowed to follow whites in the Deep South?* Except his surveillance wasn't threatening; it was concerned. The three youths were watching out for their neighbors because Crack's movements around town came off like he was planning some kind of crime. Which was accurate.

The salvager was more than relieved when he reached his next stop, the local police department. Crack asked to speak with their public-affairs spokesman, and was led into an office with a football in a display case on the desk. The captain said he was writing for one of those metal-detector hobby magazines, and he wanted to ask about some rumors he'd been hearing.

"Oh, so that's why you've been driving around here all suspicious like," said the sergeant.

"You know I've been driving around?" said Crack. "Then I need to tell you there were these dangerous characters following me."

"How do you think we found out you were driving around?" said the sergeant. "The guys following you called us on their cell phones. And they're not dangerous; they used to play on the football team. They just thought you were up to something. Are you?"

"Me? What? Huh?" Crack displayed upturned palms. "Just working on my article. I heard some folklore about a sugar kingpin who supposedly went missing in the 1928 hurricane, along with some artifacts of historical significance and maybe a couple coins."

"I've heard the same." The sergeant smiled. "And that's exactly what that is. Folklore."

"But I also heard that children playing out in the sugarcane fields have found a few of these coins over the decades since the storm."

"Another bit of fanciful folklore," said the sergeant. "In all the years, we haven't known a single actual child who found anything. And do you think little kids can keep something like that a secret? They'd bring it to school and show it all around in class, and by the end of the day it would be confiscated by a teacher for depriving others of their education."

"But I've learned so much about the history of this sugar guy from the Dominican that it seems more likely—"

The sergeant held up a hand. "My advice to you? And I mean this politely: Forget about your article. We've got a nice friendly town here, and we mean to keep it that way. Visitors are always welcome, especially all those college football scouts. But what we don't need is a bunch of people running around like headless chickens with metal detectors, trespassing and digging up the whole place. Do you see how it could get messy?"

"Well, it also won't do my magazine's reputation any good if we direct people here and nobody finds anything." Captain Crack stood and stretched. "Not all of these article ideas pan out. Guess I'll just be getting back to West Palm."

"You seem like a reasonable person," said the sergeant. He shook Crack's hand. "Stop in anytime."

Crack left the office, and the sergeant picked up the phone. "I need you to follow someone . . . Yeah, Dodge Dakota with a magnetic sign on the door for a boat-towing service . . ."

Captain Crack tapped the steering wheel to a country music tune about only being able to trust his dog anymore. The pickup truck passed vacant concrete buildings of pink, green and blue. He checked his rearview. Just as he thought. A police tail. But it was a loose one, not meant for strict surveillance as much as making sure he kept his word to leave town.

A few minutes later, Highway 98 said goodbye to the last building, and Crack left the city limits. He looked up in the mirror again, and watched the police car make a lazy U-turn in the road and head the other way. The captain drove another half mile through nothing but cane fields, then made a sharp left onto a road usually used only by the sugar company. After a few zigzags, he navigated a wide route back into town. He deliberately parked out of sight behind a small business near Main Street.

Bells jingled.

A pawnshop owner named Webber looked up from a newspaper. *Finally,* he thought. Not a kid, not police, but a real customer. He folded the paper. "How can I help you?"

"Gold pieces."

"Only have a few." Webber opened the back of a glass display case. "But a real nice one came in a few years ago. Just haven't been able to sell it because, well, the economy around here. Saint-Gaudens double eagle, 1907. If you don't know, it's one of the—"

"I know the coin," said Crack. "How'd you come by it in these parts?"

"I'm sorry, but that information is confidential." Webber set the coin on the counter for Crack to examine. "We strictly protect the privacy of all our customers."

"It was a kid, wasn't it?"

The pawnshop owner's head jerked up straight on his neck. "How'd you know?"

"Been doing my research. I'll bet you've had a number of kids bring these in over the years. What can you tell me about them?"

The owner stepped back with hands on his hips. "Mister, what's really your business here? You didn't come to buy a coin."

Crack opened his wallet. "How much?"

"You're really going to buy it? You haven't even looked at—...I mean I usually have to work harder for a sale." He glanced at the gold circle still sitting on the counter. "In that condition it books for . . ."—Webber adjusted the number upward in his head mid-sentence—". . . seventeen hundred."

Crack pulled money from the billfold. "Would you settle for, say, two thousand? In cash."

Webber scratched the top of his head. "You sure have a funny way of negotiating."

"There's a catch."

"That, I assumed."

"I'll also need the name and address of the person who sold it to you."

Webber paused again. "So you really believe kids are bringing these coins in?"

"Sure, why not?"

"Because the police think I'm fencing stolen collections."

"That's because they haven't done their homework. Do you know anything about an early sugar baron around here named Fulgencio Fakakta?"

"Everyone's heard the stories," said Webber. "Especially the part about his hidden treasure lost in the Great Hurricane . . . Wait, you're not looking for . . ."

"I never said anything about treasure. You did." Crack leaned down to the counter. "Why? You don't believe that these kids found pieces of the baron's stash?"

"Not really," said Webber. "As I was telling the cops, from the dates on these coins, that's when there were all these juke joints—"

"I've read up on the local history," said Crack. "The name and the coin? Do we have a deal?"

Webber considered the stranger a moment, then began writing on a blank sheet of paper.

"On second thought," said Captain Crack, pulling out more bills. "Make it an even three thousand."

"Another catch?"

"I was never here."

Webber handed him the paper. "You're already a ghost."

"One more thing." Crack gave him a business card. "If any other kids come in here with more coins, call me and I'll buy them. Same price and terms."

"You got it."

Bells jingled.

Chapter 20

FORT PIERCE

The gold Plymouth Satellite rolled up to the corner of Avenue S and Seventeenth Street. Serge got out and looked at another sign.

GARDEN OF HEAVENLY REST.

For a cemetery, it was sparsely populated. No big monuments or even large headstones. The rows of modest markers and slabs were widely separated in an otherwise sunny grass field where kids would have room to play ball. Coleman looked side to side as they walked past graves. "I'm guessing you have a cool story to drag me out here."

"One of the best stories yet!" Serge continued on until they reached the middle of the field. A single grave sat in the grass, surrounded by a small brick walkway. The whitewashed slab was raised slightly higher than the others, although the headstone was still only knee-high. It was the only one where people had been by recently to leave flowers. There was a candle. Some had left rocks on the headstone in the Jewish tradition.

Serge got down on a knee and placed his page over the letter Z. He began rubbing. "Hurston's undeserved obscurity had become so complete that her grave was unmarked for years and nobody could precisely pay their respects. Then the story takes a hairpin turn, extending beyond the grave to Zora's proper place in the public's awareness."

"It was only right," said Coleman.

"The year? Nineteen seventy-three. The person? Alice Walker." Serge rubbed on. "Walker was still nearly a decade away from writing her Pulitzer Prize–winning novel, *The Color Purple*. But back in the early seventies, the budding writer, still only twenty-nine years old, stumbled across Zora's works and became intrigued, even obsessed to the point of visiting Florida to get the vibes of Zora's life. She started in Eatonville, where she learned Zora was buried anonymously somewhere in Fort Pierce. So she drove out here to the coast and—this part I love—she fibbed that she was Zora's niece to get locals to open up about her 'aunt.' To her surprise, most had never heard of her, even those now living near Zora's last home. Finally, with a history-researching tenacity to which I can only aspire, she located the lost grave and bought this headstone for it." Serge began rubbing the words on the next line: A GENIUS OF THE SOUTH. "Two years later, Walker wrote a watershed article for *Ms.* magazine, 'Looking for Zora,' using her grave search as a vehicle to showcase the forgotten literary lion. That first-person piece slowly but surely rekindled interest in Hurston's work until she now stands in the pantheon. Oh, and she's from Florida!"

The gold Plymouth left the cemetery and headed south on U.S. 1, down through Jensen Beach and Stuart.

"Where to now?" asked Coleman.

"Our next stop," said Serge. "But first I need to make a *stop* before our next stop."

He pulled into a strip mall and opened the door.

"I'll wait in the car," said Coleman.

"As a general rule, that's the best plan." Serge went inside . . .

Coleman was unconscious when Serge returned, head resting against the passenger window and trademark drool stringing down from his lower lip.

Onward, south. Hobe Sound, Tequesta, Jupiter.

Coleman stirred from his liquid-induced nap. "Hmm, huh, where am I?"

"Still in the car."

Coleman reached down between his legs and popped a Schlitz to restore chemical equilibrium. "Did you get your meerkat back at that pet store?"

"No," said Serge, racing south into Juno Beach. "I didn't have any clue that they're like a thousand bucks, and they'd have to order one. Plus the pet-store guy told me that meerkats may be social creatures among themselves, but they're a little confused by the whole pet concept. Some never conform to domesticity, constantly screeching and jumping on lamps, and the ones that do work out will keep peeing on your clothes to mark you as their owner."

"That's messed up," said Coleman.

"Not exactly the definition of a support animal," said Serge. "I want a pet to wind me *down*."

"You'll figure something out." Coleman took a long swig of beer. Suddenly: "Ahh! Shit! What the hell?" The can of Schlitz went up in the air, Coleman batting and bobbling to catch it, foam everywhere.

"Are you spraying beer all over my car again?"

"Not my fault." Coleman finally got a handle on the can and pulled his neck way back in alarm, looking down in his lap in terror. "What the fuck is that thing?"

Serge glanced over. "Say hello to Mr. Zippy, my new ferret."

"Ferret?"

"When a meerkat became a non-starter, the pet-store dude suggested a ferret because they're roughly the same size and cuteness factor, easier on the wallet, and they don't pee on you. Not much."

The ferret began chattering at Coleman. "Get him off me! Get him off!" Beer flew again.

"You're frightening Zippy!" said Serge. "You need to win him over. Give him that Cheeto."

"Where?"

"Where else."

"Oh." Coleman picked it off his shoulder and tentatively extended a hand. Mr. Zippy snatched it, munching away. Then he climbed over the shoulder of a wide-eyed Coleman. "Where'd he go?"

"To explore the back seat."

"You're just going to let him run loose in the car?"

"It's what I'd want if the roles were reversed," said Serge. "Now back to live action! Our next stop is some more Florida connective tissue, this time leading from Hurston. In her now-acclaimed 1937 classic, *Their Eyes Were Watching God,* Zora depicts the hard life of African Americans along the southern shore of Lake Okeechobee early last century, culminating with the Great Hurricane of 1928—"

The ferret jumped on the dashboard and ran along the windshield, then jumped down and disappeared again.

"Jesus, Serge, how can you drive with that going on?"

"It's actually quite comforting." A calm grin crept across his face. "After the storm, Zora described the formidable task of dealing with almost three thousand bodies, so many that it took at least four burial sites . . ."

The Plymouth entered West Palm Beach and navigated south on Tamarind Avenue, into an economically scuffling section of the city, or, among the whites, the other side of the tracks. They parked on the corner of Twenty-Fifth Street.

"Hurston's novel described the mass burial activity here, but the site became so forgotten that even those who knew about it didn't have the exact location, and a warehouse was almost built on top of it. Luckily, community leaders stepped in and hired a Miami firm that used ground-penetrating radar to discover a seventy-by-thirty-foot trench." Serge placed paper against stone. "This is the granite memorial they erected in 2003."

Coleman curiously watched Serge.

"What?"

He pointed. "Where'd you get that?"

"This?" Serge looked down at something new on his chest attached to shoulder straps. "From the pet store. It's like those things that moms wear to carry infants."

Mr. Zippy poked his head out the top of the canvas pouch and looked around.

"He's growing on me," said Coleman.

Back to the car. A couple miles south on Dixie Highway, another stop.

"There's the Norton Museum of Art. Remember? From the Everglades mural?"

"We're going there?"

"No, other side of the street."

"On one condition," said Coleman.

"Now you're setting conditions, are you?"

Coleman told him what it was. ". . . *Pleeeeeease!*"

The pair walked through a grand stone archway into Wood-lawn Cemetery.

"Because of segregation at the time of the hurricane, the mass grave for the whites was here. Unlike the others, they got pine boxes . . . How's it working out over there?"

Coleman smiled and looked down at the pouch on his chest.

"I think Mr. Zippy likes me." A burst of chattering and then a tiny head disappeared. "So you came to see another mass grave?"

"Not this time." Serge led the way through the ancient grounds until stopping at a stone with the name Charles William Pierce.

Coleman gently patted the pouch. "Who's that?"

"A bonus find unconnected to the hurricane, so how can I not stop?" Serge knelt to rub again. "In 1888, Charlie became one of the state's first legendary 'barefoot mailmen.' Because there was no land route back then between West Palm and Miami, mail carriers would make a six-day, hundred-and-thirty-mile trek, much of it traversed on foot along the beach, hence the name . . ." He turned and began running back to the car. "We're off!"

"Come on, Mr. Zippy!"

Chapter 21

FOUR YEARS EARLIER

A loud bell rang nonstop.

The local junior high was dismissed for the day. Kids poured out the doors like the Berlin Wall had fallen. Backpacks, skateboards, cell phones. Someone pushed someone else into the bushes.

A Dodge Dakota quietly eased up to the curb across the street.

A girl texted as she crossed the road.

"Excuse me?" Crack hung out the window. "Miss?"

She looked up. Uh-oh. Stranger Danger.

"Don't be scared," said Crack, checking the scrap of paper from the pawnshop. "I'm just looking for my nephew. Do you know a Ricky Aparicio?"

She pointed back at the school gates.

Captain Crack stretched his neck. "Which one?"

"I thought he was your nephew."

"Been a long time."

"Red shirt, blue shorts." She hurried along on her way.

The boy headed north on the opposite side of the street, along with a dozen other loud, laughing kids. Crack started up his truck and drove slowly. Parts of the gang peeled off as they reached the streets to their homes. It was down to just a few when Crack hung out the window again.

"Ricky! Ricky Aparicio!"

The boy looked over. "Who are you?"

Crack waved with his left hand. "Come over here. I need to ask you a question."

"Don't go," said one of the other boys.

"See what he wants," said another.

Ricky decided to split the difference and walked halfway across the empty street. "What do you want?"

"Come closer," said Crack. "I won't bite."

"I'm staying right here until you tell me what this is about."

"It concerns the gold coin you sold to the pawnshop."

"I didn't steal it!"

"Nobody says you did." The captain held out a piece of currency. "I just need some information. I'm writing an article for a hobby magazine."

"Ricky!" yelled one of the boys on the other curb. "Don't get any closer!"

"Ricky!" yelled another. "That's a hundred-dollar bill!"

Ricky got closer. "Exactly what kind of information?"

"I've been doing some research on your town, the hurricane and everything, and I think you might have stumbled onto something historic. I'll pay you a hundred dollars to show me where you found that coin."

Ricky stood like a statue. A beeping car drove around him.

Crack hung farther out the driver's window. "Listen, I know what you've been taught about strangers. But how would I know all this information about what you found? Besides, all those warnings are for little kids. You're practically a man now."

Ricky remained a stone.

"What do you say?" Crack waved the bill tauntingly. "Hundred bucks. Going once, going twice—"

"Okay, okay, but give me the money first."

"Once you're in the truck, or you'll just run away."

Ricky got in, and the Dodge drove off. The other boys dashed home to tell their parents . . .

It was ten minutes of dubious directions from the youth. "Take this left. Wait, the next left, that's it. No, that's not right. It's farther up."

"Are you sure you know where we're going?"

"Positive." Ricky clutched the hundred as if it was life itself. "Uh, could we go back to town and start again? I can figure it out better if we're coming from Main Street. From this other way, I'm not so good."

"Jesus," Crack said under his breath. But greed had gotten the better of him, and he was locked in for the ride, seeing nothing but piles of those coins.

The Crossroads.

If the intersection had one of those signposts with wooden arrows pointing different directions with names of places and mileage, all the arrows on this post would have said Nowhere.

Three of the corners were empty except for concrete-block ruins with collapsed roofs, and weeds now grew where there had been carpeting.

On the fourth corner sat a gas station that sold as much malt liquor as unleaded.

Signs said No Loitering, at least under the spray-paint graffiti.

Three young men lounged on a stoop. All high school graduates, all football players, all with onetime dreams of making the NFL. Now they spent their days here. This was not the NFL.

Wasn't their fault. Life had dealt them truly cruel hands of cards. If you take a hundred successful Wall Street types and have them born at the very bottom with no breaks, see how far they go. This particular trio all had jobs. The operative word was *had*. When the economy coughed, The Muck got pneumonia, and layoffs were a lifestyle. The three currently had a bunch of job applications submitted all over town, but where were the jobs? So they hung out here until something turned up.

"Remember that pass I caught in the fourth quarter? Right sideline?"

"You and that one freaking pass! All we ever hear: 'Remember? Right sideline?' Shit, I had three receptions that game."

"But all short yardage over the middle."

"Moved us into scoring position, didn't it?"

"Both of you are bullshit," said the third young man. "Just remember who *threw* all those passes."

They stopped talking and watched as a lone vehicle slowly rounded the corner at the station and accelerated east. Magnetic door sign for a boat-towing company. They all sprang to their feet.

"That son of a bitch!"

"He's back!"

"And he's got Ricky!"

They piled into a low-riding Datsun and took off.

"I knew that asshole was up to something, but I didn't know what. He's a pedophile!"

"He'll kill Ricky for sure if we don't stop him!"

"Shouldn't we call the police?"

"Screw that! We can take care of our own . . ."

A mile out of town, Ricky pointed. "Turn here. This time I'm sure."

"If you say so." The Dakota made a skidding left onto a dirt road.

Moments later, a tricked-out Datsun sailed by the turnoff. "I don't see his truck anymore."

"Drive faster. We'll catch up . . ."

Back in the cane field, Ricky hopped down from the pickup's cab and climbed through a couple rows of stalks. "It was right around here somewhere."

"You don't seem that sure."

Ricky stopped and stomped a foot into the black soil. "Right here."

"Exactly?" said Crack.

Ricky nodded vigorously. "Take me back now."

"Are you joking? I gave you a hundred. Show me!"

"How?"

"Dig!"

"What?"

"If you're so fucking sure, dig!"

Panic now. Ricky got on the ground and scooped dirt with shaking hands.

"Don't keep looking up at me!" yelled Crack. "Pay attention to what you're doing! Dig! . . ."

Up the road, parked on the right shoulder, more panic. "We just got Ricky killed!" said the wide receiver.

"Don't say that!" yelled the tight end.

"I knew we should have called the police," said the quarterback.

"What's done is done. We need to chill out and figure this thing out. What would a pedophile do?"

They looked all the way around the horizon. "Bring him out in a cane field," said the wide receiver. "For privacy and body disposal."

"Don't say that!" snapped the tight end.

"He must have taken a turnoff." The quarterback swung the car around. "Keep your eyes open . . ."

Somewhere out in the stalks, small hands flung dirt. A whimper.

Captain Crack had gotten back into the Johnnie Walker, swinging the bottle by his side. "What the hell are you crying about!"

"I want to go home."

"Shut up and dig!"

"I want my mommy."

Ricky never saw the open-handed slap coming. It cupped the side of his head over his ear and sent him sprawling.

Louder crying now. "I didn't find the coin. A girl did."

"You've been lying to me all along?" Slap. "Who is this girl?"

"I don't know! I swear!"

Slap.

"Kathy? Karen? I can't remember . . ."

Back on Highway 98, a Datsun was on a slow roll.

"Wait! Stop!"

"What is it?"

"Back up! I saw his truck!"

The quarterback threw the car in reverse, then barreled down the dirt road toward the parked Dakota. It skidded to a stop just as Ricky came bursting through the cane stalks, bloody nose, crying, ripped shirt.

The quarterback got down on a knee and hugged the boy tight.

Then another voice from an unseen source a few cane rows over. "Come back here, you little fucker!" The boat captain broke through the final row and stopped.

The quarterback stood up. Without looking down at Ricky, he placed a hand on the boy's shoulder. "Go wait in my car."

Crack Nasty pointed at them with the hand not holding the bottle. "Now you listen here! I gave him a hundred dollars and we had a deal!"

It was a short chase.

They gang-tackled the captain only a few steps from where he started. The ensuing beating was not for the squeamish. Savage kicks to the ribs and head as Crack desperately tried to crawl for sanctuary that wasn't there. More kicking and stomping in rage. It wasn't thug life. It was family life. One of them found a stick and smashed it over his neck. Another hit him with a rock. A few more kicks and Crack finally rolled onto his back, an unconscious, bloody mess. But the kicking continued.

The quarterback jumped in and grabbed the others. "Guys! Guys! Stop or you'll kill him!"

"So what?" Kick.

"I feel the same way, but if you think our lives are shit now . . ." He looked back at the Datsun. "Plus we need to get Ricky home. His mother must be worried sick."

They took turns spitting on Captain Crack.

Then the Datsun drove away.

Chapter 22

The gold Plymouth picked up two-lane State Road 710, also known as the Bee Line Highway: an odd, almost perfectly diagonal shot northwest up through the unpopulated part of Palm Beach County, along the railroad tracks, through the Loxahatchee Slough, up past the old Pratt & Whitney aircraft-engine plant that brought thousands of transplants to the county in the early sixties. They reached Indiantown, and turned decidedly west on Route 76, into more and more nothingness.

Coleman petted the pouch on his chest and looked out the window at scraggly woods. "Are we actually heading anywhere?"

"Lake Okeechobee," said Serge. "Another of our crown jewels, so huge it dominates photos taken from the Space Shuttle. And to hell with it: I'm going on the record right now, and will take on all comers. At seven hundred and thirty square miles, Okeechobee is the largest freshwater lake in the country. Oh, sure, everyone else says it's the *second* biggest, behind Lake Michigan. But that one's open at the top, mixing with Canadian water. How is *that* the record? Where were the referees on that one?"

"It's just not fair."

"Canada, Christ." Serge shook his head. "*Our* lake is a damn force of nature. I like to think of it as Florida's moon."

"How is it a moon?"

"Give me some latitude on this, Judge Coleman, and I will show the relevance," said Serge. "Earth's moon is an oddity of our solar system, far closer and proportionally larger than any of the other planets' moons. So much so that it creates our ocean tides, affects the seasons and even stabilizes Earth's rotation, doing nothing less than making life possible at all. On a smaller scale, same thing with our freakishly large lake. Most Floridians have never seen it, and even fewer realize the overwhelming effect it has on the rest of the state. First, it collects much of the watershed in Central Florida, from the Kissimmee River and other sources. Then below it, the lake feeds the Everglades. And the extensive matrix of canals that were dug to channel its runoff created entire agricultural industries and—even more mind-blowing—the very dry land that allows much of South Florida, from Miami to Fort Lauderdale, to even exist. Otherwise, all the residents would be tits-deep in lily pads and gators instead of blissfully working skimming nets to scoop leaves from their swimming pools."

"I had no idea." Coleman held his beer away from the pouch and looked down at his chest. "You're not old enough."

"But here's the kicker, and it's a beauty . . ." Serge slowed and tracked their position on a GPS. "The Okeechobee hurricane of 1928 is still whipping up changes in the way we live, even to this day!"

"How can a storm that old still be messing with us?"

"I'll tell you!" The Plymouth slowed even further. "The three thousand souls that were lost made it the second-worst natural disaster in the nation's history, behind only the Galveston storm in 1900. Nobody saw it coming. Everyone was always preparing for storm surges from the ocean, but then that monster storm made a direct hit on the lake. And if you ever doubt how big that body of water is, imagine a tidal wave covering hundreds of square miles, much higher than virtually every house. First the storm's rotation flooded all the communities along the southern shore. Then the backside of the hurricane hit, pushing water north through the city of Okeechobee. After all the burials, the federal government stepped in to prevent such a tragedy. They built the enormous Herbert Hoover Dike, a thirty-foot-high, one-hundred-and-forty-three-mile-long earthen berm surrounding the lake. That's why so many people crisscrossing the state above and below the immense body of water never see it; they just dismiss it as a long grassy hill and have such screwed-up priorities that they aren't curious to take one of the access ramps to the top and marvel. That's why I've decided to carve out time and make the lake the culmination of our tour. Zora led us here."

"So we're almost at the end?" asked Coleman.

"Actually just beginning, but time folds in on itself." The gold Satellite pulled over on the side of an empty road without a sign of life. "I intend to drop anchor, explore the lake in every detail and get a bone-deep understanding of her people. It's an amazingly disparate culture: the old-cracker cattle ranchers up north with their rodeos, western-wear shops and steak houses; the impoverished farmworkers to the south; and all around, the visiting bass fishermen hoping to land that prized lunker."

Serge got out of the car with another large sheet of paper. He approached a green metal historic marker and began rubbing.

Coleman arrived with the ferret peeking around. "Where are we?"

Rub, rub. "Can't you read?"

"My eyes are having that focus problem again."

"We're at Port Mayaca, a ghost town with ghosts." Rub, rub.

"Out in that field somewhere lie the remains of sixteen hundred victims of the storm. As usual, people finally realized they needed to erect this sign decades later."

"Sixteen hundred?" Coleman blinked a few times.

"Right under our feet." Rub, rub. "It's important to remember."

"Shit! Dammit!"

"I know the storm was a heartbreak—"

"No, not that!" Coleman pointed.

"How'd you let Mr. Zippy get away?"

"He was too fast."

They began running around the field.

"Hold on," said Coleman. "I think I have some Doritos in my pocket."

"In your pocket?"

"Just in case." Coleman tossed one forward. "I think he's going for it."

"Here, let me have one." Serge crouched down and extended a hand. "It's working." The ferret stopped to nibble, and was gently picked up. "Give me that pouch!"

"No!" Coleman turned sideways and clutched it. "I want to carry him."

"You're obviously a bad influence," said Serge.

"I can change."

"Are we going to have a custody battle? The courts won't look fondly on your substance intake."

"What about you waxing dudes?"

Serge walked the legal proceedings through his head and saw them inevitably leading to foster care. "Okay, for *now*. Just keep on top of him."

The Plymouth drove a short distance farther west, over the train tracks, reaching Highway 98 and more emptiness. "Port Mayaca is another Florida settlement abandoned by time. Besides the cemetery, about the only other thing left, like a sore thumb out here, is that big white plantation-style house coming up on our left: the historic Cypress Inn, currently a private residence and on the National Register. Hard to imagine now that there was ever enough business to support the hotel, but once upon a time the constant, northbound winter railroad traffic of fresh vegetables made this a bustling corridor."

The Plymouth turned off the highway and drove up the incline of an access road. Serge got out with his camera, hitching a camping product to his belt.

Coleman petted Mr. Zippy. "What's that thing you put on your waist?"

"Canteen for my coffee." He uncapped it for a big chug, then re-capped it. "I just completed a blue-ribbon time-motion study on myself, and someone needs to get fired. The canteen was the number one recommendation in the report, because I'm so often reaching out a hand for coffee and coming up with a fistful of empty."

Coleman pointed in another direction. "Did we drive all the way to the ocean?"

"No." *Click, click, click.* "We're on top of the dike. That's the lake."

"*That's* the lake?" said Coleman. "I can't even see the other side. And we're way up honkin' high!"

"That's how it got its name." *Click, click, click.* "The Seminole word for *big water.*"

"There's like a row of weird clouds all spaced out," said Coleman. "Wait, each of them has a little thing stretching to the ground like a tornado. But they're black like smoke. Is something on fire?"

"That would be the sugarcane fields burning over the horizon on the opposite shore. The size of those clouds should give you some idea of the scale of those blazes. They need that to get rid of the leaves and weeds before the harvesting machines come through."

Coleman looked the other way, at something much closer. "What's that?"

"The Port Mayaca Lock and Dam." *Click, click, click.* "Something else people don't realize is that you can sail clear across the state of Florida, from Fort Myers to Stuart, along the Caloosahatchee and St. Lucie rivers. But there's a series of five locks in order to raise the vessels to get to the lake, then a clear shot across a bass fishermen's paradise before the rest of the locks lower the boats back down to sea level. Like the Panama Canal except bigger. Not as wide, but much longer. So I'm going on the record right now with that as well. Fuck 'em."

Coleman looked left and right. "If this is Port Mayaca, where's the port?"

"Pretty much just that lock," said Serge.

"What's the big gate-looking thing next to it? Part of the lock?"

"No, that's the spillway," said Serge. "Remember when I told you the 1928 hurricane was still surprising people in ways they never dreamed?"

"Not really, but go on."

"So remember when we were on the coast in Stuart last year? Remember the *smell*?"

"Oh, my God! That stink is still in my head again," said Coleman. "I've never smelled anything so nasty in all my life!"

"That's what everyone said." *Click, click, click.* "And at first, because they don't know how the state's ecosystem is interconnected, they couldn't figure it out. They just saw all this thick green sludge completely blanketing the coastal inlets, up through the Intracoastal Waterway to the boating canals behind homes, like an ice floe. The stench was so bad that it emptied beaches and restaurants, and residents were held prisoner in their homes with scented candles, praying the air-conditioning didn't give out."

"What was it?"

"It all started here, forty miles away," said Serge. "The Hoover Dike is getting old, and the Army Corps of Engineers has been sounding the alarm for years that it's in desperate need of repairs or the next hurricane could breach, just like the levees failed in

New Orleans during Katrina. So when the water levels get too high, as a precautionary step they open the spillways, releasing millions of gallons of water. Same thing simultaneously happened on the Gulf coast when they opened the gates at Moore Haven."

"But how did that cause the stinky green slime?"

"The Corps of Engineers caught a lot of flak, but it wasn't their fault. Their only responsibility is protecting life and property from a dike failure. The problem is that, over the years, the lake has become chock-full of nitrogen-rich fertilizer runoff. Some is back-pumped into the lake by Big Sugar, but probably just as much or more was carried down the Kissimmee River from the pasture and cattle land south of Orlando. The resulting algae bloom could easily be seen from space—I'm kind of hung up on the reference point right now. But oddly, it didn't get much national press, and if you weren't there, you couldn't imagine the extent of the environmental disaster. Beautiful, flowing waterways just choking to death, rotting fish, no-swimming signs. For the first time, thousands of people on both coasts became acutely aware of this faraway but dominant lake. Our moon."

Coleman used a single finger to scratch a furry head. "Mr. Zippy, you don't like algae blooms, do you?" He looked up at Serge. "He says he doesn't . . . Ow, damn!" He quickly yanked his finger back. "Mr. Zippy just bit me!"

"What kind of sickness did you inflict on him?"

"Nothing, I swear."

"Did it draw blood or was it just a little nip?"

"Just a nip." Shaking a finger. "Still hurts."

Serge nodded in understanding. "The guy at the pet store explained it to me. If they're scared or pissed off, they can really bite, but if it's only a nip, it's because they're so smart."

"How is biting me smart?"

"Their intelligence requires constant mental stimulation, and they let you know it. That's what is known as their *I'm-bored-as-shit-please-entertain-me* bite."

Coleman looked down at the pouch, wiggling silly fingers next to his ears and sticking out his tongue. Mr. Zippy squeaked. Coleman petted him.

"He bit me again."

"Here," said Serge, passing his smartphone across the front seat. "Let him watch some stuff on YouTube."

"Like what?"

"Zany ferret videos. There's like a thousand for every occasion. One thing YouTube has taught me is that other people are drilling deep into ways to waste their lives."

"Okay, let me try . . ." Coleman got a video going and held the phone to the pouch. "I think it's working. He's getting into it."

Serge glanced over. "What's it playing?"

"There's a ferret in a sweater, and now two more are losing their minds in a pile of packing peanuts, another one is rolling a watermelon across the kitchen, another is riding on the back of a house cat like a jockey, one just crawled completely inside an empty tube of Pringles . . . I had no idea they were so talented."

Serge got out of the car and stood gazing across a stunning vista. "Time to take in one last sunset look from the top of the dike before we proceed." He unhitched a camping canteen from his belt and slugged cold coffee.

A minivan came up the access ramp and parked nearby. The vehicle's sliding door opened, belching out children, who promptly began screaming as they ran in pointless circles. Exhausted parents climbed down from the front seat.

"A family!" Serge quickly chugged and capped the canteen. "People still care! I must congratulate and share the good news!"

The parents leaned against the minivan's bumper, soaking up the view and eating granola bars. Serge blustered over, jumping like he had a pogo stick. "Thank God you made it! You don't see anyone else up here. That means you're special for caring!" He bobbed on the balls of his feet. "You just *have* to visit the mass grave next, I insist. Your thoughts on the algae bloom? Seen it from space? That lake is our moon." Serge tapped the side of his head. "Let it set in. Did you know that the top of this dike is part of the thirteen-hundred-mile Florida National Scenic Trail? My faithful pal here is Coleman, and that's Mr. Zippy, my service animal. Mental condition, nothing you need to worry about. Others, maybe." He pointed at the kids, still running randomly and screaming. "Children have the best sense of hearing, and yet they're always shouting at the top of their lungs at each other, especially in motel pools. Could never figure that one out. On the other hand, kindergarten is my religion. The children will lead us . . . Coleman, you ready?"

"I'm in."

The pair began running aimlessly around the top of the dike, screaming shrill gibberish to mimic the children: *"Wa-wa-wa-wa-wa!* . . . *Yi-yi-yi-yi-yi!* . . . *Blobidy-blobidy-blobidy!* . . . Coleman! Tag! You're it! Can't catch me! . . . Can't catch me! . . . Try to catch me!—"

A panel door slammed shut. Serge stopped and watched the minivan race back to the highway. "Man, they must really want to see that cemetery . . ."

Chapter 23

FOUR YEARS EARLIER

I fell down some stairs."

The doctor glared at Captain Crack. "Only if the stairs then got up and fell on your head. Someone clearly beat the crap out of you. Probably more than one."

"How much longer?" snapped Crack, butterfly bandages across his eyebrows and cheeks. "I have to get back to work."

"Hold on, just need to finish taping up these ribs."

Crack didn't really have to lie. It was one of those off-the-books doctors, the kind you call for a GSW—that would be gunshot wound—when you want to avoid the mandatory reporting to police that the law requires. Every city's got a few, and all the shady types have them on speed dial.

The doctor finished treating the captain underneath a stuffed wahoo, and left Crack's office. Captain Nasty had some more people on speed dial who didn't advertise in the yellow pages. He punched buttons on his cell phone.

"Fallon, it's me, Crack," said the captain. "I know you probably don't remember, but we met a while back through a mutual friend. Vic Carver . . ."

The people the captain was contacting were consummate professionals, the kind he'd like working for him on his boats, but he couldn't afford their price tag for that sort of long-term employment. On the other hand, it might be for the better, because he wouldn't look forward to having any kind of business dispute with these cats.

". . . The reason I'm calling is I have a job for you. . . . No, I'm calling from a burner phone. . . . Okay, check me out with Vic and then we'll meet . . ."

The next day, Captain Crack stood on the side of the Flagler Bridge over the Intracoastal Waterway to Palm Beach. It was one of those old, low concrete drawbridges that the people who couldn't afford boats fished from. The fish were apparently biting because the bridge was unusually full. Mainly blacks and Latinos. Straw hats. Someone reeled in a flopping catfish and tossed it in a pail. There was talk, time and again, over on the wealthy island about passing some kind of law to get rid of the people on the bridge, but it never really worked out.

Captain Crack cast a lure out into the water and began reeling. The midday sun was a challenge, even with his ventilated fishing shirt, and patience wasn't among his virtues. He kept checking his watch. He looked one way toward the modest skyline of downtown West Palm Beach, and then the other toward the tony waterfront mansions with Spanish barrel tiles and royal palms. He heard someone next to him and turned.

Another fisherman set a bait bucket down on the cement next to Crack's bucket. Both pails were orange and white. The new arrival then cast a line in the water without speaking. He was a head taller than the captain, thinner, more muscular in a formfitting black T-shirt that matched his black hat and jet-black wraparound sunglasses. A formation of pelicans glided along the bridge's ancient railing. A cheap radio somewhere was playing Cuban salsa music.

"It's all in the bait bucket," said Crack. "Instructions, money, just like you told me on the phone."

The taller fisherman stared down at Crack with unseen eyes behind the sunglasses. It meant: *The instructions also were not to talk to me.* What did he not understand about standing next to a stranger on a bridge and simply switching identical bait buckets?

"Sorry," said Crack.

The man brusquely picked up the captain's bucket and left the bridge.

A white blop of pelican poop hit Crack's arm.

T he sun had just gone down behind an emaciated gas station. The horizon was low and clear over the cane stalks from all four corners of the intersection. Someone walked out of the station scratching an instant lottery ticket with the edge of a dime. Someone else uncapped a bottle in a brown paper bag. The social circle on the stoop was more animated than usual.

"Jamal, if I have to hear about that stupid pass reception one more freaking time, I swear to God I'll slit my wrists."

"But it was an ESPN highlight moment!"

"In your dreams maybe."

A low-riding Datsun sat nearby with purple neon glowing underneath. All the doors were open for the listening pleasure of an over-powered stereo with the new Grenade sub-woofer. The song changed to Hendrix.

"*. . . I went down to the crossroads . . .*"

The traffic light changed, and a Dakota thumped to a stop in the intersection. Hank Williams blasted out the open windows.

"...*Kaw-Liga!*..."

The light turned green. Someone waved out the driver's window. A middle-finger salute. "Suck my dick, porch monkeys!"

One of the trio stood up from the stoop. "I don't believe my own lyin' eyes."

"What is it?"

"That son of a bitch is at it again!" said the tight end.

"You'd think he'd learned his lesson," said the wide receiver.

The quarterback angled his neck forward in the growing darkness. "And it looks like he's got another little kid with him!"

It was déjà vu all over again. The Datsun blasted out of the parking lot like before, except this time they took it careful not to overrun a detour down a cane road. For whatever reason, the driver of the Dakota made it hard to miss his vehicle. He drove the speed limit and left his high beams on, lighting everything up like a prison break. He turned into a cane field.

"There he is!"

"I ain't going to worry about killing him like last time!"

The Datsun raced down the dirt road following Crack's headlights. When they pulled up, they figured Captain Nasty would take off running and shitting his pants. Instead, they found him leaning against his driver's door, calmly smoking a cigarette. "What's up, boys?"

"You took another kid!" shouted the wide receiver.

"What kid?" Crack took a deep drag. "I don't see any children around here."

"In your pickup cab!" yelled the tight end. He ran up to the passenger window. "What the heck?"

"What is it?" asked the quarterback.

"A small mannequin."

"What?"

The young man pulled the straw-stuffed human figure from the car and walked back with it for all to see. "He tricked us!"

"But why?"

They were off-balance, staring back at the pickup truck with confused eyes.

Crack Nasty chuckled and snubbed out his cigarette. "Nice knowing you."

Suddenly a dark, windowless van crashed through the sugarcane in front of them. The side panel flew open and four men in black jumpsuits leaped out. There was no Hollywood final banter. They simply opened up with ridiculous firepower from the latest battlefield mercenary weapons.

At least death was quick.

Helicopters and TV trucks converged on the field the next day. Police found a burst-open bag of cocaine in the Datsun, and more residue on the bodies. The three victims had no criminal records. But they were known to be young, black and hanging out with no employment. Everything pointed to a drug deal gone south. Locals weren't buying it. They brought in the larger outside law enforcement agencies, and a joint task force went in front of the TV cameras, swearing they would never rest until their investigation brought the killers to justice. But given the area and the evidence, not really.

Captain Crack Nasty was getting away with it again.

Chapter 24

COW COUNTRY

A gold Plymouth Satellite headed up U.S. Highway 98. A Styrofoam takeout dinner box sat on the back seat.

"One thing that should be mandatory on every Floridian's bucket list is to drive completely around Lake Okeechobee."

A ferret ran from one of Serge's shoulders to the other.

"I think Mr. Zippy wants to know why," said Coleman.

"Because it will recalibrate your sense of place. That's what we're doing now. One hundred and twenty miles of dynamically changing culture and landscape. And this empty section between Pahokee and the city of Okeechobee is one of the coolest!"

"He nipped me again," said Coleman. "He needs more stimulation."

"It's like channel-surfing inland Florida," said Serge. "We're on the east side, where the highway hugs the rim of the lake, through flats with sabal palms and heron swooping over the road. Moss-draped oaks, bogs and marsh, grassy straightaways with just that looming dike. Plus it continues following the thread, which I will recap for Mr. Zippy: Rawlings to Stetson to Zora to the West Palm Beach cemetery in her book to the Port Mayaca mass grave, and now circumnavigating the lake with more interrelated stops. And people think I'm just winging it . . ."

A deep horn blew.

Serge quickly checked his mirrors and skidded off the road.

"What are you doing?"

"Waiting for the train to catch up," said Serge.

"Huh?"

Another horn blast.

"Along the east side of the lake, the old train tracks that carried fresh produce up north almost a century ago still have traffic, and they lie in that short strip of easement between this road and the Hoover Dike. You haven't lived until you've raced a train up Lake Okeechobee . . . Here we go!"

Tires spun, black smoke, screeching. The Plymouth hit the road as if shot by a slingshot.

A yellow-and-black locomotive gained quickly from behind, and Serge pressed his right foot down all the way. He began honking and waving. One of the engineers glanced over. Serge leaned out the window, making a pumping gesture with his fist for the engineer to blow his horn.

A long blare followed, and the train pulled away.

Serge fell back in his seat with an afterglow. "It doesn't get any better!"

"Then why that frown?"

"Incoming thought," said Serge. "What's the deal with sales receipts these days?"

"Are we playing another round of tangent?" asked Coleman.

"I'll go in a darn CVS or Walgreens drugstore to buy a single toothbrush, and I get a receipt that reaches to the floor. You can't be doing that to people. It's a drugstore, so they have to know a certain wedge of their clientele have disorders. And now the pressure is on me to read the whole fucking thing because *you never know*. But it's always a bunch of coupons for back-to-school supplies or feminine products that make me blush. On the other hand, the receipts at gas pumps are these teensy-weensy little bastards you can barely read. We regulate the size of eggs, but where's the quality control on this one?"

Coleman nodded. "Half the long receipts seem to have a pink stripe somewhere."

"This is what I'm talking about!" said Serge. "And another thing: Society now has something called 'revenge porn.'"

"Is that where someone steals all your porn?"

"So you'd think," said Serge. "But I just heard through the grapevine that in the middle of a sixty-nine, people are pulling out their cell phones."

"This is really going on?"

Serge nodded. "You'd think a quaking orgasm would get a thank-you, but no, now it has to be in high def."

"What do they do with it?"

"Save it for the breakup," said Serge. "And it's never pretty: 'You know how you said I could trust you and ask the most embarrassing thing that you'd like me to do in bed? Well, I have a request . . .' And the next thing you know, a bunch of coworkers are in their cubicles glued to a text video involving handcuffs and a zucchini."

"Ouch."

Serge shrugged. "If those people are going to judge me on that . . . I mean, it was someone else."

The Plymouth began curling around the northwest shore of the lake. A roar came up from behind and whipped past in the opposite lane.

Coleman's head spun as he grabbed the dash. "There must be twenty motorcycles!"

"It's a popular touring route for them," said Serge. "Which means we're on the right track. Bikers are a noble breed, stripping away pretense to live in the *now*. You can always count on them to bird-dog the finest scenic byways."

More wetlands and vines and scrub brush went by. Drivers in other vehicles wearing camo baseball caps and pulling airboats.

"Now we're talking!" said Serge. "Florida's bayou country, the whole area like a Credence Clearwater album!"

He fumbled to start a boom box.

"*. . . Comin' up around the bend . . .*"

The scraggly vegetation gave way to wild palms surrounding the first wisps of the mobile-home parks.

Serge nodded to himself in contentment. "Lake Okeechobee is Florida's heart, and its beat ripples a pulse far and wide."

"I thought the lake was the moon," said Coleman.

"Since when are you listening to me?"

The road wound past more evidence of population hugging the edge of the lake. RV dealerships and RV parks. Bass boats, a country store, a honky-tonk bar, a swamp buggy on tank treads. Signs for gravel and cremation. Then the trailer parks. Trailers on wheels, trailers on blocks, trailers on slabs. Trailers with screened porches, hot tubs and gazebos. There were flowerpots with no flowers, decorative stone turtles next to real ones, and a mailbox shaped like a lighthouse. Someone was casting a fishing line on his front lawn, and someone else walked by on the side of the road in shorts, sandals and a Santa Claus hat, indicating the breadth of the human condition.

Then the local economy. Big Lake Eye Care, Big Lake Bail Bonds, the Big "O" Flea Market.

American flags everywhere.

Another roar came up behind the Plymouth. Coleman turned around. "A bunch more bikers." They began streaming by the Plymouth. "Except these are all the three-wheel kind. Why are they riding separate from the others?"

"Probably unresolved tension between the groups that goes way back to an incident nobody can remember now," said Serge. "Most likely a few too many longnecks on a Sunday afternoon, and then one guy started some shit about the number of tires, threats were made, women disrespected. Best to let them sort it out among themselves."

The Plymouth reached the outskirts of the civilization. Signs for bait, fishing licenses and fried catfish.

"Where are we?" asked Coleman.

"The city of Okeechobee, also known as Cow Town." The Plymouth pulled into a parking lot. "We need to resupply before our excellent visit."

Twenty minutes later, they came out of the store. Coleman was pushing a shopping cart, and Serge was dragging a sales receipt across the pavement. He suddenly stopped and violently balled it up. Then into a garbage can—"Motherfucker!"—slamming the lid five times.

"What's the matter?"

"I don't want to talk about it."

Soon, they were checking into another economy motel. This one had a warning sign at the reception desk.

Coleman moved his lips as he read. "Serge, what are blind mosquitoes?"

"Tiny suckers that don't bite but sometimes swarm in biblical numbers off the lake after dark, and you have to keep your mouth closed unless you want extra protein. But they can still get in your eyes, ears and nose."

"Jesus."

"They're attracted to light, so that's why that sign asks guests to turn off all the lamps before leaving the room in the evening and close the door quickly. It's a whole different set of rules out here, and they're not in the humans' favor."

A young wrangler-Jane type stood behind the counter with a genuine smile. "I wouldn't worry too much. The mosquitoes are bad on the few nights they're out, but it's mostly quiet. What freaks newcomers most are the frogs."

"Frogs?" said Serge.

She nodded and held her hands apart a good half foot. "We have these giant ones that come out after a big rain, and people open their doors at night and see them all over the sidewalk and parking lot. They're harmless, but sometimes one or two will hop in a room. That's a lot of my night service calls."

"Service calls?"

Another nod. "I have to go in rooms and capture them because people say they can't sleep with those things under their bed making noise and just being creepy, and they're too squeamish to catch them on their own . . . So what are you fellas doing in town?"

"Historical research," said Serge. "Following connective tissue."

"History? Really?" She brightened further. "I love history!" She got out a paper and pen and began jotting feverishly. "Here are the area's high points . . ." She got to the bottom of the page. ". . . Finally, don't forget the Brighton Seminole reservation. There's a visitors' center with exhibits and souvenirs, plus they have a twenty-four-hour casino where you don't have to dress up. I usually go in my pajamas."

They retired to the room as the sun began to set.

Coleman stood in amazement. "This is like the best budget place we've ever stayed in. It's got a giant full kitchen and everything!"

"Scoped it out years ago, and now it's the only place I'll stay around here." Serge hung his toiletry bag on a mirror. "Where else can you rent a former condo unit at a bargain price? And there's always vacancy. That's why I'm keeping it a secret."

Rinnnnng! Rinnnnng!

Serge jumped. "What the fuck was that?"

"The phone," said Coleman.

"Of course it's the phone! But who could possibly know we're here?"

Rinnnnng! Rinnnnng!

Serge gingerly picked up the receiver. "Hello?"

"Hi! It's me, Cheyenne, from the front desk. I just thought of a couple more places that I forgot when I was making your list. Have a pen handy?"

Serge urgently lunged toward writing materials like he was taking a call for ransom demands. "Hit me!"

The call eventually ended, and the receiver went back in its cradle.

"Who was that?" asked Coleman.

"Our little history helper from the front desk. My love for country folk just keeps growing."

The pair commenced their respective chores. Coleman spread dope on the counter and swilled malt liquor. Serge unpacked notebooks, guidebooks, pamphlets, and recording devices. Coleman made a bong from a souvenir plastic cowboy-hat penny bank that he'd bought at the store.

"TV?" asked Coleman.

"Leave it off. I have other plans." Serge carefully arranged a configuration of needed materials on the nightstand: antiquarian novel, portable stereo, Styrofoam to-go dinner box. He took a deep breath in anticipation. Then he kicked off his shoes and lay on top of a bedspread in his stocking feet. "Here . . . we . . . go! . . ."

"What are you doing?"

"A lost art: constructing the perfect moment!" Serge bunched the pillow up under his head. "It requires the precisely engineered intersection of sensory, mental and emotional input: First, the motel room is in the ideal location: From the comfort of my bed, I have a fantastic view just outside the window of the Hoover Dike in the setting sun. Next"—he pressed a button on the portable stereo, and a growling voice came to life—"'Little Black Train' by Blind Joe Taggart, just the kind of blues song they would have been playing in the 1920s juke joints surrounding the lake's bustling packing houses . . ." He opened the Styrofoam box on his stomach ". . . And this is my soul-food takeout from that shack in Pahokee of smothered pork chops, pigeon peas and collards. Standard dinner fare in those old days . . ." Serge finally grabbed the book off the nightstand. "And last but not least, a collectible early copy of Zora Neale Hurston's masterpiece recounting the 1928 storm that struck right out there! . . ."

Serge became quiet. He turned up the tiny stereo, stuck a fork in a pork chop, opened the book and stared out the window. ". . . I'm starting to feel it. I'm getting tingly . . . Here it comes! . . . Here it comes! . . . It's almost here! . . . It's here!" Serge's eyelids fluttered uncontrollably as his pupils rolled up in his head like he was possessed. Then, a few seconds later, it was over. "Coleman, did you see it? The Moment! . . . It was just here . . . See? There it goes . . ." He closed the book and swallowed a bite of pork. ". . . Whew! Exhausting! . . . If everyone could experience motels like this, prostitution as we know it would end."

"They would have to get other jobs," said Coleman.

"Then one day you order a pizza and open the door: 'Hey, didn't you used to be a hooker?' 'Shut up.'"

Serge paused curiously and considered the closed book next to him. He opened it again and read down a page. "Wait . . . just . . . a minute!"

"What is it?"

He ran for the desk and opened another, thicker green book. "I need my bible."

"The *Bible* Bible?"

"No, the Florida bible. WPA Guide published in 1939, two years after Zora penned *Their Eyes Were Watching God* and around the time when she was crossing the state with Stetson Kennedy. The government commissioned the Depression-era guide series to put writers to work, and all these incredible people of letters contributed with flourishes never seen before in a travel guide. But nobody got a byline, and all the writing is uncredited . . ." Serge found the page he was looking for and thrust a fist in the air. "I knew it! I knew it!" He grabbed Coleman's arms and danced in a circle. "I rock tonight!"

"What did you find?"

Serge plopped down at the desk again, holding up one of the books. "I knew I recognized it from somewhere! Hurston's novel described the Seminoles evacuating ahead of the storm because of how the sawgrass bloomed." He set the book down and picked up another. "And in the guide, virtually the same description. I just discovered an anonymous Zora passage! Prostitution is history!"

"Woo-hoo."

Serge stopped and held the open books side by side, one in each hand. He looked out the window at the sunlit dike, then down at the books, up at the dike, books, dike, books, dike. His eyelids began fluttering again and his pupils rolled back up. Then it passed. "Whoa! . . . Two in a row!"

"Remember that time you had—"

"I know," said Serge. "But this is better than orgasms, give or take . . . There's nothing else in life to compare . . . unless I can figure a way . . ." He let his thought trail off.

"Figure a way what?"

"I don't want to jinx it." Serge reached in one of their shopping bags and pulled out a copy of the morning's *Okeechobee News*.

Coleman popped another can of malt liquor. "I think I'm going to use all the extra space in this room to run around again."

"Knock yourself out."

"Yi-yi-yi-yi-yi . . . Wa-wa-wa-wa-wa . . . Oops, that's enough."

"Why'd you stop so soon?" asked Serge.

"The key is to stop just before you spit up in your mouth."

"I think you've just nailed what to put on your tombstone."

Coleman strolled over to a spacious desk. "What's that? What are you doing now?"

"*Trying* to read the newspaper," said Serge. "I'm required to buy a local newspaper whenever I arrive somewhere, to get in rhythm with the residents. And these small-town papers are the best! No bullshit about celebrity Twitter feuds or a cabinet member spending ten grand on a wastebasket. Check out this front page . . ." He held it up to his pal. ". . . Big photo at the top, 'Veterans Honored,' and another photo of a teen holding up two fish that won a tournament. Over in a box on the side where the weather forecast would normally be: 'Lake level 15.51 feet.' And last but not least, a front-page story you would only find in a paper like this: 'Ball of Light Reported over Lake Okeechobee,' complete with a photo someone took with a cell phone."

Coleman leaned closer. "It's just a black square with a fuzzy circle in the middle. Looks like a streetlight."

"Good a guess as any." Serge grabbed something else. "I get the feeling a lot of people around the lake are often staring up at the sky: 'Sweet Jesus! The aliens are landing again!' 'You're looking at a streetlight like last time, Uncle Biff. Why don't you hand me that beer.' . . . And here's the free town flyer with announcements for lawn-mower races, taco night at the American Legion, and a dunk tank for charity." Serge flipped through the paper until he came to a full-page ad. He leaped up. "Coleman!"

"What?"

"There's a rodeo tonight!"

"What's that mean?"

Serge tossed a duffel bag on the bed. "It means we have to get our uniforms ready . . ."

Chapter 25

SEPTEMBER 17, 1928

The twangs of a guitar floated down the dirt street in pre-dawn hours. A gusting wind picked up pieces of cardboard and newspaper. Men in grimy pants and overalls sat on the porch steps of one of the many juke joints in Belle Glade and Pahokee that stayed open around the clock: small cabins with patrons stumbling in and out, some sleeping in the grass by the back door. Cats and dogs foraged for scraps.

The front of this particular saloon was a random patchwork of corrugated sheet metal. There were signs for Nehi and Royal Crown Cola and Atlantic Ale. Inside the cramped room, loud conversation and thick smoke from filterless cigarettes. A poker game became heated. Under a window stood a wooden pinball machine with a racehorse theme. At the front of the bar, a sweaty, rotund gent sat on a stool that looked like it might collapse from physics. He was the only one wearing a suit, but the jacket had long since been removed, and perspiration pasted the white dress shirt to his chest. A kerosene lantern illuminated other beads of sweat generously cascading down his cheeks. He hunched over his Gibson Archtop guitar, strumming a three-chord Chicago progression and howling the lyrics to "Rope Stretchin'" by Blind Blake. They don't call it the blues for nothing.

In the back corner, beneath other signs for Ice Cold Jax Stout and Cobbs Creek Blended Whiskey, three men huddled over brown bottles.

"I am so sick of this shit," said Johnson.

"Me too," said Cabbage.

"How does he get away with it?" asked Mozelle.

"How? What color is his skin?" said Johnson. "I lost two weeks' pay."

"Then you had it good," said Cabbage. "I was the fool who worked a third week after he kept puttin' me off."

"Somebody needs to do something about that asshole!"

"And end up like Jacob? You weren't there."

"I also heard he got run out of the Dominican for pulling a bunch of the same bullshit."

"They say he doesn't trust the banks or anyone since," said Mozelle. "Keeps everything in gold, who knows where?"

"That's just a crazy rumor," said Johnson.

"Is it? I know a guy who saw him at the bank—"

"I thought he didn't trust banks."

"Not to deposit," said Mozelle. "To change his cash into twenty-dollar gold pieces. Had a big-ass sack of 'em."

Johnson lit a Lucky Strike, and they got another round of Blatz. They sat looking at each other.

"You thinking what I'm thinking?" said Cabbage.

"I'm in," said Mozelle.

"No time like now," said Johnson.

They quickly finished their beer and headed out into the wee hours . . .

After brief trips home, they crept through the night with Colt revolvers and a crowbar, across tomato and strawberry fields. Then they entered rows of tall stalks yielding in the whipping wind.

"You heard about this storm that's supposed to come?" asked Cabbage.

"We always get storms," said Johnson.

"But what about that hurricane two years ago?"

"Lightning doesn't strike twice. Like that's going to happen again so soon."

A gust came through, knocking them off-balance.

"I don't know," said Mozelle. "I heard the Seminoles already came through before sunset for higher ground. They tend to be right."

"They tend to be Indians," said Johnson. "We going to do this or not?"

They finally crouched on the edge of the cane field. Ahead, one of the nicest homes for miles. Columns and a second-floor wrap-around veranda. Johnson took off running, and the rest followed until they were crouched again by a side door. They all reached in their back pockets and pulled out canvas flour bags with holes cut in strategic spots. They pulled them over their heads.

Johnson stuck the crowbar in the frame and cracked the door open. They charged inside and up the stairs to the master bedroom. Fakakta was snoring.

"Where's his wife?"

"This other bedroom," said Johnson, quietly closing another door in the hall.

Mozelle stuck his gun to the baron's head and shook his shoulder. A whisper: "Wake up."

Fakakta finally roused, then sat up quickly. "What do you want?"

"Gold."

Then it all went south in an urgent hurry.

"I recognize your shirt from the fields," said Fakakta. "Blue stripes. What was your name? Mozelle something?"

"Fuck!" He yanked off his flower bag. "Where's the gold?"

"Mozelle, put your bag back on," said Cabbage.

"Why? If he wasn't sure about my name already, you just repeated it!" He swung his gun back to Fulgencio and pressed it between his eyes. "The gold!"

"What gold?" said the baron. "Go ahead and shoot. You're all dead men anyway."

Mozelle cocked the hammer. "You don't seem to be taking this seriously. You think you can just steal from everyone around here and get away with it? Not to mention lynching Jacob. You may not have known, but he was my cousin."

A loud crackle outside as lightning laced the sky. The wind was now up to a roar, whistling through the clapboards and eaves. The shutters began coming loose, banging with a violent rhythm against the side of the house. Other stuff in the yard became airborne and crashed into things. Then another crash, but this one was different. It was inside. The trio saw glass and water explode on the wall over the headboard. Mozelle spun with his pistol.

Bang.

A thud in the doorway.

"Jesus!" yelled Cabbage. "You just shot his wife!"

"She threw a vase at me!"

"We've got more trouble."

They heard footsteps pounding up the stairs. Fulgencio's adult son and chief enforcer, Pablo. With a rifle.

Johnson dashed to the door and fired his Colt, easily picking Pablo off before he reached the landing. The body slumped and tumbled backward down the stairs.

Cabbage grabbed his own head with both hands. "Shit! This was a bad idea! We never should have come!"

"We're way past that now." Johnson smacked the side of Fakakta's head with his pistol. Blood spattered. He smacked him again the other way, then a third time.

"Damn!" said Mozelle. "Aren't you going to ask him any questions?"

Another crack to the skull. "I don't like to repeat myself."

He raised the gun again, and Fakakta raised his hands. "Okay, enough. I'll take you to the gold."

Everyone marched out the back door and leaned forward in a driving rain. Fakakta led them out behind a falling-down old barn that came with the property. He placed his back against the wall, then counted out twenty measured paces. He stopped and pointed down.

Johnson shoved him out of the way and fell to his knees. "Keep him covered." His hands clawed at the dirt. About a foot down, his fingers found netting. He grabbed it and stood, pulling hard. Earth flew. They all froze. An open pit with crate after wooden crate stacked to an unknown depth. Johnson opened the first box. Gasps.

"Look at all that money!"

Then they were all on their knees, running their fingers through the coins. "How much do you think is here? . . ."

Fakakta knew the effect gold had on people. He'd been waiting for his chance. He slowly inched backward, then all at once took off for the house.

"He's running!"

Johnson stood and didn't hurry his shot. Careful aim.

Bang.

Fakakta fell forward into the mud.

"He's crawling," said Cabbage. "He's not dead."

Mozelle calmly crossed the thirty or so yards, until he had walked around in front of the slithering Fulgencio.

The sugar baron raised his face to see the barrel of a gun.

Mozelle cocked it again. "This is for Jacob."

Bang.

"We're definitely going to have to leave the state," said Cabbage. "I got some relatives in Natchez."

"First things first." Johnson grabbed the initial crate and heaved. "Let's get all this out of the ground."

The wind and rain became a brutal impediment, but they were motivated. Soon, crates were spread everywhere.

"He just left all this in a hole?" said Mozelle.

"It ain't going to spoil," said Johnson. "Gold doesn't even tarnish. We need to go back and get your brother's pickup truck. And it'll take more than one trip."

Cabbage wiped water from his eyes and looked up. "Shouldn't it already be getting light out?"

"We just lost track of time," said Mozelle, falling down in the wind and struggling to rise.

"I'll stay here and watch this," said Johnson. "You guys go get the truck—"

There was a sharp cracking sound. Louder than a rifle.

"What the hell was that?"

Then another loud report. More and more followed in quick succession.

"It sounds like trees snapping, but that can't be—"

"Shut up!"

They all stared silent at the woods a quarter mile north of the home. More savage cracking until it was a constant chorus. They strained with their eyes but couldn't make out anything. The noise became a roar of ground-level thunder.

Finally, the last rows of trees on the edge of the woods gave way and splintered and were gone. They looked up in the darkness.

"What the hell is that?" said Cabbage.

Whatever it was, it was traveling fast, at least sixty miles an hour.

When they finally figured out what they were looking at,

it was too much for their brains to process. A couple hundred yards away, they watched the plantation home explode and disappear.

Seconds later, it was right in front of them. Nothing to do but freeze and conjure one last thought: *That fucking lake.*

In surrender, they simply stared straight up into the black, twenty-foot-high tidal wave.

Part Two

Chapter 26

RODEO NIGHT

S erge drove north with a high-end tape recorder in his lap and a microphone in his hand.

CAPTAIN FLORIDA'S LOG, STAR DATE 376.693

The city of Okeechobee rests on the northern tip of the lake by the same name. You just have to love a town that runs off the cliff with its identity, and you never need to be reminded you're in cattle country: the Brahman Theater, Brahman Restaurant & Lounge, Okeechobee High School (Home of the Brahmans), Cowboy's Barbecue, the Cowtown Café, the Cattlemen's Association rodeo arena. The economic center of downtown is the bustling Eli's Western Wear. You can be driving down Main Street on a Tuesday morning and suddenly realize you desperately need a two-thousand-dollar saddle, lassos, spurs, rhinestone belt, and five-foot-long decorative steer horns to hang over the TV. You're in luck! Eli's has amassed a staggering supply. Then there are the cows themselves. Cattle dot the fields all over Central Florida, but nothing like here, where they vastly outnumber the humans, in herds not seen since buffalo covered the prairies in *Dances with Wolves*. Billboards everywhere along the pastures: BEEF, IT'S WHAT'S FOR DINNER, next to grazing livestock unaware of the advertisements for their impending execution.

Speaking of downtown, Main Street is actually called Park Street and there are two of them laid out parallel through the center of the city. Between the pair runs a wide, shaded green space like a series of football fields, starting with a military display of a Vietnam-era Huey helicopter, M60 Patton tank and a couple pieces of heavy ground artillery. From there, the public park has nowhere to go but mellow, with quiet benches, picnic tables, thatched-roof huts and vintage-style lampposts. But wait! There's more! Get ready to seriously crap yourselves! I've kind of been hung up on murals lately, and I'd completely forgotten my favorite part of Okeechobee! It's Mural City, USA! Remember the batshit town-identity thing? And just when you thought the insanity had reached critical mass. That's right: They found more mass! Most antique communities have lots of old brick buildings with empty brick sides, and the residents think nothing of it. Not the fine people here! Sometime back, they went on the mural version of a crack binge, and now you can't throw a cow pie in this place without it sticking to public art. There's a mural celebrating the arrival of the railroad in 1915 with scenes of ice delivery and catfish; another touts an important cattle drive with happy people waiting at the end; there's a car dealership that opened in 1933, and a pioneer hardware store. The side of the Big O drive-through liquor barn has marsh birds flying over the lake, and a country restaurant sports a mural within a mural: a painting of one of those old postcards, Welcome to Okeechobee, with each of the giant letters in the city's name a separate homage. And you know how a lot of main streets have abandoned buildings that are simply boarded up with plywood, and jerks spray-paint gang symbols and Fuck the System and giant penises? I think we can all agree that's not going anywhere special. But at the historic and defunct 1923 tan-brick Okeechobee bank, instead of plywood, the town painted all the windows to look like a bunch of customers in period clothing are still inside conducting business! And finally the cherry on the sundae: There's even a mural depicting the history of local phone service ("First Operator, Byrd Sizemore"). I thought something like that would only reach an audience of one. Me. But these are my people! I must stop dictating this now and interact with them . . .

T he convenience store had cedar slats. It was sparsely stocked and otherwise empty except for a retired couple at the counter. A wagon wheel leaned against the front of the building, intended to drum up business, but now there were doubts.

Serge and Coleman walked up behind the old people.

The couple was taking an extra-long time with the clerk. An involved conversation, and it wasn't about a transaction.

"Serge, are you going to do anything crazy like the other times?"

"No."

"But when people take forever in convenience stores, you always flip out."

"This is different. I want to listen to small-town talk." Serge blew across the top of a Styrofoam cup. "I already have my coffee, so I can drink it while waiting. Legally they can't touch me as long as I pay."

The old woman clutched a purse in front of her with both hands. "When does Charlie come on?"

"He doesn't work here anymore," said the clerk. "Actually, I'm his son."

"You're Billy?" asked the old man. "You've really grown. I remember when you were this high."

"Billy's my older brother."

"Then that makes you Donny," said the woman. "You've *really* grown."

"Where does your dad work now?" asked the old man.

"Retired," said the clerk. "Just smokes cigars on the porch with the dogs."

"We've always thought the world of Charlie. Your whole family," said the woman. "Can you give him our best?"

"Absolutely."

The couple thanked him and left, and Serge stepped up.

The clerk smiled cordially. "How's your day been going?"

"Magically!" Serge set a cup on the counter. "I already love your family, and we haven't even met!"

The clerk looked down. "It's an empty cup."

"I know the rules." Serge slapped down a couple of dollars. "Technically, I'm still in my lane, so there's no need for trouble."

"No, I mean, don't you want coffee in it?"

Serge patted his stomach. "Already in here."

The clerk leaned over the cup. "Oh, yeah. I see the drops." He smiled again and rang Serge up. "Will there be anything else?"

"Yes!" Serge tossed the cup in the trash. "A side order of country-fried conversation."

"Uh, what?"

"Like you were having with those old folks. I love small-town friendliness!"

"Then you've come to the right place," said the clerk. "If we got any friendlier, people would think we were trying to sell something."

"You are," said Serge. "You're a clerk in a store. Isn't that the program here? Just because the wagon wheel out front didn't fulfill the big dreams, the answer isn't Communism."

Coleman raised his hand. "You should get a mannequin of a hot chick and stick her by the road."

"Coleman! Shhhh!" said Serge. "I'm talking to the guy here. The mannequins draw the wrong crowd, who just want to use the restrooms and aren't too precise about it."

The clerk chuckled. "You guys are funny. What brings you to town?"

"The *town*!" said Serge. "I love everything about it. Right now I'm mentally rocking out to your murals."

"Oh, the murals," said Donny. "Aren't they fantastic? My personal favorite is the telephone one."

"Me too!" said Serge. "Byrdie Sizemore! I know her name is Byrd, but I like to refer to her as Byrdie because it's a free country. I'm always thinking about her. Was she musical? Petulant? Did she find her life's work fulfilling, or just start smashing telephones near the end? And exactly what switchboard call was she connecting in that mural? A family reunion at the old Forsythe place? Gossip about the preacher and the Widow Milsap? An emergency involving moonshine and a two-person tree saw?"

The clerk chuckled again. "Never quite thought about it."

Serge pointed at the duffel bag near his feet, then at the corner of the store. "Can we use your restroom? I actually made a purchase, so we're not from the mannequin crowd. But I will need a while because we have to get dressed for work. Really important gig."

"Take as long as you want," said Donny. "If there's a problem, I'll tell everyone to use the women's room."

"You're good people . . ."

Donny sat back on a stool and resumed flipping through a

magazine with blueprints for patio decks. After a couple minutes, he thought he heard something. He leaned over the counter, looking down the hall to the restrooms. There was a muffled banging sound, then a crash and arguing in hushed tones. *"Let go of me!"* *"Don't screw this up again!"* Another bang. A clanging noise. The door opened and Serge stuck his head out with a grin. "Almost done. There's nothing unusual." The door closed. Bang, bang, bang. *"Dammit!"* *"Shit, my bad."* Then a suspiciously long pause. The door finally opened again.

Serge and Coleman stepped out, and Donny stepped back, scratching his head. "What exactly is this job you do?"

Serge told him.

"Ohhhh." Donny nodded with understanding.

"Don't fib," said Serge. "At first you thought this was weird. Anyway, pleasure to meet, thanks for use of the restroom, and any damage in there was from the other guys."

They left the store, and a gold Plymouth sped off north through the fading light on U.S. Highway 441. Pot smoke wafted out the windows.

"I'm beginning to see why you like country folk so much," said Coleman. "First your little history helper at the motel desk, and now that cool guy in the convenience store."

"Country folk are the best!" said Serge. "That is, most of the time."

Puff, puff. "What do you mean?"

"Don't get me wrong: Everything is usually finger-lickin' fantastic," said Serge. "Until you get lost driving through deep fog in the woods at night with no cell service or GPS. Then you notice a tiny light on in the distance at an isolated farmhouse. So you knock on the door for directions, and the next thing you know, you're handcuffed to a radiator while a family in bib overalls giggles and rubs mice on your face, and one of them says, 'Go get the twins.' And someone else opens a cellar door, and these two little albinos with pointy teeth show up, and you're like, 'Where in the fuck is this going?' But you know that all the signs so far are not positive, and then somehow you free yourself and run outside. Your car is just feet away and the keys are still in your pocket, but for some reason you tell yourself, 'That's a stupid idea. I'll run for a barn way out in that dark field.' You dash inside the rickety structure to find all kinds of thick chains hanging from the rafters with hooks and rusty scything blades, and a mottled hand is reaching up from a fresh grave in the dirt floor. Then a chain saw roars to life outside and you dive behind bales of hay as flashlight beams pierce through slats in the barn wall. And that's if you're lucky. Sometimes the family is into Amway: 'No, I don't want to join!' 'It'll change your life!' And then they're chasing you to the barn with pamphlets and brochures."

"Amway," said Coleman, shaking with the willies.

The Plymouth pulled off the road. "Here we are."

Other cars were already parked, many more arriving. People streamed toward what looked like an old minor-league baseball stadium in Oshkosh. Erector-Set girders and rusty metal sheeting over the stands in case of rain.

Serge and Coleman made their way to the entrance of the rodeo arena. A cashier in the ticket booth gave their outfits a double take, then asked for the admission fee.

Serge shook his head. "We're clowns. We're authorized."

"You're in the show?" asked the cashier.

Serge adjusted the red ball on his nose. "Why else would we be dressed like this? Just because we decided to pretend like we work here?"

"But the clowns have already arrived."

"They called for backup." Serge flashed a clown badge. "There could be trouble tonight. I'd count on it."

She shrugged and let them pass.

Coleman slapped floppy shoes on the walkway. "What do we do now?"

"Act like we belong."

They arrived at a fence along the side of the dusty arena. A cowgal in scarlet-fringed riding chaps went by on a horse. Sandy-blond locks flowed out from under her black Stetson hat. She proudly raised a giant American flag as they played "The Star-Spangled Banner."

Coleman nudged his buddy. "Look who it is."

"I know," said Serge. "My little history helper. Imagine that."

Coleman nudged him again. "She's wearing a plaid shirt."

"Shut up."

After a few preliminary announcements over the PA system, a galvanized metal gate burst open. A cowboy swung a free arm in the air as a bronco fiercely fought to dislodge him. After eight seconds, he hit the dirt in a nasty spill. The crowd stood in silent concern. The cowboy jumped right up and waved to them with his hat.

The PA announcer: "Let's hear it for Sundance Cassidy."

Wild cheering.

Serge wound his way through spectators along the fence— "Excuse me, excuse me, coming through . . ."—until he came to an access gate and a security guard. "Thank you for your service. Could you please open that?"

"Who are you?"

Serge looked at Coleman. "Who are we?" Then back at the guard. "Who does it look like we are? Is this your first rodeo?"

"But the clowns are already out there."

"New liability insurance rule: more clowns."

"I'm going to have to check with a supervisor."

"Go ahead," Serge said as a bronco thundered by, throwing the rider into the fence. "Meanwhile, someone gets hurt, lawsuits fly, and then you're stuttering on the witness stand about why you withheld lifesaving clown procedures."

PA: "Let's hear it for Blueridge Grymes!"

"Well, okay, you seem authorized."

Serge and Coleman waved to the crowd as they strolled across the dirt. Coleman stopped and looked at something stuck to the bottom of one of his big floppy shoes.

"Seriously?" said Serge. "Already?"

"It's everywhere."

Serge pointed. "There's our command post."

They took up positions behind a pair of oak barrels, leaning with their elbows.

"This is it? This is a job?" Coleman whistled. "Clowns have it all figured out."

"The clowning life is extreme boredom punctuated by bursts of sheer terror."

"I remember those birthday parties."

PA: "Let's hear it for Omaha Kid Sloane!"

Gate after gate flew open, and cowboy after cowboy flew through the air. More names from the PA were announced and applauded: Boone Cartwright, Doc Hickock, Austin Buck, Dead-wood Dixon, Medicine Hat McCoy.

"What are those big animals over there?" asked Coleman. "They look nasty."

"They are," said Serge, resting his chin on top of a barrel. "Brahma bulls. Unlike horses, they have vicious horns. Only the bravest ride them."

"People *ride* them?" said Coleman. "And we're going to be *out* here? What if they come after me and I get scared?"

"Just get inside one of these barrels. That's what they're for."

Coleman nodded. "You know what I'm thinking about now?"

"The panel is stumped."

"My taste buds."

"Still goose eggs. Please proceed."

"You know how you loved some foods as a kid, but unless you make it a point, you don't get the chance anymore?" said Cole-man. "I miss SpaghettiOs."

"This is your news flash?" said Serge.

"Just sayin'."

"But I do feel your pain," said Serge. "Our taste buds have changed, despite all my efforts. It's no coincidence that Chef Boyardee has two different gustation formulas for kids and grown-ups, developed through rigorous kindergarten focus groups. Same thing with the little McDonald's hamburgers. They needed a gateway drug to get kids hooked, but adults were unreliable test subjects, so the winning formula had to be the result of random permutations screened by the preschool set. How else would you explain the counterintuitive final strokes of adding a dollop of mustard and diced pieces of sautéed onions? I remember when I was five taking one of my hamburgers apart: 'I must learn what kind of party is going on in this thing because Mom never comes close!' And the next time she made hamburgers at home: 'Mom, I'll get the mustard and you grab the little translucent squares.'"

"I still like peanut butter and jelly," said Coleman.

"Those sandwiches are critical to keeping your childhood taste buds in shape, or you end up an asshole in a restaurant mispronouncing *foie gras*— . . . Shit, terror time!"

"What is it?"

"That cowboy's starting to slide off the horse but it looks like his left foot is stuck in the stirrup! . . . We're on!"

Serge dashed out into the arena, just as the bronco rider hit the ground and began being dragged through the dirt. Other clowns ran in from the other direction, trying to distract the horse and slow it down. The rider was taking a beating.

Then something nobody had seen before. Serge kicked off his clown shoes, running alongside the slowed horse to get his timing right. Suddenly he leaped, grabbing the saddle knob, getting a foot in the right stirrup and pulling himself aboard. He had the advantage of being able to use both hands, while the horse was hampered by the weight of what he was dragging.

Serge leaned all the way forward, wrapping his arms around the horse's neck, stroking it and whispering in a big brown ear.

The horse began to calm until it stopped. They freed the rider's foot as Serge hopped down and walked around to the front of the horse. He said a few more words in private. The horse whinnied, nickered and snorted. Serge patted him above the nose.

Nearby, the fallen cowboy leaped to his feet.

"Let's hear it for Kyle Lovitt!"

Thunderous cheers.

An older man in a white Stetson ran out onto the dirt. "What have you done?"

"Official clown business," said Serge.

"You broke my bronco!"

Serge patted the side of the horse's head. Another whinny. "He doesn't look broken."

"I mean he won't buck anymore," said the ranch owner. "He's useless at rodeos now."

Serge held out upturned palms. "No good deed goes unpunished..."

Meantime, the thrown rider named Kyle had walked over to one of the officials at the fence, who relayed a message up to the PA booth.

"Ladies and gentlemen, this is quite unusual, but just before our intermission Kyle is going to ride again. Of course it won't count in the official standings, but it's the least we can do for one of our brave military veterans."

More wild cheering.

Kyle climbed onto another saddle, gripped tightly with one hand and nodded that he was ready...

Chapter 27

A FEW MONTHS EARLIER

Senior year.

Coach Calhoun had finally resigned himself to wearing bifocals.

He was sitting behind his desk going over the tryout sheet for the upcoming season. Seemed everyone wanted to play for Pahokee. He ran a finger down the list of names. The finger stopped. A slight smile. No surprise there.

A knock at the door.

He removed the glasses. "Chris, come in."

"Thanks, Coach." She'd gone through a growth spurt over the last three years and was nearing five ten. The chair on the other side of the coach's desk was getting small.

"As usual, you want to talk about something?"

"I'm not asking for any favors . . ."

"I already know where this is going," said Calhoun. "You signed up again for tryouts."

"Four years in a row," said Chris. "This is my last chance."

The coach took a deep breath with paternal eyes. "Chris, I want you to listen carefully to me and take it to heart. I never saw this coming when we first met, but I can't tell you what a pleasure it's been. You make all this worthwhile. You're the kind of student that inspires teachers to teach, and coaches to coach. You've got the best attitude, been the best manager, but most important, you've kept your grades way up."

She sat silent and serious.

"Look," said Calhoun. "Yes, a lot of these boys are going to get athletic scholarships, but I'd be more than shocked if you didn't land an academic one. You're going to go on and make everyone at this school proud."

"Thank you. It means a lot." She looked down.

The coach sighed in frustration. "Chris, you're asking the unrealistic." He held up the tryout sheet. "Do you know how many students we're going to have to cut as it is?"

"Coach, I don't care if I have to ride the bench. I don't care if I never play. I would just be proud to wear the uniform." She placed a hand on her chest where the numbers would go. "As I said, no favors. If I don't earn it, so be it. But I've really been working on my kicking over the summer. Can you just come out to the field and take a look?"

Calhoun slowly began to nod. "Okay, you've more than earned a look. But promise me that this won't get your hopes up . . ."

T he receivers coach, the one named Odom, had been promoted to the head position a couple seasons back. He heard a knock on his office door.

"Lamar, come in. What's up?"

The coach pulled out a chair. "I want you to keep an open mind."

"Uh-oh, I've heard that one before."

Calhoun explained what he had in mind. "What do you think?"

A long pause. "Lamar, I know how fond you are of Chris. And you know I am as well. But we already have two solid place kickers coming back from last year, and an even better punter."

"A lot of teams carry three place kickers," said Calhoun.

"I know, in case of injury or ineligibility," said Odom. "But often the third-stringer plays another position. We have a corner-back who can easily fill in."

"Would you send him out for a field goal in the final seconds?"

"Are you trying to tell me Chris will be our best kicker?"

"No, third best. But a solid third," said Calhoun. "Can you do me a favor? . . ."

Minutes later, both coaches stood with folded arms on the side of an empty field. Chris was waiting at the thirty-yard line with a big sack of footballs spilled onto the ground.

"Okay, Chris!" shouted Lamar. "Show him what you showed me."

She teed up a ball between the hash marks, took the requisite steps back and stopped. She let her arms dangle in concentration. Then she loped forward and let it fly.

It was a perfect end-over-end kick—that hooked left of the up-right.

Calhoun looked sideways. "But it had plenty of distance." Odom didn't respond.

She teed up another. It split the uprights.

"See?" said Calhoun.

"That's just one-for-two," said Odom.

Chris proceeded through the rest of the balls on the grass. Except for one that bounced off the crossbar, they were all true down the middle.

"What do you think now?" asked Calhoun.

"It's different in helmet and pads," said Odom. "Even more so in game situations . . ."

The next day, all the returning players and would-bes covered the field. Whistles blew. Students were sorted according to position. And a handful collected around the coach in charge of kickers. They started at the fifteen-yard line. The coach made notes on a clipboard as each player took shots at the goalposts.

The field had been such chaos earlier, with so many more players than usual, that they didn't notice. But now they did, nudging each other and pointing downfield at a particular player with the number 00.

Chris kicked a modest-length field goal. Then the players didn't pay any more attention. They were too busy trying to make the team. They moved the kicking tees back ten yards and the hopefuls went at it again . . .

Tryouts continued pretty much as they all do. Triage. The ones who were definitely going to make the team, the ones who had no prayer, and the middle group clinging to a dream.

The day of reckoning came. Tryouts were over. Players filled a hallway, nervous silence, waiting. A door opened and they perked up. The head coach came out of the locker room and taped a sheet of paper on the wall. The final list. Students lined up single file, taking turns, one by one, looking for their name. Then either an under-the-breath "Yes!" or demure heartbreak.

Chris's nerves couldn't take it. She had deliberately placed herself at the very end of the line, because she didn't want anyone else around when she got the news. Finally there was only one boy left in front of her. He read down the list, twice, then hung his head and walked away. She watched until he was out of sight, and took a deep breath. "This is it."

She stepped up to the wall and read down the first column with no luck. Her eyes started down the second and she had to take a break from the tension. There weren't a lot of names left, and that would be it. Chris summoned courage and went back to the list. Almost exactly where she had left off, she immediately saw it. And her hand went over her mouth. "Oh, my God."

Her name.

She kept blinking and checking again because she didn't trust her eyes. But each time it was still there.

The empty hallway echoed with joy. *"Wooooo-hooooooooo!"*

She jumped up and down and spun around, crashing into Coach Calhoun. He steadied her by the arms. "Easy, you don't want to hurt yourself before the season."

"I didn't know you were there. Where'd you come from?"

"I kind of wanted to be here."

"Oh, thank you! Thank you! Thank you!"

Now Calhoun grabbed her wrists and pulled them back. "Okay, new rule. You don't hug coaches."

"Sorry, it's just . . ."

"I know." He began walking away. "Get some sleep. Practice starts tomorrow."

Chapter 28

OKEECHOBEE RODEO

The gate burst open wide with an explosion of horse.

It was the encore performance everyone had been awaiting from the service veteran. This bronco bucked even meaner than the first, but Kyle Lovitt was more than up to it. This time, the ride went flawlessly through the required eight seconds, and Kyle jumped down like a dismounting gymnast to stick the landing.

The PA announcer needn't comment. The crowd was already on its feet.

A smaller gate opened, and a cowgal ran into the arena. She tearfully hugged Kyle. "You were magnificent!"

Serge strolled over. "Hope I'm not interrupting anything."

The woman turned, and suddenly Serge had tight arms around

his neck. "I saw what you did for Kyle! Thank you! Thank you! Thank you! . . ."

"Easy now." Serge grabbed her wrists to pull them down. "All in a clown's day, Cheyenne."

"Thank you . . . Wait, how do you know my name?"

The clown removed his red-ball nose and replaced it. "It's me, Serge, from the motel. You're my little history helper."

"Serge?" Cheyenne said in surprise. "I didn't know you were with the rodeo."

"Neither do they," said Serge. "So I guess Kyle's your boyfriend."

"No, silly. My brother."

Serge extended an earnest hand. "I always appreciate a chance to thank one of our heroes who protects the cornucopia of freedoms in this land."

Kyle shook the hand. "I'm not a hero."

"And that's exactly what every single hero says, or they wouldn't be heroes," added Serge. "If you walked around all day bragging about how great you are, I guess you'd be . . . I don't know, elected something?"

Cheyenne squeezed his hand. "Thanks again for helping him with that horse."

"And thanks again for his service," said Serge. "Kyle, where were you stationed?"

"Two tours Afghanistan, one Iraq."

The cowgal glanced around. "So is your friend with you?"

"Coleman?" Now it was Serge's turn to look around. "I completely forgot in all the excitement. Where is that idiot?"

They checked in every direction, until Serge's eyes stopped. Smoke was drifting out of one of the barrels. "Excuse me," he said. "This will only take a sec . . ."

The lid of a wooden barrel was raised, and Coleman looked up. "Hey, Serge."

"What the hell do you think you're doing?"

"Nuthin'."

"I never thought I would utter this sentence, but you can't smoke dope in a clown barrel."

"I got scared," said Coleman. "Just trying to take the edge off."

"Well, don't!" snapped Serge. "Now get out here. There's someone I want you to meet . . ."

Serge grinned with embarrassment as he led his pal back across the arena. "Coleman, I'd like you to meet Cheyenne's brother, Kyle, one of our nation's military heroes."

Coleman stared at an empty sleeve in Kyle's cowboy shirt. "You only have one arm."

"Coleman! For God's sake! You can't just go up to people and say they only have one arm. *Especially* when they only have one arm." Serge turned. "My deepest apologies."

"Don't worry about it," said Kyle.

"What happened to the arm?" asked Coleman.

"Jesus!" Serge smacked his forehead.

"That's all right," said Kyle. "IED went off outside Kandahar. We lost a good woman that day. She was my flank. Next to that, the arm's nothing."

Serge lowered his head. "Your breed never ceases to amaze me. Living by your own high moral code when the rest of us seem to be living by an anti-code. Just so you know, I also live by my own code, drawn from ancient Greeks, Renaissance thinkers, the Age of Reason, President Lincoln and Stones lyrics—'the better angels of our nature,' and 'you can't always get what you want'—if you catch my drift. A lot of my code still doesn't make sense, but that's the whole point, isn't it? Kant borrowed from the Roman poet Horace the Latin phrase *sapere aude,* which translates to 'dare to know,' or essentially, 'Challenge yourself to accept hard and inconvenient truths,' as opposed to the current prevailing wisdom: 'Fuck you and the facts you rode in on.' I don't know the Latin for that."

A pause. "What are you talking about?" asked Kyle.

"I'm not sure," said Serge.

"Uh, you don't know what you're talking about?"

"No, I mean that's the title of my life's philosophy. The only thing I'm absolutely certain of is that *I'm Not Sure*," said Serge. "It's my catchphrase. Walk through the concrete human rain forest with that perspective, and ninety-nine times out of a hundred you'll be more correct than the people who *are* sure. Why? you ask. Okay, hold on to your hat, Kyle, because you've been out of the country for a while . . ." Serge leaned closer and dropped his voice ". . . believe it or not, it's now totally okay to make up every single thing that comes out of your mouth." He stopped and nodded hard. "I know, I know. It's hard to believe, but it's so widespread it's often the person standing right next to you."

"I agree," said Coleman, "because pot makes me smart."

"Excuse me." Cheyenne pointed to activity in the starting gates. "Intermission's ending. We need to be going before the Brahma bulls start."

"Good talk!" said Serge, glancing toward the far side of the arena. "Back to live action . . ."

Elbows rested atop the barrels again. A gate swung open. A bull bucked.

"Those were some good folk," said Serge. "Gives me hope."

"One arm, geez."

"Can you stop?"

"No, I'm just trying to remember what not to say. Anything else?"

"If someone has a mole on their face the size of a pepperoni," said Serge.

"How many times do I have to apologize for that?"

"But did you actually have to use the word 'pepperoni'?"

Yelling and gasps from the crowd.

"Uh-oh," said Serge. "We're needed again."

Serge took off across the dirt, and Coleman dove in a barrel.

A frenzy of clown activity swirled in the middle of the arena. The rider had been thrown clear, but the bull came back to stomp and gore, as they're prone to do. The clowns jumped and whooped to distract the ton of fury from the hapless cowhand... Across the arena, a curious head popped out of a barrel and peeked around, puffing a joint.

For some reason, this interested the bull. He turned and stared toward the barrel.

Coleman casually looked around the arena as he puffed. Until his eyes locked with the bull's. He shrieked in alarm. The joint went flying, and the bull came running.

"Crap!" Coleman pulled the lid back down on top of the barrel and squeezed his hands together in prayer. "Please, please, please..."

Thundering hooves approached. The point of a long white horn pierced the barrel, and the whole thing was suddenly on its side. Another horn attacked the wood as the container began to rotate across the dirt under the momentum of the raging steer. If it had been a car wreck, it would have been called a barrel roll. In this case, it literally was a barrel roll.

Coleman looped and spun and looped some more in an unending violent cascade down the length of the arena. He covered his mouth between bulging cheeks. "Starting to get a little sick in here..."

Meanwhile, everyone else was able to flee to safety either through hurriedly opened gates or by wildly scrambling over fences. After he helped vault the last person's butt up over the barrier into safety, only Serge was left.

He spun in highly emotional concern. "Coleman, my best pal!..."

Angry horns drove the barrel forward, rolling by in front of Serge.

"I don't like this anymore," Coleman yelled with an echo, as if he was shouting from the bottom of a well. "I'm too high."

"Hang tight! I'm so sorry for getting you into this! I'll never forgive myself!"

The rest of the clowns reemerged with the other rodeo staff, who were expert in handling this most dangerous aspect of the event. They surrounded the bull, speaking softly with calm movements. Then they lassoed its horns and brought the beast under control before guiding it into a secure chute.

The clowns righted the barrel, and Serge pulled off the lid. "Buddy! Are you okay?"

"What's happening?" Coleman had made himself into a ball. "Is it over?"

"You're safe now."

Coleman slowly stood up in the barrel. As soon as his curly red wig was visible, the crowd went wild.

One of the top rodeo officials trotted over in seriousness. "We saw everything that happened. We know what was going on."

"You do?" said Serge.

The official nodded. "And you guys aren't on our official list. What's your name?"

"Serge."

"No, him."

"Uh, Coleman."

"Coleman, come with me . . ." They pulled him out of the barrel, and the official took him by the arm. "This way."

Serge ran alongside. "I can explain."

"Save your breath." They reached the center of the arena, and someone handed the official a wireless microphone. He tapped it to make sure it was on, and the sound bounced off the metal roofs. "Ladies and gentlemen, we have just witnessed an amazing display of heroism. While Idaho Jack was in danger of serious injury, and the other clowns weren't having luck controlling the bull, Coleman here . . ." He turned. "It's Coleman, right? Coleman here took stock of the situation and swung into action without regard for his personal well-being, getting the bull's attention and bravely provoking it to attack his barrel, thus averting tragedy . . . Coleman, to what do you owe your quick thinking?"

Coleman leaned toward the microphone. "Pot makes me smart." He stood back up straight and grinned extra wide.

"Uh ..." said the official. "Well, there you have it. Let's hear it for Coleman."

The standing ovation was deafening.

Serge stood next to Cheyenne and Kyle. "Unbelievable."

The quartet of new friends grabbed nachos and sat at a picnic table on the side of the rodeo.

Serge scooped salsa and sour cream. *Crunch, crunch.* "Normally I never eat sporting-event nachos because they're covered with the kind of kiosk-vat molten cheese that you're forced to deal with later, so I'm baking that into my schedule ahead of time. Don't let it affect your appetite . . . Kyle, what's next for you?"

Kyle looked at his sister. "I have that thing tomorrow morning, so I need to come by and get the flags."

"What thing?" said Serge. "What flags?"

"A funeral," said Cheyenne. "North of here an hour."

Kyle wasn't eating. "Someone from my unit."

"Sorry for your loss," said Serge. "So the flags? You're in the color guard or something?"

"I wish it was like that." He pushed his cardboard container of chips toward the center of the table. "No matter how hard I try, I just can't understand it."

"Understand what?" asked Serge.

"Protesters," said Cheyenne. "They picket military funerals."

"Come again?" said Serge. "You're stringing words that don't go together."

"And they shouldn't," said Cheyenne. "But here we are."

"What on earth can they be protesting?" asked Serge.

"Our nation's growing tolerance for gays in general, and those serving in uniform in particular," said Cheyenne. "The protesters claim that *all* our fallen heroes—gay, straight, whatever—are

God's punishment for our wicked ways. I can't bear to repeat what's on the signs they wave."

"Wait," said Serge. "Is this that wacko church in Kansas?"

"They may have started it and gotten the headlines," said Kyle. "But the movement's spread. They also picket recruitment centers and pride parades and even other Christian churches that they consider too inclusive. But the worst are the funerals."

"Not to make any excuses," said Serge, "but relative to the size of the country, we're talking about an extremely tiny number."

"How few is an acceptable number when you know the person being laid to rest?"

"True, true."

"But you raise a good point," said Kyle. "The idiots yelling in the streets are a small fraction. The problem is the complicit silence of a large segment of the population. They may not care for that kind of cruelty at funerals, but they're plenty cruel the rest of the time."

"Please elaborate."

"The bellwether is political campaigns," said Kyle. "One thing politicians can be counted on is to follow the polls, regardless of what they personally believe or who gets hurt. A while back it was 'don't ask, don't tell.' Then society evolved, or at least fifty-one percent did, and that cynical ploy is no longer reliable. So now when some elected cretin needs a poll bump, they've moved on to attacking one of the last acceptable targets—transgender citizens—which is code for broader hate that's not exactly cool to articulate anymore. And these leaders wouldn't be doing it if the polls didn't tell them enough of the public was behind them. That's what really hurts . . ."

Serge didn't know what to say, so he did the right thing and didn't say anything.

"Those of us out in the field know these people. We *are* these people, whether it personally applies or not, because all we have out there is each other, and when you know you can trust someone with your life, you wouldn't notice or care if they're a Martian. When all is said and done, you realize these are some of the finest people you'll ever meet in life. That's why it's so hard to fathom our political leaders today. Can you imagine what it's like to be in a gun battle, and you're fighting shoulder to shoulder with a member of your unit who just heard on the news that morning that some idiot back home is trying to score votes by saying people of his faith aren't welcome in the very country that he's risking his life to protect? And people cheer this shit in large arenas. The funeral protesters are just the spearhead."

"So this cause of yours is a liberal thing?" asked Serge.

"Not remotely," said Kyle. "It runs the whole spectrum. We got artsy-fartsy types, bikers, pointy heads, guys with shotguns in the back windows of their pickups. Most of us are vets, and the one principle that unites us all is: Don't mess with our brothers-and sisters-in-arms."

Serge nodded. "Explain the business about the flags tomorrow."

"Courts have ruled that the protesters are protected by the First Amendment, which I agree with because that's part of what I fought for—"

Serge inadvertently glanced at an empty sleeve.

"—But they also ruled that the picketers must stay at least three hundred feet away from the funeral. Me and my friends, on the other hand, aren't protesting, so the buffer zone doesn't apply to us. We arrive early and line up twenty feet in front of the protest with our huge, overlapping American flags that completely block the view of those at the cemetery paying their respects."

"But I'm sure the protesters are shouting," said Serge.

"That's why we play inspirational music on boom boxes," said Kyle.

"Like what?"

"Like 'This Land Is Your Land.'"

"Where do I sign up?"

"Can you carry a flag? . . ."

The night eventually wound down, and the friends bade each other good night with plans to meet in the morning.

Serge went back in the motel room, heading for the fridge. "I'm already regretting the nachos." He uncapped a bottle of water and turned around. "Coleman!"

"What?"

"You left the door open! Here come the frogs!"

Coleman looked down at something huge leaping through the wickets of his legs.

"Dammit!" Serge dropped to the floor and crawled under the bed. Coleman screamed and ran out the door.

Serge snagged the jumbo amphibian and scooted backward out from under the box spring. As he did, two more frogs hopped under the bed. "The door's still open! Where's that fool?"

He headed for the sidewalk to release his captive and almost bumped into someone.

"Cheyenne! Sorry, didn't see you." He bent down to let the creature hop off into the dark parking lot. "What are you doing back here?" He checked out the cowgal outfit she was still wearing. "I thought this was your rodeo night."

"If you work at a motel, you accept the hours." She gestured back over her shoulder at a sheepish Coleman. "He said you needed a frog rescue."

"Not me, but Coleman definitely needs a rescue, and frogs are the least of it." Serge looked up at a small swirl of insects around one of the porch lights on the motel's walkway. "Are those the blind mosquitoes?"

"That's them."

"What's the big deal everyone's talking about?" said Serge. "I've seen worse swarms of butterflies."

"Oh, that's not remotely close to a swarm. Just a few stragglers out for a stroll. But it does mean they're coming."

"How long?"

"Could be a day, could be three." Cheyenne didn't even know

she was doing it, but she leaned against the doorway with subconscious body language. "You know, you were pretty good out there tonight. Most clowns just run around randomly to create confusion in the animals."

Serge noticed she was absentmindedly rubbing the tip of a cowboy boot on the ground. He cleared his throat: "Uh, you wouldn't happen to have any more vacant rooms tonight?"

"Sure, right next to yours. Why? Expecting anyone?"

"Something's come up. We'll take it."

"I'll go get the key . . ."

She returned in a moment, opening the second room herself. "There you go."

Serge grabbed Coleman by the arm, shoving him inside. "And there *you* go."

"Hey!" yelled Coleman. "What's the deal? . . . Ah, frogs came in! Help!"

"And there are plenty more where that came from if you open this door. Now stay put!" Serge slammed it shut.

"What's going on?" asked Cheyenne.

"Coleman's a crowd. Please, come in."

The second the door closed, Cheyenne's head slowly swiveled around the room with open eyes. "If you're a motel manager, you develop instincts, but I didn't peg you for the damage type. Did you invite a rock star you didn't tell me about?"

Serge threw his arms up in exasperation. Just about everything was knocked over. Broken lightbulbs, torn curtains, pillows disemboweled. "It's Mr. Zippy."

On cue, a ferret jumped up to the TV, standing on his hind legs and chattering demonically. Then he hopped down and scattered Coleman's empty beer bottles like bowling pins. "He's wrapped way too tight, and I'm afraid we're unfit parents. But I've been putting off the inevitable because I didn't want it to reflect poorly on the adoption rights of two dudes."

"No problem," said Cheyenne. "This is a family-run place, and we have a large cage in the back room for the day manager, who has an older cat that needs care. I can put the ferret in there, and I know lots of pet people around here who would be more than happy to take him."

"Thank God," said Serge. "He was getting on my last nerve."

"Be right back." Cheyenne lovingly grabbed the ferret and disappeared.

Then she returned. As soon as Serge opened the door, she slammed into him without warning, and they fell onto the still-made bed. Violent kissing and groping. Clothes flew in all directions. "Can you leave the boots on?" asked Serge. "You can make requests, too."

"Shut up!"

"Haven't had that one before."

They were soon going at it like—well, they deserve *some* privacy. Shrieking and banging came from both sides of the wall connecting Coleman's room to theirs.

Serge raised a hand. "Can I talk now?"

"Sure, just don't stop."

"That's not really my call," said Serge. "If you haven't noticed, you're the one on top."

"*Oh, yes, yes, yes, yes!* . . ."—pounding the headboard—". . . *Yes! Yes! Yes!* . . . Before we go any further, I need to ask a question."

"Further?" asked Serge. "I don't see any more stop signs."

"It's about commitment. You're not one of those guys, I mean . . ."

Great, Serge thought. *Here we go again.*

Cheyenne continued thrusting. "Did you just roll your eyes at me?"

"No, that was a twitch. Please, ask your question."

"Every once in a while I'll find a guy where there's the perfect combination of a meeting of the minds and broiling animal attraction. But more often than not, they turn out to be clinging vines."

"Wait," said Serge. "*That's* your commitment question? You were worried I'd be the smothering one?"

She nodded and thrust. "I hope you understand. There's too many places I've got to see. I'm sure you've heard the song."

"In my sleep," said Serge. "Believe me, you have no worries. And I completely understand about the travelin' jones."

More screaming from Coleman's room. A crash against the wall. "*Frogs!*"

Thrust. "Is your friend okay?"

"Not even close. I just tune out the meltdowns."

Thrust, thrust. "The whole history thing is what first attracted me to you."

"Really?" said Serge. "Me too! Would you like to see my tombstone rubbings?"

"Now?" Cheyenne thrust harder as she whipped her hair side to side. "Isn't that part supposed to come before, when you're trying to *get* me in bed?"

"You're right," said Serge. "Life is all about timing."

"Man, you're weird," said Cheyenne. "For some reason, that just attracts me more."

"And this concludes the slow middle movement of our song. Now it's time for the triple-guitar crescendo." Serge quickly flipped her on the bed, and moans became shrieks, louder and louder. To the point where Coleman stopped shrieking himself and became more afraid of the sounds coming from the next room . . .

The lovers finally collapsed on their backs in pools of sweat.

Serge wiped stinging perspiration from his eyes. "My compliments to the chef."

"I'm still fluttering," said Cheyenne. "And speaking of fluttering, what was that deal with your eyelids and your pupils going up in your head?"

"I had a simultaneous."

"Don't you mean *we* had a simultaneous?"

Serge shook his head. "Just me. I came *and* had A Moment. Thinking about all the murals in town and early telephone service."

"You're shitting me."

"You'd rather me think about old girlfriends, or picture you wearing a walrus mask?"

"I'm not sure." She turned her head on the pillow. "Let's find out."

"Serious?"

She nodded eagerly.

"Where's your cowboy hat?"

"In the office." Cheyenne jumped out of bed. "I'll go get it."

She wiggled into her blue jeans and opened the door. A truck with a full rack of amber lights was pulling up. "What the hell is that?"

"Ordered a rental fishing boat," said Serge. "They attach a temporary hitch on your car and everything. I always figure if you're going in, go big!"

"If you say so."

"Just realized something," said Serge. "What if other guests are trying to call you at the front desk with an emergency?"

"Screw 'em. They're just frogs."

Chapter 29

PAHOKEE

The Blue Devils were an early-season favorite, and they lived up to the hype. Pahokee tore through their district schedule, undefeated after six games. And it wasn't even close. All double-digit victories. You could always pick out the loudest voice on the bench shouting encouragement. Guess who?

A few weeks earlier, before a game, Coach Calhoun was smiling behind his desk as Chris sat on the other side. He actually looked forward to her visits now, and felt something conspicuously missing on the days she didn't show up.

She was wearing her shoulder pads and game jersey: 00. He noticed she was unusually serious.

"Is something wrong?"

"Oh, no, no, no," said Chris. "It's just that I feel awkward asking you for something."

"Never stopped you before."

"But you've done so many favors for me in the last few years."

"What's one more? Fire away."

"But I promised you."

"Promised me what?"

"That I didn't care if I never got on the field," said Chris. "I just wanted to wear the uniform."

"And?"

"I learned that to earn a varsity letter, you have to be in at least one play during a regular-season game."

"Is that so?"

"Coach, in several of these games we've had big leads late in the fourth quarter."

"Some actually huge."

"What I'm asking is, if we're leading by several touchdowns near the end and we score, uh—"

"You'd like to kick off?"

She nodded.

"All right, you've asked," said Calhoun. "We'll just see how it goes. Now, if I could have the office, there's a few things that need dealing with before tonight."

That evening's game proceeded like the previous six Fridays. The Blue Devils built up an early lead, and the defense held their opponent to only three first downs. By the beginning of the fourth quarter, it was 35–0. It was raining.

Calhoun walked over to the head coach for a private talk. By the body language, it seemed that Lamar had to be persistent. Finally, and in no small part simply in order to get Calhoun off his back, the head coach said: "We'll just have to see."

Rain poured harder and the field began turning to mud. Runners lost their footing and passes were impossible to catch. Referees had towels on the field to wipe the ball down between each snap.

It was time to call running plays from here on out. Not to move the ball, but to burn the clock. It was also one of those unwritten rules of football decorum. Don't pass and run up the score at the end. That's why the entire team on the field was second and third string. And even then, Pahokee was unstoppable. They consistently moved the ball five to ten yards a play. They entered the red zone, which means the twenty. Three minutes left.

Lamar Calhoun finished another chat with the head coach and walked back over to the players' bench. "Chris?"

She was leaning forward, wrapped up in the game and still shouting encouragement. She raised her eyes. "Yes, Coach?"

"Start warming up."

It froze her.

"Did you hear me?"

An eager nod. She sprang off the bench and began running toward the practice kicking net.

"Aren't you forgetting something?" Calhoun pointed back under the bench. "You're going to need that."

Chris raced back and snatched her helmet.

Pahokee scored again even faster than expected. Chris barely had time to stretch, no practice kicks. She ran onto the field with ten boys as the rain whipped even harder. Some of her teammates raced past her, slapping her shoulder pads. "Show 'em what you got, Chris."

As she teed up the ball, shouting came from the opposite sidelines. The other coach frantically waved his clipboard at his receiving team. They had just realized a girl was kicking. "Move up! Move up!"

The visiting team advanced ten yards.

The clipboard kept waving. "More!"

The players positioned themselves fifteen yards ahead of where they normally fielded a kick.

Chris stared down at the ball and took a few steps back. Thunder boomed from the clouds over the stadium lights. She looked left and right down the Blue Devil line. Boys nodded back, helmets dripping. The referee blew a whistle for play to resume. Chris ran forward and put her shoe into the leather.

Now here's the thing about kickoffs: they're live balls. Which means that after it travels ten yards, either team can grab it for possession.

It was an exceptionally high kick, which, along with the rain, threw off the receiving team's depth perception. They began slowly backpedaling. Meanwhile, the Pahokee line was sprinting full speed. By the time the visiting team realized the ball was seriously over their heads, all the players were at roughly the same spot on the field.

The ball bounced at the two-yard line and rolled into the end zone. Now it was a full-out race to see who could get there first. A player in a blue jersey leaped horizontally and landed on the ball just before it rolled out of bounds. The referee raised two arms straight into the air.

Touchdown.

The home crowd exploded.

All eyes were on the end zone. They didn't notice it at first. But back toward the other end of the field, whistles were blowing and numerous yellow flags had flown.

Pahokee wasn't trying to run up the score. But the other team felt they had done something far more insulting to rub their opponent's noses in it. They'd sent in a girl.

So here's what happened when the play began. The forward players of the receiving team usually begin moving back to set up their blocks. This time, however, the two players in the middle ran forward as fast as they could. The game was so unwinnable that penalties didn't matter anymore.

Chris had stood alone, watching the ball sail. Two seconds later, she was clobbered by a pair of players coming in from both sides. They sent her flying onto her back. That drew the first whistle and flag. After a few more seconds, as Chris started to push herself up, they pounced again, making sure to push her helmet hard into the grass. "Stay down, girl!"

More whistles and flags. People in the stands began to notice and point, and the celebration in the end zone ceased. The Pahokee team watched two cocky players trotting away from where their kicker was faltering as she tried to get up, a big chunk of muddy turf stuck in her face mask. "Chris!"

The offending players never made it back to their sideline. The Pahokee bench emptied and they were swarmed, then the visiting team entered the fray. It took a while to untangle, but coaches and cops were ultimately able to pull everyone apart.

For a victory, it was unusually silent in the Pahokee locker room. Normally a fight, let alone a bench-clearing brawl, would receive a tongue-lashing from the coaching staff. The players were waiting for the rebuke that never came. Everyone knew what wasn't said aloud. Chris may have been viewed in the past as just a girl, but now she was a Blue Devil, and nobody but nobody does that to one of theirs.

Chapter 30

THE NEXT MORNING

The sun had just peeked over the eastern sky of Lake Okeechobee when a Dodge Ram pickup with all the chrome and jacked-up tires and everything else it stands for rolled into the parking lot. There was the full complement of bumper stickers and decals: black POW-MIA logo, the yellow-green-red bar for Vietnam, silver parachutes for airborne, silver dolphins for submarine service, Purple Heart, Rangers, et cetera, et cetera.

Another pickup rolled in behind, a black Chevy Colorado with more decals, flying flags, American, Marine Corps. The pair of vehicles stopped outside an off-brand motel on the northern shore of Lake Okeechobee. The cabs of the trucks were already full, and more people squatted in the beds of the pickups as if there had been a pre-dawn street-corner call for migrant workers: *"We need ten for six hours . . ."*

A motel room door opened, and Serge and Cheyenne stepped out. He walked to the next door and knocked.

"Just a minute."

"Coleman! Come on! People are waiting!" said Serge.

"It's okay," said Cheyenne. "They have to stop anyway for the others to catch up."

"Others?"

The door opened and Coleman appeared. "All set to go."

Serge stared at a lumpy spot below Coleman's collarbone. "You're wearing the chest pouch?"

"That's right."

Ribbit, ribbit . . .

"A frog's in there?"

Coleman nodded and patted the pouch. "We worked things out last night. We're friends now."

"You do realize they're not like ferrets," said Serge. "I don't think he has any idea what's going on."

"You couldn't be more wrong." Coleman stroked the canvas. *Ribbit.* "And you wouldn't know it to look at him, but he's a raging maniac."

"Don't tell me."

"I found out that it's almost impossible to get a frog to smoke a joint—"

"Another sentence I never thought I'd live to hear."

"—So I grabbed one of the empty plastic bags that come with the trash cans in the room, and put the frog in it. Then I took a mondo, triple-clutch hit and blew it into the bag."

"I realize that among your people such gestures are tokens of goodwill, but we're bordering on animal unkindness here."

"He didn't mind at all." Coleman peeked down through the opening. "He liked the beer, too."

Serge covered his eyes with a hand.

Coleman reached into the pouch. "I know you and Cheyenne had your own thing going on in your room last night, but you missed the real fun."

"Did we?"

Coleman scooped out the frog, stroking its head lightly with an index finger. "Isn't that right, Jeremiah?"

"You call your frog Jeremiah?"

"Because he is a bullfrog."

"Naturally," said Serge. "But back to giving him beer."

"Three Dog Night let their frog drink wine, so I don't see the big fuss."

"Technically their frog *brought* the wine," said Serge. "Didn't that tell you there was some artistic license going on?"

"I don't know what that means, but you should have seen him last night," said Coleman. "When this little sucker gets his swerve on, look out! He was jumping straight up, sideways, even a back-flip. We had a contest."

"You jumped with him?"

"Duh!" said Coleman. "Then I used the plastic ice bucket to make him a little boat in the tub. But what he really liked was the toilet. Don't worry: I taped up the flush handle in case I forgot. I was responsible. And some of those blind mosquitoes had gotten into the room, and I was able to capture a few, but only crushed them a little, and then I sat on the edge of the tub throwing bugs to Jeremiah in the toilet. I wish someone had a camera."

"I can't picture anything more precious."

"I know," said Coleman. "He really had the munchies."

"But don't you think you should be releasing him now?" said Serge. "He probably wants to get back to his own kind."

"I think he's happy," said Coleman. "Remember how they were jumping all over the parking lot last night? Look at him now, happy to sit in my hand."

"Coleman, his eyes are closed. He's still fucked up."

"Then the nice thing to do is let him sleep it off." Coleman opened the pouch. "Back in you go."

A roar erupted from an unseen point around the bend, growing louder and louder until it was vibrating stuff. The source came into view and pulled into the parking lot.

The bikers had arrived.

Harleys, helmets and star-spangled bandannas. Most had black leather vests, festooned with medals and patches from every branch of service.

"Time to saddle up," said Cheyenne, and the three climbed in the bed of the second truck. The caravan pulled out of the parking lot and headed north.

Serge sat against the back gate next to Coleman. "I think I might have a problem."

"I'll do anything I can."

"It's not that kind of problem. It's Cheyenne." Serge searched for words. "She doesn't want a commitment."

"I don't see the problem."

"*That's* the problem," said Serge. "Almost every woman I've ever met wants a commitment. Some act like they don't at first, but it eventually comes up, and I'm a ramblin' kind of guy."

"I get it," said Coleman. "You think she's acting?"

"No, I think she's on the level."

"Then you're home free."

Serge was quiet a moment. "I can't describe it, but it's having some kind of effect on me. I'm oddly attracted to this. She's a ramblin' kind of *gal,* and that makes *me* want to commit. And then I'll be trapped following her around a Pottery Barn with an armload of guest towels and that feeling that I can't breathe."

"Jesus!" said Coleman. "Get a grip. You can't let her split us up."

"Thanks for thinking of me."

"No, seriously," said Coleman. "I don't know how to survive."

"You'll do fine."

"Serge!" He grabbed his friend tightly by the arm. "Don't mess around. You know I'd end up in the woods behind a 7-Eleven living on an old mattress."

"I see your point."

"Maybe it's all a trick," said Coleman. *Ribbit.* "If you find out that she secretly wants to commit, then you won't be attracted anymore."

"For once you speak as a sage, my finely toasted friend. And I know just how to find out . . ."

The patriotic procession of trucks and hogs cruised up through Osceola County, wind flapping hair and scarves. Serge scooted across the bed of the pickup until he settled in next to Cheyenne.

She smiled coyly. "Well, look who it is."

"Hi, Cheyenne. Uh, uh, I mean, uh, what I'm trying to say is, uh . . ."

"Wow, I've never known you to be at a loss for words."

"Cheyenne, would you like to go steady?"

"Is this a joke?" She had a good laugh. "Are you in seventh grade?"

"I've given this a lot of thought." Serge nervously picked at his fingernails. "I'd like to give you an ID bracelet with our names engraved."

"Whoa! Stop!" said Cheyenne. "You *are* serious. I thought I could trust you when we talked about this last night."

"You *can* trust me. That was just a test, to make sure what you said wasn't a trick."

"You sure?"

"When was the last time you were in a Pottery Barn?"

"Like, never."

"Case closed. You passed with flying colors."

Serge's butt scooted back across the pickup's bed until he was at the gate again.

"Well?" asked Coleman.

"It's worse than I thought. She's never even stepped foot in a Pottery Barn."

"Good God!" said Coleman. "How can you not love a woman like that?"

"I know, I know," said Serge. "I must think of something. She's just got to have some kind of a big turnoff that's a deal breaker."

"Maybe when she laughs really hard, she sounds like a donkey."

"She has a great laugh."

"You're fucked."

Nearly an hour later, the ad hoc motorcade arrived and parked along a remote country road where the only building had a steeple. Across the street, tombstones in a neatly manicured field. Nobody had arrived at the cemetery yet. Funeral workers had already set up the rows of folding chairs under a white sun canopy. A brass contraption with heavy-gauge straps sat over a freshly dug hole.

Across the street was a different story. Bullhorns, tightly screwed faces, and some of the most vile signs that have ever been painted.

Over a distant hill on the straight highway, various vehicles headed toward them. Moments later, the pickup trucks emptied and motorcyclists dismounted.

The new arrivals were heckled as they carried their flags toward the protest line. The malcontents noticed the size and nature of the people coming toward them, particularly the bikers. The protesters took an intimidated step back. "You touch us and we'll sue! We taking video of all of this!"

Not a word was spoken among the flag people. They formed a precise line from rehearsal, turning their backs to the picketers and presenting fifteen huge renditions of Old Glory that formed an effective red, white and blue curtain.

"Hey, you can't block us like that! We have rights!"

No response.

Up the road came a solemn line of cars with headlights on at noon.

Someone reached down and pressed a button on a boom box. "*... This land is your land ...*"

The funeral procession pulled though the cemetery gates, and the hearse parked near the sun canopy.

The protesters screamed louder. The boom box was turned up.

Men with white gloves slid the casket out the back of the hearse and ceremoniously placed it on the support straps over the grave. It had its own American flag. An honor guard gave a salute with guns. A trumpet played. Two of the people with white gloves removed the flag from the casket and, with measured cadence, folded it into a triangle. One of them bent down to present it to a widow with small children.

The protesters had so much anger baggage, you wouldn't have thought there was room for more. But the flags in front of them were just too much. Not only did they block their view of the service, but more importantly, they blocked the mourners' view of their signs. On top of that, the boom box. It just wasn't fair!

"I'll fix this!"

The leader of the protest, a pastor, ran around the end of the line and stood facing them, waving his sign and screaming into a bullhorn.

Kyle Lovitt and the others looked up and down their ranks. They had been over this before in their meetings. In case the picketers ignored the court order: No violence. Don't even move lest there be inadvertent physical contact that could become courtroom fodder. Just get out cell phones and document the violation of the buffer zone.

Serge hadn't gotten the memo.

He handed Coleman his flag and ran over to the protest leader. "Excuse me, but you're out of your comfort zone. I suggest you slither back behind the buffer line."

"Go to hell! You and your queer buddies are interfering with our First Amendment rights. You're forcing us to step forward."

"There's the little matter of the court order," said Serge.

"What about it?" said the leader. "I don't see anybody here to enforce it."

"Oh, but I do." Serge swiftly nailed him in the chest with a stun gun, and just as quickly stashed it away. The leader collapsed, and his followers came running.

Kyle glanced back and forth. "Turn off your phones! Erase those files! . . ."

Serge nonchalantly sauntered over to his group as the picketers dragged their leader back behind enemy lines.

Kyle grabbed him by the arm. "Why did you go and do that?"

"What are you talking about?"

"You're just lucky that our flags blocked their video cameras."

"If you say so." Serge opened a brown billfold and removed a driver's license. "Hmm, his name's Jebediah."

"What's that?"

"A wallet I just happened to find on the ground." Serge replaced the license.

"Why'd you take it from him?"

"You don't want to know."

"And you didn't tell me that."

Chapter 31

PAHOKEE

C oach Calhoun strolled down the corridor outside the locker room. He heard slapping footsteps on the wax floor. A student ran past him practically in tears.

"Chris! Come back here!"

She stopped, embarrassed, trying to hide emotion.

"What's wrong?"

"Nothing."

"Don't 'nothing' me. In my office, now."

Chris sat quietly in a familiar wooden chair. Calhoun kept trying to get her to open up, but it was like prying answers from a hostile witness. She was staring at the floor, lips trembling, so shaken that the coach's mind ran through the menu of worst cases that can befall teenagers. The list was long and ugly in these parts.

All she kept saying was that it was "her fault." That only made the list grow in Calhoun's head. Finally, the coach was able to drag out enough details to learn that the problem was academic, and he practically collapsed with relief. But then puzzlement. What kind of problem could Chris have in class? So many straight A's now that he barely glanced at her report cards.

"Chris, I can't help you if you won't talk."

It wasn't that Chris was resisting the coach. She was one of those people who can hold in crying as long as they don't talk, or it all erupts. She couldn't have that. So she silently reached in her backpack with a quivering hand and pulled out a term paper.

Calhoun took it and looked at the top of the first page. A big red *F*. Now he was really confused. Chris never got an F in anything. Plus, this was a science paper, her best subject.

"Okay, Chris, I know you're upset, so can you come back here tomorrow, same time?"

She nodded.

"And can you leave the term paper with me?"

Another nod. She left.

Coach Calhoun leaned back in his chair with the paper and didn't know what to make of it. But the game plan for that Friday night's gridiron contest had just been put on hold. He scooted his chair up and logged on to his computer. Surfing the net, checking her footnotes. To himself: "What the heck is dark energy?" More clattering of the keyboard. "Quarks? Photons? Planck time?"

The next afternoon, the final bell of the school day rang. Minutes later, Coach Calhoun entered a classroom. The only person still there was a teacher behind his desk, starting to grade quiz papers. He had been a midterm replacement for the previous science teacher, who had left to accept a higher-paying position at a private school on the east side of the county.

"Mr. Garns?"

"Yes?"

"Coach Calhoun." They shook hands.

"How can I help you?"

"It's about one of your students, Chris Maples."

"Oh." Garns turned serious and looked down, making a mark on a test paper. "I guess she went running to you about her last grade."

Calhoun hit pause in his brain. This was not how he expected the conversation to begin. He reassessed. "She didn't come running to me. But I did see her paper. I've known her for a while, and I'm trying to understand this F."

Garns, not looking up: "She used the Internet."

"What does that mean?"

"Students aren't supposed to rely on the Internet for sourcing. It's unverified," said the teacher. "I made that extremely clear when I came on board."

"I agree," said Calhoun. "But I went through her footnotes. These weren't bulletin boards or blogs. They were scientific research journals with articles from professors at Caltech, MIT, Carnegie Mellon. I asked other teachers, and those Internet sources are allowed."

"The footnotes weren't in the proper format."

Calhoun took another deep breath. "I looked at your strike-throughs on her paper, like where she cited dark energy as the reason why gravity isn't slowing down the expansion of the big bang."

"We haven't covered that in class. And I don't believe it exists."

"She noted it as a theory. It has support in the research journals."

"You're a science teacher now?" Garns stood. "Second-guessing me?"

"Not in the least. I'm just trying to sort all this out."

"She also has a big attitude problem."

Calhoun's head practically spun on his neck. "Are we talking about the same person?"

"She undermines my authority."

"She talks back? That would surprise me."

"No, just smug like she's too smart for my class, challenging me in front of the other students."

"Challenging?"

"Interrupting to ask cynical questions, like the dark energy thing."

"I think she's just trying to learn."

"I see where this is going," said Garns. "You *coaches.*"

"What's that supposed to mean?"

"Pressuring teachers to keep players eligible."

Calhoun stopped again, this time to check his temper. He knew there was a widespread stereotype about coaches tampering with grades. But in reality, the vast majority take a holistic approach to developing a student, both as an athlete and a person, getting to know their parents, talking to their teachers.

"Can we dial this back a bit?" said Calhoun. "It's not about us. It's a student's welfare."

"So you coddle your players?"

"We don't need to continue in this direction."

"You sports guys think you have so much influence."

Calhoun took a final pause to choose words, because a bridge was about to catch fire. "I've seen you before. Not often, but enough to know."

"Seen me?"

"Some of the finest people in the world are teachers. They work tirelessly for little pay. But what really makes them so special is they're like parents to the whole community. They find no greater joy than helping students succeed to their utmost potential . . . Then there's some of the worst people in the world. Also teachers, the rare ones here and there. Bitter because their lives didn't work out the way they'd hoped. And when they see a great kid with a bright future, they don't take pride in helping them along. Instead, they're jealous and try to crush their spirit. That is unforgivable."

The coach walked around the desk and got face-to-face with

Garns. "But you're right about one thing. Coaches do have undue influence in our culture. I make it a rule not to use mine. I also make exceptions."

Calhoun stormed out of the classroom and slammed the door.

C oach Calhoun sat in the principal's office. He'd finished laying out his case, and now the ball was in the other court.

"I find all this hard to believe," said the principal. "But since it's coming from you . . ."

"So you'll look into it?"

"With due diligence. If it's true, this is very disturbing news. It has no place at my school."

The principal kept his word. He interviewed students and parents, and the feedback was uniform. Some teachers use a tough style of teaching, but only to push the students to do their best. This new science teacher just seemed to genuinely dislike the kids.

By the end of the week, Garns was packing up his belongings in a cardboard box. And swearing he'd find a way to get even.

Chapter 32

OSCEOLA COUNTY

C reeping was afoot.

Two suspicious figures on their hands and knees inched forward in the night. North of St. Cloud, Florida. North of sanity.

Coleman raised his right hand and sniffed the palm, then held it to Serge.

"Get that out of my face." Serge's back was like a leopard's. "You're just going to have to deal with it."

They crawled forward across the pasture like a sniper team. At least Serge did. Coleman's stealth was more like that of something in a playpen. Serge looked up: "Full moon. That's the worst for our mission, but we were in no position to pick our timing."

Ribbit.

"You brought Jeremiah?" asked Serge.

"He's good luck."

"He's loud," said Serge. "He'll give our position away."

"Not my Jeremiah!"

"Shhhh! Keep it down!" Serge lowered his chin in the tall weeds. "People are up . . ."

Moments earlier, the gold Satellite had left the highway for the concealment of a dirt road that ran through pine hardwoods. From there, Serge drove across the bumpy pasture as curious cattle watched the silhouette of the Plymouth in the moonlight. They continued on until reaching some new-growth woods and brush at the edge of a property. That's where they left the car and commenced their crawl. Now they were in the perfect position that Serge had scoped out in advance with Internet help. Ahead: the target.

A white farmhouse sat atop a small hill.

It was a large farmhouse, as they go, two stories with an addition on back. The owner's budget apparently favored size over condition. A tin roof sagged above the front porch. The wood siding had termite damage and missing paint from the sun. A pond sat off the driveway. And now two strangers lay in the woods just a stone's throw from the front door.

"What do we do?" asked Coleman.

"Wait and watch." Serge got out binoculars and scanned windows. "I picked the best spot to launch our operation, but that's where my plan ends. I knew this extraction would be tricky because I figured he didn't live alone. We must recon the social structure of this abode and find its soft underbelly."

"What's going on in there?"

"Remember the pastor from the funeral protest? He just went in the kitchen. I've picked up five other people inside, but they're all young women. Long dresses and bonnets. They're holding candles like it's some kind of ceremony."

"No guys?"

"Something weird's going on in there."

Coleman kissed his frog on the mouth. "Weird how?"

"Looks like one of those cults where the leader preaches strict obedience to the gospels in order for him to have sex with everyone."

"Is that what the gospels are about?"

"I hate to judge without all the facts, but I'm guessing he's taking liberties." Serge handed Coleman the binoculars. "Stay here."

"Where are you going?"

"To get more facts."

Serge darted ahead toward the farmhouse, sweeping around the west side, which was shielded from the moonlight. He plastered his back against the building, creeping sideways. Soon he was under a window. He slowly rose on tiptoes until his eyes were just above the sill.

Inside the living room, the women stood in a line with heads bowed over their candle holders. The pastor held an open Bible with one hand and gesticulated wildly with the other. Then he stepped forward. The women's chests heaved with anticipation. He looked up and down the row before blowing out one of the candles. He took that woman by the hand and led her into another room.

Serge resumed creeping along until he came to another window. This one was a bit higher. He found some loose bricks on the side of the house and fashioned a little stack. Two eyes again rose above a sill. It was a bedroom. Mirrors everywhere, including the ceiling. A video camera sat on a tripod in the corner. Serge watched the pastor taking off his shirt. The young woman took off her bonnet and reached for the top button under her neck.

"Holy mother," Serge said to himself. "There's no way she's even close to eighteen. I can't watch."

He crouched down below the sill, and when he did, a couple of the bricks at his feet toppled. "Shit." Serge hit the ground and rolled himself as tightly as possible against the lattice along the farmhouse's crawl space. He looked sharply up and saw the shadow of the pastor's face against the windowpane. Serge held his breath as the shadow moved from one side of the window to the other, clearly convinced something was out there.

After the longest of times, the shadow left the window, and voices could be heard inside.

"Whew!" Serge scurried in a big loop around the side of the house and dove back into the brush next to Coleman.

"What did you see?"

"It's worse than I thought," said Serge. "First, I don't see any way of extracting the pastor without raising general mayhem from the women. They've been brainwashed. So we must abort the mission and put him under surveillance until we can identify an interception point away from his flock. Second, I think the one he's about to have sex with is underage. I should burst in there under general principles to stop it. But what if I'm wrong or she's older than she looks, or some kind of common-law wife?"

"Maybe you could phone in an anonymous tip."

"That's a great idea." Serge pulled out a disposable burner phone with prepaid minutes. He looked up as clouds drifted across the moon, cutting the light. "And our luck might be turning. We're getting extra cover of darkness . . ." He began pressing buttons.

A tap on his shoulder.

"Not now, Coleman. I'm phoning in the important information."

Another tap. "Uh, Serge . . ."

"I told you I'm busy!"

Tap, tap, tap.

"Dammit, Coleman! What is it that can't wait?"

A crunching of leaves. "*Who's out there!*"

Serge looked up to see the pastor aiming a double-barrel twelve-gauge shotgun.

"Damn," Serge whispered. "Keep your head down and don't move."

"I said, who's out there!"

The pastor kept walking, straight toward them.

The gun cocked, now only feet away. Just a thin, single row of

bushes between them and discovery. The clouds began thinning and drifting away. The moonlight grew brighter on the leaves.

"Come out with your hands up or I'll blast ya!"

Stone silence. Then:

Ribbit . . .

The shotgun's twin barrels bore down on an exact spot in the bushes.

Jeremiah slipped out of Coleman's pouch, and before the pair could react, the amphibian leaped from the brush. Another big jump, and it landed at the pastor's feet.

"For heaven's sake! I'm giving myself a heart attack over a stupid bullfrog!" The pastor propped the shotgun on his shoulder and turned back toward the farmhouse.

That was all the opportunity Serge needed. He sprang from the vegetation and caught the pastor in the small of his back with the stun gun. The victim fell inert.

Serge and Coleman grabbed him under the armpits and dragged the limp body from view as several curious people in bonnets appeared in the front window . . .

J ust after midnight, the gold Plymouth returned to the motel on the north shore of Lake Okeechobee. It backed up to their room.

Serge stood idly next to the car like he was bored.

"What are you waiting for?"

"Cheyenne."

"You're bringing her in on this?"

"Just the opposite." His eyes scanned every conceivable direction. "I have to make sure she doesn't get the slightest whiff of what we're up to. I'm taking a wild stab this is a touch worse than romantic commitment."

Serge began to whistle as he leaned against the back of the car,

slowly rocking. "That's long enough. She's not around. Open the room and I'll get our guest from the trunk." He bent down and began inserting a key in the lid.

A woman's voice: "There you are!"

"Jesus Christ!" Serge leapt up and landed sitting on the lid of the trunk. "Where the hell did you come from?"

"Uh, just around the corner," said Cheyenne. "What's gotten into you? You're awfully jumpy."

"Nothing, nothing," said Serge. "Almost had an accident up the road. Heart's still pounding."

A wary eye. "Are you sure that's it?"

"Definitely!"

"If you say so." An off-hand smile. "I didn't know where you went, because I was kind of hoping . . . uh, you could show me your tombstone rubbings."

"Yes, yes, sure. How long are you on tonight? I just have a couple pressing business matters to tie up, and then it will be a freaking tombstone jamboree."

"Are you positive you're okay?"

"I'll ring you in the office when I'm free."

"I'll be waiting." She headed back to her office, glancing over her shoulder in suspicion. Serge had a toothy grin and waved to her with wiggling fingers. Then she was gone.

"Hurry, Coleman!"

The trunk popped, and soon a familiar scene.

Two people sat next to each other on the edge of a motel bed. Coleman smiled and petted a frog. Serge petted a roll of duct tape.

A brief scream as the pastor regained consciousness and looked down at all the tight rope and his uncomfortable chair.

Ribbit.

"Where are my manners?" said Serge. "Jebediah, meet Jeremiah. Sorry, but he didn't bring his wine."

"What do you want from me?"

"Damn, you're fast." Serge began cleaning under his finger-

nails with the tip of a large-bladed hunting knife. "My conditions are nonnegotiable. First, release all the young women at your farmhouse. We both know what's going on. Second, no more protests outside military funerals. Make that anywhere in the world while we're at it."

"You can't do this!" said the pastor. "You're abrogating my First Amendment rights!"

"Couldn't agree more," said Serge. "Few things are as important to me as our blessed Constitution."

"You agree?" said the pastor. "Then how can you do this?"

Serge shrugged. "I'm wrong. Sorry."

The pastor fumed with flared nostrils. "You're going to hell!"

"Meet you in the elevator."

The pastor threw a tantrum in his chair, making the legs tap-dance on the wooden floor. "Who do you think you are?"

"An angel," said Serge. "Avenging or merciful. You make the call!"

"You're no angel!"

"I was using poetic slack," said Serge. "'The better angels of our nature.' That was Lincoln. And I want you to embrace all your fellow citizens as children of God."

"I don't want to."

"'You can't always get what you want.' That was Jagger."

"You won't get away with this!"

"I don't have to get away with anything if you agree to my simple terms."

"Never, you pervert! Not in a million years."

"I was kind of hoping you'd say that, because I have so been wanting to try this." Duct tape quickly went over the mouth, and the chair began being dragged backward.

Minutes later, Serge sat at the steering wheel of the Plymouth. "Coast clear? No Cheyenne?"

"Right-o," said Coleman, leaning over a bong.

"You're not even looking."

"I'm high. I have extra powers."

The gold Plymouth slowly pulled around to the dark side of the motel and the special parking area for the bass boats favored by the sportsmen staying at the inn. Serge backed up to one, got out and fastened the trailer hitch.

"You're stealing a boat?" said Coleman.

"No, this is one I rented earlier and had waiting here on standby." Serge climbed back in the car to the sound of banging in the trunk. "It's actually a pretty good deal around here. I grabbed this baby on the wings of hope that I could employ it in my next science project." The Plymouth pulled out of the parking lot and turned east . . .

Lake Okeechobee has various access points for fishermen. There are a number of ramps over the Herbert Hoover Dike to public launches. If you have a really big boat already in the water, then you have to enter through one of three locks.

"It's not a very big boat," said Coleman.

"No lock, no problem."

Serge followed the road curling south toward Clewiston until he found one of the ramps, dark and deserted. The bass boat slid into the water, including the captive, tied up again to the chair. Serge got behind the wheel and pushed the throttle just above idle.

At this part of the lake, the open water is a few miles away. In between, marshland laced with canals, including a large one around the rim, logically called the Rim Canal. Serge rode it awhile before reaching an opening off the port side, and turned left into what's known as the Old Moore Haven Canal.

From there it was a straight shot through ferocious thriving nature. Birds and bugs and bogs.

"Listen to that racket," said Coleman.

"The swamp sizzles at night," said Serge. "Humans might be at the top of the food chain, but out here we're seriously outnumbered."

"What is this place?"

"They call it Dynamite Pass. But it's nothing like the cool name of the spot where we're heading. In fact, I chose it just for the name." Serge pushed the throttle forward again, and the boat began to plane. "Florida has some of the best place-names: Corkscrew, Spuds, Festus, Roach, Howey-in-the-Hills, Two Egg, but we're about to reach my favorite one of all."

Moments later, they dropped anchor at a crossroads of canals, sitting just a short distance from the lake proper.

"Okay," said Coleman. "I give. What's the name of this place?"

Serge stood with spread arms and yelled at the sky: "Monkey Box, Florida!"

"That is catchy."

"In this case, I'm also media savvy: If you're going to pull some newsworthy stunt like this, and aren't geographically constrained, always pick a place with a name that makes the TV people go belly up. They won't be able to resist!"

Coleman turned all the way around. "But there's nothing here."

"Florida doesn't care, so why should we? Now help me with our newest best friend."

They dragged the pastor, chair and all, into the shallow water and up onto spongy ground.

Coleman kept slapping his arms and swatting in front of his face.

"They're attracted to carbon dioxide," said Serge. "Remember me telling you down in Flamingo at the tip of the state?"

"No." Coleman spit something out of his mouth.

The captive struggled fiercely in the chair. "You won't get away with this! I'll yell!"

"*I'll* yell," said Serge. "Ahhhhhhhhhhhhhh! Damn, that feels good. You should try it."

"Ahhhhhhhhhhhhhh!" The hostage stopped and coughed and spit something out. "You're insane!"

"Thank you."

Coleman continued swatting and spitting. "What are these things?"

"The blind mosquitoes," said Serge. "Scientific name *Chironomidae,* also known as lake flies, and in Florida—you'll love this—chizzywinks. Guess what? The chizzywinks are back in season! I checked with the locals, and they expect them to be at maximum swarm strength tonight in the darkest hours just before sunrise. And that's just their activity level back on land away from the lake. Out here—hoo-wee! . . . Back in the 1800s, there were rampant cases of entire herds of cattle dying from insect asphyxiation in this region. Just read *A Land Remembered.*"

Serge put on a surgical mask and safety goggles, and handed an identical pair to the now-coughing Coleman. He turned to the captive. "Oops, I'm short on supplies. I guess that's where the power of prayer comes in."

The pastor was blinking rapidly and trying to breathe through his nose.

"What a nature show you're about to experience," said Serge. "Kind of like something out of the Bible."

Serge sloshed back out to the boat and helped Coleman aboard. They motored away in the direction of Dynamite Pass.

A buzzer rang on the night window of a budget motel on Lake Okeechobee.

Serge swatted away bugs. He cupped hands around his eyes and pressed his nose against the window, looking at the empty front desk.

Someone emerged from a back room. "There you are! I was wondering what kind of business took so long."

"Totally tedious," said Serge. "But I do need to report a missing chair from our room. It kind of got away from me. I'm good for it."

"You know, I still have that extra room available next to yours, if, uh, your friend would like some privacy. On the house."

"You've read my mind . . ."

A half hour later, Serge lay on his back in the bed, holding up a series of large pages like flash cards. "Here's another cool tombstone rubbing, and here's another, and this one has a little cherub on top. I'm a sucker for that. And this is Mitzi the Dolphin . . ."

Cheyenne continued massaging him below the belt. "Um, Serge? Am I doing something wrong?"

"I can accurately say no. I believe most of my gender would concur."

"But you're still looking at your rubbings."

"Precisely." Serge flipped to another page. "What you're doing down there makes me appreciate them in a whole new light."

"Serge . . ."

"O-*kayyyyyyyyy*." Serge set the pages on the nightstand and picked up something else. "What about View-Masters? No? My elongated penny collection? I thought women were into sex toys."

"Is that what you call those?"

"Who doesn't?" Serge set the penny album down. "Don't tell anyone I have all this stuff. I'd be mortified if the public knew about my kinky trove."

"What about simple vibrators?"

"You mean those things in the ads that people are using to rub tense facial muscles?"

"Those ads are kind of in code."

Serge crinkled his nose. "That would explain so much."

"Stop talking."

"What?"

Cheyenne got on her hands and knees and slowly crawled up the bed toward him like a jungle cat. She growled.

"Yikes."

Chapter 33

PAHOKEE

C oach Calhoun stuck his head in the principal's office. "You wanted to see me?"

"Come in. And close the door."

Uh-oh, that's never good. Hopefully one of his players hadn't made a mistake that couldn't be reversed.

"Lamar, I can't tell you how happy I was when you first showed up back at the school."

"It was a special day for me, too."

"I know, I know."

"But . . . ?"

"Lamar, we all kind of wondered a little bit about your missing years," said the principal.

"That would be natural," said Calhoun. "I'm sort of a private person."

"We weren't being nosy, mind you. It's just that you were so gifted, we all expected to see you someday in the NFL draft. But after a while, we simply assumed football didn't work out for whatever reason, and the rest was your business. Until you finally decided to come back to your roots."

"Life takes its turns," said Calhoun. "I worked in an auto plant for a while, then a drydock . . . But by that look in your eyes, you already know that."

It pained the principal, and Calhoun saw it all play out again like it was yesterday instead of more than twenty years ago . . .

T he winters in the upper Midwest were far more freezing than Calhoun had ever imagined. It was his senior year at the university, and while he hadn't torn up the Big Ten, Lamar was expected to go in the top six or seven rounds of the draft. He stared out at the snow that was crusting over the campus and piling up on the windowsill of the athletic dorm. His roommate was named Ted, but everyone called him Bruiser.

It was kind of a joke. Ted was a kicker, and they tend to be the smallest players on a team, usually by such a degree that they seem not to be football players at all. It held true in Ted's case. Hence, Bruiser. Ted was from a small farm in an equally small dot on the map in Missouri, and he was lost on the big campus. He didn't know the current music, how to talk to girls or even basic slang. "You mean when something's 'bad,' it's actually 'good'? That doesn't make sense." They went to a club one night, and Ted tried to dance. Lamar almost lost a lung from laughing. The huge player from Pahokee, Florida, appointed himself Ted's big brother, and they became the inseparable odd couple. That's how Calhoun first developed an affinity for kickers.

There are many scandals in big-time college sports that make headlines, and many more that never leave the practice field or locker room. The head coach was in the mold of Ohio State's

Woody Hayes, who punched a player on national TV. Which meant he was a dinosaur. It was a new era, and the assistant coaches struggled to keep him in check. It came to a head halfway through the season. Ted had shanked a thirty-yarder, costing them the game against Michigan. For the next few days, the coach's rage had been tightening in a vicious cycle until he was spring-loaded. On a Wednesday, the practice field was extra busy, pockets of activity where various specialty players honed their specialties. But the coach's eyes were locked in on the kickers. They call it staring daggers, and all the assistants went on high alert, like a domestic abuse victim detecting the first signs of that telltale mood swing.

Ted was back in form, nailing it down the middle. But the coach was just waiting. After, who knows, fifteen perfect kicks, Ted dinged one off the left upright, and the coach was on the field. The assistants chased. Before they could get there, the coach had his hands around Ted's neck. A similar incident had already hit the news, when an Indiana basketball coach was videotaped choking a player. But that was brief compared to this. It was a two-handed throttle that wouldn't let go. Ted vainly fought for breath. He was trying to cough and turning red. The assistants raced up and grabbed the coach's arms—too gently, under the circumstances, because they didn't want to lose their jobs. "Coach! Coach!" One of them looked up to an overhead booth and made a slashing gesture to stop filming practice.

Thumbs pressed harder into Ted's windpipe. A red face was becoming blue. "Coach!" They grabbed him around the waist and arms to no avail. Then, out of nowhere, a fist came flying in. It caught the coach in the jaw and he went down. So did Ted, finally free, gasping frantically before throwing up.

The assistants had a crisis on their hands. They looked around. All the other players had stopped practicing, standing and holding their helmets at their sides by the face masks. Even if they could destroy the video, there were too many witnesses. And if the coach went down, so did their assistant coaching positions. A new head coach would wipe the slate clean and hire all his own people. Panic turned into a plan. They would get out ahead of this and deflect. The solution was handed to them on a platter.

The punch.

They were initially thankful that Lamar had jumped in to help his friend. But thanks didn't pay power bills. In an instant, he was under the bus.

Handcuffs clapped on Calhoun's wrists, followed by expulsion from the team. But it was handled hush-hush, because any digging into the running back's arrest could lead back to the coach. They promised he'd stay on scholarship until graduation, to buy his silence. There was a quick plea bargain with no testimony, followed by a misdemeanor conviction and a suspended sentence.

Although it never made the papers, there was always the grapevine. Nobody knew the details, just that Lamar had attacked a head coach. It was a de facto blackball. Despite his credentials, the entire NFL draft took a hard pass on Calhoun.

He went to look for a job. "Sorry, we just can't do it." Like many athletes', his academic major was physical education, and schools weren't allowed to hire anyone with an assault conviction. Lamar began welding fenders . . .

That was then; this was now.

"I wish you would have said something." The Pahokee High School principal shook his head. "On the surface, it didn't sound at all like you. So we looked into it and learned the real circumstances, and then it all made sense. If we had known earlier, we might have figured something out, some kind of exemption, or gotten it expunged."

"But now?"

The principal held up a sheet of paper. "You didn't disclose it. You filed a false job application."

"I used bad judgment," said Calhoun. "It was just so long ago.

I wanted to put it behind me, and I wanted to get back to the kids."

"Dammit!" said the principal.

"I know this is putting you through a lot. I'm sorry."

"No, not you," said the principal. "That asshole Garns."

"Who?"

"The science teacher I got rid of."

"Oh, I remember him now," said Calhoun. "But what's he got to do with any of this?"

"He couldn't simply go quietly and get on with his life," said the principal. "I wish he was still here just so I could fire him again."

"I'm not following."

"He must have spent weeks digging, and then I still don't know how he found out," said the principal. "He's the one who reported you."

Calhoun sat a moment in helpless thought as the pieces of realization fell into place. "Someone like that has no business being around our kids. It was still worth it."

"Not from where I'm sitting," said the principal. "I wish there was something I could do."

"You've done enough." Calhoun stood. "I'll go get my stuff."

Chapter 34

OKEECHOBEE

The next morning it was breakfast in bed. Then Serge and Cheyenne took a brisk five-mile stroll along the Florida Trail on top of the Hoover Dike.

By ten o'clock, they were back in the room, making plans for her day off. By eleven, a crash against the wall from Coleman's room. "He's up."

By noon, it was on the news.

Law enforcement needed airboats to reach the scene, and they now sat clustered near the northern bank of the Old Moore Haven Canal.

TV correspondents in even more airboats began broadcasting from behind police lines.

"This is Soledad Torres reporting live from a place few have heard of. I'm standing here in Monkey Box, Florida, where a trio of bass fishermen heading out to Lake Okeechobee made a grisly early-morning discovery of a body in this remote swampland. The sheriff's office is releasing few details, but confidential sources tell me the victim may have been the leader of a controversial church infamous for picketing military funerals around the state. Sources also describe the murder victim as being bound and tortured with what are known in these parts as blind mosquitoes, also known as chizzywinks, which occasionally swarm in ferocious numbers. The most probable cause of death was asphyxiation, but prior to the victim's demise, the insects likely also filled his ears, eyes and even the sinus cavity via the nose, where he could feel them moving around behind his eyes. Sorry for ruining your lunch. This is Soledad Torres in Monkey Box, Florida. Back to you, Chet and Angela."

The broadcast switched to a pair of anchorpeople behind a desk in the home studio, sharing light banter and a chuckle. "I think she just likes saying Monkey Box . . ." "I like saying it, too. Monkey Box." "We'll be right back after these commercial messages. Monkey Box."

Cheyenne stared. "What exactly was your business last night?"

"Fake news! Fake news!" Serge clicked the set off and clapped his hands a single sharp time. "I'm famished! What do you say we grab a bite to eat?"

"Actually, I'm supposed to have lunch with my brother," said Cheyenne.

"Kyle? Fantastic! We'll make it a family affair," said Serge. "My treat. I insist!"

A knock at the door. Serge jumped and spun. "Who the hell is that?"

"Probably my brother. I told him where I was." She cast a suspicious eye over her shoulder as she went to the door and opened up. "Hey, Kyle."

"Hi, sis." He stepped into the room and glared at Serge without speaking.

Serge spread his arms. "What?"

The glare lasted a moment longer. "I just watched the news."

"That? Ha, ha, ha!" Serge waved a dismissive hand that signaled silly talk. "Where do they dream up all the crazy stuff they're putting on the air these days? I mean, death by chizzy-winks? Is there even such a bug? Such a *word*?"

Cheyenne wanted the subject changed. "Serge has offered to take us to lunch."

"Damn straight!" said Serge. "It's the least I can do for your service to the nation. The only condition is I get to pick the place. I've been dying to try one of Okeechobee's famous steak houses.

A loud crash on the other side of the wall, followed by a scream and a thud.

Serge pointed. "I'll go get Coleman."

A gold Plymouth pulled into a parking lot.

Kyle looked up at the sign. "I thought you wanted to go to one of our famous steak houses."

"I do. This is it!" Serge slammed down an empty coffee mug. "No finer choice!"

"Golden Corral? But you can eat at these anywhere in the country."

"Accept no substitutes!" said Serge. "Golden Corral is the pulse of America, where the Forgotten Fly-Over-Country People dine, and I mean that as a compliment. Pundits mention the Forgotten People like they genuinely care, but there's an unmistakable subtext of condescension. This is why the elitists can never get their predictions right. Whether it's elections, consumer confidence, shifting social tectonics, just chuck your fancy algorithms and scientific polls. Golden Corral is the Rosetta stone, the Oracle of Menestheus and the Magic Eight Ball rolled into one. The reasons are myriad, but one rises above all others: They have a chocolate fountain. There can be no greater symbol of straight-shootin', salt-of-the-earth integrity. As the pinnacle of the Corral's ziggurat, the chocolate fountain cannot be surpassed or even questioned."

The Plymouth slowly crawled through the gridlocked parking lot. "Wow, is this place jammed! Their food must be extra popular in these parts."

"It's veteran appreciation day," said Kyle.

"What's that mean?" asked Serge.

"Across the country, all veterans eat free today."

"The chocolate fountain has just been eclipsed."

An old man in a USS *Iowa* baseball cap suddenly jumped in front of the Plymouth with hands urgently raised for them to stop. At several other nearby points, more vets halted other cars.

"World War Two vet pulling out!"

Others were positioned behind a Buick Regal, using hand signals to help the driver inch backward like a snail. Serge jumped from his car and joined the flag-less semaphore team directing the vehicle. "God, I love these people! . . ."

Inside the restaurant, a color guard and a small contingent from the high school band. Most of the people at the tables wore some kind of hat or vest commemorating their service.

Serge grabbed a plate. "I've inadvertently entered an overkill of positive vibes." He led his group along the salad bar. "Let me show you how to make a salad. Most people simply throw a salad together because it's just a salad. But it's actually a statement. Please stand back . . ." They gave him space as he became a windmill of motion. Ingredients filled his plate, first in meticulous layers, then quadrants. ". . . A true salad is about architecture and engineering. I'm borrowing from the Romans for my potato salad basilica, and now for the victory arch . . ."

The packed dining room was a southern aroma symphony. Catfish, barbecued chicken, roast beef, okra, hush puppies, popcorn shrimp, three kinds of gravy.

Kyle pointed with a fork. "Serge, aren't you hungry?"

Serge sat back in his chair with his head tilted sideways. "This salad is way too damn big." His fork hovered over the single cherry tomato on top. "How does one even approach eating this without an avalanche?"

Cheyenne took a bite of beef. "So, Serge, what are you up to next?"

"Communing with these fine folks and learning their ways." He leaned toward the next table, where four old guys in suspenders and U.S. Navy caps were cutting steak. "Excuse me! Yoo-hoo! You know my new motto? Remember the Forgotten People! I think it's got legs. Don't pay no mind to the New York–L.A. cultural axis. There's an untapped reservoir of values and enlightenment in this room."

"Are you okay?" asked one of the guys.

"Fantastic, except for this ridiculous salad. But I've learned to accept what I can't change." A grin. "So tell me, what does Golden Corral have that those pointy-headed ivory tower types don't understand?"

One of the old guys continued chewing. "A chocolate fountain."

"Bingo!" said Serge. "It *looks* like an ordinary chocolate fountain, but you and I know what it really means." Wink. "All across the country there's an economic Mendoza Line, below which the middle and lower classes are secretly viewed by our oligarchs as the *livestock* class. How else can it be explained? Our paycheck-to-paycheck toil created their staggering fortunes. In return, all our safety nets are under siege in the name of corporate greed that won't be quenched until our lives are reduced to perpetual white-knuckled freak-outs hurtling toward premature, pre-existing-condition death. Who could do that in good conscience to another human being? On the other hand, if they see us as livestock instead of people, then it all makes sense: A political consultant stands at the front of a conference room with a projector. 'Our research shows we can easily convince the beef cattle to vote for the owners of the slaughterhouse. First we get them pissed off at the *dairy* cows—'"

"Quick," Kyle told his sister. "Grab his coffee."

"Just talkin' 'bout the chocolate fountain," said Serge. "It's the secret symbol of recognition among our people, like that creepy eyeball atop the pyramid on the back of a one-dollar bill."

Cheyenne smiled. "When I asked what you were up to next, I meant where are you going?"

"Oh, that's different." Serge stuck his fork in the salad, triggering a rockslide of croutons. "You're all witnesses. Not my fault . . . Anyway, I'm continuing my Florida odyssey of sweeping ramifications, but aren't they all? This one involves connective tissue that is pulling us in a tractor beam toward the lost town of Ortona, then Clewiston, before whipping under the bottom of Lake Okeechobee and visiting Belle Glade and Pahokee, collectively known as The Muck, for its rich earth. The welcome sign to Belle Glade says 'Her Soil Is Her Fortune.' The sign to Pahokee just says 'Pahokee.' It's hard to figure people out."

"I know all those places," said Kyle.

"Me too," said Cheyenne.

"How so?" asked Serge. "You're from the north side of the lake."

"But I played football," said Kyle. "We had away games. My father was one of the coaches in Okeechobee, and around the lake, all the coaches pretty much knew each other. From the time I was a little kid, we were always having dinner at someone's house in another small town."

"I was a cheerleader," said Cheyenne. "It's hard to believe now with the way many of those towns are boarded up, but I heard that back in the 1930s the whole area was called the 'winter vegetable capital of America.' It was a twenty-four-hour operation with refrigerated warehouses and trains constantly coming and going to rush the produce north while still fresh, not to mention thousands of workers filling the juke joints and gambling houses at all hours near the shantytowns that sprang up."

"Look at the Florida knowledge on you," said Serge.

"I'm your little history helper, remember? I've heard lots of stories about the whole lake region, some not on the books."

"Such as?"

"Lost treasure," said Cheyenne. "That was a favorite on the school yard. Trunks of precious metals supposedly went missing during the hurricane of '28."

"I'm sure a lot of everything went missing in that one."

"Yeah, but this tale had other scary and mysterious details," said Cheyenne. "Like a vicious sugar baron whose body was discovered with bullet holes and buried before the authorities found out."

"Then how did you and your schoolmates hear about it?" asked Serge.

"The guys who did the burying allegedly told their families, and the story was passed down generation to generation by word of mouth. But it's probably just that, a story." Cheyenne's fork toyed with the food on her plate. "It must be fun to take road trips like you do."

"I'm sure you've taken a million."

"Not really."

"But what about you saying there's too many places you've got to see?"

"That's why."

"Okay, then come with us." Serge collapsed the other side of his salad. "Shit."

"Really?"

Kyle touched her wrist. "What about the motel?"

"I've piled up a ton of vacation."

The brother grabbed his cowboy hat from under the chair. "Then I guess I'll need to make it a foursome. When do we leave? ..."

Chapter 35

PAHOKEE

Senior year of high school arrived with all the fanfare of raging hormones.

Social calendars filled up. A few students now had cars. Others got new clothes for the merciless battlefield that is popularity. And of course there was football season, with the mandatory post-game gatherings at burger joints. Yes, they still do that.

Chris was blossoming with her own crowd. The varsity team, the cheerleading squad, the marching band and various hangers-on. She was welcome at their restaurant tables, where they laughed and relived big plays and threw french fries at each other.

But Chris was still different. She didn't have any money. Others always chipped in for her food and told her not to worry, but good luck with that.

She never stopped smiling, but it began eating at her stomach, figuratively and literally.

One Thursday afternoon that fall, Chris thought hard about a dilemma that she'd been twisting in her mind and rotating to inspect from all angles. She made her choice. After all, how much difference can *one* make?"

That night, she left her grandmother's apartment and quietly headed down the stairs. Chris glanced around one last time before running off into the darkness behind the building and disappearing like a ninja . . .

The next afternoon, community fever grew as hours counted down to another huge gridiron contest in The Muck. The Blue Devils were still undefeated, and it was the second-to-last game of the season; the last before the Big Game. Signs that normally advertised breakfast specials and free tire rotation now had their letters rearranged into some variation of BEAT CARDINAL NEWMAN! The barbershop was full of experts and bullshit.

At a storefront on a downtown street, bells jingled.

The pawnshop owner's hand was shaking a Rolex that had stopped working. He looked up. He saw her letterman jacket. "We going to win tonight?"

"Bank on it," said Chris.

"Are you one of the cheerleaders?"

"No, a kicker."

"You're on the team?" He paused with a finger to his mouth. "Wait, I heard something about you . . . Well, that's great. So how can I help?"

"I need to sell something."

"Let's see what you've got."

Chris pulled a shiny coin from her pocket and placed it on the glass counter.

"Wow, that sure is pretty." He turned it over. "Says twenty dollars. But of course you realize that they don't use these anymore."

"I know. We effectively went off the gold standard under Roosevelt," said Chris. "Some technically argue Nixon. Now it's full faith and credit."

"What do you say I give you—"

Chris removed a book from her backpack and placed it on the counter. *The Red Book,* the bible of coin-collecting price guides. "With all due respect, I know exactly what it's worth."

It was the last thing the pawn man expected. "Okay, I'm sorry. I'm not exactly killing it here in this town business-wise. Straight up, I need to make a profit, and who knows how long till I sell it. How about half of what it books for?"

"How about the melt value of the gold?" asked Chris. "That way you can't lose, and you get the whole numismatic collecting up-charge."

The pawn man thought: *Where did this kid come from? Most adults don't negotiate this well.* He slowly began to nod. "I can live with that. You just need to fill out this form. I'll get money from the register." He began counting out hundreds . . .

The football game went pretty much as expected. The home crowd had everything to cheer about all night as Pahokee took an early lead and never looked back for the trounce. There was even a late kickoff return that went all the way for a touchdown, crowning the night.

Revving convertibles and trucks, stereos blaring, converged again on Max's Shake Spot. It was a nicely converted old gas station from the thirties in the period's art deco design. Max had used old photos to replicate the original green-and-orange neon that trimmed the building all the way around to the outside restroom doors. Team pennants and banners filled the walls, along with a couple of framed jerseys and photos of former players who had gone on to the pros. The school's fall schedule and results had been dutifully tallied on a chalkboard. All the chairs were filled in the dining room, and the crowd spilled outside to the picnic tables on the porch.

"I can't believe about Coach Calhoun!"

"What have you heard?"

"Just rumors, but they can't be true."

"We have to do something!"

"Chris, you were pretty close to him. What do you think?"

"I feel the same as you," said the kicker. "But I know what he told me: Don't worry about him. And don't let anything distract us. We have to win the Muck Bowl."

The Muck Bowl.

More than historic.

Pahokee versus Glades Central. David and Goliath. Except David always had his slingshot. Either team could go undefeated the rest of the year, even win state championships in their separate divisions, but it wouldn't mean anything if they didn't prevail in the end-of-the-regular-season rivalry.

"The Muck Bowl." Nodding around the table. "Coach Calhoun is right. We'll deal with it later . . ."

The waitress came over and they ordered. It was pay in advance, and Chris stood up with her wallet. "I've got this."

"Chris, since when do you have money?"

"Since I started doing some odd jobs."

"Put your money away," said a starting lineman. "We always got you."

Then they saw the hundred-dollar bill . . . "Please, pay away."

The jumbo basket of buffalo wings arrived first and they dove in. Some of the loyal crowd were ex-students who had graduated in the last couple of years and were still trying to get in gear. They had minimum-wage jobs, unable to figure a way out. But they all looked forward to Friday nights in the fall, the connection to their true family. They wore their old team jackets.

The kicker felt a slap on her back.

"Chris, how's it going?"

She turned around. A young man named Ricky, who used to push her down in the dirt.

"Don't you mean 'Milk Crate'?"

"Sorry about all that," said Ricky. "And I think I owe you a football or two. Anyway, great game."

"I didn't even play."

"Still, you made the team. That's something."

"Thanks." She scooted over to make room. "Have some wings."

ORTONA

Kyle Lovitt looked out the rear window of a gold Plymouth speeding down the western shore of Lake Okeechobee. "Nobody can accuse you of letting moss grow."

"Why noodle around? When it's time to ramble, it should just be a matter of packing your bags and throwing them in the trunk," said Serge. "Of course in my case, my bags are usually already packed in the trunk, unless there's no room because . . . Let's leave it at that."

Ribbit. Coleman petted his chest. "Easy, Jeremiah."

Serge looked across the front seat. "Been meaning to ask. Cheyenne is such a fetching name, yet all the parents today go for Brittany or Kirsten. How come?"

"Because I'm Native American."

He pushed her shoulder playfully. "Get out of town!"

"Supposedly full-blooded, but I think someone in my family was fucking around and lying about it."

Coleman reached over from the back seat and tapped his shoulder. "Serge, a chick who says 'fuck.' That is so hot."

Serge smacked his hand away. "Shut up, you . . ." He turned. "Sorry about that on multiple male levels. But full disclosure: It *is* hot. Don't let that affect your level of lurid lexicon, for more or less . . . Please continue."

"So that's why I'm Cheyenne." The Plymouth's A/C was broken, and the wind from the open windows made her grab a rubber band and fashion a ponytail. "Imagine me. A Native American raised in Okeechobee. Half Indian, half cowboy."

Kyle stared at Coleman a moment, sitting next to him in the back seat, trying to give beer to a frog with an eyedropper. "So what's this next stop of yours? Ortona? I've never heard of it, and I've lived my whole life around here."

"It's the best!" Serge chugged coffee with a single brown rivulet running from the corner of his mouth. "A tiny hamlet down a long, inspiring country drive through our unspoiled nature. I would say it's a forgotten place, if it was ever known in the first place. There's a modest collection of canal-front homes down by the Caloosahatchee River, and that's about it for population. Otherwise, just a wild stretch of Route Seventy-Eight between LaBelle and Moore Haven. With one major exception: an incredibly important historic site that is right-on-point relevant! Which can mean only one thing."

"What's that?" asked Kyle.

"We must balance out relevance with non sequitur or The Man imprisons us in his plastic cage of linear thought. And we all know where that leads. Except I don't know where it leads because I've escaped the cage. See how it works? . . . Coleman, ready for another round of tangent? Get the list."

"Cool." Coleman reached in the glove compartment. "Next topic: best cowbell songs."

"Right!" said Serge, reaching under his seat.

"You brought a cowbell?" asked Kyle.

"I always have a cowbell nearby for any circumstance. Why? Without warning in polite cocktail-party society, you might need to urgently change the subject: 'Serge, did your friend Coleman just scratch his butt and sniff his finger?' You can interrupt and yell 'Gas leak!' or, if a stampede isn't needed . . ." He began hitting the bell with a drumstick. ". . . Get where I'm going with this? . . . *'Honky-tonk womannnnnnnnn!'* . . ."

"Shouldn't you be paying more attention to the road?" asked Kyle.

"The other hemisphere of my brain is at the wheel." *Clang, clang, clang.* "*'Mississippi queen!'* . . ." *Clang, clang.* "*'Fool for the city!'* . . . Remember the Chambers Brothers? *'Time has come to-day!'* . . ." *Clang, clang.* He threw the cowbell back under the seat. "Enough of that shit. Coleman?"

Coleman checked the list. "Homeland security."

"This is an important one," said Serge. "They say that our main strategic weakness against the terrorists is failure of imagination. But I'm just the guy to fix that! Two words: toupee bomber. Are we on that one?"

"Serge—"

"Hold that thought," said Serge. "We're here."

The Plymouth pulled up to the edge of the Caloosahatchee, and everyone got out.

"Is this the historic place?" asked Cheyenne.

"Not the main one," said Serge. "We need to build up to that or we could lapse into history shock. This is the Ortona Lock and Dam, part of a system of such structures that raise and lower boats traveling across the state on the one-hundred-and-fifty-four-mile-long Okeechobee Waterway. As opposed to, say, only forty-eight miles. I'm looking in your direction, Panama Canal."

"We've got a lock like this back near the motel," said Cheyenne.

Serge walked closer to the edge, carrying a paper sack.

"What's in the bag?" asked Kyle.

"You'll find out." Serge drank in the vista. "I love locks for their engineering feats. And especially the whirlpools."

"Whirlpools?" asked Coleman.

Serge nodded and aimed an arm. "When a boat's coming over from the coast and enters the lock, valves are opened, and water from the high side flows into it, raising the vessel like a rubber duck in a bathtub. But so much fluid rushes inside that it creates a vast vortex just outside the lock's upstream doors. In fact, this lock was recently closed two weeks for repairs because, among other things, serious whirlpools were forming *inside* the lock when lowering boats. Not good for the canoe people."

"Here comes a boat now," said Cheyenne.

"Let's watch the whirlpool." Serge led them up a path to the lock's eastern doors. "I love watching whirlpools the way cats watch a toilet flush."

"The whirlpool's starting," said Coleman. "Wow, it's getting big."

"I had no idea," said Kyle. "Forget canoes. It's a monster."

"Videos of these physics spectacles are all over YouTube, and someone just posted incredible footage from the Demopolis Lock in Alabama." Serge pulled something from his paper bag. "Watch this!"

"You carry a rubber duck around?" asked Cheyenne.

"A close second behind the cowbell." He heaved the yellow toy far out into the water.

They all watched it splash, then rotate in a wide but tightening circle until it was violently sucked under.

"Ta-da!" said Serge.

"Uh, you do realize you just littered," said Cheyenne.

"What? Oh, shit! I usually play with it in the tub, so there's rarely difficulty retrieving it. I wasn't thinking." Serge covered his face with his hands. "This negates my whole moment. I must atone." He ran back along the bank and stared at the water and waited. Finally, a rubber duck popped to the surface inside the lock. He cupped hands around his mouth. "Hey, you in the boat! I need a big favor! I just accidentally littered because I was watching water like a house cat. See that rubber duck about to float by? If you could just snag the sucker, it would center my karma . . . Thanks." Serge wiped his forehead. "Whew! Another close one! . . . Back to the car!"

They drove a short distance until three people were standing beside a Plymouth, watching Serge standing proudly atop a small hill.

"And this is one of the fabulous Ortona mounds, believed to have been created seventeen hundred years ago by the Calusa, who were the busy bees of early Florida, also digging a network of navigable canals . . . Back to the car!"

Another short drive. Serge leaped from the Plymouth. "You've been properly warmed up, so here it is! But first look around and let the context sink in: nothing, deserted, not even cars on the road. The closest thing to *anything* is that remote and idle quarry we passed on the way in. And I can't get enough of it! Dig!" Serge walked fifty yards out into a roadside field that was blanketed in yellow. He called back to the gang: "Florida, literally the Land of Flowers, and all these beautiful babies around me are the state's official wildflower, coreopsis." He stretched out his arms and began spinning joyously amid the blooms. "'*The hills are alive with the sound of—*' . . . whoa, getting a little dizzy again." He staggered back to the road. "And now for our feature presentation."

Serge opened the Plymouth's trunk for his gravestone-rubbing supplies. A brief hike followed. "This is the Ortona Cemetery. It's hard to imagine now with all the surrounding emptiness, but for a few days in 1928, this was one of the busiest spots in the state. That year's hurricane was so devastating that it required three mass graves, including this last one." He placed his oversize sheet of paper against a historical marker and began rubbing. "We're back in Zora country! Can you dig it?"

"Uh . . ." said Kyle. "This has been an . . . interesting day."

"This is nothing," said Serge. "I'm getting a familiar tingle in my bones. That means the biggest day of this entire tour is about to dawn and blow your hat off! Come on! . . ."

Chapter 36

WEST PALM BEACH

Captain Crack Nasty grabbed a stuffed wahoo by the tail and ripped it off the wall. He smashed it over and over against the edge of his desk until it was almost dust.

His treasure business was turning to shit. The losing streak had reached six wreck sites that he had been sure would pay off like slot machines. All he had to show for it was another cannonball. Some of his workers left in frustration, and the rest found a way back to prison.

He fell in his chair and grabbed a bottle and fumed. He began thinking of an older "can't miss" treasure site. The one that had slipped through his fingers.

Crack Nasty had indeed gotten away with that ugly business out at the lake with those three young men. Four years had quickly passed without a knock on his door from the cops.

But he had also screwed himself.

Pahokee was too small a town, and he had been too visible. If he wanted to keep getting away with the killings, he had to stay extremely clear of the area. Dammit! Why did he let emotions make business decisions? And after the homework he'd put in. He had been so close he could taste it. He grabbed a nautical map, out of habit, to look for another offshore site. "What's the point!" He threw it and grabbed the bottle instead.

The phone rang.

"Hello? . . . No, I don't know who this is. . . . Been a long time? You said to call and you'd pay? If you say so. . . . What do you mean, 'prepare for happiness'? . . . What! Seriously? I'll be there this afternoon . . ."

Captain Crack pulled the magnetic door sign off his pickup truck, kicked caution to the curb, and headed west into sugar country.

Bells jingled extra hard as Crack burst into the pawnshop. "When did it come in?"

The owner stuck a clarinet on a shelf. "A few weeks ago, but I couldn't find your business card until this morning." He reached into the display case for a coin dated 1911.

Crack held it to his face as waves of dormant greed resurfaced. "Who sold it?"

"Young girl from the local high school." The owner pulled out a ledger book. "Her name was Chris something . . . Yeah, here it is. For whatever reason I didn't get her address, but she plays for the football team." He scribbled on a sheet of paper.

Crack laid a stack of hundreds on the counter and snatched the coin. "Remember . . ."

"I know. You were never here."

Bells jingled.

The owner shook his head. "I will never understand white people."

The gold Plymouth swung down under the lake and passed a welcome sign: AMERICA'S SWEETEST TOWN.

"This is it," said Serge. "Clewiston. Epicenter of Florida's sugar industry. Here we begin our exploration of the southern lake culture, moving on to South Bay, then swinging northeast along the shore. See the plumes of smoke dotting the horizon, as well as these recently burned black fields we're passing?"

"We're familiar with the harvesting process," said Kyle. Still, it was always a sight, and he and Cheyenne leaned toward the window.

"Then I'll tell Coleman," said Serge. An elbow. "Coleman, you awake?"

"Just resting my eyelids. They've been going all day."

"Look alive. We're in a hallowed place." He startled everyone by swinging into a convenience store at the last second, and running for the far wall.

Coleman caught up. "Coffee. What a surprise."

Serge shook a small packet and ripped it open. "Know what I'm pouring in my coffee?"

"Sugar?"

"History!" He tore open a second packet. "And since I'm in Clewiston, I need a second helping of heritage. From the molasses and rum trade routes to modern-day Florida, the sugar industry has sparked economy and controversy. Back to the car!"

Moments later, the quartet stood quietly in the middle of a large, gleaming space.

"Have to hand it to you," said Cheyenne. "You sure can pick 'em. This is incredible."

"The Clewiston Inn? Easy call." Serge swept an arm through the air. "Now *this* is a lobby! Other lobbies today are sterile nightmares that disagree with my colon: a few chairs, artificial flowers, rack of tourist pamphlets, and the counter where they lay out the free breakfast, which has been reduced to a plastic bin of Froot Loops where you have to turn a crank like a gumball machine. And then strictly at ten A.M., they actually *lock up* the Froot Loops! Will the madness never end? But not here! I can't get enough of a lobby that is a virtual church of varnished dark-wood walls, with the original mail slots behind the vintage counter, antique sofas and bookshelves with more old stuff that makes you want to leave your room just to sit in the middle of bygone days. Check out the hotel's preserved switchboard next to the fireplace, with the old cables and everything. And this coffee table over here is a glass display case. See those shiny metal things in there that look like a baseball catcher's shin guards, except if they'd come off a medieval suit of armor? Those are the old sugar cutters' leg protectors, because back before mechanized harvesting they were working so fast and swinging such sharp machetes to slice down the stalks that they kept hitting their legs, which was no good for anybody. And next to the protector things is one of the ancient cane blades. Notice the size and width of that bastard. If I ever have to attend a machete fight, that's what I'm bringing." He marched back to the receptionist's desk, where they'd just checked in.

"Sorry to bother you," said Serge, "but could I trouble you to open up the lounge for me and my friends to see art?"

"Wait, I remember you." A smile from behind the counter. "You're the mural guy."

"In some circles."

"No problem." She grabbed keys. "Follow me."

The quartet soon stood in another fabulous space, turning slowly to take it in.

"What do you think?" asked Serge. "Snazzy, eh?"

"I had no idea," said Cheyenne, stepping toward a wall to inspect a spoonbill. "I've driven by this place a million times but never stopped in because who needs a hotel when you live so close?"

"The history we most often overlook is in our own backyard." Serge parted blinds to look out one of the lounge's windows. "It's the little things about a small town, and in Clewiston it's stuff like that bank-style sign by the road, where in any other place the lightbulbs would display time and temperature, but here it's the lake level, just over fifteen feet. Wow, that's getting pretty high."

Serge pulled out a chair for Cheyenne, and they all sat at a table in the middle of the bar.

"Ladies and gentlemen!" Serge zestfully rubbed his hands together. "Our timing here is no accident! I have a surprise! But first an essential background briefing, which is mainly for Coleman . . . *Coleman!*"

"Huh? What? Right here."

"Can you at least raise your forehead off the table when I'm talking to you?"

"Crap. Always more work. Just give me a minute . . . Okay, I'm looking at you."

"As our journey continues, we're about to enter a most amazing place." Serge raised his arms to the heavens. "Some of the hardest-working folk you'll ever meet, with an astounding sense of family and community. It's actually two separate small towns ten miles apart on the southeastern shore of Lake Okeechobee— Belle Glade and Pahokee—but they're collectively referred to as The Muck, from the rich, dark soil—"

"Wait, what's the date?" asked Kyle. He checked his cell phone and smiled. "Now I know why your bones were tingling for the biggest day of your tour. The Muck Bowl."

"Ding, ding, ding!" said Serge. "We have a winner!"

"The Muck Bowl?" said Cheyenne. "That's so cool! I've never seen one."

Coleman looked left and right at the table. "What's the Muck Bowl?"

"Just the biggest high school football game in all of Florida," said Kyle. "Forget state championships. The rivalry between those two towns is more electric than anything. I played against both teams when I was in school, and they're unbelievable."

Serge nodded. "Go to any Muck Bowl, and a few years later you're liable to see several players on TV in the NFL."

"So you have tickets?" asked Kyle.

"I was going to pick some up when we got into town."

"You can't just *pick up* tickets to the Muck Bowl, unless you want to wait in line forever."

"What do you suggest?" asked Serge.

"I know one of the coaches in Pahokee, Lamar Calhoun." Kyle got out his phone again. "He might be able to hook us up."

"Lamar Calhoun?" said Serge. "Why do I know his name?"

"Because he used to be one of the best blue-chip running backs in all the state."

Serge snapped his fingers. "That's right. He was incredible, one that I would have bet for sure would make the pros. But then nothing. What happened?"

"I don't know," said Kyle. "I wasn't even born when he graduated, but our fathers were both coaches at opposite ends of the lake, and they became great friends over the years from crossing paths on the circuit. I even met Lamar at his dad's house a few times when he visited for the holidays. I heard he moved back to coach himself a couple years ago, and I've been meaning to call, but you know how that goes."

"I remember us having dinner at their house several times when I was a little kid," said Cheyenne. "Wonderful family." She turned to her brother. "Did you read where Pahokee has a girl on the team this year?"

Kyle shook his head, listening to his cell phone before hanging up. "No answer. They must have all left school for the day."

"She's a kicker," said Cheyenne.

"Who?" asked Kyle.

"The girl on the Pahokee squad," said his sister. "I saw a small thing about it in the paper, so I started following the team this year. I always get a good feeling when I see a girl making those kinds of strides against the odds."

Serge nodded. "And I always get a bad feeling when I see Internet trolls babbling that some successful girl is just a token who only made it through favoritism. Give me a break! I've been witnessing the behavior of my gender for years. Do you have any idea what it's like to be a woman in a man's world?"

"Yes."

"Okay, well, I don't," said Serge. "But I know the burden of the kind of brains we guys have to work with . . ." He grabbed Coleman by the hair and lifted his head up off the table again. "Exhibit A." He lowered the head. "And I can't believe the crassness I observed directed at women on the street."

"And that's only the stuff that guys like you overhear," said Cheyenne. "For us, it's such a perpetual, day-in-day-out gauntlet of leering and vulgar remarks that you eventually become numb."

"Coleman and I were discussing the phenomenon the other day," said Serge. "And I want to offer my deepest proxy apology for the dudes making slurping sounds and calling out anatomy by non-medical names. Personally, it confounds me. Putting the rudeness factor aside for a moment, on the mating level this is also their intelligence audition. It's like if a guy goes to a supermarket cashier a hundred days in a row and says, 'I don't have any money,' and she says, 'Then you can't have any food,' and he says, 'Okay, same time tomorrow?'"

"Did I just start a tangent with you?" asked Cheyenne.

"Well played," said Serge.

"So we're going to the Muck Bowl," said Kyle. "I'll just need to keep trying to reach Coach Calhoun. What in the meantime?"

Serge flipped open a notepad. "There's something huge that's been looming on my Florida bucket list. And now is the perfect opportunity to strike it off."

"What is it?" asked Kyle.

"This one is best left to be revealed in real time . . ."

An hour later, two flatbed pickup trucks sat on the side of a road with nothing around but a setting sun over vast acreage. Behind the trucks was a gold Plymouth and two people leaning against the fender with folded arms.

"What do you think they're doing in there?" asked Cheyenne.

Kyle covered his mouth as he began to cough from the smoke. "I have a good idea."

Serge dashed as fast as he could down the black-dirt rows. He crashed through stalks and dove on the ground over and over. Then running full speed again, smashing through more cane and another dive.

Exhausted, he rolled over onto his back and lay in the dirt, looked up into a circle of a half-dozen children's faces. Some of the kids were grasping cottontails. They giggled at Serge and ran off.

A few rows over, Coleman also lay on his back. Eyes shut tight. *Ribbit.* A bullfrog crawled out of a chest pouch and hopped away.

Serge got up and raced about, obsessively not giving up. But then it became just too dark. "Coleman! We have to head back to the car! . . . Coleman! . . ."

Coleman roused from an anesthesia fog. "Wha—? What is it?" He raised his head. "Oh, hello. It's another of my little nature friends." While Coleman had been unconscious, something had crawled onto his chest and found his girth, warmth and breathing to be a soothing elixir. He began stroking its back. He sat up and snuggled it under his chin, gently slipping it down into his chest pouch. "I'm coming, Serge!"

Over at the road, kids began jumping back into the pickups that had brought them. Most had sacks and makeshift chicken-wire cages with rabbits. Serge collapsed empty-handed over the hood of the Satellite.

"Jesus!" said Cheyenne. "You look like you're about to have a heart attack!"

"There's no other way to do a job than to end up looking like you're nearly in cardiac arrest. But you're a witness: I gave it my all."

"And then some," said Cheyenne.

The truck beds were noisy with animated tall tales from the cane fields. Then they went silent, all looking in the same direction.

Coleman strolled ho-hum out of the cane field, petting his newest furry friend. He looked up to see all eyes upon him. "What?"

Kids jumped down from the trucks and gathered around the plump, stumbling stranger. *"What's your secret?" "How'd you catch a jackrabbit?" "You must be super fast!"*

There was a banging sound. Serge's forehead against the hood of his Plymouth. Accompanied by fists.

"Easy," said Cheyenne. "You'll catch one someday."

"You're right." Serge stood and collected himself. "Besides, the big game is tomorrow. We need to be heading for the hotel to get our rest."

The gang piled back into the Plymouth and turned south on Main Street.

"Serge, why are you pulling over?"

"Just one last stop of the day on the way to the inn."

The Plymouth pulled around behind a government building.

"What is this place?" asked Cheyenne.

"Used to be the library," said Serge. "Now a museum."

Three people headed for the doors. One went another direction.

"Serge," yelled Kyle. "The entrance is this way."

"We're not going in the museum," said Serge. "Follow me . . ."

The foursome soon stood on the lawn on the north side of the building. All staring up at the same thing.

"This is just like our hotel," said Cheyenne. "I've driven by a thousand times but never stopped to really take a look."

"One of the most emotional historic monuments in all the state," said Serge. "Statues of a family of four: father, young son, and mother cradling an infant, all running for their lives and looking back up at the sky in terror, the parents raising futile arms to shield their heads. And on the monument's base, a stone-relief sculpture of giant waves washing away homes and snapping palm trees. And if you look real close in the water, there's a bunch of tiny people drowning beneath a simple inscription: 'Belle Glade 1928.'"

"Whew," said Cheyenne. "What can you say?"

"You can't," said Serge.

The monument was too much to take in at once, so they didn't.

"Every now and then, being at a place pulls at me in a way I don't understand," said Serge. "I get an odd feeling."

"Who wouldn't at a monument like this?" said Cheyenne.

"It's not the monument," said Serge. "Another kind of feeling. My bones again, but different this time. Like something big is looming just around the corner."

They all became quiet again, respectfully taking in the sight as the sun departed.

Chapter 37

GAME DAY

There had been talk of rain, but it never came. Instead, the departing clouds over Lake Okeechobee left the night air cool and crisp under the stadium lights. The faint smell of smoke from the surrounding cane fields competed with sausage grills in the concession stands.

Spectators had started arriving at the gates when the sun was still high. You had to for this one if you wanted any kind of decent seat. Those who arrived late were still more than happy to stand or watch from outside the fence, fingers clinging to chain link.

Twenty-five thousand were expected tonight. Insane for a high school. But the Muck Bowl was no ordinary game. The number of college scouts in the stands confirmed that. They always came out for the annual battle of the rabbit chasers.

The hype had been building for weeks among the nearby

communities. Signs outside restaurants and dry cleaners and lube shops cheered on the Blue Devils and the Raiders. They talked about it in the post office and the supermarket lines. Tailgate parties were planned with the logistics of military campaigns. And now it was time.

School buses arrived after the ten-mile drive up the rim of the lake from Belle Glade, and the players streamed out. Bands played, police directed traffic. The Blue Devils were already on their home-field sideline. Their uniforms were slightly different from the usual. It was the players' idea. On the front of each of their jerseys, just above the numbers, a strip of tape with lettering in Magic Marker: CALHOUN. It was unauthorized, but all the coaches looked the other way.

The cheering from the stands was like a jet taking off. And this was only the warm-ups . . .

. . . A gold Plymouth Satellite rounded the bottom of the lake.

"You sure we got tickets?" asked Serge.

Kyle nodded. "Coach Calhoun said they'd be waiting for us at the booth, but it might be standing room."

The Plymouth continued north. Even if they hadn't known there was a big game, they would've been able to tell something was definitely up. Everyone in motion, piling in cars, honking, good-natured yelling in traffic, making last-moment dashes into stores, well-wishes painted on the windows of homes and offices.

"This is what I'm talking about," said Serge, gripping his fingers against the steering wheel. "Small-town pride. The fabric of the community coming together like a Kevlar vest."

They left Belle Glade behind and then it was just an empty stretch of cane fields that connected destinies. The sun finally set over Pahokee, draping the town in darkness, except for the strings of headlights pouring in from all directions.

"There it is," said Serge.

The brilliantly glowing football field stood out in the surroundings like Yankee Stadium.

"Looks like we have a bit of a walk," said Cheyenne.

They parked down the street from the overflow lots and hiked to the entrance booth.

"Coleman, you let the jackrabbit free," said Serge. "Why are you still wearing the chest pouch?"

Coleman reached inside and pulled something out to show his buddy. Then put it back inside.

"Why are you carrying a doughnut in your pouch?"

"Emergencies."

Tickets were waiting as promised. This time Kyle took charge, leading them along the fence in front of the home section until they reached the area behind the Pahokee bench.

"Coach Calhoun!"

Lamar turned. At first there was a lack of recognition.

"It's me, Kyle."

Then Calhoun brightened, and a reunion hug. "I heard about your dad. Sorry."

"Heard about yours, too," said Kyle. "They were good men."

"Coach!" A hand extended to shake.

"And you must be Cheyenne." Lamar lowered his right palm to the height of his waist. "Last time I saw you, you were this tall."

"The years fly by," she said. "So you're back home coaching now?"

Calhoun rested a forearm on the top of the fence. "That's a complicated story."

"Where's this kicker I've been reading about?"

"Chris? Right over there. She's quite something."

They all looked down the bench at a slender girl with a pony-tail, leaning forward with spring-wound intensity.

Then more coiled intensity from another direction. "Coach! I'm Serge! Huge fan!"—shaking hands vigorously—"Can't tell you how much all of this means to our nation! Connective tissue from Stetson to Zora! This is Coleman . . ."

Coleman waved. "I caught a bunny."

"Don't listen to him," said Serge. "So what's the big plan for tonight? Razzle-dazzle, Statue of Liberty, flea flicker, fumble-rooski, triple-reverse sting operation, bark at the moon to confuse the blitz?"

Calhoun glanced over at Kyle. "You know these people?"

"Actually, yes," said the young man. "But they're harmless. Maybe not to themselves . . ."

Cheyenne pointed at the color guard marching out onto the field. "Looks like we're starting."

After the national anthem, thunder from the stands as the Devils took the field to kick off. They formed a rigid line. A referee blew a whistle. A ball sailed high under the lights.

The Belle Glade receiver took it on the fifteen and charged straight up the field, waiting for his wall of blockers to form. Then he abruptly swung left, and used ridiculous speed to curl around the end and race up the sideline. The blocking wall held. One by one, the defenders were picked off. The path to the end zone now clear.

Well, almost clear. The kicker was left, outmatched by at least eighty pounds and staring in headlights. Normally a tackle would have been impossible. But the receiver was running down the sideline. It wasn't necessary to *tackle,* just knock him out of bounds. So the kicker, as they say, took one for the team. He ran as best he could toward the edge of the field, left his feet and laid out. Which meant just diving and sacrificing his body horizontally in front of the runner.

It was a wincing collision, but it did the trick. Out of bounds at the thirty. The kicker didn't get up. Coaches ran over. They held fingers in front of his face. They gave him a pop quiz.

The referee leaned in. "What's the story?"

They shook their heads. "Concussion. He's out."

A rare moment of silence in the stands as medics wheeled the stretcher toward the waiting ambulance that had backed up through the gates. Then an eruption of applause from both stands as the player, still prone on the stretcher, raised a fist with a thumbs-up.

That bit of drama was the first of many. Key fumbles and interceptions. Lead swings. Fourth-down pass completions. Safety blitzes and trick plays. Spectators held their stomachs and hearts, not sure how much more they could take . . .

. . . Police officers kept an eye on the darkened parking lots. Every space was taken. Even spaces that weren't spaces. Vehicles up on curbs, in no-parking zones, blocking fire hydrants. It was the unwritten fine print of a small town: no parking tickets during high school games.

Just after halftime, a pickup truck arrived and drove up and down packed rows until parking on the grass behind a dumpster. The driver bought a standing-room ticket and stood as Pahokee kicked off. But the new spectator wasn't watching the field. He was looking at the bench.

Chris wasn't hard to spot. The players on the bench had their helmets off. Just look for the only girl.

Captain Crack Nasty reached into his pocket and rubbed the gold coin he had just purchased at the pawnshop. He smiled to himself and decided to enjoy the rest of the game . . .

With five minutes to go, the Blue Devils were down 27–21 and driving inside the five. But play stalled on a third-down shot out the back of the end zone. They were too close to risk another touchdown attempt and give up the sure three points. They sent out the kicker, who made good: 27–24.

The kicker trotted off the field as teammates slapped his pads in congratulation. Then he suddenly began hopping on his left foot and dropped down on the bench. His helmet came off with a grimace. The trainer arrived, then other staff.

"What is it?" asked the head coach.

The trainer rotated the leg slightly, and the player almost screamed. "Looks like a pulled groin."

"So how's he going to be?"

"He's in no condition for even an onside kick."

"Are you kidding me?" said the coach. "Can't you do anything? Tape it up?"

A headshake. "He might even need surgery."

Teeth gritted; then: "I know, I know. Shouldn't have even asked. Their welfare comes first." A frustrated kick in the dirt. "But why in a three-point game? One field goal to tie and send it to overtime? What am I supposed to do?"

"I guess you're just going to have to try for the touchdown and the win."

They carefully took off the kicker's jersey.

Chris was leaning way forward, trying to make out the commotion at the other end of the bench. She saw them removing the shoulder pads of the second-string kicker, who was in obvious agony. She leaned back. "Shit."

The Devils defense made a clutch stop on third down in enemy territory, and the Raiders had no choice but to punt. The Pahokee offense took the field. Time was running short, so they had to manage the clock. Which meant passing. And Belle Glade knew it. They loaded up deep and played soft for the short, underneath stuff. Pahokee started with a sideline route that went out of bounds for a four-yard gain. Then another for five yards. Then a short pass over the middle for a first down that stopped the clock at just over a minute. It was working, but it was taking far too long.

Chris would have been biting her nails if she did that sort of thing. Instead, her right knee nervously bounced up and down. She glanced over her shoulder at the roaring overflow crowd. She did a double take. She jumped off the bench and ran to the fence. "Coach Calhoun!" She hugged him over the top of the chain link.

"Easy now."

Chris let him go. "What are you doing here?"

"You kidding? I wouldn't miss this for anything."

She hadn't noticed because of the excitement at seeing the

coach, but someone was standing with him. He was home for a break from college.

"Reggie!" Another hug.

"Chris," said Calhoun. "There's time for this later. You need to get your head back in the game."

"Did you see what happened to our kickers?"

Calhoun nodded.

"What should I do?"

"I suggest you start warming up."

Chris nodded and dashed off. She found a spot behind the bench away from the others and began stretching.

The Blue Devils continued a consistent march down the field. But it was all still more short stuff, eating up way too much time. Both sides knew what was coming. The quarterback took the next snap and dropped back farther than before to give the receivers time to extend their routes. He looked right and saw tight coverage. He ducked and stepped up in the pocket as a defender leaped and flew by. He reached back with everything he had and launched a perfect spiral with plenty of air. It couldn't have been more on target, arcing down toward the back corner of the end zone. But Glades Central had time to shift an extra defender, and now the Pahokee receiver was double-teamed. The ball was swatted away.

Fourth and long. At the outer edge of field-goal range. The clock stopped at ten seconds. The head coach glanced at Chris, warming up at the practice net. "Time out!"

The roar of the crowd was a rattling blare of sheer white noise. Nobody had taken a seat for the last fifteen minutes. Even the cops were cheering.

The teams went to their sidelines, panting, gargling water and spitting it out. Nobody could say they weren't leaving it all on the field. Both sides had nothing left, and that's when the boys at the lake always found more. The head coach called the play. The players ran back onto the field.

Chris stayed behind the bench at the practice net.

Pahokee lined up identical to the last play. Spectators grabbed their heads and pulled their hair. The ball was snapped. The fastest receivers streaked down both sidelines. The quarterback dropped back deep. He cocked his arm to launch another long one. Then he pulled the ball in. It was a delay play. The tight end threw a block on the right tackle, then slipped over the line five yards. The quarterback stepped forward and hit him running full speed. The defense was covering all the long routes and had left the middle open. Bedlam in the stands. The end raced up the clear middle of the field. Ten yards, fifteen, twenty. The defenders converged. The end tried to get around the left side, but one of the Raiders dove for a perfect ankle tackle. The runner went down right on the hash mark at the fifteen-yard line. A second later, a horn on top of the scoreboard blared. No time on the clock. Final score: Glades Central 27, Pahokee 24.

One side of the field jumped in ecstasy, the other in furious protest. The referees were already huddling. They already knew they had a serious mess on their hands. They realized the implications of what they had to do, and in the back of their minds were thinking how to get out of the parking lot as fast as possible when it was all over. The runner was down, but the scorekeeper up in the booth hadn't stopped the clock in time. The refs all nodded in agreement, and the head official broke their huddle and signaled to the booth to put a single second back on the clock.

Now emotions reversed in the opposing stands.

The Pahokee coach yelled at a ref and made a T with his hands. "Time out!"

Then he turned. "Chris!"

There wasn't need for any strategy discussion. It was a straight field goal. If she made it, then overtime. If not . . .

"You got this one, Chris," said a teammate, slapping her on the butt. "Oops, sorry."

"Don't worry about it."

The crowd was apoplectic. Spectators dug fingernails into each other's arms. Some gasped for air. Others grabbed their hearts. Coleman reached in his pouch for the doughnut.

The intermission ended, and the players trotted back out under the bright lights.

To this day, almost everyone involved remembers what happened next like the climax of a sports movie, drawn way out in extra-excruciating drama. Not that it needed any more.

Chris stepped up to the holder and addressed where the ball would be placed. Then she took measured steps backward and two more to the left. She shook her dangling arms at her sides to loosen nerves. She looked up at the home stands. Berserk people jumping and clapping. She saw their mouths shouting but she couldn't hear them. She couldn't hear any sound. Then a shrill ringing grew louder in her ears, and a pounding heartbeat. She looked toward the holder and nodded. The holder turned toward the blocking line and nodded at the center. People held breaths, prayed.

The ball was snapped.

It was ultra-slow motion. A tenth of a second ticked off the clock. Shoulder pads violently collided. Chris had done this a million times. She began running toward the holder, synchronizing her approach with the arrival of the ball. *Click*. Another tenth of a second. The ball seemed to hang in the air forever on the way to the holder. More shoulder pads crashed. She saw the linebackers take their first step forward for their leaps to attempt the block.

The ball reached the holder's hands. *Click*. She could see individual laces. The ball went toward the ground. Chris took another step and got ready to plant her left foot. There would be another step after that. Her kicking leg would swing.

The holder got the ball to the ground. *Click*. He spun the laces away.

Chris was suddenly hit in the chest with utter terror.

While spinning the ball, the holder had muffed it. The ball slipped out of his hands and it now lay sideways on the ground.

He tried to right it, but too late. Chris was already there. She had to pull up and abort the kick.

The team had a plan for such a misplay. They'd drilled it and drilled it in practice. But it was never conceivably meant with Chris in mind. Nonetheless, she had dutifully gone through all the practices with the other kickers, and now it was the mindless instinct of repetition.

Click. The horn sounded. The clock read zero.

Chris swung out of her kicking approach, running wide right. The holder pitched her the ball. She caught it in stride. The Belle Glade defense had loaded up for the block, and now most of their players were entangled in that snarl of limbs at scrimmage, allowing Chris to round the end. And damn if she wasn't faster than anyone would have guessed. Rabbits.

But all appeared to be for naught. The Raiders were anything but slow, and a pair of them bounced outside and swept toward her path. The farther one was toward the middle and had a ways to go, but the closer was almost straight ahead and in perfect position.

He'd placed himself to be able to beat her to the sideline. Unless she wanted to run out of bounds and end the game, her only option was to do what he wanted: to veer inside toward the middle of the field, where he'd have help from the other player, and maybe more. She'd easily be tackled.

Either way, checkmate.

She kept running full sprint. Then she did something the defenders didn't expect. She began curling *toward* the sideline. Those in the home stands who had been holding their own heads began slapping them. *"What's she doing?" "He'll run her out of bounds!"*

The closest player couldn't believe his luck. *Must be her lack of experience, probably thinks she can beat me to the corner and tightrope it into the end zone.* He adjusted his course along with hers. Then Chris surprised him even more. She increased her angle toward the sideline. He thought: *Has Christmas come early?*

They were only yards away, a split second left. He leaned forward to shove her out of bounds.

Chris took a last stride with her right leg toward the sideline. But instead of continuing, she dug her foot into the turf, hitting the brakes. The player flew by in front of her. His feet went out from under him as he tried to reach back, but Chris had already hit the gas again.

She still couldn't hear the crowd, but now it was because they were almost silent, mouths open.

The last defender had expected to merge with his teammate and sandwich her just inside the five. That was off the table now, and the footrace was on. He had the edge in distance and speed, but nothing was settled yet.

Chris had no more "Reggie" cuts in her bag of tricks. No argument that she'd be tackled inside the two. It was just a question of geometry.

She reached full sprint speed and left her feet like a track star in the long jump. Except this time it was headfirst. The Raiders player had been expecting that, and dove to hit her at the waist, hoping to drive airborne Chris off the field.

As she was coming down, Chris stretched out an arm and reached as far left as she could, swiping the tip of the ball against the orange pylon in the front corner of the end zone.

The referee's arms went up. Touchdown. No need for that overtime.

Players and fans swarmed the field. The insane jumping in the home team's stands would have registered on seismic instruments.

Calhoun and Reggie stood on their toes at the fence. They couldn't have been happier as they watched the team carry Chris off the field on their shoulders.

Chapter 38

CELEBRATION

C ar horns honked nonstop all over town. Screaming on Main Street. People whipped team towels in circles over their heads. The epicenter of the bedlam, of course, was Max's Shake Spot.

Chris was the talk and the toast. She was still carrying the game ball that the head coach had presented to her. No way she would be allowed to pay for anything tonight. And not just Chris. Max himself came out and made the announcement personally: All players eat free tonight.

"Hooray!"

The revelry continued into the night, players becoming bloated on free burgers, chocolate shakes and root beer floats.

"Pahokee! . . . Pahokee! . . . Pahokee! . . ."

Players took selfies and group photos with cell phones. The

students, especially the seniors, knew this was a night they would well remember into the decades to come.

And for the first night all season, there were an unusually large number of white people. It wasn't suspicious. It was the usual suspects from the scouting ranks across the southeast and all the way up to Ohio and Michigan. They knew the delicate line of what they could and couldn't say to avoid violating eligibility. All night long: *"Great game! Here's my card. Florida State ..." "... Here's my card. Georgia Tech ..." "... Auburn ..." "... Ole Miss ..."*

Former coach Calhoun arrived and headed toward a picnic table, smiling bigger than he had in years. Chris suddenly noticed him in the crowd. She jumped up and gave him a strangling hug. "Thank you! Thank you! Thank you!"

"Easy, you'll break my neck," said Calhoun. "And I should be the one thanking you. At my age, you don't think there's much more to learn in life, but you've taught me so much."

A Plymouth pulled up and emptied. Serge led the gang through the crowd.

"Uh-oh," said Calhoun. "I think you have some more fans."

"Chris!" said Serge, shaking her hand. "I've heard so much about you! Such an inspiration in our times of crisis!"

"Uh, do I know you?"

"No, but I'm a friend of a friend of Coach Calhoun."

"Then you're my friend."

More students arrived and crowded round the table. *"That was fantastic!" "You were great!"*

Cheyenne tugged Serge by the sleeve. "We should let her be with her friends. It's her big night."

"I was going to start a wave in her honor, but I'll defer to your female judgment," said Serge. "That's my new life motto: When in doubt, ask a woman. Because us guys are doing such a bang-up job, right?"

She tugged his sleeve harder. "There are some seats in back ..."

Chris said she had to go to the bathroom.

"Too much information."

"Just hold my seat."

She walked around the dark side of the building for the restrooms.

"Chris!" someone yelled. "Great game!"

She turned around. "Thanks . . . Do I know you?"

"Doubt it," said the man in the cab of the pickup. "I'm a college scout. If only you were a boy . . . I didn't mean that like it sounded."

"I know what you meant." She grabbed the handle of the door to the women's room.

When she walked out moments later: "Could you come here a second?"

"Why?"

"We don't recruit girls for football in Division One, but you're a natural," said Crack. "There are a number of sports you could easily adapt to."

Chris walked halfway to the truck. "Like what?"

"Tell me what else you play," said the captain. "You're probably thinking we're just trying to comply with Title Nine, which we are. But this is no charity: You can definitely play. Full scholarships rarely come along for girls. Ever try volleyball? Lacrosse?"

A couple more steps. "I really haven't tried any other sports."

Captain Crack opened his door and stepped out. "Let me show you these brochures from the school I represent."

"What school did you say that was?"

"I didn't."

And before Chris knew it, Crack had her by the arm, twisting hard. She yelped as he tried pushing her into the pickup. She was putting up a lot more fight than he had expected from a girl, but a sock in the jaw ended that nonsense.

Two boys came around the side of the building, yucking it up. Chris screamed from the open window as the pickup patched out.

The boys raced back to the picnic table. "Some guy just snatched Chris!"

"What? Who?"

"I got a picture on my cell phone." He held it up.

Someone leaned over his shoulder. "I know that truck!" yelled Ricky. "I know that *guy*. I'll never forget him as long as I live!"

It took mere seconds for alarm to sweep the crowd. Serge burst through and saw the phone. "I overheard you say that you know where he took her?"

The boy nodded.

"What's your name?"

"Ricky."

Calhoun frantically pushed his way in. "What's going on? Where's Chris?"

"No time," said Serge. "Seconds are precious . . . Ricky! Coleman! Come with me! . . . Coach, take the others in your car and follow us!"

Soon the Plymouth was barreling out of town, out into the darkness of flowing cane stalks. The needle spiked at over a hundred, leaving Calhoun and the others in the dust. Ricky filled Serge in along the way: His own beating in the cane fields years earlier, sure he was going to die until his rescue. Then the murder of his rescuers in the exact same spot, which the authorities ruled to be a drug deal gone sour, but Ricky knew better.

"Slow down," said the boy. "The turnoff's coming up."

The Plymouth rolled to a crawl.

"There it is," said Ricky.

Serge couldn't see anything down the dirt road, but he did make out fresh tire tracks leading into the field. "Ricky, you need to trust me. Get out and wait here by the road for the others for your own good. This is my specialty and I work alone." He pulled something from under the seat and Ricky opened the door. "And you didn't see this."

"What gun?" Ricky closed the door.

Serge hit his high beams and sped off into the black desolation of the cane field . . .

Soon, other headlights came up the highway. They caught Ricky waving madly on the side of the road. Calhoun pulled alongside. "What's happening?"

Ricky stuck his head in the window. "He went in after him. And I'm not supposed to tell you, but he has a gun."

"Shit!" Lamar cut the wheel and raced his car down the dirt road . . .

Serge's lights eventually hit the back of Captain Crack's pickup. Dark and empty. Bad sign. "Coleman, wait in the car. I may need you to drive this out of here in a hurry."

Serge planted his feet in the soil and crouched to listen. A brief gust of wind carried a snippet of noise. He crept like a ghost in its direction, quietly parting cane stalks. The sound grew louder. Voices. Soon they weren't hard to follow. The captain had chucked all his business rules. He chugged Johnnie Walker straight from the bottle as Chris lay crying in the dirt at his feet. "Please don't hurt me."

"Shut up!" A swift kick to her ribs. "Just dig!"

"I'm trying!"

More weeping, more kicks, more Scotch. Chris trembling too much to make progress in the soil. It wasn't going anyplace good.

"What the fuck is wrong with you?"

She heard a click and looked up and saw the cocked pistol. "No!"

Then another sound, unexpected. The clack of metal on skull.

Captain Crack thudded to the dirt like an unhooked punching bag. In the space where he had been standing, another person now stood. Chris recognized him as someone she had just met back at the burger joint.

She ran crying into his arms.

He quickly held Chris out by the shoulders. "You have to pull yourself together. I know you can do it! Others are counting on you, okay?"

She nodded and stifled her sobs down to sniffles.

"Good," said Serge. "If I'm correct, Coach Calhoun should be arriving just about now. I need you to walk straight down this one row of cane and start calling out for him."

"What are you going to do?" asked Chris.

"You and Ricky and the other kids deserve to be happy. And safe. And that will never happen under the status quo." Serge nodded in the direction of the cane. "Now get going. And don't look back . . ."

"Coach Calhoun! Coach Calhoun! . . ."

Lamar's headlights had just hit Serge's Plymouth parked behind a pickup truck. He slammed the brakes and got out.

"Coach Calhoun! Coach Calhoun! . . ."

Lamar looked at Kyle and Cheyenne. "Did you hear that?"

"It's coming from over there!"

They crashed through stalks. "Chris! We're over here! We're on the way!"

Moments later, they all burst through the last rows of cane, and everyone embraced in terrified relief.

"What happened?" asked Calhoun.

"I don't know," said Chris. "The guy was going to kill me for sure. I just know it. But then that friend of yours came out of nowhere."

"And where are they now?"

She shrugged. "He just told me to leave and not look back."

Kyle and Cheyenne glanced at each other. They heard sirens in the distance. A lot of them.

Calhoun took off his Pahokee football jacket and wrapped it around Chris's shoulders. "We need to get you to my car."

Back at the highway, Ricky was waving a long line of police cars down the dirt road. Blue and red lights flashed through the crops as the speeding vehicles kicked up a long plume of black dust.

The officers arrived at Calhoun's car just as the former coach and the others emerged safely with Chris.

But the '69 Plymouth and pickup truck were gone.

HIGHWAY 78 REVISITED

High beams pierced the black countryside.

Nothingness for miles. The pickup's windows were down, allowing a cool night breeze to accompany the peaceful, silent, green glow from the instrument panel.

It hadn't started that way. In the passenger seat, the captain had been quite chatty. *What do you want? I have money. I'll give you anything. Blah, blah, blah.*

Serge put a stop to the annoyance with another bloody skull crack from his Colt .45. Calmly as a librarian: "Shhhh . . . I'm enjoying the tranquil drive." He kept the pistol in his left hand, aiming across the pickup's cab as he steered with his right.

It was indeed a mellow ride. Dim fields of wildflowers under the economic light of a crescent moon. More miles of blood-pressure-reducing serenity through the wilderness.

Finally, Serge let off the gas, and the pickup truck from a marine-towing company uneventfully rolled to a stop with the sound of small crushed white rocks under the tires. He ordered the good captain out of the car at gunpoint.

A gold Plymouth arrived and parked behind. "Coleman, wait here until I get back."

A hike began. Crack Nasty looked around in the night landscape. Emptiness only led to even more emptiness. His thoughts pinballed as they can at a moment like this. Heaven, hell, God, the devil. *Anything you want! I'm begging!* Crack!

Another half hour.

Serge poked a gun barrel in ribs. "Walk down the bank and watch your step."

It was precarious, with loose soil and gravel collapsing and rolling down the incline under their feet, but they made it with only a couple of stumbles. They arrived at a modest shoreline.

"We're here," said Serge. "Sit down."

"What are you going to do?"

"Wait for someone."

"Who?"

"I don't know."

"I don't understand."

"That's your problem," said Serge. "Your least."

They sat, as they say in kindergarten, crisscross applesauce, amid sounds of insects and bullfrogs and rustling leaves.

Serge's ears perked, and he stood. "Here they come."

"Who?"

"Like I said, I don't know."

"You're insane, aren't you?"

"My gain is your loss."

Crack Nasty opened his mouth to scream, but Serge bashed him once more before he could get it out. "Try to yell again, and it's game over. Two taps to the head. But play nice and you might get away. Here's my offer: If you behave and wait until I release you, you're free to swim for it. But utter a peep, even in the water, and I can plug you way over here. Deal? Just nod."

He nodded.

"Great! A cooperator! Sit still . . ." Serge listened intently as the distant motorized sound grew louder. "That's the person I've been waiting for. Okay, Florida Man, take off all your clothes."

"You want me to get naked?"

"I'm doing you a favor." Serge stretched out his shooting arm. "Play your cards right, and you could become an Internet heart-throb."

"But—"

"You'd rather stay here with me? How sweet."

"No, no!" Crack quickly ripped off his shirt and pulled down his pants. "I'll skinny-dip . . ." He looked around. "But where is this person you were waiting for?"

"They're arriving by boat." Serge aimed his pistol. "You're free to go. Swim . . ."

Crack didn't need to be told twice. He dove in the water and swam like it was the Olympics. He neared the halfway mark across the river and found he was veering in the wrong direction. He lifted his head and corrected course. It happened two more times, but no matter how hard he tried, the captain always found himself swinging back to face Serge. What was going on?

Then it became clear. He didn't know the name of the place he was at, but he understood the concept. Captain Crack began spinning wildly, screaming with abandon as he stared up at the large metal wall at the Ortona Lock and Dam towering over him.

And the violent, twenty-foot-wide whirlpool flushed him down like a turd.

Epilogue

As football signing day approached, college scouts again descended on The Muck like a migration of birds. Or locusts.

One particular scout from a perennial midwestern contender was interested in the star running back. The principal pulled him aside and reminded the scout that, years earlier, his university had recruited another of their running backs.

"That's right," said the smiling scout. "I remember him."

Then the principal adopted a grave tone and explained how it would be.

Now, mere mortals cannot comprehend what the power and money of big-college football are able to accomplish, just short of interstellar travel. And even that's arguable. It's only a matter of motivation, and the college boosters really wanted this tailback. The principal's conversation was highly inappropriate and totally the right thing to do.

A few weeks later, a knock at the front door of a modest concrete-block ranch house on Pahokee's south side.

"Principal Jennings, what brings you around?"

"May I come in?"

"Be my guest," said a former running back named Calhoun.

"Lamar, funny thing. We took another look at your situation, and it turns out there are no records whatsoever of any incident between you and a coach." He opened a file with stamped pages. "We've received notarized statements from both the university and local police department that your name is squeaky-clean up there."

"What? But how—?"

"Lamar, listen to me . . ."—telegraphing the unspoken with his eyes—". . . there are no records."

"Uh, okay."

The principal headed for the door and turned around just before he left. "Why don't you swing by my office Monday morning. I'd like to hear your plans for the team this year."

The body of Captain Crack Nasty was discovered sticking halfway out of an underwater valve at the Ortona Lock and Dam. Due to his blood-alcohol content, nudity and other factors, it was officially ruled death by misadventure, as if someone had planned it that way. Some of the locals had other theories about an unusual stranger who'd breezed through town, but none felt the slightest inclination to come forward.

Cheyenne Lovitt actually cried after opening the letter that had been slipped under the motel office door in the middle of the night: "For reasons that are now all too obvious, I must go away for a while and not have any contact with you or your brother, for your own protection. I guess there are too many places we've *both* got to see. I can't say when, but I promise after things blow over, I'll find a way to get back in touch with my little history helper. Serge."

Kyle Lovitt's passion for the rodeo only grew, and he became a crowd favorite on the southern circuit. He was back home again a year later for the annual Okeechobee Rodeo. It immediately got dicey in the starting chute. An extra-ornery bronco named Diablo crashed and bucked against the railings. Until now, nobody had been able to complete a ride, and most no longer dared try. "Hold on!" yelled one of the rodeo hands trying to steady the horse. "No, I've got it," said Kyle. "Just get that gate open fast." He practically had to jump into the saddle, and the horse blasted off. It was a magnificent ride, and after the full eight seconds, Kyle jumped down to a standing ovation from the crowd.

Cheyenne had begun nursing school, but still always found the time to slip into her cowgal duds and proudly carry the American flag to open each rodeo. After Kyle dismounted Diablo, she ran out across the dirt to congratulate him with a hug. "You were fantastic! Listen to that applause!" As their eyes moved around the arena, taking in all the standing, cheering people, they happened to look at the far end of the dirt and a pair of barrels. Suddenly, two clowns popped up and waved. Then ran off into the night.

"Did I just really see that?" asked Cheyenne.

Kyle turned to his sister. "Is this good or bad?"

C hris never played organized sports again.

Instead, she received a full academic scholarship to Johns Hopkins University. She had the grades and aptitude to become a highly paid, top-notch specialist in any number of disciplines, but her personal calling required her to become a general practitioner.

After graduation, she hired a lawyer. He had never heard such a story, about a little kid who discovered treasure in a cane field and patiently carried a little bit home every day until, over the course of years, she had buried, well, a lot of it in the woods behind her grandmother's apartment. He researched applicable law, and sure enough, the hurricane had given her the same salvage rights as if it had been a Spanish galleon. The question of a proper lease and trespassing were another matter, but the land had since changed hands, wiping the slate clean. She was free and clear. He set up a trust and took care of taxes.

Chris used the trust and her degree to return to The Muck, where she opened a much-needed pediatric health clinic. She accepted all kinds of insurance and Medicaid. If you didn't have any of that, it was free. She couldn't have been happier, and neither could the town.

This is how much the community loved Chris for all she had given to them: Four decades later, in the wrinkled winter of her career, they unveiled a bronze statue of a young girl running with a football.

A few days after that, Chris and her staff finished a Friday afternoon of treating the latest crop of local kids who came through her door. The staff and patients had all gone home, and Chris stayed behind to deal with some government forms.

A number of professionals in various walks of life like to decorate their offices with mementos of success: diplomas, plaques, trophies, medals and ribbons. Chris had her own idea of decorating.

She finished the paperwork and grabbed her briefcase. Just before turning out the lights, Chris did what she always did at the end of each day. She looked around at the various walls, completely covered with overlapping photos of children and thank-you cards.

Finally, Chris's eyes went over to her favorite trophy, displayed on a bookshelf. And she smiled.

She was looking at a milk crate.

ABOUT THE AUTHOR

Tim Dorsey was a reporter and editor for the *Tampa Tribune* from 1987 to 1999, and is the author of twenty-three other novels: *Florida Roadkill, Hammerhead Ranch Motel, Orange Crush, Triggerfish Twist, The Stingray Shuffle, Cadillac Beach, Torpedo Juice, The Big Bamboo, Hurricane Punch, Atomic Lobster, Nuclear Jellyfish, Gator A-Go-Go, Electric Barracuda, When Elves Attack, Pineapple Grenade, The Riptide Ultra-Glide, Tiger Shrimp Tango, Shark Skin Suite, Coconut Cowboy, Clownfish Blues, The Pope of Palm Beach, No Sunscreen for the Dead,* and *Tropic of Stupid.* He lives in Tampa, Florida.

LETHE

APOCRYPHA OF THE BLUE PHOENIX

KIMJIN

Lethe

Story and Art by Kimjin

English translation rights in USA, Canada,
UK, NZ, Australia arranged by
Ecomix Media Company
395-21 Seogyo-dong, Mapo-gu,
Seoul, Korea 121-840
info@ecomixmedia.com

Produced by **Ecomix Media Company**
Translator **Michael Han**
Editor **Philip Daay**
Managing Editor **Soyoung Jung**
Cover Design **purj**
Graphic Design **Eunsook Lee, Hyekyoung Choi**
President & Publisher **Heewoon Chung**

P.O. Box 16484, Jersey City, NJ 07306
info@netcomics.com
www.NETCOMICS.com

ISBN: 1-60009-054-0

First printing: October 2006
10 9 8 7 6 5 4 3 2 1
Printed in Korea

Preface

At the end of the century, Earth was becoming an uninhabitable planet. The entire planet's eco-system was being destroyed by selfish policies of the most powerful nations and the survival tactics employed by the weak countries.

Voracious development of increasingly scarce natural resources, raging wars, opposing alliances causing the destruction of entire regions, collapsing economies and depressions all repeated again and again with no stop. Before long, humanity found itself facing the worst scenario imaginable.

Alarmed by signs of the imminent collapse of the world's environment, a group of people drew up a plan they named 'Ark', by which they would flee Earth's solar system to survive. The Ark program included machines that would manage the human genome and contained programs to establish human settlements on other planets.

The main computer systems launched into space by Ark were known as the Constitution Series. These self-evolving machines stayed in communication With each other and continued monitoring developments on Earth.

The colonists scattered into seven new solar systems, while those left behind on earth spiraled towards destruction. Guided by the constitution series, a new mankind flourished in the universe and became the genetic standard of humanity. They called themselves the Blue Phoinix Union.

However, one of the Constitution computers malfunctioned.
Cut off from the others, the stray supercomputer created flaws in
its human genome and wandered alone into the outskirts of the galaxy.
This supercomputer controlled and perpetuated defects in its colonists.
Finally, the colonists rebelled against their Constitution computer and
destroyed it. Thus, a new empire of human deformity called Gorgonia rose
to challenge the hegemony of the Blue Phoinix Union.

Then, in the Universal Year of 967, under the rationale of defending
mankind's genetic purity, the Blue Phoinix Union waged all-out war upon
Gorgonia and seized control of the empire's technology and resources.
They attempted colonizing Gorgonia with their own people and the Gorgonians
were redefined as lower-class humans.
This conflict later became known as Universe War I.

On November 27th, 987 Universal Year, the starship Neptunis of the Achaean
Naval Academy returned to Achaea from a graduation voyage. The ship was
attacked and destroyed by a Gorgonian special forces unit named Cyllene.
Lux Phoebus, Achaea's crown prince, and 49 cadets were on board.

The assassination sparked Universe War II, a war of vengeance by Gorgonia
against the Blue Phoinix Union.

Lethe tells the story of an incident immediately following the outbreak of conflict.

6

8

THERE'S NO NEED TO BE SO AFRAID.

YOU'LL FORGET EVERYTHING BY THE TIME YOU LEAVE THIS PLACE AFTER THE TREATMENT.

SOME BASTARD GAVE THIS KIND OF THING A ROMANTIC NAME...

LETHE–.

ONCE, THEY USED TO JUST CALL IT WHAT IT IS. 'EXECUTION.'

AND,

YOU

HAVE THE RIGHT TO A NEW IDENTITY,

YOU'LL RECEIVE A NEW SOCIAL SECURITY NUMBER,

AND YOU'LL START A NEW LIFE IN A DESIGNATED LOCATION.

SO...

THAT WOMAN'S JOB IS

EXECUTIONER, THE HEADSMAN.

SOMETHING LIKE THAT.

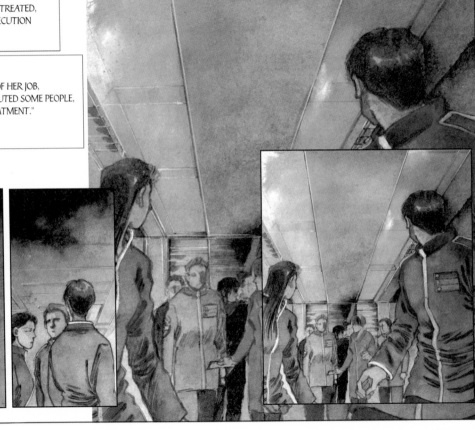

SO... I'M NOT GETTING TREATED, I'M GOING TO THE EXECUTION GROUND.

AND FOR THE SAKE OF HER JOB, THAT WOMAN EXECUTED SOME PEOPLE, NOT "PERFORM TREATMENT."

THEY PROBABLY THINK THEY'RE THE ONLY ONES DOING THIS TYPE OF WORK,

BUT ACTUALLY...

NOT TOO LONG AGO, I TOO...

I BROUGHT A GUY I KNEW THROUGH THIS HALLWAY BEFORE.

THIS CIRCUMSTANCE IS PRETTY MUCH THE SAME AS THAT TIME, EXCEPT THAT THE ORDER IS CHANGED.

FOR OUR GENERATION, THIS IS THE STATUS QUO.

I TOLD HIM EVERYTHING, EXACTLY IN THE SAME MANNER AS THAT WOMAN.

IT'S THIS GENERATION'S MISTAKE...

TO KEEP YOU ALIVE.

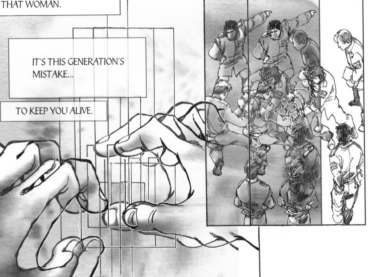

THE PRICE WE HAD TO PAY FOR GETTING RID OF CAPITAL PUNISHMENT

HAS BEEN PILES OF HUMAN TRASH.

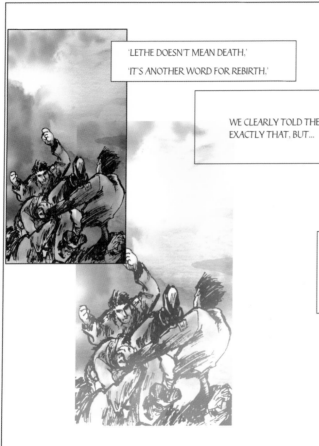

'LETHE DOESN'T MEAN DEATH,'

'IT'S ANOTHER WORD FOR REBIRTH,'

WE CLEARLY TOLD THE TRASH
EXACTLY THAT, BUT...

THEY BECAME ENRAGED...
THEY WANTED TO RUN.

...EVEN THOUGH
THE PREMISE OF LETHE
IS THAT WE WOULDN'T
KILL THEM.

THE GUY YELLED AT US.

YOU CAN KILL ME, BUT YOU DON'T HAVE THE RIGHT TO ERASE ME.

KILL ME!

KILL ME!

PLEASE KILL ME--!

WE ERASED HIS REPULSIVE SENSE OF IDENTITY.

I KNOW

BECAUSE I TRACKED GUYS LIKE THEM DOWN MYSELF, TOO.

16

THE BEST WAY, OF COURSE,

IS TO GET OUT OF HERE
WITHOUT BEING CAUGHT OR KILLED.

BUT, THAT KIND OF PLAN'S BEEN
IMPOSSIBLE FROM THE BEGINNING.

HE REALLY DID FOLLOW THE ADVICE.

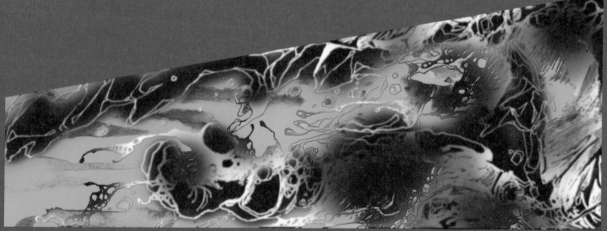

BY STAYING FROZEN THERE
FOR A LITTLE WHILE

AND SIMPLY DISAPPEARING,
SHATTERED INTO PIECES.

HE DIDN'T NEED TO STOP...
TO CONSIDER WHAT HIS FUTURE WOULD BE,
OR WHAT HIS IDENTITY MIGHT BECOME.

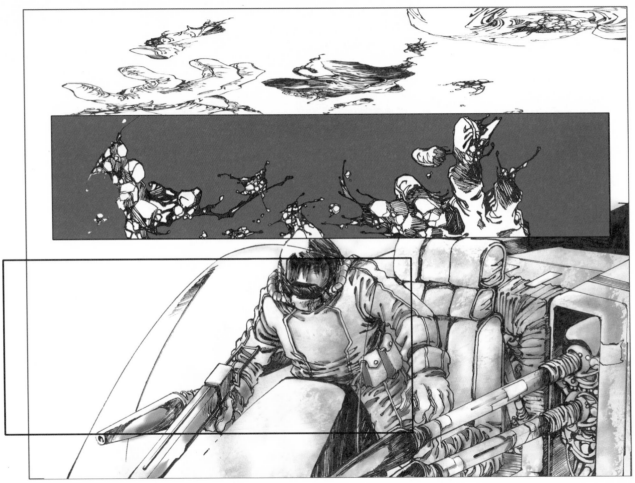

NOW WE'RE THE ONES WHO HAVE BEGUN TO WORRY ABOUT PETTY LETHE–.

MAZDA HUN, WHO ARE YOU?

NO MATTER WHAT THE REASON,

WE WON'T BE SYSTEMATICALLY MURDERED.

MY FRIENDS SAID THAT
OUR WHOLE REGIMENT TOOK PART
IN THE REBELLION.

THEY ALSO SAID NO ONE EXCEPT
THE CAPTAIN KNEW THE REASON
FOR THE REBELLION.

AND NO MATTER THE PURPOSE,
IF WE JOIN THE REBELLION, THEY
WORRIED THAT WE MIGHT LOSE
OUR PENSIONS WHEN WE'RE FINALLY
DISCHARGED FROM SERVICE.

ANYWAY...
WE DIDN'T PLAN THE REBELLION
AGAINST THE GOVERNMENT.

OUR ENEMY HID SOMEWHERE
A BIT MORE TACTFUL
AND OUT OF REACH.

THAT ENEMY
REIGNED OVER US

WITH MANY NAMES.

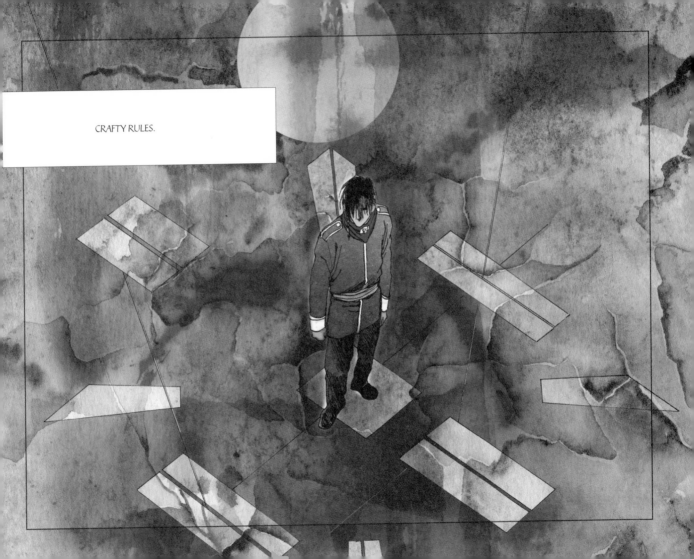

CRAFTY RULES.

WE WONDER ABOUT THESE RULES.

WE LIVE WITHIN SOME UNKNOWN
BASTARD'S MIMICKED CONSTRUCT.

THE CREATURES HE HAS MADE
GATHER AT THE COURT
TO PASS JUDGMENT ON ME.

MAZDA HUN,
YOU HAVE BEEN DESIGNATED
AS A DANGEROUS ELEMENT
TO THIS WORLD.

OUR CONSENSUS IS TO ERASE
THAT DANGEROUS IDENTITY OF YOURS.

WHO AM I?

30% OF THE WORLD'S HUMAN
POPULATION IS ALLOCATED
TO MONGOLOIDS LIKE ME,
AND ABOUT 10% ARE ALLOCATED
TO OTHER MINORITIES.

IT GOVERNS OUR ALLOWED %
AND IT ALLOCATES THAT %

LET'S SAY THAT I, WHO LIVE IN
THAT ALLOCATED %, SIDED WITH
THE REBELS BECAUSE I RESISTED
THAT STANDARDIZED
PERCENTAGE.

I'M A BEING THAT FELL WITHIN
THEIR MARGIN OF ERROR,
A TROUBLEMAKER.

I HEARD THAT
THEY HAD TO DECIDE

WHETHER TO SCRAP ME
OR REPAIR AND REUSE ME,

AND, IN THE END,
THEY DECIDED TO REPAIR
AND PROCESS ME
FOR THE SAKE OF
PUBLIC SANITATION.

SO, OKAY~.

REPAIRING HUMANS LIKE THAT
IS CALLED LETHE~.

LET'S SAY I'M THE ONE
WHO'LL BE REPAIRED THAT WAY.

WHO AM I?

BEFORE BEING PUT THROUGH LETHE,

THE GOVERNMENT PROVIDES COUNSELORS
SUPPOSEDLY TO PUT THE PERSON'S
PSYCHOLOGICAL STATE AT EASE.

*HUNS: A NOMADIC PASTORALIST PEOPLE WHO INVADED EUROPE IN THE FOURTH AND FIFTH CENTURIES A.D. AND WERE DEFEATED IN 455.

THERE WAS A GIRL I ONCE KNEW,

BUT SHE NEVER-NOT ONCE-
KISSED ME IN THIS COLD, CALLOUS WAY.

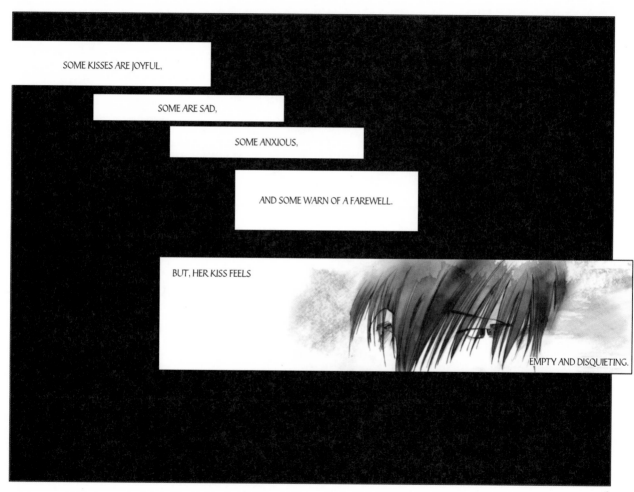

SOME KISSES ARE JOYFUL,

SOME ARE SAD,

SOME ANXIOUS,

AND SOME WARN OF A FAREWELL.

BUT, HER KISS FEELS

EMPTY AND DISQUIETING.

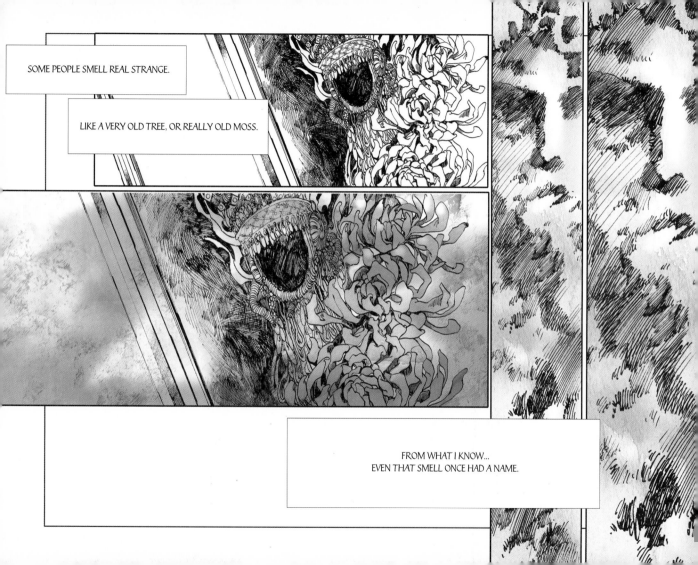

SOME PEOPLE SMELL REAL STRANGE.

LIKE A VERY OLD TREE, OR REALLY OLD MOSS.

FROM WHAT I KNOW...
EVEN THAT SMELL ONCE HAD A NAME.

IN ANCIENT MYTHOLOGY, THE GODS CURSED A WOMAN TO HAVE SNAKES FOR HAIR. HER NAME WAS MEDUSA.

SNAKES

SYMBOLICALLY REPRESENT WISDOM

OR YOUTH.

OR SOMETIMES REPRESENT MEDICINE AND IMMORTALITY...

ACCORDING TO MYTH, IT ISN'T DANGEROUS

WHEN PEOPLE SEE HER HAIR

AS BLOSSOMING FLOWERS.

BUT, ONCE THEY START SEEING THEM AS SNAKES

THEY EITHER TURN TO STONE OR ARE POISONED.

IF OTHER HEADS THAT ARE ATTACHED TO MINE START BECOMING SELF-CONSCIOUS, DOES THAT MEAN I BECOME A MEDUSA OR SOMETHING?

...I HAVE TO BREAK UP
WITH THIS WOMAN...

WITHOUT EVEN
LOOKING BACK
......
SHE LEFT.

WHEN I BRIEFLY THINK ABOUT IT...

I MOVED MY STUFF, AND TRIED TO SEE
HOW OUR FURNITURE MIGHT FIT TOGETHER
BECAUSE I WAS THINKING IN TERMS OF
LIVING WITH HER.

SHE WAS IRRITATING AND I TOLD HER TO GO,

SO THE WOMAN I WANTED TO SPEND TIME
WITH WAS GONE... AND THE REASON TO
MATCH THE FURNITURE WAS GONE WITH HER.

WHAT COULD THIS BE?

THE THREE-HEADED DOG IS CERBERUS,
AND THE SNAKE WITH A HUNDRED
HEADS IS THE HYDRA.

HEL IS THE GODDESS OF HELL.
SHE MAKES HER BOAT OUT OF
THE HAIR AND NAILS OF THE DEAD.

SOME MEMORIES ARE CALLED
KNOWLEDGE, AND WITH ENOUGH
MONEY YOU COULD BUY SOME AND
HAVE THEM PUT INTO YOUR HEAD.

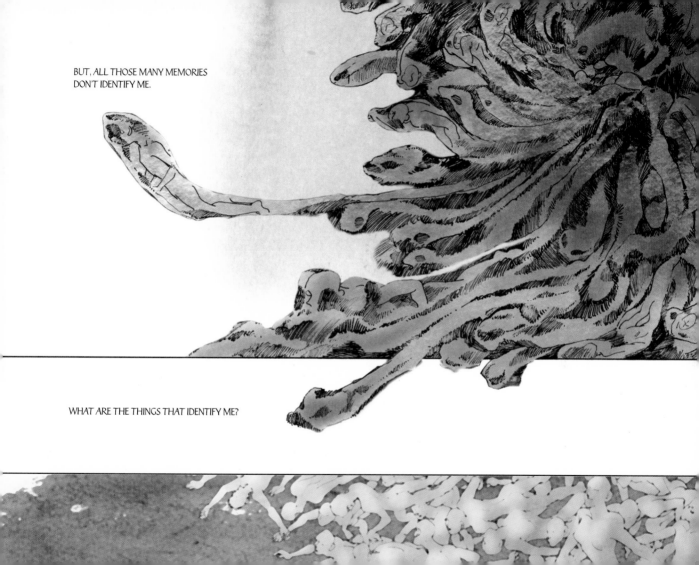

BUT, ALL THOSE MANY MEMORIES
DON'T IDENTIFY ME.

WHAT ARE THE THINGS THAT IDENTIFY ME?

MAZDA HUN... WHO ARE YOU?

THEY'RE KILLING HIM...

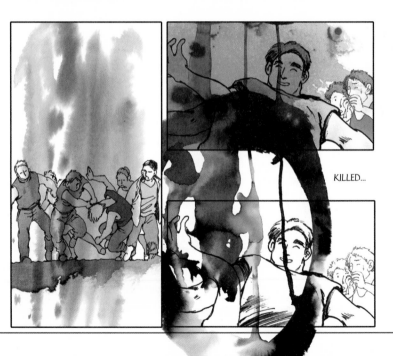

KILLED...

61

WHAT IF I'M NOT ONE,
BUT MANY?

WHAT IF HALF OF THE WORLD IS ME?

WHAT IF I WANT TO KNOW ABOUT
THAT "ME" THAT I DON'T KNOW

THROUGH YOU?

THE THOUGHT
CAME TO ME

THAT SHE REALLY MEANT IT.

SHE...

66

MAY HAVE DIED MANY TIMES.
SHE HAS THAT KIND OF SMELL.

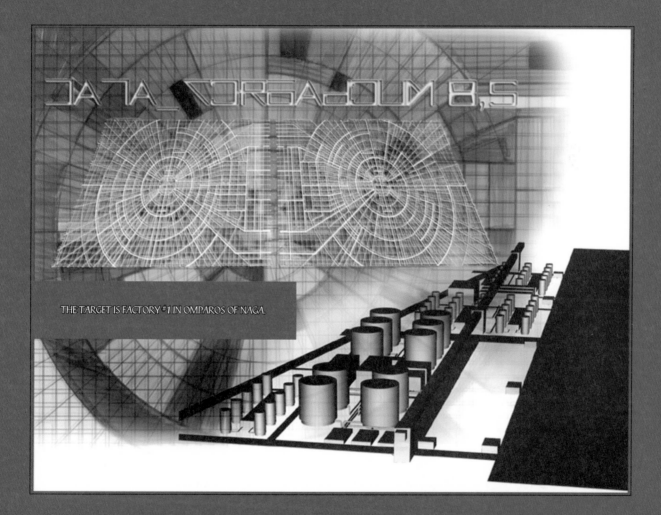

THE TARGET IS FACTORY #1 IN OMPAROS OF NAGA.

THE PALS WHO SOLD THE CRAPPY WEAPONS AT EXTREMELY HIGH PRICES

AND HAVE BECOME FILTHY RICH

HAVE ENSHRINED OUR TAXES IN THE FACTORY.

LET'S BRING IT AS THE REPRESENTATIVES OF OUR REGIMENT.

THE GOVERNMENT WAS GOING TO USE IT,

BUT THE CAPTAIN WAS GIVEN IT AS OUR SHARE WHEN HE PROCLAIMED A REVOLUTION AT THE SILVANUS SEA.

A WARRANT FOR OUR ARREST WILL BE ISSUED IMMEDIATELY, SO OUR COMFY VACATION COMES TO AN END NOW.

LET'S DIVIDE OURSELVES INTO A GROUP THAT WILL BE CAUGHT IN ORDER TO DIVERT THEIR ATTENTION AND A GROUP THAT WILL ATTACK. WHO WANTS TO BE THE STARS?

LET'S DIVIDE INTO TEAMS.

MY CONTRACT ENDS SOON, BUT FOR THE CAPTAIN WHOM I LOVE

I'LL STICK AROUND A LITTLE MORE.

IF YOU DON'T KEEP UP YOUR STUDIES

AND GET A BETTER LICENSE

AS TIME PASSES, THE BALANCE BETWEEN US WON'T BE EVEN!!

I'M NOT A CERTIFICATE-COLLECTING MANIAC LIKE YOU.

I'M LAZY, SLUGGISH,

INCONSISTENT.

IF YOU BECOME A STORK, THEN I'D BE A CAMPBELL. AND IF YOU BECOME A PHOENIX, THEN I'D BE A SPARROW.

I'M NOT SAYING THIS TO PUT YOU DOWN!

I CAN IMAGINE–.

SHE WAS YOUNG.

BUT, ISN'T IT STRANGE?

MANKIND HAS BEGUN

MORE THAN A THOUSAND
REVOLUTIONS SINCE
THE BEGINNING
FOR THE SAME REASON.

SO, WHY A NEW
REVOLUTION NOW,
WHEN NONE OF THEM
HAVE EVER CHANGED
THE WORLD?

DON'T

SHUT ME OUT.

I WANT TO KNOW

WHY WE DID IT.

SOME JERK, THE KIND
OF PERSON I HATE THE
MOST IN THIS WORLD,

SAID THIS TO ME.

WE DON'T KNOW
WHAT IDENTIFIES US.

MAZDA HUN, WHO ARE YOU?

A LONG TIME AGO,
THERE WAS A CHICKEN
THAT LAID GOLDEN EGGS.

IT LAID ONE GOLDEN
EGG EVERY DAY.

TEAR US APART AND DIG INSIDE ALL YOU WANT, AND SEE IF YOU CAN FIND THE GENETIC CODE OF YOUR SOULS.

HACK UP ALL THE WIDE OPEN MUSCLES, CELLS AND ORGANS AND SEE IF YOU CAN FIND THEM.

SEE WHICH CODE OF YOURS OUR SOULS BELONG TO.

WHEN PEOPLE FACE DEATH THEY WANT TO LEAVE SOMETHING BEHIND.

SOME GO INSANE WANTING TO LEAVE CLONES OF THEMSELVES.

THAT'S WHY PEOPLE ARE SEEDY LIKE THIS.

SINCE SEEDY PEOPLE LEAVE BEHIND SEEDY GENES.

PEOPLE FEAR DEATH BECAUSE THEY BELIEVE

THAT THEY HAVE NO CONTROL OVER THE FUTURE OF THEIR SOULS.

HA!

IF I BELIEVE THAT I CAN'T BE
TURNED INTO ANYTHING ELSE BUT ME—

THEN WE DON'T NEED ANY SUPPLEMENTAL
MEANS TO IDENTIFY ONESELF...
SINCE OUR EGO WOULD VERIFY OUR EXISTENCE.

BUT,
IF AN ETERNAL EGO THAT NEVER FORGETS EXISTS,

AND APPEARS ENDLESSLY IN THE WORLD,
IN DIFFERENT MANIFESTATIONS,

WHAT IF THOSE WHO
HAVE SUCH EGOS

COME BACK TO LIFE
ENDLESSLY?

AND IF MY OBSTRUCTOR

IS BORN ENDLESSLY
WITH AN ILL WILL AND
CONTROLS MY LIFE?

I CAN BE FREE ONLY IF I DESTROY THAT PERMANENTLY.

MY ENEMY.

THE MEMORY THAT IS BORN CEASELESSLY
AND CHANGES ITS SHAPE.

THE OBSTRUCTOR OF MY LIFE,
AND A CO-OWNER OF MY MEMORY.

HOW DO I GET RID OF THAT?

THE NAME OF MY CURRENT EXISTENCE IS MAZDA HUN.

A PLAUSIBLE NAME I GOT FROM SOMEWHERE,
WHICH COMES FROM AHURA MAZDA,
THE ANCIENT GOD OF FIRE,
PLUS THE NAME OF FEARSOME NOMADS...

BUT THAT NAME DOESN'T ATTEST TO MY BEING.

DOES MY EXISTENCE RULE MY CONSCIOUSNESS?
DOES MY CONSCIOUSNESS RULE MY EXISTENCE?

MARX SAID THAT EXISTENCE RULES
CONSCIOUSNESS.
I DISAGREE, AND AGREE.

IF SO,
WHAT PROVES WHAT I AM?

MAZDA–
WHO ARE YOU?

LETHE IS ERASING CONSCIOUSNESS FROM EXISTENCE.

WHATEVER EXISTENCE
MAY BE—

IT LEAVES BEHIND A TRACE.
THERE'S NOTHING THAT APPEARS WITHOUT A TRACE
AND THEN DISAPPEARS WITHOUT A TRACE.
I KNOW YOU–.
WHO
ARE YOU?

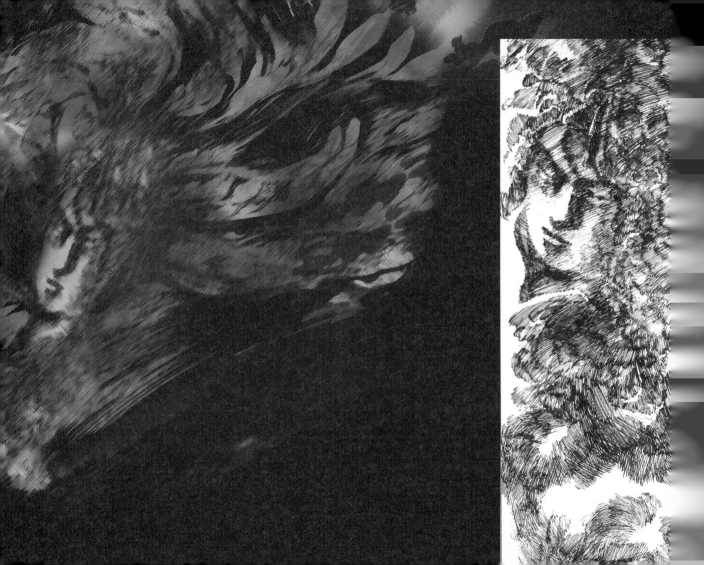

I KNOW YOU!!!

103

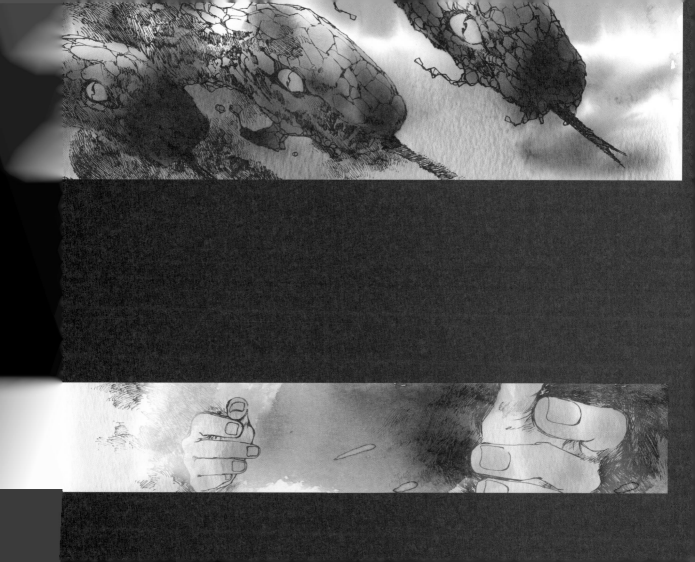

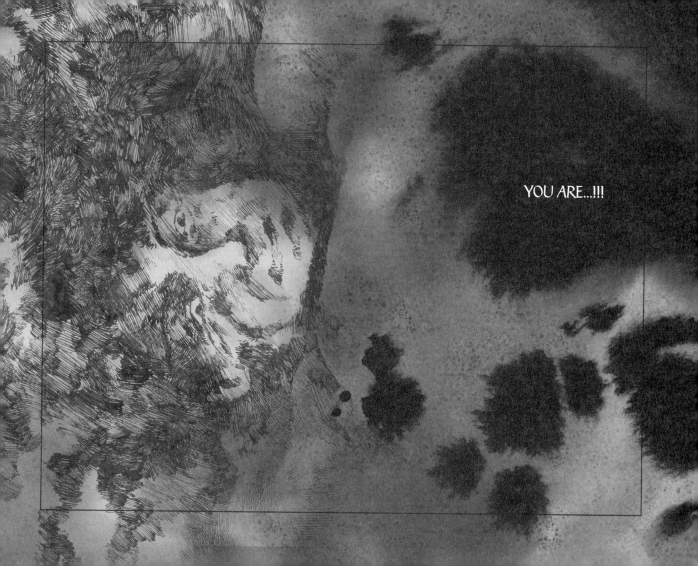

SHE MAY HAVE A DIFFERENT FACE,
A DIFFERENT AGE, AND A DIFFERENT GENDER,

BUT I KNOW THIS WOMAN.

THIS SMELL,
THIS FEELING,
THIS TOUCH...
EVEN THIS HATRED...

I DON'T. EVER. WANT TO MEET HER. AGAIN.

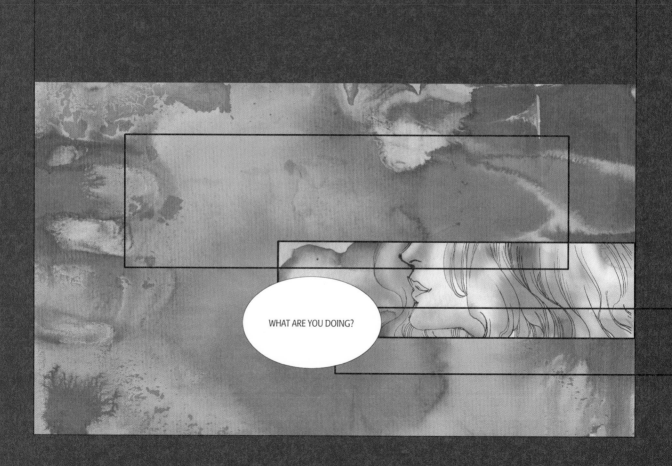

KISS~.

I WON'T DO THAT KINDA THING WITH YOU.

WHY?

BECAUSE I DON'T KNOW YOUR IDENTITY.

WHAT IS 'IDENTITY'?

WHO KNOWS WHAT IT IS?

HOW DO I KNOW WHO YOU ARE?

115

118

PEOPLE SAY THAT HUMAN EXISTENCE
REQUIRES COOPERATION IN THIS WORLD.
IN LIFE, I'VE FOUND THAT TO BE ROUGHLY TRUE QUITE OFTEN.
PLUS, THERE ARE TIMES WHEN YOU HAVE NO CHOICE
BUT TO DO WHAT YOU'RE TOLD.

HOWEVER, SOME NEVER COOPERATE,
AND YET THERE AREN'T ANY PROBLEMS FOR THEM...
THEY EVEN RECEIVE PROTECTION.

OUR CAPTAIN HAS ATTACHED
A PLAUSIBLE REASON FOR THE ONE WHO
HAS TO REMAIN ALIVE, EVEN IF WE ALL DIE.

AND ONCE THE ONE WITH VESTED INTERESTS IS GONE, THE STANDARD WOULD CONTROL THE WORLD.

AS HUMANS BEGAN TO STANDARDIZE HUMANS, THEY REDUCED THE MARGIN OF ERROR FOR DEFORMITY.

QUITE A LONG TIME AGO,

PEOPLE LOGICALLY ANALYZED HUMAN BEINGS AND CREATED SOMETHING CALLED A GENOME STANDARD.

FOR EXAMPLE, IF THEY WANTED TO RESURRECT THE EXTINCT DINOSAURS, THEY COULD DO IT USING THE GENOME STANDARD.

THEY MADE THE STANDARD FOR THAT REASON.

THE ONE WITH VESTED INTERESTS WOULD CONTROL THE WORLD'S STANDARD.

THE EXISTENTIAL EXPERIMENT OF LIFE WAS CASTRATED. THUS, EVOLUTION CAME TO A STOP.

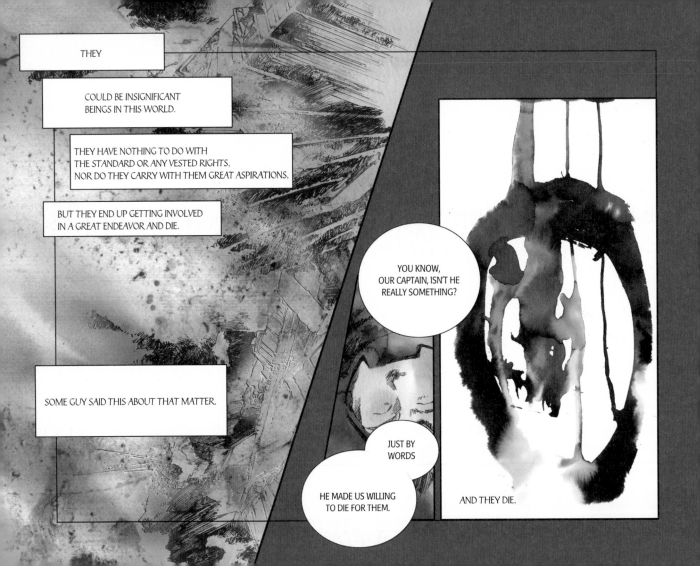

WHILE FIGHTING FOR THE DREAM OF SOMEONE
WHO DOESN'T EVEN REMEMBER THEM.

THE HUMAN TURNS INTO A STONE AND LOSES HIS EGO.

---DAMN!!

FROM AFAR, SHE CAME.

SHE LOOKED PALE AND SHABBY.

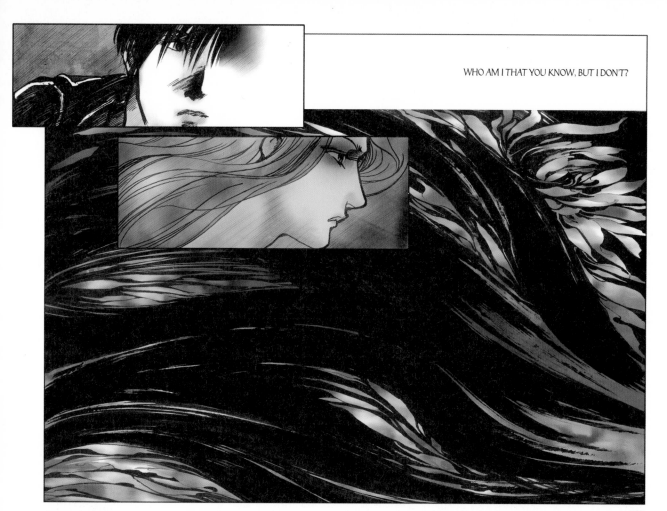

WHO AM I THAT YOU KNOW, BUT I DON'T?

–WHO AM I?

–WHO AM I?

TELL ME WHO AM I
THAT YOU KNOW, BUT I DON'T?

WHO AM I?
WHO AM I?

AUTHENTICATE ME.

TELL ME ABOUT ME!!

WHO AM I?!!

WHO AM I?!

148

SHE...   CROSSED THE RIVER AND CAME TO ME.

BUT...

MAZDA...

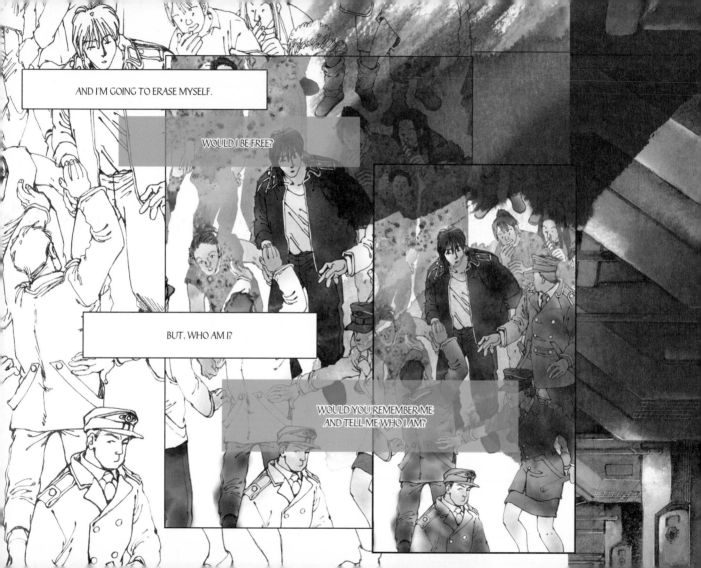

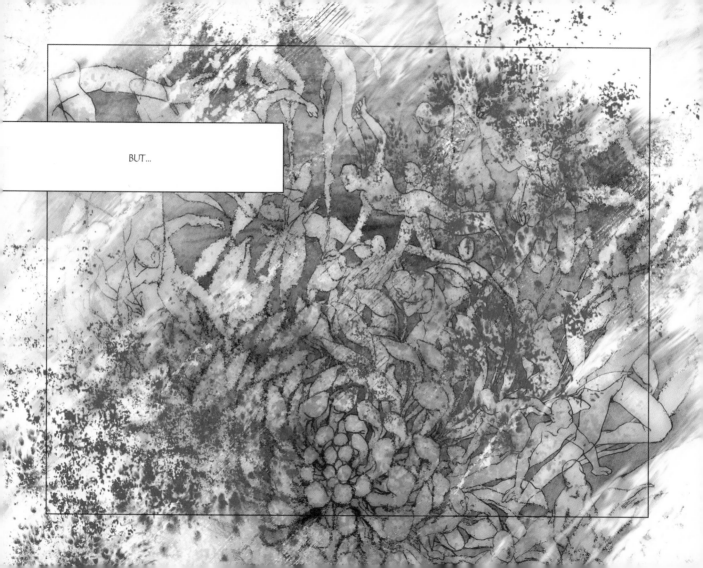

BUT...

BUT...

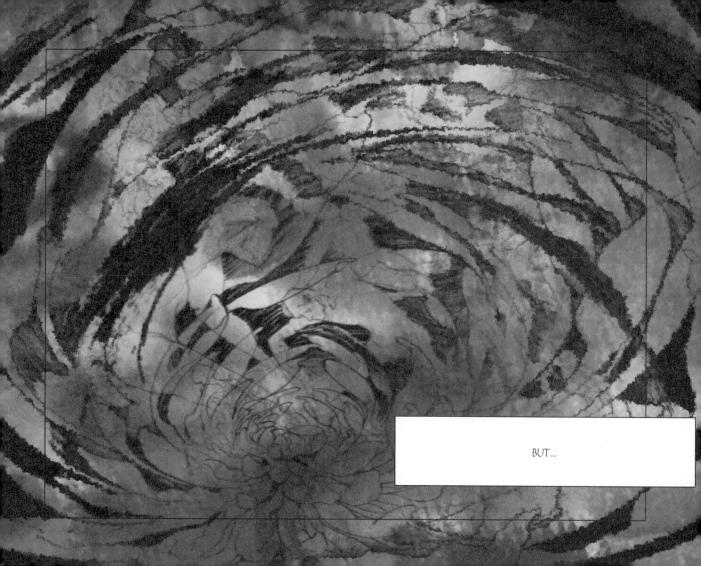

BUT...

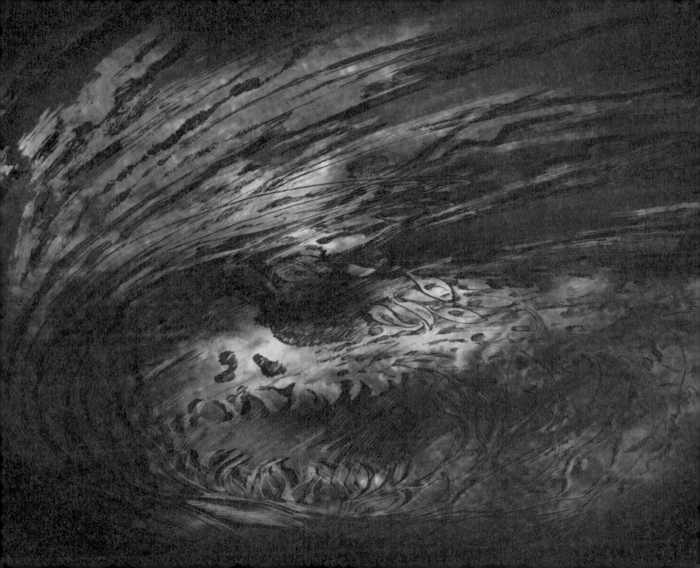

BUT...

WHO AM I?

WHO ARE YOU?

SOME BASTARD GAVE SUCH WORK
A NAME...'LETHE.'

A DISHONEST NAME.

AN EXECUTION FOR
ECONOMIC REASONS.

AMNESIA THAT'S FORCED UPON US,
WHO ARE GLUED TO THE WORLD
SHAPED ALONG SOME BASTARD'S
DREAM AND AMBITION.

I REFUSE IT.

YOU CAN'T MAKE ME ACCEPT A ME THAT I DON'T KNOW.

I AM MY OWN SELF, AND THAT HAS TO BE.

MY IDENTITY DEMANDS THAT FROM YOU.

YOU CAN KILL ME, BUT YOU CANNOT ERASE ME!!